DAY HIKING

Mount Hood

A Year-Round Guide

DAY HIKING

Mount Hood

A Year-Round Guide

Eli Boschetto

MOUNTAINEERS BOOKS

For John

MOUNTAINEERS BOOKS is dedicated to the exploration, preservation, and enjoyment of outdoor and wilderness areas.

1001 SW Klickitat Way, Suite 201, Seattle, WA 98134
800-553-4453, www.mountaineersbooks.org

Printed in Korea
Distributed in the United Kingdom by Cordee, www.cordee.co.uk
First edition, 2020

Mountaineers Books and its colophon are registered trademarks of The Mountaineers organization.

Copyeditor: Kerry Maynes
Design: Mountaineers Books
Layout: Jennifer Shontz, www.redshoedesign.com
Cartographer: Pease Press Cartography
All photographs by the author unless credited otherwise
Cover photograph: *Mount Hood rises majestically above Laurance Lake (Hike 6).*
Frontispiece: *Enjoy a big Mount Hood view from Bald Mountain (Hike 10).*

The background maps for this book were produced using the online map viewer CalTopo. For more information, visit caltopo.com.

Library of Congress Cataloging-in-Publication data is on file for this title at https://lccn.loc.gov/2019040956

Mountaineers Books titles may be purchased for corporate, educational, or other promotional sales, and our authors are available for a wide range of events. For information on special discounts or booking an author, contact our customer service at 800-553-4453 or mbooks@mountaineersbooks.org.

Printed on FSC-certified materials

MIX
Paper from responsible sources
FSC® C140526

ISBN (paperback): 978-1-68051-124-6
ISBN (ebook): 978-1-68051-125-3

An independent nonprofit publisher since 1960

Contents

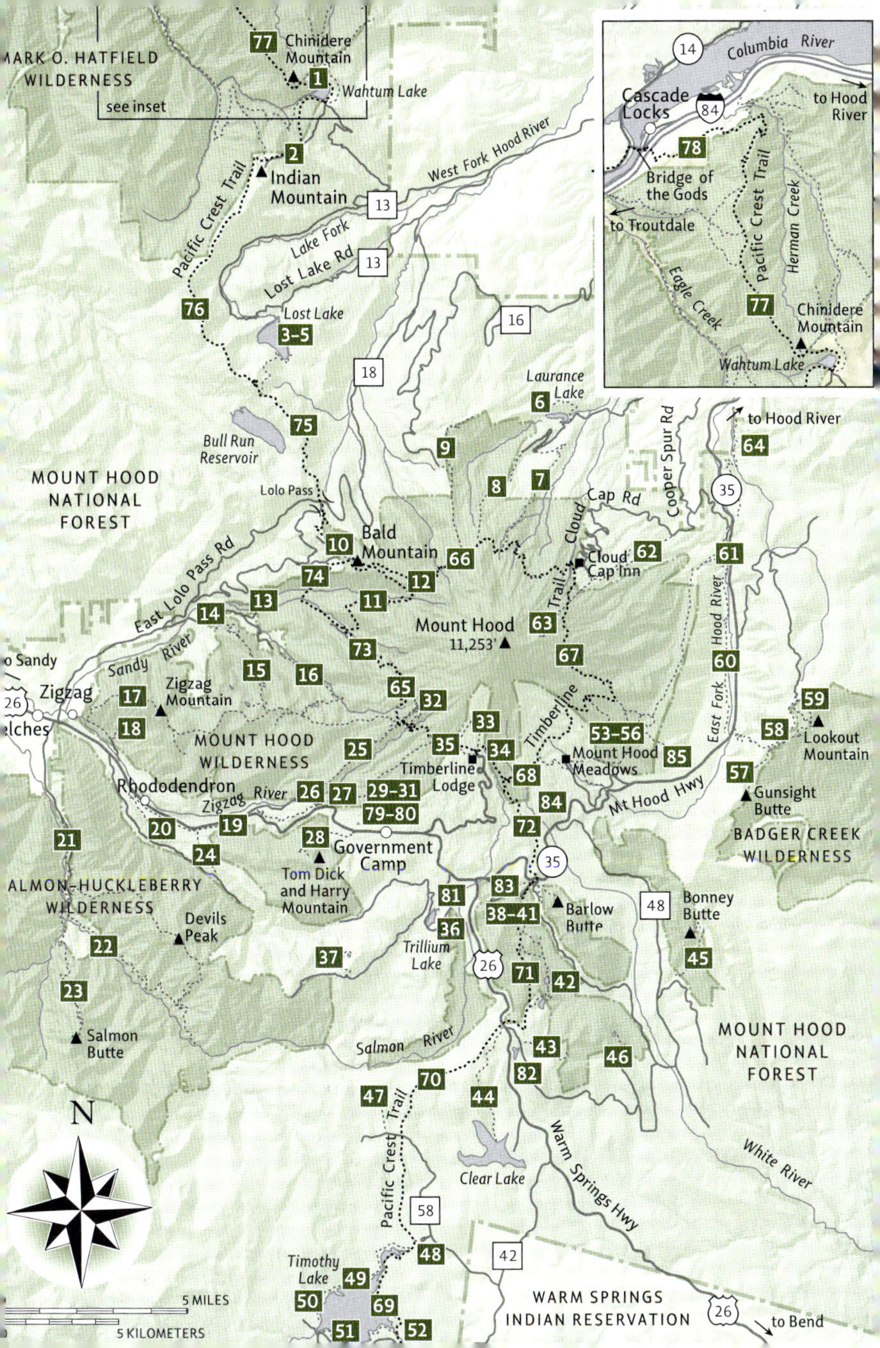

MARK O. HATFIELD WILDERNESS
see inset
Chinidere Mountain
Wahtum Lake
Indian Mountain
Pacific Crest Trail
West Fork Hood River
13
Lake Fork
Lost Lake Rd
Lost Lake
16
18
Laurance Lake
Bull Run Reservoir
MOUNT HOOD NATIONAL FOREST
Lolo Pass
Bald Mountain
Cloud Cap Rd
Cooper Spur Rd
to Hood River
35
Cloud Cap Inn
Cloud Cap Trail
East Lolo Pass Rd
Mount Hood
11,253'
to Sandy
26
Zigzag
Sandy River
Zigzag Mountain
Welches
MOUNT HOOD WILDERNESS
Timberline Trail
Mount Hood Meadows
Timberline Lodge
East Fork Hood River
Lookout Mountain
Rhododendron
Zigzag River
Mt Hood Hwy
Gunsight Butte
BADGER CREEK WILDERNESS
Government Camp
Tom Dick and Harry Mountain
SALMON-HUCKLEBERRY WILDERNESS
Devils Peak
Barlow Butte
48
Bonney Butte
Trillium Lake
Salmon Butte
Salmon River
MOUNT HOOD NATIONAL FOREST
White River
Warm Springs Hwy
Clear Lake
N
58
42
Timothy Lake
WARM SPRINGS INDIAN RESERVATION
to Bend
5 MILES
5 KILOMETERS
14
Columbia River
Cascade Locks
84
to Hood River
Bridge of the Gods
to Troutdale
Eagle Creek
Herman Creek
1
2
3-5
6
7
8
9
10
11
12
13
14
15
16
17
18
19
20
21
22
23
24
25
26
27
28
29-31
32
33
34
35
36
37
38-41
42
43
44
45
46
47
48
49
50
51
52
53-56
57
58
59
60
61
62
63
64
65
66
67
68
69
70
71
72
73
74
75
76
77
78
79-80
81
82
83
84
85

Hikes at a Glance

HIKE	DISTANCE IN MILES (ROUNDTRIP)	RATING	ELEVATION GAIN
MOUNT HOOD NORTH			
1. Chinidere Mountain	4.9	****	1370
2. Indian Mountain	8.9	*****	2080
3. Lakeshore Trail	3	*****	280
4. Lost Lake Butte	3.2	****	1200
5. Buck Peak	11.8	***	3050
6. Laurance Lake High Loop	5.8	***	1550
7. Elk Cove	9.4	****	2970
8. Pinnacle Ridge	6.6	***	2500
9. Owl Point	4.2	****	970
MOUNT HOOD WEST			
10. Bald Mountain	2.2	****	890
11. Bald–Ramona Loop	10.4	*****	3470
12. McNeil Point	9.2	*****	3210
13. Ramona Falls	7	****	1230
14. Sandy River	3.6	**	360
15. Cast Lake	11.2	***	3590
16. Burnt Lake	6.6	****	1560
17. Zigzag Mountain Lookout	11.3	****	4400
18. Castle Canyon	1.8	***	970
19. Pioneer Bridal Trail	7.7[†]	**	2270
20. Flag Mountain	3.7	**	1570
21. Old Salmon River	4.9	***	470
22. Salmon River	11.6	***	3340
23. Salmon Butte	10.8	****	4160
24. Still Creek	3.1	**	910
25. Paradise Park Trail	13.9	*****	3670
26. Hidden Lake	3.8	**	990
27. Zigzag Falls	0.6	***	250
MOUNT HOOD SOUTH			
28. Mirror Lake	4.1	****	970
29. Multorpor Fen	2.3	**	330
30. Enid Lake	1.2	**	210
31. Crosstown Loop	2.4	**	390
32. Paradise Park Loop	12.2	*****	3470

[†] One-way mileage

DIFFICULTY	KID-FRIENDLY	DOG-FRIENDLY	WILD-FLOWERS	VIEWS	WATER-FALLS	HISTORICAL INTEREST	GOOD ON CLOUDY DAYS	WINTER
3		•	•	•				
4		•	•	•		•		
1	•	•					•	
3		•		•		•		
5				•				
3	•	•		•			•	
5		•	•	•				
5			•	•				
3		•	•	•				
2	•	•	•	•				
5			•	•	•			
5		•	•	•		•		
4			•		•		•	
1	•	•					•	
5		•		•			•	
3	•	•		•		•	•	
5		•		•		•		
4							•	
1–2	•	•				•		•
4		•					•	
1	•	•			•		•	
4	•	•		•			•	
4		•	•	•		•		
2	•	•					•	
5			•	•				
3		•					•	
1	•	•			•		•	
3	•	•		•				
1	•	•		•				•
2	•	•					•	•
2	•	•					•	•
5			•	•	•			

HIKE	DISTANCE IN MILES (ROUNDTRIP)	RATING	ELEVATION GAIN
MOUNT HOOD SOUTH (CONTINUED)			
33. Mountaineer Loop	2.8	***	1170
34. Buried Forest Overlook	3.1	****	920
35. Timberline Gardens	3	***	350
36. Trillium Lake	1.9	***	110
37. Veda Lake	2.8	***	950
38. Grave Trail	1.9	**	480
39. Barlow Butte	2.9	**	1340
40. Devils Half-Acre	2.2	**	480
41. Palmateer Point	5.4	***	1160
42. Twin Lakes	7.3	***	1160
43. Frog Lake Buttes	3.8	**	1430
44. Blue Box Peak	7.8	**	1900
45. Bonney Butte	5.2	****	1840
46. Catalpa Lake	1.7	***	290
47. Jackpot Meadows	2.6	*	240
48. Little Crater Lake	0.3	***	0
49. Timothy Lake Loop	12.4	****	660
50. Meditation Point	2.8	***	290
51. Southshore Trail	6	***	250
52. Clackamas Lake and Oak Grove Fork	4.4	***	480
MOUNT HOOD EAST			
53. Heather Canyon	9.6	*****	2130
54. Umbrella Falls	3.9	****	940
55. Elk Meadows	5.5	***	1200
56. Gnarl Ridge	6.8	****	1600
57. Gunsight Butte	7.8	**	2450
58. Lookout Mountain	10.3	****	3120
59. High Prairie Loop	2.5	****	530
60. Tamanawas Falls	3.3	***	820
61. East Fork Hood River	6.2†	**	1270
62. Polallie Ridge	5.5	***	2000
63. Cooper Spur	6.6	*****	2680
64. Dog River	6	***	1700
TIMBERLINE TRAIL			
65. Timberline Lodge to Bald Mountain	15.4†	*****	3310
66. Bald Mountain to Cloud Cap	11.7†	*****	4220

† One-way mileage

DIFFICULTY	KID-FRIENDLY	DOG-FRIENDLY	WILD-FLOWERS	VIEWS	WATER-FALLS	HISTORICAL INTEREST	GOOD ON CLOUDY DAYS	WINTER
4			•	•		•		
3	•	•	•	•				
1–2	•	•	•	•		•		
1	•	•		•			•	
3		•		•			•	
2	•	•				•	•	
3		•						
2	•	•				•	•	•
3		•		•		•		
3	•	•					•	•
4		•						•
3		•					•	
3		•		•		•		
1	•	•					•	
1	•	•					•	
1	•	•					•	
3		•		•			•	
1	•	•		•			•	
2	•	•		•			•	
2	•	•					•	
5			•	•	•			
3	•	•	•		•		•	
3			•			•	•	
4				•				
4		•		•				
5			•	•		•		
2	•	•	•	•		•		
2	•	•			•		•	
2	•	•			•		•	
5				•		•		•
5				•		•		
3	•	•		•				
5			•	•	•			
5			•	•		•		

HIKE	DISTANCE IN MILES (ROUNDTRIP)	RATING	ELEVATION GAIN
TIMBERLINE TRAIL (CONTINUED)			
67. Cloud Cap to Mount Hood Meadows	10.8†	*****	2680
68. Mount Hood Meadows to Timberline Lodge	4.9†	*****	1860
PACIFIC CREST TRAIL			
69. Timothy Lake to Little Crater Camp	5.8†	****	330
70. Little Crater Camp to Wapinitia Pass	7.8†	**	1290
71. Wapinitia Pass to Barlow Pass	4.8†	***	880
72. Barlow Pass to Timberline Lodge	5.3†	*****	2200
73. Timberline Lodge to Sandy River	12.2†	*****	1300
74. Sandy River to Lolo Pass	6.9†	***	2290
75. Lolo Pass to Lost Lake	6.3†	**	1340
76. Lost Lake to Wahtum Lake	14.3†	****	3200
77. Wahtum Lake to Herman Camp	13.2†	****	1630
78. Herman Camp to Bridge of the Gods	5.6†	***	1790
WINTER TRAILS			
79. Glacier View	1.4	***	440
80. Summit Trail	4.4	**	530
81. Trillium Lake	4.4	****	500
82. Frog Lake	2.1	***	160
83. Buzzard Point	4	***	530
84. White River West	3.1	****	690
85. Bennett Pass	5.4	***	1060

† One-way mileage

DIFFICULTY	KID-FRIENDLY	DOG-FRIENDLY	WILD-FLOWERS	VIEWS	WATER-FALLS	HISTORICAL INTEREST	GOOD ON CLOUDY DAYS	WINTER
5			•	•	•	•		
5				•	•			
2	•	•		•			•	
3		•		•			•	
3		•	•	•				•
4		•	•	•		•		
5			•	•	•			
5			•	•				
3		•					•	
5		•	•	•			•	
5		•		•			•	
3	•	•					•	
2	•	•					•	•
2	•	•		•			•	•
3	•	•		•			•	•
1	•	•					•	•
2	•	•					•	•
3	•	•		•				•
4	•	•		•			•	•

Ramona Falls is a magical destination that will have you wondering when you left Oregon and entered Middle Earth (Hikes 11, 13, 65, 74).

Introduction

Everybody needs beauty as well as bread,
places to play in and pray in, where
nature may heal and cheer and give
strength to body and soul alike.
—John Muir

Chances are, relative to the fact that you're holding this book, that you've seen Mount Hood from a highway, an airplane, a calendar, a postcard, or by a hundred other means and said to yourself, "I want to hike that!" The good news is, with this book, you've just taken your first step.

Welcome to Oregon's premiere outdoor playground. After all, where else can you spend a summer day skiing in the morning, hiking in the afternoon, and kicking back with a microbrew and an alpenglow view in the evening—*all in the same place!* Whether you're new to the Northwest and looking for help getting outdoors, just visiting and want to explore some amazing mountain wilderness, or a longtime resident and looking for a fresh take on familiar territory, you've come to the right place. The following pages will offer a fresh and fun perspective on many of Mount Hood's classic trails, as well as a few lesser-known routes, and is intended to help you get out and enjoy your own brand of peace, solitude, discovery, and adventure in a rich and dynamic landscape of old-growth forests, volcanic ridges, and sparkling glaciers. But before getting too far ahead, let's set the stage . . .

Known to the Multnomah tribe as *Wy'east*, 11,240-foot Mount Hood is the highest peak in the Beaver State, and dominates the horizon in much of northwest Oregon and southwest Washington. It is the fourth-highest peak among the entire Cascade Range, following Mounts Rainier, Shasta, and Adams, and has the distinction of being the most recently volcanically active—behind Mount St. Helens, of course—merely 235 years ago. This was near the same time that the Lewis and Clark Expedition was arriving in the Oregon Territory. More than one million years old, Mount Hood is a composite volcano formed by repeated spectacular, explosive eruptions of andesite and dacite lava domes and flows, pyroclastic deposition, and tephra fallout—thus its high, pointed peak and rugged features. Presently considered "dormant," Mount Hood is still geologically active.

What intermittent eruptions do to build up Mount Hood, ice and water work to tear it down. Blanketing Mount Hood's flanks are eleven named glaciers and snowfields, with numerous additional perennial snow features. Over the course of several ice ages, Mount Hood's glaciers once radiated up to 9 miles from the mountain's crown. Presently, the largest glaciers on the mountain are the Coe and Eliot on the north and northeast flanks, respectively. An estimated three million cubic meters of ice and snow combined remains on the mountain. In addition to the glacier chewing away at Mount Hood's flanks, massive lahars (debris flows) have scoured the southern and western drainages, creating huge scar-like canyons. As you gaze over, and hike through, these canyons, you can examine the denuded walls and make out the varying layers of Mount Hood's anatomy laid bare.

ORIGIN STORIES: MOUNT HOOD

According to the ancient Multnomah peoples, Wy'east is a monument created by the Great Spirit Sahale. Legend says that Sahale's two sons, Wy'east and Klickitat, fought for the love of a beautiful maiden, Loowit. The battle resulted in great destruction to forests and villages. This enraged Sahale, inciting him to smite all three. In his grief, he erected three mountains as monuments to the fallen lovers: Loowit (Mount St. Helens), Klickitat (Mount Adams), and Wy'east (Mount Hood). More recent history states that Mount Hood was "discovered" by Lieutenant William Broughton, a member of Captain George Vancouver's Discovery Expedition of the 1790s. Broughton christened the "high, snowy mountain" after Lord Samuel Hood, an admiral in the British navy. A few years later, the mountain was sighted by the Lewis and Clark Expedition, who, at the time, dubbed the peak Timm Mountain, translated "Falls Mountain" by the local natives, for its proximity to Celilo Falls on the Columbia River. Shortly afterward, the expedition learned that the mountain had already been designated Mount Hood.

Despite it being a natural and geologic wonder, Mount Hood is most recognized as a beacon for outdoor recreation, mostly for its ski resorts and hiking trails, in addition to being one of the most-climbed mountains in the United States. Here you'll find more than 4600 acres of skiable terrain, including the country's only year-round ski slope on Palmer Glacier—thus the aforementioned summer skiing. When it isn't covered in snow, you have more than 1000 miles of hiking trails available for exploring the mountain's ridges and valleys, meadows and wetlands, lakes and rivers. The mountain's signature hiking trail, the Timberline Trail, built in the 1930s by the Civilian Conservation Corps, circumnavigates the mountain on a 43-mile loop. The centerpiece of this mountain wonderland is the historic Timberline Lodge. Built in the 1930s, and perched high on the volcano's southern slopes, it is a popular tourist and dining destination, as well as the launch point for a variety of hiking and backpacking adventures.

So if you're ready to go on your own journey of discovery, consider this guidebook your personal Mount Hood tour guide. In addition to the many hiking opportunities you'll learn about, there are also references to camping, dining, and other local resources to help you prepare for your first, fifth, or fiftieth visit to Mount Hood. In no time at all, you'll find yourself standing at a trailhead ready for your next step.

PERMITS AND FEES

In general, a **permit** is not required to hike anywhere on Mount Hood. The Mount Hood National Forest is public land, and trails—both within and outside of designated wilderness areas—are free for exploring. Visitors are asked to register and carry a wilderness permit for some portions of Mount Hood Wilderness. These are free, self-issue permits and are generally found at kiosks near trailheads and wilderness boundaries. These permits serve two primary purposes. The first is to register your entry into an area and your planned destination(s). This informs wilderness managers that you are in the backcountry, where you're planning to go, and when you're planning to exit. This information can be critical for locating you if an incident (landslide, wildfire) or emergency (injury) occurs. The second purpose is so land managers can monitor how many people are using the trails and backcountry destinations on the mountain. This helps them identify where to focus precious maintenance staff and funding in order to keep trails in good repair. For these important reasons, it is highly recommended that you register at every kiosk you encounter.

While hiking on Mount Hood is free, there are a few nominal **fees** for parking. And while you may bristle at the thought of having to pay to visit your public lands, paying a small fee goes a long way in helping to maintain roads and trails, keep roads and trailheads plowed in winter, and keep backcountry destinations and trailhead facilities in good repair. This is especially vital in these days of ever-declining Forest Service budgets and staffing. These fees are required only at developed trailheads, typically where you find large parking areas, restroom facilities, picnic amenities, and so on. There are just as many remote, undeveloped trailheads that don't require any fees.

The two types of permit typically required for trailhead parking on Mount Hood are the **Northwest Forest Pass** (or Federal Interagency Pass) and the **Oregon Sno-Park Permit**. These passes can be obtained at a variety of ranger stations and retailers on

Summer brings an explosion of wildflowers to Mount Hood's meadows, like this bear grass near Cairn Basin (Hikes 12, 66).

your way up the mountain, or online prior to your hike. Passes can be purchased for a single day visit, season, or full year. Northwest Forest Passes are required for applicable trailheads year-round; Oregon Sno-Park Permits are required for applicable trailheads from November 1 through April 30. A handful of hiking locations in this guide are operated or managed by private entities and require their own day-use or overnight fee. You will find what kind of permit or fee is required in the info block for each hike. See appendix II for a complete list of the trailheads that require parking permits or fees and some of the locations where permits are available for purchase.

YOUR PUBLIC LANDS

The majority of trails in this guide are located on public lands, mostly in the form of national forests and designated wilderness areas. That means that you have a right to visit them and have a voice in their use and administration. However, advocating for these public lands is sometimes easier said than done, and doing so sometimes involves figuring out exactly who you're supposed to be talking to.

In this guidebook, most of the trails around Mount Hood are on **US Forest Service** land, notably, the **Mount Hood National Forest** (MHNF). Established as a reserve in 1908, MHNF encompasses more than 1600 square miles of mountains, forests, lakes, and rivers. Within the forest are eight designated wilderness areas, giving additional protection to more than 310,000 acres of especially scenic and sensitive landscapes. Also administered by the Forest Service is the neighboring **Columbia River Gorge National Scenic Area** (CRGNSA). Designated in 1986, and covering areas in both Oregon and Washington, the CRGNSA adds another 292,000 acres of mountains, rivers, and forests to the pool of public lands. Within this area is one designated wilderness area protecting 65,000 acres of old-growth forests, volcanic cliffs, and canyons.

The mission of the Forest Service, a branch of the US Department of Agriculture, is "to sustain the health, diversity, and productivity of the Nation's forests and grasslands to meet the needs of present and future generations." And while we, as hikers, like to think those "needs" mean preserving these lands as places to find peace and experience nature, these *multiuse* lands are intended to serve a variety of recreational and commercial interests, including not only hiking and camping, but also fishing, hunting, motorized recreation, and timber harvesting. And depending on the leanings of whatever administration is in charge, that mission priority, unfortunately, is usually biased.

This is why it's more urgent than ever for you to stand up in favor of preserving access to public lands and advocating for wilderness, clean water, and wildlife protections. Keep up with the activities and plans of your local Forest Service districts. If there are opportunities to attend public meetings and information sessions, go and be a voice for trails. Call your state and federal representatives and tell them that public lands are important to you. Together, as a community, we can work toward ensuring that our public lands remain protected and accessible now, and for future generations.

WEATHER

Weather on Mount Hood and in the surrounding area is *usually* somewhat predictable. Winter is cold and snowy, spring is cool and wet, summer is warm and sunny, and fall is a mixed bag. The Northwest's volcanic Cascades have the ability to create their own weather, so conditions can and do change. Without going into a bunch of complicated scientific explanation, mountain weather is usually the product of air currents reacting to land masses, temperature, and elevation. When weather and temperature are stable, hiking days are usually quite pleasant. But every now and then, Mother Nature can throw curve balls. It's not unheard of to have a sudden snowstorm in summer or a heat wave in fall.

Weather can also be quite variable from one side of the mountain to the other. While it may be cool and rainy in Portland and on the west side of Mount Hood, it may be warm and sunny on the east side. This is due to much of the Northwest's weather coming in from the Pacific Ocean, where it then gets halted by the high peaks and ridges of the Cascades. Elevation is also a factor. If you find rainy weather in Portland or the Columbia River Gorge at lower elevations, you might find it to be sunny and clear at higher elevations on the mountain. So don't automatically discount rainy days in town as nonhiking days. You may just need to get above it or over to the east side. The best way to check current weather conditions and forecasts on Mount Hood is to visit www.noaa.gov.

While we all favor warm, sunny, bluebird days as the ideal hiking conditions, remember that Mount Hood is not a summer-only hiking destination. The mountain puts on showy seasonal displays throughout the year. This means that a hike in summer may look dramatically different from the same hike in fall or winter. While spring and summer bring a lot of green meadows, wildflowers, and cascading creeks, fall paints the mountain in a mosaic of vibrant autumn hues, and winter blankets the mountain in frosty white. If properly prepared (see the Apparel and Gear section), you can enjoy Mount Hood at any time of the year. After all, that's what Gore-Tex and puffy jackets are for!

ROAD AND TRAIL CONDITIONS

Hiking trails on and around Mount Hood generally remain in good, hikeable condition from one season to the next. However, one thing this guidebook cannot tell you is what the condition of any trail is *right now*. At the time that the research for this guidebook was done, all of the trails featured were open and hikeable. Some trails did show signs of

Remote forest roads can get you to some of the most secluded trails on Mount Hood.

GIVE BACK TO TRAILS

Trails don't take care of themselves. Unlike many desert and alpine trails that remain constant from one season to the next, trails in the wet Northwest are under a constant barrage of wind, rain, and snow, where landslides and washouts are common. Every spring and summer, trail crews—many of them unpaid volunteers—pack tools and supplies into Oregon's wilderness areas to log out fallen trees, repair trail tread, install new drainages, and brush back overgrown vegetation. This is all done out of a love and appreciation for Oregon's extraordinary forests and mountains, and their desire to keep these special places open and hikeable to everyone.

You can show your appreciation for Oregon's trails by pitching in. In these days of ever-declining forest budgets and funding, volunteers are needed more than ever. And you don't even need to know how to do trail work. There are several hiking and conservation groups in the Portland and Mount Hood areas that organize trail work parties and invite the public to join in. They will teach you the skills required to fix trails and keep them open and accessible. You're likely to meet a diverse crowd of fellow hikers who share your love of trails and wilderness—and you may even meet your next hiking partner. You can find a list of local trail support and conservation groups in appendix IV, in the back of this book. Visit their websites and find out how you can support a trail near you.

damage and/or neglect, and some trails did have ongoing maintenance being performed. A small handful of trails on Mount Hood were not included in this guide due to their prolonged poor condition or difficult accessibility.

Weather—wind, rain, snow—is a significant factor affecting trail conditions. Heavy rain can wash out trails; heavy snowfall can down trees onto trails. This is especially true in areas where wildfires have damaged the landscape. These areas are much more susceptible to washouts, rockfalls, landslides, and falling trees, especially in periods of rapid snowmelt and heavy wind and rain. The same can be said of roads, especially remote and/or unimproved forest roads. Before heading out, you should call the local ranger district to inquire about any conditions or closures that may be affecting your trail of choice.

WILDERNESS AND TRAIL ETIQUETTE

This guide includes hiking trails in wilderness areas, national forests, and national recreation areas. Wilderness areas are designated to preserve the natural characteristics of especially unique, sensitive, or scenic places. Of Oregon's forty-seven wilderness areas, four are on or around Mount Hood: Mount Hood Wilderness, Badger Creek Wilderness, Salmon-Huckleberry Wilderness, and Mark O. Hatfield Wilderness. Together, these areas protect more than 220,000 acres of forests, rivers, meadows, wetlands, and alpine environments. In order to preserve the integrity of these special places, wilderness trails are open only to hikers and stock users.

Some of the trails in this guide are designated multiuse trails. These trails are located in national forest and recreation areas, and are open to hikers, equestrians, mountain bikers and, in a few cases, motorized users. If a trail is open for multiple uses, it will be indicated in the trail description. And while hiking on a popular mountain biking path may not sound especially appealing, you could be missing out on a great trail experience. Mountain bikers appreciate great scenery too. Plus, many trail-riding communities do a lot to help maintain trails and assist in backcountry rescues, so while these trail users may differ in their preferred mode of travel, we can all respect one another's enjoyment of the outdoors.

Look for usage signs at trailheads.

Leave No Trace

When hiking in forest and wilderness areas—well, when hiking anywhere—the general rule of thumb is to Leave No Trace (LNT). There are seven LNT guidelines that every hiker should take to heart in order to enjoy their outdoors experience, provide enjoyable experiences for others, and help maintain an attractive outdoors for future generations.

1. Plan ahead and prepare. You're already off to a good start with this guidebook. Use the info and resources on these pages to help you select your hikes to plan safe, fun outings. When you can, avoid peak traffic and tourist times, such as summer weekends and holidays.

2. Travel on durable surfaces. Stick to the trails—don't cut switchbacks, and don't tromp through flower meadows. Sensitive wilderness environments can take decades to recover from just one footprint. If you want to take a break, step off the trail onto a durable surface, such as dirt or rock.

3. Dispose of waste properly. All together now: "Pack it in, pack it out." There's nary an eyesore as offensive as trash in the wilderness. Be extra vigilant about managing your trash—and don't be afraid to pick up any trash you may find. Nature will bless you with good juju.

4. Leave what you find. Avoid the temptation to pick the wildflowers, or pocket an interesting rock. Follow the hiker's motto "Take only photos, leave only footprints." A photo of a pretty wildflower on your Instagram will last a lot longer than any flower you may be tempted to pick.

5. Minimize campfires. You're not likely to have a campfire on a day hike, but if you do any wilderness camping, build campfires only when and where permitted, and only in established fire rings. Be sure to *fully extinguish* any campfire before going to sleep or leaving the area.

6. Respect wildlife. When viewing wild critters, do so from a respectable distance. This will keep the animals from getting stressed out. If they get frightened and charge, you don't want them charging at you! Also, don't feed wildlife. This puts both you and the animal at risk.

7. Be considerate of others. Everyone deserves to have enjoyable outdoors experiences, whether they're fellow hikers, trail runners, equestrians, hunters, or mountain bikers. See the next section for some suggestions about how you can demonstrate top-notch trail courtesy.

For more information about Leave No Trace, visit www.lnt.org.

Sharing the Trail

In the wilderness, as in life, a little kindness goes a long way. While having a mountain lake or summit viewpoint all to yourself may be the ideal situation, it's just not that likely—especially with the increasing numbers of people escaping to the forests and mountains for a little rest and relaxation time. Instead of being annoyed by others, just take a deep breath and appreciate that they're out there for the same reason as you. After all, the more people that use and appreciate our natural spaces and public lands, the more people will take part in protecting it.

Stay to the right. Just like you do on the road or bike paths—unless you live in the UK—stay to the right side of the trail. This will allow hikers coming the other way easy passage without any awkward run-ins. If you're hiking with companions, especially on narrow trails, try to hike single file.

Yield to uphill hikers. Hiking uphill is a lot more work than hiking downhill. And restarting an uphill slog after pausing takes a considerable amount of effort. If you're joyously skipping downhill and encounter other hikers heading up, step to the side and let them pass.

Take breaks off-trail. When you need to stop for a drink, catch your breath, or snap a pic, step completely off the trail (onto a durable surface), so as not to be a blockade for other hikers who may need to pass. Also, make sure your pack or trekking poles aren't tripping hazards for others.

Give the right-of-way. When encountering equestrians, step off the trail and let them pass. It is best to step off downslope where safe so as not to spook horses. If on multiuse trails, do the same for mountain bikes. Official trail right-of-way usage suggests that mountain bikers should yield to hikers, but in most cases this is just not practical. As a hiker, you have more agility to move than they do, and it's easier for you to start walking again than it is for a cyclist to restart their ride. You can avoid confrontations with wheeled trail users by taking the high road and just stepping aside to let them pass.

Use your quiet voice. When chatting with your hiking companions, be considerate of others. Most hikers would rather hear the soothing sounds of the wind and water than a heated debate over who shot first, Han Solo or Greedo. (It was Han Solo. It was *always* Han Solo.)

Taking care of #2. If you suddenly have the need to engage in the backcountry squat, find a private place at least 100 feet off-trail and 200 feet from water. Make your deposit in a hole six to eight inches deep, and pack out your used toilet tissue in a zip-top bag. It's a good idea to pack along a little toilet kit for those just-in-case moments, even on day hikes. Use a small stuff sack to carry a lightweight trowel (for digging your hole), some toilet tissue, a zip-top bag, and some hand sanitizer for cleaning up.

Get good trail karma. When encountering other hikers, a little kindness goes a long way. When passing others, it's always nice to give a wave or a "hello." If you see someone lost or struggling, try to offer assistance. Above all, be a good steward to the forest and Galadriel will smile on you.

HIKING AND SOCIAL MEDIA

Like it or not, social media is a fact of life. If you're an enthusiast of social media, you're probably bombarded on a daily—nay, hourly—basis with all manner of news, photos, updates, memes, videos, recipes, and so on. For better or worse, social media can both influence and inspire. It can also impact. Studies have shown that pretty travel and outdoors destinations shared on social media experience significant increases in visitation because viewers see these images and say, "Hey, I want to see that, go there, do that." This includes hiking trails.

If you have a large social media following and you post a picture of a cascading waterfall, a flowery meadow, or an awesome summit view, and tag it with a "look where I am!" message, you're essentially inviting your entire audience to come visit that location. And many of them—since they admire you by following you—will take you up on that invitation. Suddenly, your favorite trails are more crowded, trailhead parking is more difficult, and there's more trash left on the ground. In a few extreme cases, land managers have responded to these increases in visitation by imposing trail quotas, parking limits, and additional fees.

This isn't to suggest that you shouldn't take and share photos of our amazing public lands. People need inspiration to get outdoors and discover the beauty and healing power of nature. However, you don't need to give away the farm. When you post your images, it is recommended that you be vague about your location tagging, so as not to steer your entire audience to a single location. For example, instead of posting a photo as "Bear Meadows on Mount Lotsabears," post your photo as "Pretty meadow in the Lotsabears Wilderness." This can show the appeal of a location while inviting your audience to discover the wider area on their own, thus reducing high impacts in a single place—or on a single trail.

Hiking with Dogs

With just a few exceptions, you are welcome to hike with your furry friend on most of the trails in this guide. If there are specific restrictions concerning dogs on a trail, you will find this information in the **Notes** section of each hike. As a dog owner, you are responsible for your pooch. Please bear in mind that not every hiker loves dogs, and small children are often frightened of large animals. When hiking with your four-legged pal, consider the following:

Follow the rules. Be aware of any regulations an area or trail may have concerning dogs. This will usually be posted at trailheads and/or park entrances. Some locations in this guide do not permit dogs on trails, and some require dogs to be leashed at all times. Be aware of any conditions that may not be suitable for your dog, and consider visiting popular and/or heavy-use trails when they're more likely to be less crowded.

Keep your dog under control. It is good practice to keep your dog leashed while on-trail. This will prevent Fido from frightening wildlife and other hikers, trampling sensitive plants and wildflowers, or getting into thorny or poisonous shrubs. When approaching or passing other hikers, heel your dog to your side to prevent them from encroaching on others, especially small children. The same goes for encountering equestrians; step to the side of the trail and keep your dog under strict control.

Choose dog-friendly trails. While most of the trails in this guide are *open* to dogs, that doesn't mean they're *suitable* for dogs. All of the hikes in this guide give some indication about the type of terrain the trail crosses. Challenging terrain that can be rough for booted feet can be doubly challenging for little doggie paws. Also consider the elevation gain/loss and distance of a trail, and whether your furry friend has the stamina to complete the hike—or if you'll be carrying it!

Gear up Fido. You should outfit your pooch just as well as you do yourself for a good day on-trail. Put a pair of trail booties on your dog to protect their paws from sharp rocks, sticks, and thorns. Dogs get cold too, so pack along a rain jacket or insulated cover for Fido, just in case the weather turns. Dogs can contract *Giardia* from contaminated water the same way humans can. Carry enough clean water for your dog to keep it hydrated, as well as snacks and treats to keep its energy up.

Pack out poop. Leave No Trace applies to dogs just as much as humans. If your dog poops on the trail, pick it up with a disposable doggie-dropping bag and pack it out with your trash. *Do not leave dog waste bags on the side of the trail to be picked up later.* Chances are, you'll forget about it, or forget where you left it, and someone else will feel obliged to pick it up and pack it out—*and no one wants to clean up after your dog.*

As a dog owner, you are an ambassador for all of dogkind. It is your responsibility to demonstrate good doggie practices so that your fellow hikers feel safe on-trail and are not disturbed by your animal's behavior or messes. Remember, while you may be a dog lover, not everyone else is. If your dog gets aggressive or overly excited around strangers, consider hiking lesser-used trails or just leave your dog at home in order to avoid conflicts with others.

WILDLIFE

When you venture out into the woods and wilderness areas on and around Mount Hood, you are a guest in the home of all the winged and furry critters that reside in the mountain's hills, trees, and waters. The majority of these are mild-mannered creatures that spend the majority of their days searching for food, raising their young, and keeping up their homes. When you spot wildlife on the trail, enjoy the experience from a distance. This will keep the animals from getting nervous or aggressive in case they perceive you as a threat.

While catching a glimpse of large animals is always a thrilling experience, the majority of animals you are likely to see around Mount Hood are small squirrels, chipmunks, and Canada jays. All of these, especially the latter, are more than willing to invite themselves to your snack breaks, so keep an eye on your food. And while they're cute, don't be tempted to share your trail mix with little critters and birds. This conditions them to bad feeding habits and can make them aggressive.

What you're less likely to see on Mount Hood are deer, elk, skunks, porcupines, bobcats, coyotes, black bears, and cougars (mountain lions)—even though they are all up there. These animals want little to do with humans, so they tend to stay away from popular camping and hiking areas, and will often vacate an area before you even know they were there. Although encounters with these intriguing and majestic animals are

Black bears do live on Mount Hood, but they're rarely seen.

extremely rare, they occasionally happen. So while you shouldn't be afraid to go into the woods, it's good to know how to respond to a large animal encounter so you can share the tale when you get back home.

Be Bear Aware

The only type of bear found in Oregon is the black bear (*Ursus americanus*). These are the smaller cousins of the mighty grizzly (or brown) bear. And while they are named "black" bears, their coloring can range from cinnamon to brown to black—so if you've ever heard anyone share their encounter with a grizzly bear on Mount Hood, it's more likely that they encountered a brown black bear. These typically timid animals grow five to six feet in length, weigh 125 to 250 pounds, and sustain themselves on a mostly vegetarian diet of berries, nuts, grasses, and insects; only occasionally will they dine on small animals, fish, and carrion. They are extremely wary of people and prefer to be left alone to forage, feed, and raise their young.

If you are fortunate enough to spot a black bear on Mount Hood, it is a truly magical experience. From late spring to midsummer, keep your eyes peeled in the morning and early evening hours, when bears are most active. In fall, they're often active all day, as they're gorging on goodies to fatten up for their long winter naps. When on the trail, watch for bear signs such as footprints, scat piles, and scratched-up trees. So as not to startle a bear—one of the things that can make them act aggressively—it's good to make noise by talking loudly, singing, or clapping when hiking through overgrown brush (especially berry bushes) or when approaching blind curves.

If you do encounter an aggressive bear, it's likely feeling threatened and defending its cubs or food source. Startled bears will pop their jaws, huff, and slam their paws to the ground to tell you that you've crossed the line. **Avoid eye contact,** which bears perceive as a challenge, and **talk calmly** to identify yourself as a human—that is, not a menu item. **Never turn your back on a**

bear and never, *EVER* run, but **back away slowly**. Occasionally, a bear will bluff charge (charge and stop short) to try to scare the holy hell out of you. **Stand your ground** and avoid eye contact, while trying not to soil yourself. Once the bear is gone, leave the area immediately. If a black bear does attack, summon the power of Thor and fight back with all you've got.

Cougar Country

Oregon recorded its first fatal cougar attack on Mount Hood in 2018. And while that may give you pause about venturing out into the woods, you can take heart in knowing that you're more likely to be struck by lightning or win the lottery before becoming the next cougar victim. Also, that cougar was promptly tracked down and killed so it would not inflict any further harm. That said, the odds of seeing a cougar are quite slim, much less even seeing the footprint of one of these shy, solitary animals. Similar to bears, cougars are often in the wind long before you're aware they were even nearby.

In the ridiculously rare instance that you do cross paths with a cougar and it gets curious about you, **maintain eye contact.** Cougars rely on being stealthy and hidden, so staring a cat down tells it you're aware of its presence. Next, **make noise and get crazy**. Wave your trekking poles or pull your jacket up to make yourself look larger and more like a formidable enemy. If you have children or a small dog with you, pick them up and keep them high, as cougars usually target the smallest, easiest prey. **Never run from a cougar**, as this may trigger the cat's instinctive urge to chase. Instead, **back away slowly** and never turn your back on the animal. Once the animal has gone, vacate the area immediately and notify the local land agency. If a cougar does attack, do not play dead but **fight back and fight dirty**. Punch it in the nose, poke it in the eyes, and hit it with rocks.

The Creepy Crawlies

While we relish wandering the woods with cute critters and cheerful birds, we also need to be aware of the less cuddly mountain residents: snakes and insects. Oregon is home to several species of **snakes**, including two types of poisonous rattlesnakes. The good news is that Oregon's rattlesnakes reside in the southern and high central and eastern regions of the state. If you see a snake while hiking around Mount Hood or in the Columbia River Gorge, it's most likely going to be a harmless garter snake.

There are plenty of little biting and stinging buggers in Oregon's forests. Unless you're allergic, simple topical treatments from your first-aid kit will relieve most bug bites and stings (see the Ten Essentials section). The only crawlies you really need to be concerned with are **ticks** and **mosquitoes**. Ticks typically reside in warm, grassy areas, such as the eastern Columbia River Gorge and high prairies on the east side of the Cascades. They don't fly but rather hop aboard their intended hosts. Ticks are capable of transmitting various diseases, including Lyme disease. If you're going to be hiking in tick country, the best way to avoid picking up one of these unsavory hitchhikers is to wear long sleeves and pants, tuck your pants into your socks, and apply an insect repellant to any exposed skin. After your hike, do a thorough check to make sure you didn't pick up any ticks. If you find a tick attached to you, remove it with a pair of tweezers by pulling it straight out. Monitor the location of the bite, and if you notice any changes, or begin feeling any unusual symptoms—headaches, fever, rash—seek medical attention.

Unfortunately, mosquitoes in the woods are just a fact of life these days, and they seem to get worse every year. They are most prevalent in late spring and early summer—just when Oregon's skies are clearing and you're itching to get outdoors. By midsummer, the little buggers are usually gone—or at least significantly diminished. While reported cases of mosquito-borne West Nile virus in Oregon are extremely rare, you should still take precautions to protect yourself. If you're willing to brave the bugs to frolic in the flowers, it's not so much trying to avoid getting bitten—*because you're going to get bitten*—it's how to minimize how much you're bitten. Armor up by wearing loose-fitting long pants and sleeves, as well as a hat, and apply a good bug repellent. A head net might also help you keep your sanity. There are some bug-repellent products you can purchase to treat your hiking clothing (i.e., permethrin); however, these can be quite toxic, so follow their directions carefully if you choose to use. An after-bite treatment or balm can help soothe the bites you do get.

FORAGING

The hills and woods on and around Mount Hood are home to a variety of wild berries and fungi—many of which are quite tasty! These include huckleberries, thimbleberries, salmonberries, and wild strawberries, as well as oyster, chanterelle, morel, matsutake, and other mushrooms. You are welcome to pick small amounts of berries and mushrooms to snack on while you're hiking. Gathering large amounts of berries and/or mushrooms, and transporting them out of the forest for personal and/or commercial use requires a harvesting permit. These are available through the Forest Service, and

Wild huckleberries are a tasty trail treat in late summer.

have limits and fees associated with the type and quantity of product being gathered. See the Passes and Permits page on the MHNF website for more information.

If you're mushroom hunting, you should absolutely, positively, *100%* know what it is you're picking. While there are many delicious morsels to be found around Mount Hood, there are just as many toxic and dangerous specimens as well. Some of the latter, such as the fly amanita, are even dangerous to touch. If you're even remotely unsure of what a specimen is, it's best to leave it be. A couple of good resources that can help you identify many of the fungi species you may find on your outings are *Northwest Foraging*, by Doug Benoliel, and *Mushrooms of the Pacific Northwest*, by Steve Trudell and Joe Ammirati. Be advised that mushroom hunting can be quite competitive. If you enter an area and observe someone already actively searching for tasty treats, it's best to go and find a new place to search.

Foraging tip: The best berry and mushroom gathering is usually done away from popular trails, as the treats that are right alongside the trails are typically snatched up or picked through as soon as they appear. If you're going to wander off trail for some tasty treasure hunting, make sure you're carrying a map and compass (or GPS) and constantly paying attention to where you came from and where you're going. A common irony among foragers is that they're usually most successful at finding themselves lost.

HIKING IN HUNTING SEASON

Hunting is permitted on many of Oregon's public lands. Seasons vary depending on the location, type of game, and the health of the population. Many popular hunts take place in late summer and early fall, coinciding with some great late-season hiking opportunities. For complete hunting regulations and seasonal openings, visit the Oregon Department of Fish and Wildlife website (see appendix IV). Here are some general guidelines if hiking during hunting season:

Wear bright-colored clothing. Pick a hat, shirt, jacket, or pack that will be clearly seen and identify you as a hiker. Orange and red are recommended; avoid white, khaki, and brown.

Make noise as you hike. Hunters typically avoid high-traffic areas that frighten away game. Talk, sing, or whistle to let hunters know that there are hikers in the area.

Avoid peak hunting times. Hunters favor dawn and dusk, when animals are most active. If hiking in low light, wear a headlamp.

Avoid off-trail travel. Hunters are scoping for game away from populous trails, so avoid tromping through brush where a hunter might be awaiting his next target.

Leave Fido at home. If you hike with a dog, hunting season is a good time to leave him at home. If you do take a dog, put it in its own bright-colored vest and keep it leashed and at your side.

APPAREL AND GEAR

Day hiking does not require carrying a lot of gear. Most of what you need to enjoy yourself is what you choose to wear and what can go into a small backpack. Start with a good pair of trail shoes or lightweight hiking boots. Choose footwear that fits comfortably for your foot size and shape, and consider sizing up a half size larger than your regular street shoes to give your feet a little room to swell once you get moving. Along with your footwear, choose a good pair of breathable socks, preferably of moisture-wicking wool or a synthetic material, with a moderate amount

Pack along a small trash bag and help keep Mount Hood's trails clean while you hike.

of cushion. If you're prone to blisters, adding a thin sock liner can help reduce friction in the sensitive spots. On longer hikes, when your feet are likely to get good and sweaty, you may want to carry an extra pair of socks to change into halfway through your hike to help keep your feet dry and comfortable.

During the regular hiking season in Oregon (spring, summer, fall), days typically start cool and warm up gradually. This makes the layering system the best approach to planning your trail apparel. Start with breathable, moisture-wicking base layers (top and bottom). These will help keep you cool, dry, and comfortable as your body heats up. The best base layers are made of wool, silk, or synthetic materials. Next come your middle layers. Up top, choose warm and insulating layers that you can get into and out of easily to adjust for changes in the day's temperature. Down below, choose garments that will protect your legs from overgrown brush, poison oak, and other scratchy things. Top it all off with a light windbreaker or rain jacket for those high, exposed ridges and just in case the weather gets wet. A few other good things to pack along are a light, compressible puffy jacket, a warm beanie, and a light pair of gloves. Cotton apparel is not recommended as it soaks easily when you sweat or get it wet—and once it gets wet, it can lead to uncomfortable chafing on warm days and potential hypothermia on cool ones.

If you plan on winter hiking in the rain and snow, choose heavier, water-repellent insulating layers that are still breathable and easy to get in and out of. Even if it's freezing outside, you can still work up a sweat slogging through mud and snow. Jackets and pants with zippered vents are ideal for regulating body temperature on winter hikes. Many seasonal pants may even be equipped with internal gaiters to help keep snow and water out of your socks and boots. Heat escapes quickly by way of your extremities, so top off your winter wear with a warm hat to keep your noggin toasty and a pair of gloves to keep your digits from turning blue.

Along with your footwear and apparel, you should carry a few essentials in a small backpack (see the Ten Essentials section). One of the most important things you should have in your pack is a **map and compass**—*and know how to use them!* While most of the trails in this guide are relatively easy to navigate, and most trails on Mount Hood have good directional signage, it's still possible to lose your way if you take an unplanned detour or wander too far on an unmarked path. After all, wilderness invites exploration. Being able to identify your location on a map and find your way back to your starting point can be vital, especially if bad weather rolls in and visibility decreases. Every year, hikers get lost on Mount Hood and require rescue. Don't be one of them.

Carrying a dedicated GPS device or smartphone with a GPS navigation app while you hike can also be beneficial for helping you keep track of your location. And just like with a traditional map and compass, you should know how to use them, as they won't do you any good in a pinch if you don't know which way is which. Many outdoor gear shops offer courses in electronic navigation. If you're unfamiliar with the workings of your navigation device or app, consider looking into a course. And most importantly for electronic navigation devices, they're only helpful for as long as their batteries last. If you're going to use a GPS or smartphone on the trail, carry extra batteries or a spare battery pack for recharging—especially for the latter, as GPS apps on smartphones tend to drain batteries rapidly.

A few extra items can help ensure an enjoyable experience on-trail. Consider a small, packable camp chair. You're likely going to be hiking to many a spectacular viewpoint, so having a comfy place to sit while you eat your lunch and enjoy the view can be quite delightful. Carry a small nature guide to help you identify some of the trees, plants, flowers, or wildlife you may encounter on-trail. Some of these are available in small brochure form or as apps for your smartphone. This book highlights many of the common things you will see, but there is so much more to discover.

Ten Essentials

Whenever you're heading out on a hike—no matter how short or long—you should always pack your Ten Essentials developed by The Mountaineers. These are a selection of just-in-case items that can help you out in a pinch, such as sustaining a minor injury, experiencing a gear failure, or needing to spend an unplanned night in the wilderness.

1. **Navigation (map and compass):** Download or purchase a map of the area you plan to visit. Familiarize yourself with your hiking area, such as trailhead locations, connecting trails, significant landmarks, and so on, to help keep you on track. A cell phone with a navigation app or GPS unit are good to have along too. Remember, if you carry an electronic device, be sure to pack along extra batteries or a battery pack.
2. **Illumination (flashlight, headlamp):** If your hike runs late and you're caught out after dark, you'll be glad to have a light source to help you find your way back to the trailhead. Having a light or lamp can also be a source of comfort if you wind up spending an unplanned night in the wilderness. Don't forget spare batteries for this one, too.
3. **Sun protection (hat, sunscreen, sunglasses):** It's much easier to get

sunburned at higher elevations where the air is thinner and you're closer to the sun. Use a sunscreen rated at least SPF 30, and wear sunglasses and sun-protective clothing. Mountainous terrain (e.g., volcanic rocks and snow) can reflect the sun back at you from all sides, so it's wise to apply sunscreen even if wearing a hat.

4. **First aid:** For day hiking, carry a small kit containing bandages, antiseptic, blister prevention supplies, tweezers, pain relievers, and perhaps a small how-to manual. For longer or overnight outings, consider adding gauze, tape, scissors, anti-inflammatory and anti-diarrheal tablets, and topical antibiotics. Don't forget any important personal prescriptions. If you have allergies (e.g., pollen or bees), carry antihistamine tablets or an EpiPen, and instruct your hiking partners about what to do in case you need assistance.
5. **Repair kit and tools (including a knife):** Pack along a small kit of just-in-case items that can help you out in the event of a gear failure. Basic repair items such as duct tape, safety pins, a length of lightweight cord, and a tube of superglue can work wonders in a pinch. Keep a small pocketknife or multitool in your kit as well.
6. **Fire tools (matches and firestarter):** Spending a spontaneous night in the wilderness is not likely, but a campfire can provide welcome warmth in an emergency. Carry a butane lighter or waterproof matches in a zip-top bag. A small, lightweight firestarter, such as dryer lint soaked in petroleum jelly or commercially prepared firestarter tabs, can come in handy.
7. **Emergency shelter:** If a sudden storm blows in, or you have to spend the night outdoors, a lightweight shelter can help keep you warm and dry. This can be as simple as a garbage bag or a rain poncho. There are also lightweight tarps, heat-reflective emergency blankets, and compact bivvy sacks you can carry that can double as picnic blankets or seat pads.
8. **Nutrition (extra food):** Hiking burns a lot of calories, so pack along enough food and snacks to keep your energy up through your hike. Foods and snacks high in calories and protein are best for sustained energy, for example, nuts and nut butters, energy bars, and meat jerkies. Bring a little extra. If you wind up spending the night outdoors, you're going to get hungry.
9. **Hydration (water treatment):** Bring enough water to stay hydrated for the length of the trail you plan to hike. Keep weather and temperature factors in mind. On sweltering days at higher elevations, you will drink more than on cooler days at lower elevations. Use an electrolyte supplement to help replenish essential minerals you'll sweat out. In addition, it's a good idea to carry a water purification method (filter, pump, or treatment additive) in case you need more, or due to an extended outing.
10. **Insulation (extra clothing):** Weather and temperature can change quickly in the mountains, so it's advisable to carry an extra insulating layer (e.g., fleece or sweater) and raingear. Pack additional layers needed to survive the night in the worst conditions that you may realistically encounter. Be sure to include a warm beanie, gloves, and extra socks.

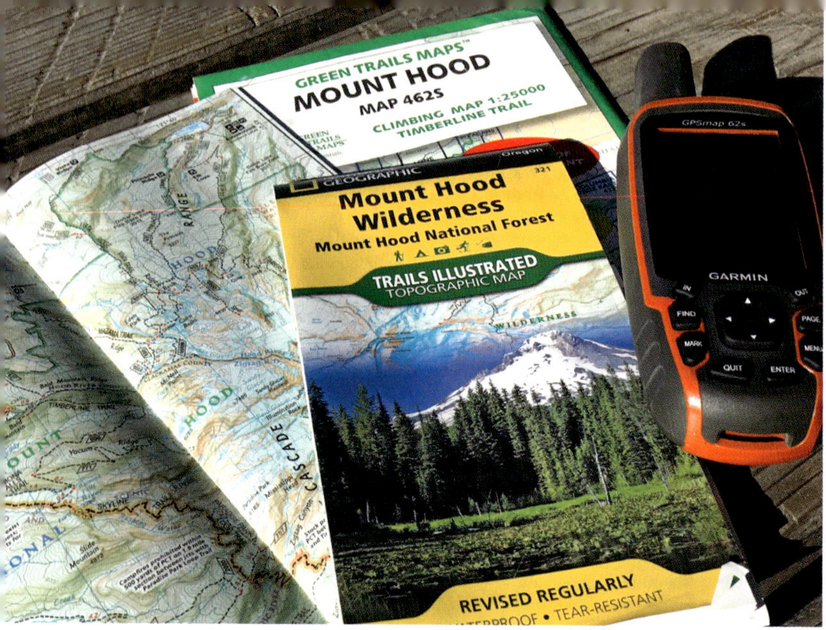

Always carry your Ten Essentials, including a good trail map.

Food and Water

With all of the trails in this guide being single-day outings, there's no need to overload your pack. For shorter outings, you may just want to bring along a few snacks. For the longer ones, snacks and a lunch or dinner are a good idea. There are a lot of hikes in this book that culminate at good viewpoints, and having a tasty meal to enjoy along with the view just makes the day that much better—so go ahead and pack along that sub sandwich and fudgy brownie. If you're going longer distances, it's good to snack often on items high in calories and protein to keep your energy up and balanced. Pack along a few extra snacks, just in case your hike takes longer than expected or you need a little extra boost.

Staying hydrated while hiking is important to keep muscles and joints in optimal condition, improve performance, reduce fatigue, and replace fluids as you sweat. As a general guideline, when hiking a moderate trail in moderate weather, drinking a half liter of water per hour is good practice. When hiking strenuous trails, in warmer weather, or at higher elevations, one full liter per hour is recommended. You may also want to add an electrolyte supplement to help replenish some of the minerals you'll be sweating out. While you may not always be thirsty—especially when hiking at high elevations or in cooler weather—it is important to remind yourself to drink.

While there is often plenty of running water on and around Mount Hood, it is not necessarily safe to drink. Unfortunately, many mountain water sources contain tasteless protozoa such as *Cryptosporidium* and *Giardia*. These waterborne pathogens can cause flulike symptoms, including vomiting and diarrhea that can last for six weeks—or in some cases up to a year. So while fresh mountain water may look clean and inviting, it takes only one bad swig to do you in. If you're inclined to indulge in tasty mountain water, you should only do so after properly filtering it.

Water-treatment devices range from UV-light pens that kill bacteria and viruses to carbon or ceramic filters that eliminate bacteria and unpleasant tastes. Almost all are lightweight, portable, and extremely effective. There are also water-treatment tablets, usually made with iodine or chlorine dioxide; the latter is better, not having a nasty taste. When drawing water from the mountain, choose a water source that is clean and flowing. Avoid milky, silty water on Mount Hood, as this often contains particles of silica (glass) that can clog filters and wreak havoc on your digestive system.

TRAIL SAFETY

Going for a walk in the woods is generally a safe and enjoyable experience. You don't have to have the latest high-tech hiking gear, carry a bunch of gadgets, or be an expert in vulcanology to have a good hike. However, there are a few situations that can throw a curve ball at you, such as missing signs at trail junctions, unmapped reroutes, and swollen rivers. And it can be quite easy to get disoriented in inclement weather or if you encounter snow on the trail. The best thing to help ensure a safe and successful outdoors experience is exercising some good ol' common sense, whether you're hiking solo, with a partner, or in a group.

Leave your hiking itinerary with a friend or family member. In 2003, outdoor adventurer Aron Ralston became trapped in a remote slot canyon and spent five days stuck there before cutting off his own forearm and hiking out. Rescuers had been called when friends became aware of his absence, but they had no idea where to look because he hadn't told anyone where he was going. This is a worst-case scenario, but a good reason to leave your hiking plans with someone at home who can notify authorities if you fail to return on time, and tell them exactly where you are.

Your hiking itinerary should include the trail(s) you plan to hike, your intended destination(s), and your estimated return time. If you can, print out a copy of your trail map showing your hiking plan to accompany your itinerary. Once your hike is complete, call or message your contact and let them know you've safely returned. Give yourself a little padding, time-wise, so your contact doesn't get worried if you don't call in exactly at your estimated return time, just in case your hike takes longer than expected, or you take a little extra time to eat lunch at an exceptionally good viewpoint.

Recognize your own skill level, and know when to turn around. You don't need to be Bear Grylls to take a hike on Mount Hood. Most of the trails in this guide can be hiked by anyone with a little stamina and a good pair of boots. That said, be realistic with your expectations and know your own limits. If you're new to hiking, don't go for the longest, highest, steepest trail as your first outing. Start with something easy and build up to the bigger stuff. If you're not used to hiking at higher elevations, start low and work your way up.

There's no shame in turning around if you get tired, aren't comfortable crossing a raging river, or lose the trail in snow. Unless you have skill and experience in routefinding and wilderness navigation, especially when it comes to winter conditions, you're better off calling it a day and trying again at a later date. You don't want to put yourself, your companions, or, potentially, the people who might have to come and rescue you in danger. Remember the old adage "Better safe than sorry." The mountain will still be there next week, or next month.

Ford rivers only when it's safe. There are several large rivers on Mount Hood that do not have bridges for crossing. In spring and early summer, these can be raging torrents of whitewater and potentially hazardous. If a waterway looks too high, too fast, or too deep to cross, it is not worth the risk. Just head back and try the trail again later in the season. If a waterway does look manageable, here are some river-fording tips:

- **Cross in the early morning hours.** This is typically when snow- and glacier-fed streams are flowing at their lowest. However, if you'll have to recross later, during the warmer part of the day, it's possible that the water level can increase dramatically and prevent another safe crossing. Consider this when choosing trails that will require significant water crossings.
- **Look for straight, shallow, wide, and gentle water.** Also, you don't have to cross right at the trail, as this may not be the safest location. Scout up- and downstream for a safe crossing with calmer water. Before scouting, identify where the trail continues on the other side so you can find it again if you have to go far to find a safe crossing location.
- **Scan for "strainers" and tripping hazards.** Look for any debris that could trap you if you get swept downstream, or

Many of Mount Hood's rivers do not have bridges. Use caution and scout for the safest crossing.

anything underwater that you could get snagged by or slip on.

- **Don't cross if the water is above your knees.** Any higher than that, and the current can suck you downstream. If the water is calm and flat, you may bend this rule of thumb.
- **Keep your boots on.** Bare feet can slip on rocks and wet logs, plus you risk jamming or breaking toes or puncturing your feet on sharp rocks. Use trekking poles to help you balance.
- **Unbuckle your pack's waist belt.** Your pack might shift as you slosh across, but having an easy exit strategy could save your bacon if you go for an unexpected plunge.

Keep these tips in mind if you become lost or injured. Most of the hiking trails on Mount Hood and in this guide are pretty straightforward and easy to navigate under normal conditions. But if you're not paying attention, it is possible to take a wrong turn or wander off the trail. If you break off the trail to check out a view or take a bathroom break, try to keep the trail within visual range so you can find your way back. If you've wandered too far off the trail, taken a wrong turn, lost the trail in snow, or lost visibility due to a sudden change in weather, the first thing to do is keep your head and *not panic*.

If you're hiking with companions, or hiking solo and have seen other hikers nearby, and you don't know which way to go, the first thing to do is try to get someone's attention. The easiest way is just by shouting for help. If you have an emergency whistle on your backpack strap (or in your Ten Essentials kit), give it three quick, loud blasts. This is the universal signal for help. Stay where you are and wait for a response. If you don't get a response after a few minutes, try again. If after several attempts you still don't get a response and haven't found your way back to the trail, it's time to **S.T.O.P.**:

- **Stop** and take a few deep breaths. Sit down and have a snack and a drink of water. By remaining calm, you'll keep from panicking and making rash decisions. As you consider your next steps, you can be thankful that your companions are likely looking for you, or—just in case—you left your hiking itinerary with someone back home who knows, generally, where you are.
- **Think** about your situation and your location. How long has it been since you remember being on the trail? Were you traveling uphill or downhill to get where you are? What were the last significant landmarks you observed? If you've been taking pictures, look back through them to see if you can identify anything that might lead you back the way you came.
- **Observe** your surroundings. If you're above the trees, try to identify any significant landmarks and find them on your map. If you're in the trees with no outward visibility, look to see if you've left any footprints that you may be able to follow back. Scan for signs of a trail, such as blazes or notches on trees, logouts (fallen trees cut through for a trail), and cairns.
- **Plan** your next steps, and take a quick inventory of your food, water, and gear. Consider how much daylight you have left, and what the weather is doing. If you have a lot of daylight left and the weather is favorable, try methodically finding your way back to the trail. If daylight is waning, you should take shelter and prepare for a night outdoors so as not to wander aimlessly in the darkness.

If your attempts at regaining the trail don't pan out and you're carrying a cell phone or an emergency beacon, now is the time to fire it up. Cell phone service in the wilderness is spotty at best. If you're in the woods and can't get a clear cell signal, try to find a clearing or get to higher ground. Carrying an emergency beacon or personal locator/communicator that operates via satellite connection can be a worthy investment for traveling in the backcountry. These devices are more reliable than cell phones, are fairly affordable, and can connect directly to emergency services—a worthy little bit of insurance if the need arises, and nice for giving peace of mind to friends and family back home.

While you wait for your rescue, settle in, try to get comfortable, and be thankful you're carrying your Ten Essentials. If you can, try to find a spot near a meadow or clearing so you will be visible by any rescuers searching from the air. The most important thing you want to do is keep warm and dry. If the day is cooling off, put on all the extra layers you're carrying. If it's safe to do so, try building a campfire. It will keep you warm and the smoke will be visible to rescuers. Have something to eat and stay hydrated. While you may be tempted to while away the time by playing Plants vs. Zombies, don't wear down your phone battery. You may be able to use it the next day to call or text for help if you can get a signal.

If you're lost *and* injured, it's extra important to stay calm—or at least try to. First, do what you can with your first-aid kit to treat your injury. Second, proceed through the S.T.O.P. method to determine your next move. If you're still mobile, despite being banged up, do what you can to effect your exit. If you're unable to move, try to get as comfortable as you can by bundling up or taking shelter, then eat something, drink something, and wait for your rescue. For more information about treating trail-related injuries, there are a variety of first-aid guides available, or consider taking a wilderness first-aid course.

A NOTE ABOUT EMERGENCY BEACONS

An emergency beacon, such as a SPOT or PLB, is intended for just those types of situations: emergencies. Too many hikers in recent years have been using these devices for nonemergency incidents, such as getting rained on, experiencing a gear failure, or suffering a minor injury. This is not what these devices are intended for and puts a significant strain on emergency services, often at great expense. While you should not hesitate to activate your beacon if you are experiencing a legitimate emergency, you should ensure that it is just that, and not a minor inconvenience.

A two-way satellite communicator lets you send and receive text messages where there's no cellular service.

LEARN WILDERNESS SKILLS

If you're going to be spending more time hiking around the mountains and exploring wilderness areas, it's a good idea to learn a few skills that can help you out in a pinch if the need arises. There are many wilderness survival guides available that offer a wealth of information and instruction on everything from weathering storms to fixing broken gear. Many outdoor gear shops, such as REI (rei.com), and some community hiking clubs offer workshops on essential outdoor skills, such as packing your backpack, map and compass navigation, basic survival, reading weather, and wilderness first aid.

If you're going to rely on electronic devices in the wilderness, be sure to read all the operating instructions, understand the device's limits, and practice with it somewhere close to home before diving into the woods. With an arsenal of wilderness survival knowledge at the ready, you'll be able to kick into high gear and respond quickly and confidently to any unexpected incidents.

Where there's smoke, there's fire. With warm, dry weather comes the threat of wildfires. Most of these are sparked by lightning storms. Some are the result of careless individuals. In recent years, as Northwest summers have been getting hotter and drier, wildfires are becoming more common and more destructive. In 2011, lightning ignited a wildfire that ravaged 6300 acres of forest on the north side of Mount Hood. In 2017, a reckless teen lobbed a firecracker into Eagle Creek, resulting in a devastating wildfire that burned more than 48,000 acres and damaged and destroyed numerous trails.

If you encounter thunderstorm activity while hiking, be extra vigilant of your surroundings. Descend from high ridges and retreat from any sharp, exposed peaks. If you observe smoke or an active wildfire anywhere in your vicinity, plan to beat a quick exit. Wildfires can spread incredibly quickly, so don't assume that because a fire is in the distance, you're safe. Consult your map and either (1) turn around and exit the way you came; or (2) head out to a road via the nearest safe route. If you're unable to effect a safe exit by these means, head for the nearest body of water or large meadow, or try to safely get above the tree line. Don't flirt with trying to get around a wildfire. If the wind picks up or changes direction, it could blow the fire right at you. Dangers can also remain in past burn areas. Use extra caution when hiking in areas with blackened, dead-standing trees and loamy, loose soil, as trees may become unstable, especially in high winds.

Trail and Trailhead Crime

Thankfully, most criminals are lazy, and committing crimes on trails is usually too much effort. That said, staying vigilant and keeping a healthy level of awareness is always a good idea. Here are few tips to follow to help ensure that you have a safe experience outdoors.

Never leave valuables in your vehicle. Take (or hide) anything and everything that might look interesting. Even if it's empty, a closed sunglasses case might look like it contains an expensive pair of Maui Jims; a smartphone charger might make a prowler think the phone is still in the car.

Case the place. When arriving at the trailhead, look for anything or anyone that seems out of place. Criminals rely on stealth and may leave if they feel "made." Snap a casual pic of the vehicle and license plate, and make a note with a description of the person in question.

Trust your instincts. If you sense that someone you meet on-trail has bad intentions, allow yourself to be guarded and rude if necessary. Never tell anyone you meet where you're headed, especially if you're hiking alone. Be vague: "I'm just going for a while."

Never mention your party size. If you're hiking alone, using "we" statements might confuse a criminal. Shouting "Hurry up, Tony!" or "Let's get going, Steve!" into the bushes may deter someone who thinks you're an easy solo target.

Avoid hiking with headphones. When in the backcountry, try listening to birdsong, squeaking pikas, and whistling marmots instead of blasting your favorite Ramones album. Paying attention to your surroundings will help you hear someone, or something, coming.

A NOTE ABOUT SAFETY

Safety is an important concern in all outdoor activities. No guidebook can alert you to every hazard or anticipate the limitations of every reader. Therefore, the descriptions of roads, trails, routes, and natural features in this book are not representations that a particular place or excursion will be safe for your party. When you follow any of the routes described in this book, you assume responsibility for your own safety. Under normal conditions, such excursions require the usual attention to traffic, road and trail conditions, weather, terrain, the capabilities of your party, and other factors. Keeping informed on current conditions and exercising common sense are the keys to a safe, enjoyable outing.

—Mountaineers Books

How to Use This Book

The trails featured in this guide strike a balance between easily accessible routes and short, easy outings, good for beginning hikers and families with kids, and longer, more remote and challenging trails good for experienced hikers and those who may be conditioning with an eye toward bigger adventures, such as the Timberline Trail or Pacific Crest Trail. This guide does not include every single trail on Mount Hood. Some trails were omitted for their difficult access, their poor condition, or simply for being too long to reasonably hike in a single day. Regardless, you are likely to find more than enough suggestions in the following pages to keep you hiking on Mount Hood for many seasons to come.

This book also includes "section-hiking" guides to the 43-mile Timberline Trail around Mount Hood, and more than 70 miles of the Pacific Crest Trail (PCT) that passes through the Mount Hood area. These descriptions outline how you may hike bite-size pieces of the Timberline or PCT, one day hike at a time. And since Mount Hood spends a portion of every year slumbering under a snowy blanket, this guide includes a selection of winter routes good for snowshoeing and cross-country skiing so you can enjoy the mountain in all its sparkling, wintry glory.

The hike descriptions in this guide are presented in a way to give you all the important trail beta you need to plan and enjoy each of these hikes on and around Mount Hood. This includes general directional descriptions, permit requirements (if applicable), driving directions, and more. While each description includes turn-by-turn directions, area info, and details on natural and/or cultural history, there is much more to see than this guide can cover. Some (nonvital) details were intentionally left out in order to allow you plenty of opportunity for your own self-discovery. In some cases, additional resources are recommended to help you learn more.

OREGON'S MIDDLE EARTH

If you are a fan of J. R. R. Tolkien's works, like *The Hobbit*, *The Lord of the Rings*, and *The Silmarillion*, then you are about to embark on an epic journey into the Northwest's version of Middle Earth. Many of the trails on Mount Hood and in this guide visit ancient forests evoking Fangorn and Lórien, high passes resembling the Misty Mountains and Emyn Muil, and desolate plains akin to the Plateau of Gorgoroth. Plus, you'll come across assorted pinnacles, mounds, and outcrops that harken to some of Middle Earth's famed and notorious ruins. You'll find many references throughout this guide suggesting some of these wonders. If you're not familiar with these fantastical locations, not to fear, you will enjoy all these sights just the same.

RATINGS AND MEASUREMENTS

Each trail description in this guide begins with a selection of basic information about the hike, beginning with a **Rating**. This figure ranks the general appeal of the hike based on scenery, accessibility, typical trail condition, and a variety of other considerations. This figure is quite subjective, as everyone finds outdoor enjoyment in their own right, so the following ratings boil it down to these factors:

- ***** This is about as good as it gets on Mount Hood, with plenty of stunning views, wildflowers, waterfalls, and/or other natural features. Of course, these hikes are no secret, so plan to share the experience with others.
- **** A great hike with plenty of outstanding scenery and/or natural features. Typically popular, so be prepared for crowds.
- *** These are good hikes that may have a viewpoint and/or other natural features, but don't draw the masses, so they present good opportunities for finding some solitude.
- ** Trails that are good for a decent hike, but with few views or special features. Good for finding solitude, practicing macro photography, or just getting outdoors and trying something new.
- * A nice way to just stretch your legs and get some fresh air. These trails may be in a constant state of disrepair or with few remarkable features, but they challenge you to find the silver lining.

The next ranking each hike receives—and perhaps the more important one—is its **Difficulty**. This rating is also quite subjective, as every hiker views trail challenges differently. This score was reached by calculating several variables, such as distance, elevation gain, terrain, exposure, and other conditions, and coming up with a score that best represents an "average" calculation. For example, a short, steep trail may receive a similar score as a long, flat trail; a trail that requires routefinding or river fording is considered more difficult, even if short and flat. Considering these factors, here is what you can generally expect from each difficulty rating in this guide:

1 Easy walking on good trail; shorter distances; no challenges
2 Mild to moderate hiking on good trail; moderate distances; few to no challenges
3 Moderate hiking on uneven trail; moderate distances/elevation gain; few challenges
4 More difficult hiking on rough, steep trail; longer distances/elevation gain; some challenges
5 Strenuous hiking on rough, steep trail; long distances/elevation gain; river fords, routefinding

With regard to winter trails, their difficulty will vary significantly depending on the depth and compaction of the snow. The deeper the snow, the more challenging the trail will be to hike—even flat trails. The difficulty ratings given to the winter trails in this guide are based on moderate snow cover with some compaction. Following a significant snowfall, when snow is light, deep, and loose, foot travel over it—or more likely through it—will be more demanding. You

Paradise Park is one of the longer, more challenging hikes on Mount Hood, but with scenery like this, it's worth the extra effort (Hikes 25, 32, 65, 73).

should take this into consideration if planning to visit a winter trail with little ones or your pup.

The **Distance** given for each hike in this guide is for the total miles required to hike the trail as described, from the trailhead and back or one-way for Timberland or Pacific Crest Trail hikes. This includes round-trips (out-and-back), lollipops, and loops. Short detours to viewpoints or other points of interest are not included in this figure unless they are of significant distance. Each description will indicate the approximate amount of distance added if you choose to explore these options. These figures also do not include the distances and/or mileage for the **Extend Your Trip** options on some hikes. The additional travel distance for these options will be included in these supplements. Most of the trails in this guide (with just a few exceptions) do not exceed 12 miles.

The mileage figures used in this guide are based on hiking and surveying each trail and tracking them with a professional Garmin GPS unit using WGS 84 measurements. These surveys are then calculated using the CalTopo trail-mapping platform. While every distance figure in this guide was meticulously calculated for the highest degree of accuracy, there are numerous factors that can affect the calculations of GPS distances measured in mountainous terrain.

This includes tree cover, angle of terrain, cloud cover, temperature, humidity, and more. So while not every measurement may be 100 percent accurate, you can generally assume that they're at least 99 percent accurate.

The same can be said for each **Elevation Gain** figure—and perhaps a little more so. Each of these figures is derived from the same method as the distance measurements; however, this figure is even more challenging to pinpoint for the same reasons—especially when it comes to tree cover. These figures are based on known USGS topographic measurements and more current GPS mapping, and are calculated to be as accurate as possible, perhaps 98 percent, based on currently available data.

The elevation gain figures for each hike are for the *total elevation gain* you can expect for the length of each hike. This is not just the difference between the low point and the high point, but for every up and down, from start to finish, whether it's an out-and-back, lollipop, or loop. The elevation gains for the hikes in this guide can vary significantly. Easier trails may gain only a few hundred feet, while more challenging trails may gain several thousand feet. One of the most challenging hikes in this guide, Zigzag Mountain Lookout has 4400 feet of elevation gain!

The **High Point** for each hike is just what it suggests: the highest point you will reach on each hike. These points may not necessarily mean the end or summit of a hike. It could also represent a location along the hike where the trail reaches its highest point of elevation. The trails in this guide remain at mostly low to moderate elevations, with the highest trail reaching an elevation of 8490 feet. This guide does not include mountaineering or climbing routes.

The **Season** indicated with each hike is the typical timeframe that the trail is accessible and generally snow-free. This is more of a guideline than a rule, especially in recent years. Hiking "seasons" (the months we typically expect to be able to hike at moderate mountain elevations) used to be more predictable, but with climate change having a greater impact on weather and seasons, access to Oregon's mountains can vary greatly from one year to the next. A long winter with a heavy snowpack followed by a cool spring may result in trails staying buried under snow later than usual, whereas a mild winter with a light snowpack followed by a balmy spring may render trails accessible earlier than usual. While the recommendations in this guide suggest the time that trails *should* be snow-free, you should still check the current trail and road conditions online or with the appropriate ranger station.

The maps in this guide provide a simplified overview of each featured trail; however, due to their small size, some details have been omitted. In addition, each map covers only the specific area relative to each hike. For a larger overview of the area you'll be hiking, you should carry a high-quality topographic map on all your hikes. The **Maps** recommended for most of the trails in this guide are National Geographic's Trails Illustrated Mount Hood Wilderness #321, Trails Illustrated Pacific Crest Trail: Oregon North #1004, and Green Trails Mount Hood #462S. In some cases, there are other trail maps available for specific areas, such as community trail networks and Sno-Parks. See appendix II for a list of these downloadable trail maps.

Rounding out each info block are a few more details to help you prepare for your

LEGEND

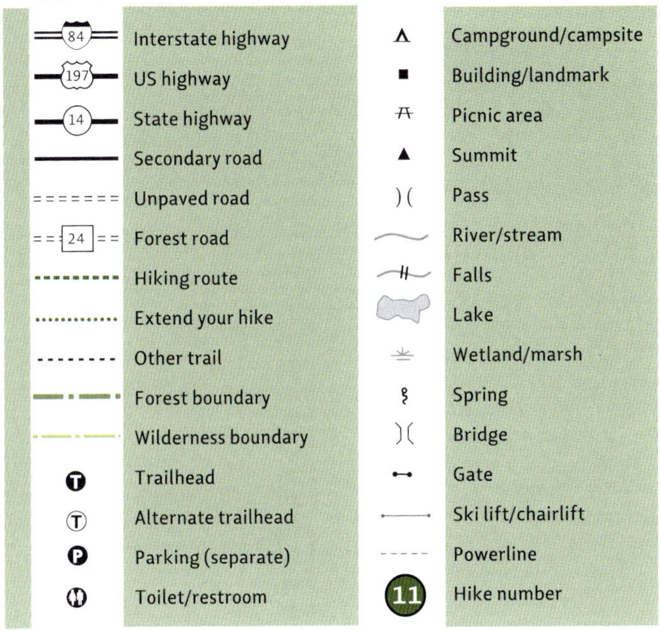

hike. **Permits** tells you whether any hiking or parking permits are required for the trail. **Contact** lets you know where to go for more information and to inquire about current road and trail conditions. Mount Hood National Forest is managed by four different ranger districts, so depending on where you're hiking, there will be different land managers who can assist you. You'll find district locations and phone numbers in appendix III in the back of this book. In addition, each hike provides pertinent **Notes** about the trail. This entry will alert you to any potential challenges or safety issues related to the hike, seasonal access limits, and may offer skill or experience recommendations. Finally, **GPS** coordinates (degrees and decimal minutes) are provided for the trailhead location of each hike. These are generally not required for accessing any of the trails in this guide, as they are all accessible from established trailheads on mostly easy, drivable roads. If you're using a dedicated GPS device or GPS smartphone app, these can help you pinpoint your starting/ending point for monitoring your location as you hike.

The nuts and bolts of each hike comes in the form of a detailed **Description**. These narratives will give you turn-by-turn directions and mileage indicators that reference significant landmarks and points of interest that will help keep you on track and point out some of the features to be seen along the way. This includes trail junctions, viewpoints, waterfalls, geographic features, and points of natural, cultural, or historical significance. To add to your enjoyment, each description also mentions some of the easily identifiable trees, shrubs, and wildflowers you might happen upon. Don't be surprised if you suddenly find references to visiting Middle Earth, Endor, or Wakanda, as Oregon's wilderness areas can be pretty fantastical. In addition to all the good stuff you will find on each hike, these descriptions will also inform you about any challenges to be encountered, such as steep and/or difficult trail sections, river fords, bushwhacking, routefinding needs, or potentially dangerous locations.

A selection of **icons** at the beginning of each description serves as a quick-reference guide for some of the features and compatibilities of each hike. **Kid-friendly** hikes are typically shorter, easier trails and often with a significant feature or point of interest at the end. **Dog-friendly** hikes are those suitable for bringing Fido along without any risks to their safety (see Hiking with Dogs). **Multiuse** trails are those that may be open to horseback riders and mountain bikers. On some winter trails, it may also include motorized users. While you're likely to see an abundance of **wildflowers**, **geologic features**, and **great mountain views** on most hikes, some are quite exceptional and are indicated as such. There are many hikes in this guide that feature **points of historical interest**, ranging from American Indian and Oregon Trail sites to old fire lookouts. While most of the trails in this guide are generally hikeable in spring, summer, and fall seasons, some are also good **winter hikes**, while **endangered trails** may be overgrown or unmaintained and may be more challenging to hike (see Road and Trail Conditions). Finally, you should exercise **caution** on trails along high ridges and cliffs, or trails that may have challenging water crossings. These trails may not be suitable for children, dogs, or inexperienced hikers (see Trail Safety).

Kid-friendly

Dog-friendly

Multiuse trail

Exceptional wildflowers (in season)

Exceptional views

Waterfall or water features

Point of historical interest

Good hikes for cloudy days

Volcanic or geological features

Nearby camping available

Accessible in winter

Endangered trail

Possible challenges or hazards

Within each hike description, you'll find detailed driving directions for **Getting There**. Most of the hikes in this guide start at trailheads on good, paved roads or highways via Sandy from the west (Portland area), or Hood River from the north (Columbia River Gorge area). Some more remote trailheads might use dirt or gravel forest roads (FR).

COMMON TREES AROUND MOUNT HOOD

1. Douglas fir
2. Mountain hemlock
3. Noble fir
4. Ponderosa pine
5. Western red cedar
6. White oak

See appendix I for common wildflowers and shrubs.

Most of these forest roads are drivable by typical passenger vehicles and do not require high clearance or four-wheel drive. A select few trails do require driving rough, challenging roads, and this will be indicated, if applicable. If you're considering hiking a trail that requires driving an unpaved road, it's a good idea to contact the ranger district and inquire about the road's condition. Unimproved roads are often susceptible to damage from winter weather and storms, and repairs on remote roads can take a while to be completed.

When available, some hikes provide opportunities to **Extend Your Trip**. These are suggestions for taking your journey beyond the hike as summarized. These suggestions may involve adding miles to visit additional destinations or viewpoints, incorporating other trails for longer outings, or taking alternate return routes. If a hike includes an Extend Your Trip suggestion, it will provide the additional mileage and/or elevation gain involved. A few of these alternatives may require going farther than a typical day hike and may be more appropriate as overnight backpacking trips.

HIKE YOUR OWN HIKE

This is the Golden Rule. Hiking is not just for über-athletes and hardcore thru-hikers. Most of the trails on Mount Hood are all-access trails that can be hiked by just about anyone in reasonably good health. This guidebook is intended to help you discover these trails in a manner that suits

There's more to Mount Hood than big views. Don't forget to enjoy the small, unusual, and colorful things, like this turkey tail fungi.

HIKING CHECKLIST

Are you ready to hit the trail? Go through this pre-hike checklist to ensure you don't forget anything.

- ❑ Pack Ten Essentials
- ❑ Pack food and water
- ❑ Wear appropriate clothing
- ❑ Check trail conditions
- ❑ Check road conditions
- ❑ Check weather forecast
- ❑ Leave itinerary
- ❑ Fuel up auto

your individual interests and abilities. If you're new to hiking, or to the Northwest, start with the easy trails and work your way up to more challenging ones. Enjoy each hiking experience for what it has to offer.

Many of the trails in this guide spend a lot of time in the trees—a product of all the Northwest rain that keeps Oregon so vibrant and green. Instead of getting bored with monotonous forest, take a closer look and discover more about what's at your feet. Oregon has a fascinating natural story, much of it found in the colorful rocks and lavas on and near the trail, as well as all the vibrant mosses, lichens, flowers, and fungi that populate the forests. Pack along a small nature guide, or download a smartphone app (Oregon Wildflowers is a great one to have handy) and turn your hike into a treasure hunt. See how many you can identify and keep a log of your finds. Give yourself bonus points if you find the elusive calypso orchid or a morel mushroom.

Now start flipping through this book and putting hikes on your to-do list. A good place to start is the **Hikes at a Glance** chart at the front of the book. This will help you quickly identify trails with waterfalls, trails with wildflowers, trails with great views, or trails to do on a cloudy day. Put a few of each on your list so when you're ready to go for a hike, you have a few preselected choices ready to go. Then you'll be ready to grab your boots and pack and head out to enjoy all that's waiting to be discovered around one of the most beautiful places in Oregon. Happy trails!

Opposite: *Enjoy sprawling wildflower meadows, icy glacial streams, and sweeping views from Wy'East Basin (Hike 8).*

mount hood north

Lose yourself in nature and find peace.
—Ralph Waldo Emerson

It takes a little more effort to access the trails on Mount Hood's rugged north side, but the rewards are often fewer crowds and bigger views than on the other sides of the mountain. However, following the 2011 Dollar Lake Fire, which burned most of Mount Hood's middle northern flank, some of these trails have deteriorated and lost some of their appeal. That's not to say they're not worth hiking. Despite these trails climbing through miles of scorched forest, the mountainside is recovering nicely, with plenty of new forest taking root and open hillsides brimming with summer wildflowers. From the top of many of the long, northern ridges, you can use the round-the-mountain Timberline Trail to explore numerous wildflower meadows, icy streams, and impressive viewpoints. Be advised, however, that many of these long, steep ridgelines have a lot of exposure to sun and wind and are short on reliable water sources. Extra water and sun/wind protection are recommended. If you're looking for something a bit less demanding, check out the trails lower on the north side. Both Lost Lake and Wahtum Lake offer more easy-to-moderate opportunities for exploring some fantastic old-growth forest, as well as several summits with equally impressive views.

Pick a bluebird day to summit Chinidere Mountain, and see how many Cascade peaks you can spy.

1 Chinidere Mountain

RATING/ DIFFICULTY	ROUNDTRIP	ELEV GAIN/ HIGH POINT	SEASON
****/3	4.9 miles	1370 feet / 4670 feet	July–Oct

Map: Trails Illustrated Columbia River Gorge #821; **Permits:** NW Forest Pass for trailhead parking; self-issue wilderness permit; **Contact:** Hood River Ranger District, MHNF; **GPS:** N 45°34.638', W 121°47.562'

Pack a lunch and a lightweight camp chair and plan to spend the afternoon kicking back atop this high perch, named for the last chief of the Wasco Indians. Here, you can just sit and watch the clouds roll by while enjoying a sweeping panorama over the Hatfield Wilderness that takes in five big Cascade peaks. Save this one for a bluebird day when you can get the clearest views that seem to go on forever.

GETTING THERE

From Interstate 84 in Hood River, take exit 62 for US Highway 30. Turn east on Cascade Avenue, then right on Mount Adams Avenue, then right again on Wine Country Avenue, which turns into Country Club Road. Drive 2.8 miles west then north. Turn left (east) on Barrett Drive and proceed another 1.2 miles. At the stop, turn right (south) on Tucker Road (OR 281) for 2 miles; veer right at the Odell Highway fork onto Dee Highway (OR 281) for another 6.3 miles. Make a slight right across some railroad tracks then veer left on Lost Lake Road (Forest Road 13). Follow this road for 5.1 miles, veer right (west) onto FR 13 for another 4.3 miles, then veer right again onto FR 1310 for 6 more miles to the Wahtum Lake Campground and Trailhead.

ON THE TRAIL

Start at the trailhead below the Wahtum Lake Campground by filling out your self-issue wilderness permit. Drop the slip in the slot, put your portion in your pocket, and begin with a 0.4-mile descent via a couple of switchbacks to arrive at a junction with the Pacific Crest Trail (PCT), just above Wahtum Lake's brushy shoreline. If you're in a hurry to get moving, you can opt for the steep wooden steps that bypass the switchbacks. Whichever way you descend, turn right (east) on the PCT and start an easy ramble around the lakeshore. Overhead, tall, mossy hemlocks and firs keep the trail, ferns, and berry shrubs mostly cool and shady.

As the trail makes a gently ascending circuit around the lake, views remain limited, as the path stays on the slope above the shoreline. A few user paths head down to day-use spaces and campsites near the water. Proceeding around the east end of the lake, the way gets muddy where several small springs and seeps spill across the path. Push your way through overgrown ferns, berries, hedge nettle, columbine, and bleeding heart, after which the trail commences a contouring ascent around the north side of the lake basin. As the trail climbs, the groundcover becomes a carpet of bear grass, and any views of the lake below are obstructed by dense forest. After rolling upward on easy tread, the path eventually turns away from the lake basin to a signed junction with the Herman Creek Trail at 2 miles.

Continue another 0.1 mile southwest on the PCT to the next junction, where the

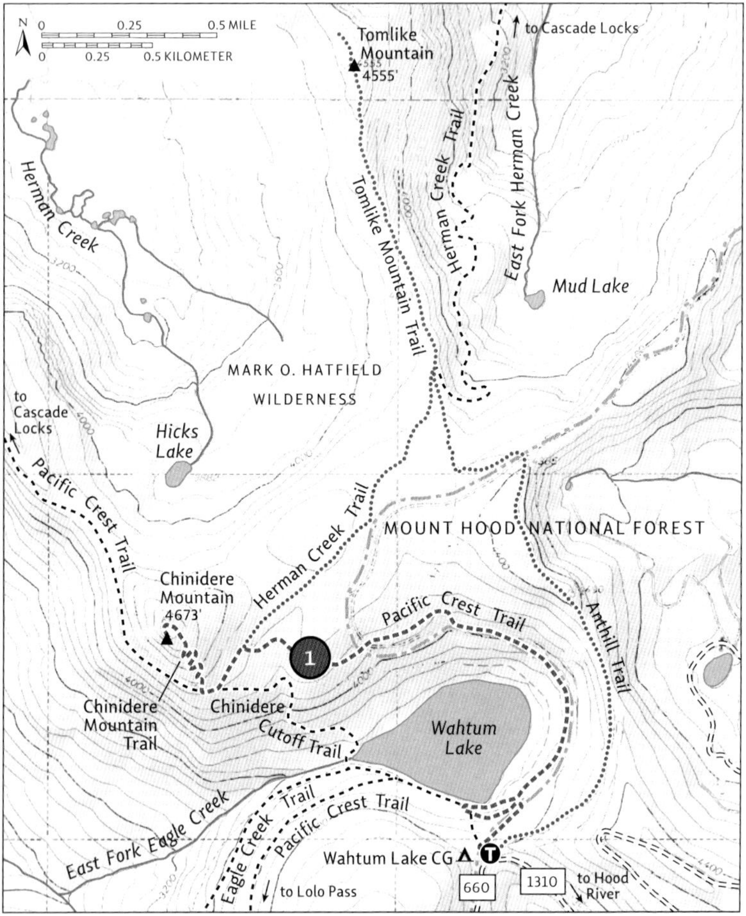

Chinidere Cutoff Trail drops steeply to the left (south), after which the Chinidere Mountain Trail climbs to the right (north). Take the latter for the mountain and start climbing a series of short, steep switchbacks. The way stays mostly under the cover of trees as it climbs the next 0.2 mile until it reaches the upper eastern flank of the mountain, dominated by a wide slope of shale-like rock slabs. Continue upward, traversing the base of the rocks until the trail swings up and across the jumble and proceeds up the spine of the mountain to its 4673-foot summit at about 2.5 miles.

The view from here is all-encompassing. In the near distance, you can take in a 360-degree sweep of Tomlike Mountain to the northeast (see Alternate Route), Benson Plateau to the northwest, fire-charred Tanner Butte to the west, and Indian Mountain to the south (Hike 2). In the farther distance to the north, Mounts St. Helens, Rainier, and Adams dominate the horizon; to the south, Mount Hood takes center stage, with Mount Jefferson over its shoulder. Below, wildflowers carpet the meadows on Chinidere's western slope; even farther below, Wahtum Lake sparkles in its tree-ringed basin. In all, not a bad spot to sit and enjoy some Northwest wilderness scenery for a while. When you're ready to head back down, you can return by the same route, or opt for a change of scenery by taking the Herman Creek and Anthill Trails (see Alternate Route).

Alternate Route

Change up your return from Chinidere Mountain with this alternate route. The additional mileage is negligible, and there's a little more climbing, but it gets you another nice viewpoint and the option of bagging a second peak—Tomlike Mountain—in the same trip (see Extend Your Trip). For this option, descend back to the PCT and backtrack to the Herman Creek Trail junction. Veer left (northeast) on this trail and commence a gentle ascent along wooded Waucoma Ridge. About 1 mile along, where the trail dips into a shallow, wooded saddle, keep your eyes peeled for a signed junction with the Anthill Trail. Turn right (south) and continue ascending to cross an old logging road at 1.5 miles. The grade begins to ease as the trail traverses the curving ridgeline that separates the Wahtum Lake basin from the Green Point Creek valley. Your viewpoint finally arrives at 1.9 miles, where the trail briefly exits the trees near the 4492-foot crest of the ridge and crosses an open rock slope. Here, you can peer down on Wahtum Lake and over the upper reaches of Eagle Creek Canyon. Complete your journey with a steady, contouring descent through the woods until the trail ends in the Wahtum Lake Campground, near your starting point.

ORIGIN STORIES: WAHTUM LAKE

Wahtum Lake is one of Oregon's chuckle-worthy geographic place names. Designated in 1901 by H. G. Langille, on a survey party for the USGS, he was obviously unaware that *wahtum* is the Sahaptin word for "lake." Enjoy your visit to Lake Lake.

EXTEND YOUR TRIP

The trail to summit Tomlike Mountain is a lesser-used route that may require bushwhacking and routefinding. If you opt for the Herman Creek and Anthill alternate return route, look for the unsigned Tomlike Mountain Trail just north of the Anthill Trail junction. The trail proceeds through the woods, then along the open, narrow ridgetop. Views are expansive, and there are some interesting, layered rock outcrops. Bagging the 4555-foot summit requires a moderate scramble up a pile of slabby rocks. The view from the top takes in the entire Herman Creek Canyon, as well as neighboring canyons and distant peaks.

2 Indian Mountain

RATING/ DIFFICULTY	ROUNDTRIP	ELEV GAIN/ HIGH POINT	SEASON
*****/4	8.9 miles	2080 feet/ 4900 feet	July–Oct

Map: Trails Illustrated Columbia River Gorge #821; **Permits:** NW Forest Pass for trailhead parking; self-issue wilderness permit; **Contact:** Hood River Ranger District, MHNF; **Notes:** Sharp, steep cliffs on mountain summit; use caution if hiking with small children or dogs; **GPS:** N 45°34.638', W 121°47.562'

There's a little bit of everything on this pleasant stroll along the Pacific Crest Trail. Amble along a mountain lake, enjoy lively woods full of berries and wildflowers, traipse through mountain meadows—with more wildflowers—and top it off with big mountain views from an old fire lookout site. You usually have to work harder for so much scenery.

GETTING THERE

From Interstate 84 in Hood River, take exit 62 for US Highway 30. Turn east on Cascade Avenue, then right on Mount Adams Avenue, then right again on Wine Country Avenue, which turns into Country Club Road. Drive 2.8 miles west then north. Turn left (east) on Barrett Drive and proceed another 1.2 miles. At the stop, turn right (south) on Tucker Road (OR 281) for 2 miles; veer right at the Odell Highway fork onto Dee Highway (OR 281) for another 6.3 miles. Make a slight right across some railroad tracks then veer left on Lost Lake Road (Forest Road 13). Follow this road for 5.1 miles, veer right (west) onto FR 13 for another 4.3 miles, then veer right again onto FR 1310 for 6 more miles to the Wahtum Lake Campground and Trailhead.

ON THE TRAIL

At the trailhead below the Wahtum Lake Campground, fill out your self-issue permit at the wilderness kiosk and descend to the Pacific Crest Trail (PCT) on a couple of switchbacks. You can also take the steep steps that bypass the switchbacks for a quicker start. Once you reach the PCT at 0.4 mile (switchback route), turn left under a mixed forest of mossy firs and hemlocks and traipse along the brushy slope above Wahtum Lake's shoreline. You'll get a few decent views of the lake as you pass a few user trails that lead to secluded campsites near the shore.

At 0.6 mile, the trail forks, with the PCT veering left (southwest) and the Eagle Creek Trail veering right (northwest). The latter was closed in fall of 2017, following the devastating Eagle Creek Fire that did extensive damage to the trail and high-walled canyon. (You can inquire with the Hood River Ranger District regarding the current status of the Eagle Creek Trail.) Sticking with the PCT, veer left, and begin a gentle ascent to contour southward around a forested butte. The hiking is fairly effortless on soft, duffy tread. Under the shady canopy, the slopes are adorned with a variety of vine maple, ferns, Oregon grape, vanilla leaf, and false lily of the valley. A few gaps in the trees offer sparing looks behind toward Chinidere Mountain.

Around 2.3 miles, the PCT bends westward to traverse a narrow ridge along the Hatfield Wilderness boundary, where it parallels a gravel forest road (FR 660). Looking ahead (west), a rocky, pyramid-

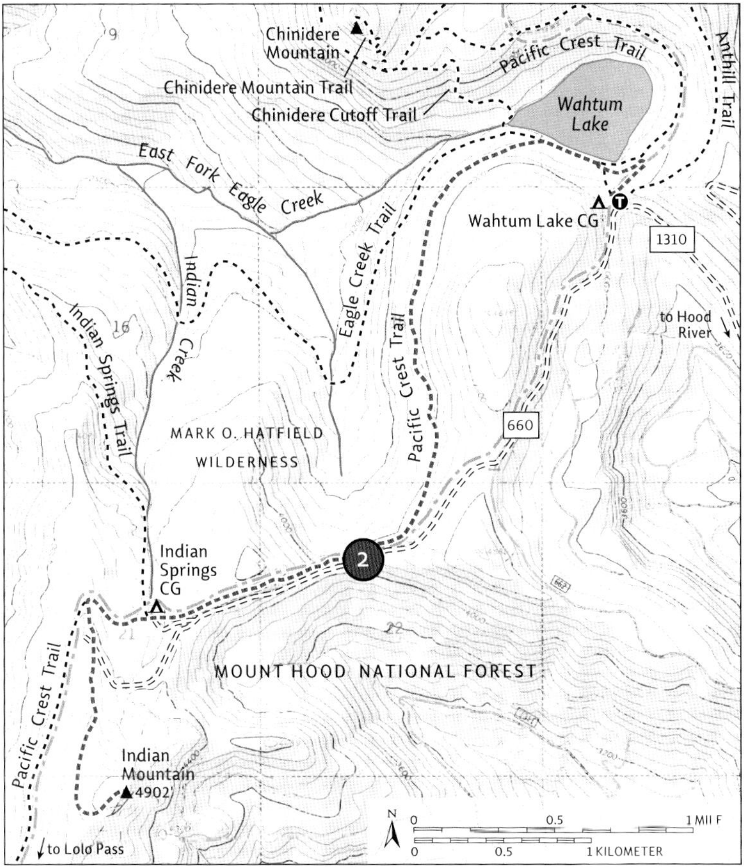

shaped butte rises beside the trail; looking south, the view looks over clear-cut-marred Sawtooth Mountain to Mount Hood. The trail dips through a shallow saddle, followed by a moderate ascent along the flank of the pyramid-shaped butte, before easing and dropping into the abandoned Indian Springs Camp at 3.2 miles. At the edge of the rough, rutted parking area sits a worn picnic table, and hidden in trees are a handful of secluded campsites—usually used only by weary PCT thru-hikers. Nearby, Indian Spring trickles out of the hillside.

Continue onward, through a brief thicket of alder, vine maple, and spiraea, then begin ascending the open east slope of Indian

A large cairn and signpost points the way to Indian Mountain.

Mountain. At the crest of the mountain's ridgeline, at 3.5 miles, the Indian Mountain Trail breaks off left (south) beside a large rock cairn. Turn off the PCT and follow this rocky ridgeline trail up through a patchwork of shale-like slabs, bare earth, and clusters of bear grass, heather, mixed wildflowers, and young noble firs. Don't forget to throw a look in your rearview for a sweeping panorama over the Hatfield Wilderness (including much of the charred Eagle Creek Canyon) and farther to southern Washington's towering Cascade peaks. Down the western slope you can spy the mountain's sprawling rock gardens bursting with summer penstemon, paintbrush, arnica, fireweed, and yarrow. Listen for the "Eeeeepp!" of cute, furry pikas darting among the rocks.

About halfway up, the path crosses an old access road, then ducks through a stretch of mixed woods filled with huckleberries and avalanche lilies, until it finally turns and exits the trees onto Indian Mountain's open, eastern summit at about 4.5 miles. Here, three different fire lookouts used to occupy this rocky high point from the early 1900s until the late 1960s. Ironically, the first two lookouts burned down from accidents not related to forest fires. Even with the lookouts gone, you can still enjoy the same impressive view of Mount Hood, fronted by Raker Point, Sawtooth Mountain, and Lost Lake Butte (Hike 4). Don't get too near the edge of the peak, as the rocks are loose and the edges are steep. When it's time to go, return by the same route.

3 Lakeshore Trail

RATING/ DIFFICULTY	ROUNDTRIP	ELEV GAIN/ HIGH POINT	SEASON
*****/1	3 miles	280 feet/ 3210 feet	May–Oct

Map: Trails Illustrated Mount Hood #820; **Permit:** Lost Lake day-use or camping pass; **Contact:** Hood River Ranger District, MHNF; Lost Lake Resort; **Notes:** You can park at any of the day-use lots to access this trail; some barrier-free sections; **GPS:** N 45°29.796', W 121°49.140'

The Lakeshore Trail at Lost Lake is one of those hikes that epitomizes the phrase "It's the journey, not the destination." With so much to gawk at—from towering old-growth trees to tiny woodland fungi, wildflowers, berries, woodland critters, watery denizens, and winged residents—give yourself extra time to take this easy 3-mile loop, as you'll likely be making plenty of stops to admire each and every natural feature and curiosity.

GETTING THERE

From Interstate 84 in Hood River, take exit 62 for US Highway 30. Turn right on Cascade Avenue, then right (south) on Mount Adams Avenue, which turns west into Wine Country Avenue, then turns south into Country Club Road. Follow this route for 3.2 miles, turn left (east) on Barrett Drive, and proceed another 1.2 miles. At the stop, turn right (south) on Tucker Road (OR 281) for 2 miles, then veer right at the Odell Highway fork onto Dee Highway (OR 281) for another 6.3 miles. Make a slight right across some railroad tracks, then veer left on Lost Lake Road (Forest Road 13). Follow this winding road for 14 miles to the Lost Lake Resort entrance and pay your fee at the booth. Proceed 0.5 mile into the resort area; turn right for the north day-use area, or left for the south day-use area.

ON THE TRAIL

Begin your journey of discovery at the Bigfoot monument, near the boat rental station and across from the general store. You may want to snap a selfie with the friendly giant. From here, follow the wide gravel path north through a section of shady trees to cross the lake's bridged outlet; there are nice views across the lake from this point. The trail then proceeds along the forested lakeshore, through the north day-use picnic area. There are numerous benches and tables along this stretch, some secluded with nice lake views, so consider packing a lunch to enjoy here before or after your lakeside hike. Near the west end of the picnic area, another view across opens up, this one with an impressive look at Mount Hood.

Now the fun really begins as the trail plunges into lush old-growth forest, where impressive Douglas firs, western hemlocks, and red cedars tower over countless woodland wonders. The first thing to note is the abundance of trailside huckleberries. This will be a signature feature of the entire loop, so if you're visiting in mid- to late summer, you may be in for a tasty treat. Also present is a profusion of bunchberry, vine maple, rhododendron, vanilla leaf, inside-out flower (duckfoot), and a variety of ferns, with a smattering of salmonberry and thimbleberry. Around the 0.5-mile mark, take note of the grove of giant red cedars that tower overhead, after which the trail proceeds across a couple of old boardwalks that appear to predate the resort and contribute to the area's lasting and organic character.

This becomes the nature of the trail for the majority of the way, alternating between comfortable gravel trail and wooden boardwalks on mostly level ground, as it traverses thriving lakeside environments. As the route circuits the western shores, watch out for thickets of thorny devil's club encroaching on the trail. In more wooded areas, look for a variety of strange and colorful fungi, including orange coralroot, chicken of the woods, turkey tails, and bear's tooth. At 1 mile, a

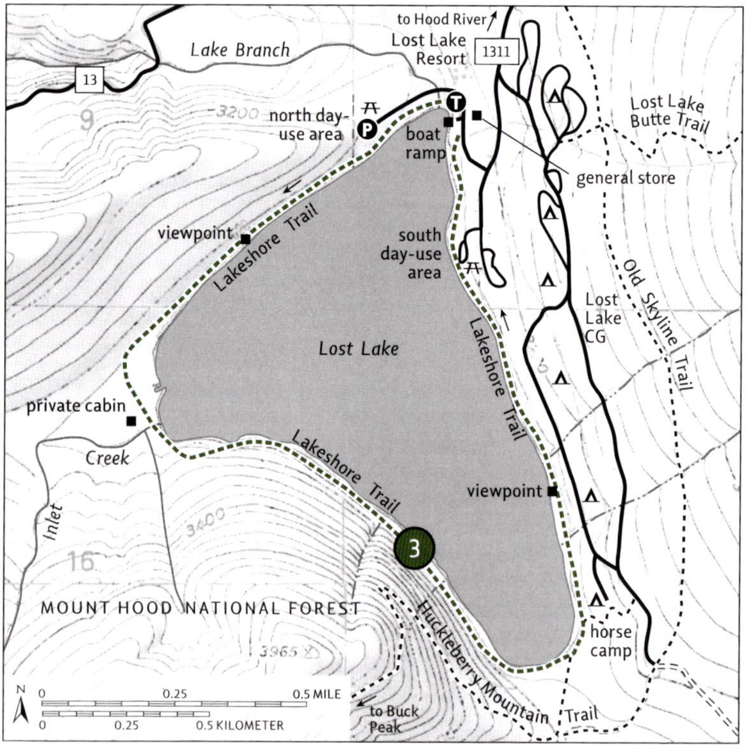

The Lakeshore Trail is a family-friendly jaunt through lush old-growth forest, with a few inspiring views of Lost Lake.

short path branches off right (west) to a small, private cabin; to the left (east) another path proceeds to a small dock on the lake where you can look for rough-skinned newts in the shallow water.

Now the trail turns a little more rugged, becoming rocky and rooty as it makes a short ascent to contour a steep hillside. Near the crest of the ascent, around 1.4 miles, a massive, ancient Douglas fir reaches for the heavens. The path then descends to the lakeshore and proceeds right along the water before crossing an exposed rock slope then diving back under cover of forest to circuit the head of the lake. At the 2-mile mark, the Huckleberry Mountain Trail branches off to the right (south) to make a steep climb to the Pacific Crest Trail and Buck Peak (Hike 5). Just beyond, another fork veers off to the resort pavilion and horse camp areas.

Now on the east shore of Lost Lake, the final mile proceeds on alternating gravel trail and elevated boardwalks, with campsites upslope and the lakeshore downslope, amid even more huckleberry, thimbleberry, and rhododendron. Around 2.3 miles, a viewing platform extends out over the lake, where you can take in a panorama that includes Preachers Peak and Devils Pulpit. As you approach the end of loop, near 2.8 miles, the path proceeds through the south day-use area, where more picnic tables—some in secluded, wooded alcoves—offer a few more nice places to kick back and enjoy the lakeshore. Close the loop by continuing past the grassy amphitheater clearing and walking the last short stretch on paved walkway to the parking area near the resort store at 3 miles.

ORIGIN STORIES: PREACHERS PEAK AND DEVILS PULPIT

According to legend, the naming of these neighboring peaks suggests that if the preacher is present, the devil is likely nearby.

4 Lost Lake Butte

RATING/ DIFFICULTY	ROUNDTRIP	ELEV GAIN/ HIGH POINT	SEASON
****/3	3.2 miles	1200 feet/ 4460 feet	June–Oct

Map: Trails Illustrated Mount Hood #820; **Permit:** Lost Lake day-use or camping pass; **Contact:** Hood River Ranger District, MHNF; Lost Lake Resort; **Notes:** The lower portion of this trail is very rough and uneven; **GPS:** N 45°29.760', W 121°48.906'

Easily done in just a couple of hours, the climb to the top of Lost Lake Butte is an enjoyable ramble through lively forest rich with rhododendron and huckleberries. Bag it in early summer when the forest is exploding with flowers, or in late summer and munch on a bounty of juicy forest fruits. There's even nice fall color here, when the summer campers have gone and the air gets cool and moist.

GETTING THERE

From Interstate 84 in Hood River, take exit 62 for US Highway 30. Turn right on Cascade Avenue, then right (south) on Mount Adams Avenue, which turns west into Wine Country Avenue, then turns south into Country Club Road. Follow this route for 3.2 miles, turn left (east) on Barrett Drive, and proceed another 1.2 miles. At the stop, turn right (south) on Tucker Road (OR 281) for 2 miles, then veer right at the Odell Highway fork onto Dee Highway (OR 281) for another 6.3 miles. Make a slight right across some railroad tracks, then veer left on Lost Lake Road (Forest Road 13). Follow this winding road for 14 miles to the Lost Lake Resort entrance and pay your fee at the booth. Proceed 0.4 mile into the resort area, following signs for campgrounds and the butte trailhead. Park

Climb through rhododendron and hemlock forest to wide summit views atop Lost Lake Butte.

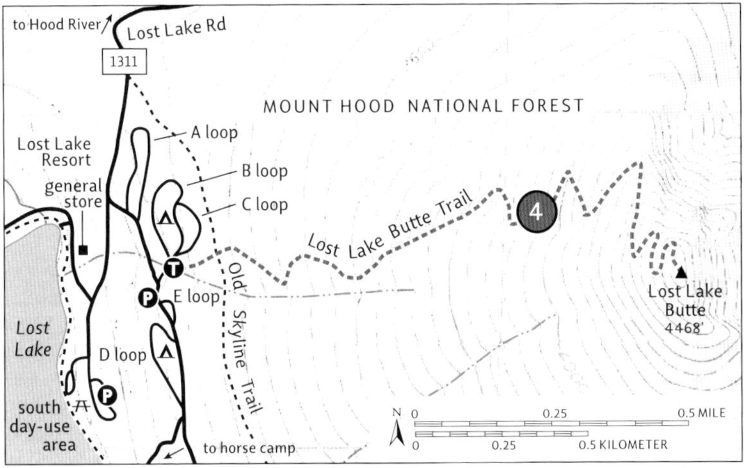

nearby in designated spaces on the road shoulder; do not park in reserved campsite or yurt spaces.

ON THE TRAIL

Find the Lost Lake Butte Trailhead between the campground B loop and the yurt area E loop. The trail starts in a cluster of silver fir and dense salmonberry, huckleberry, and rhododendron. A few paces up, there's an info board with resort and trail information, as well as an area map. Going forward, a couple of paths diverge right (south) into the yurt area, and left (north) to a vault toilet; the trail surface is rough, rocky, and rooty, and will remain so for a good portion of the way. A little past 0.1 mile, cut diagonally across the Old Skyline Trail and head uphill into mossy hemlock and Douglas fir woods. Rhododendron and berry shrubs continue to dominate most of the hillside, with bits of deer fern, vanilla leaf, bear grass, bunchberry, and pipsissewa joining the mix.

The path now snakes up the hillside on a steady, moderate grade. The surrounding forest is lush and green, with scattered rocks and fallen trees encased in vibrant mosses. It's the kind of forest you may expect to find wood elves or pixies frolicking in. There aren't any views, but that may be for the best, as the valley hillsides to the north are a patchwork of recent and recovering clear-cuts. Soon silver firs reappear, adding some floral variety. Near the 1-mile mark, the trail tread finally transitions to a nice duffy surface for more effortless walking, just as it starts switchbacking upward. The first few switchbacks are wide and lazy, maintaining the same steady grade; nearing the top, the turns get quicker and the grade starts easing. When you pass a large, knobby rock outcrop, you're almost at the top; proceed through an abrupt U-turn to reach the butte's 4468-foot summit.

Surrounded by big-leaf maple and overgrown bear grass and thimbleberry, the trail comes to a small clearing at the summit of the butte where the concrete piers and steps of the old watchtower are all that remains of the forest lookout that occupied this perch from 1950 until 1963. Continue past these relics through overgrown shrubs to the north, sunny side of the summit, where the trail pops out of the trees into an open clearing with an almost-picture-perfect view of Mount Hood at 1.6 miles. (Unfortunately, several old clear-cuts mar the foreground.) There's a big jumble of rocks amid the brushy chinquapin and boxwood bushes that makes a fine place to sit and enjoy the view for a while. When you've gotten your fill of the scene, head back down by the same route. If you're up for more rambling, and want to take full advantage of your day-use fee, take a stroll on the Old Skyline Trail, or head down to the lake and take a journey of discovery on the Lakeshore Trail (Hike 3).

5 Buck Peak

RATING/ DIFFICULTY	ROUNDTRIP	ELEV GAIN/ HIGH POINT	SEASON
***/5	11.8 miles	3050 feet/ 4730 feet	July–Oct

Map: Trails Illustrated Mount Hood #820; **Permit:** Lost Lake day-use or camping pass; **Contact:** Hood River Ranger District, MHNF; Lost Lake Resort; **Notes:** This route traverses high, steep ridges and may require minor bushwhacking; **GPS:** N 45°28.980', W 121°48.738'

This strenuous up-and-back hike ascends Huckleberry Mountain to connect with the Pacific Crest Trail (PCT) before rolling along a high ridge above the Bull Run Watershed. This often-misty route stays mostly confined to dense, primeval forest, but the payoff for your effort is an eye-popping panorama of Oregon and Washington peaks. In late summer, bring a container to collect tasty berries to snack on, as Huckleberry Mountain didn't get its name for nothing.

GETTING THERE

From Interstate 84 in Hood River, take exit 62 for US Highway 30. Turn right on Cascade Avenue, then right (south) on Mount Adams Avenue, which turns west into Wine Country Avenue, then turns south into Country Club Road. Follow this route for 3.2 miles, turn left (east) on Barrett Drive, and proceed another 1.2 miles. At the stop, turn right (south) on Tucker Road (OR 281) for 2 miles, then veer right at the Odell Highway fork onto Dee Highway (OR 281) for another 6.3 miles. Make a slight right across some railroad tracks, then veer left on Lost Lake Road (Forest Road 13). Follow this winding road for 14 miles to the Lost Lake Resort entrance and pay your fee at the booth. Proceed 0.5 mile into the resort area, following signs for the horse camp and pavilion area.

ON THE TRAIL

Begin your journey at the trailhead near Lost Lake's horse camp area, near the top of the parking loop. Follow a graded path about 100 yards west, past the pavilion, to connect with the Lakeshore Trail (Hike 3). Turn left (south) on the lake trail and plunge into shady fir and hemlock forest decorated with deer fern, wild ginger, bunchberry, trillium, and vine maple. Follow this path for about 70 yards to a wide junction signed for the Huckleberry Mountain Trail. Veer left (south) into a sea of huckleberries and proceed 0.1 mile to another fork that leads to an alternate

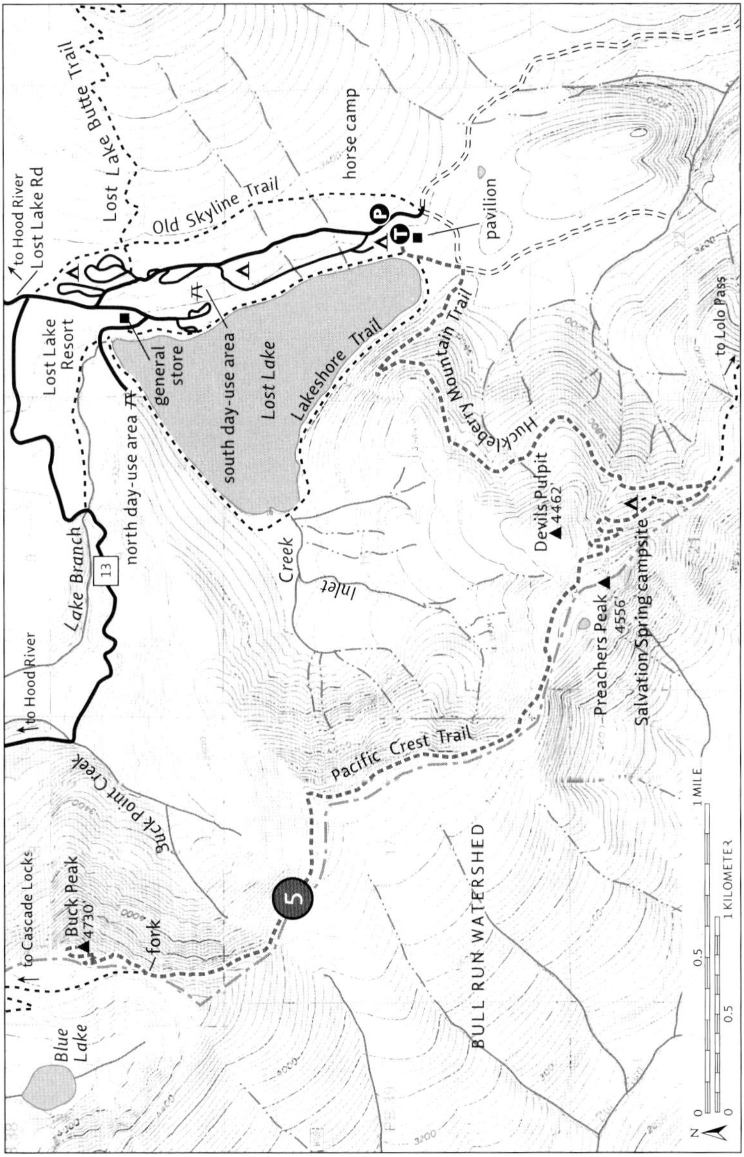
to Hood River
Lost Lake Rd
Lost Lake Butte Trail
Old Skyline Trail
horse camp
pavilion
Lost Lake Resort
general store
south day-use area
Lost Lake
Lakeshore Trail
north day-use area
Huckleberry Mountain Trail
to Lolo Pass
Lake Branch
13
to Hood River
Creek
Inlet
Devils Pulpit
4462'
Preachers Peak
4556'
Salvation Spring campsite
Pacific Crest Trail
Buck Point Creek
BULL RUN WATERSHED
to Cascade Locks
Buck Peak
4730'
fork
5
Blue Lake
1 MILE
1 KILOMETER
0.5
0
N

There are berries aplenty in late summer on Huckleberry Mountain, en route to Buck Peak.

trailhead on an old forest road. Turn right (west) at this junction and start climbing.

The trail begins a steady ascent, cutting a steep contour across the lower flank of Devils Pulpit. Near 0.8 mile, the trail makes a sharp switchback to keep climbing, even steeper. As you're making your way upward, you get a few brief looks out over Lost Lake, otherwise the trail stays mostly confined to the trees. Here and there you can admire some impressively large old-growth hemlocks, as well as continue enjoying all the berries. As you pass through the 1.2-mile mark, the grade eases somewhat as the trail contours south around the upper slopes of the Jones Creek drainage. Finally, at 2.3 miles, the trail ends at a junction with the PCT, on a high ridge above the Bull Run Watershed. Unfortunately, this does not conclude your climbing.

Turn right (north) and traipse along the PCT on nice, duffy tread, where the slopes are blanketed with salmonberry, salal, rhododendron, and vanilla leaf. There aren't any views yet, but the walking is easy (for now) and the cool, shady woods harken to the forests of Endor. Around 2.5 miles, just before the grade picks up again, a narrow, brushy path dips off to the right (north). This leads to the Salvation Spring campsite, a small wooded clearing near a trickling spring. This is followed by a steady climb though a handful of switchbacks to pass through the saddle between 4556-foot Preachers Peak and 4462-foot Devils Pulpit (see sidebar). The trail then dips through a shallow saddle, where it gets narrow and brushy with overgrown thimbleberry, penstemon, and cow parsnip as it makes a slippery traverse around a very steep, very deep forest basin.

Where the path makes an abrupt left (west) turn, at 4.5 miles, the route gets a little less harrowing and dips through another viewless saddle, where a primitive campsite can be found beside the trail. Then comes another steady ascent along the flank of an unnamed butte to a (possibly unsigned) fork at 5.5 miles. To bag Buck Peak, veer right (north) off the PCT and continue the final

0.4 mile up through overgrown huckleberry to the rocky, 4730-foot summit at 5.9 miles. The panorama, from south to north, takes in Mount Hood, Lost Lake, Raker Point, Sawtooth Mountain, and far-off Mount Adams. After soaking it all in, return to your starting point by the same route.

6 Laurance Lake High Loop

RATING/ DIFFICULTY	ROUNDTRIP	ELEV GAIN/ HIGH POINT	SEASON
***/3	5.8 miles	1550 feet/ 3950 feet	June–Oct

Map: Trails Illustrated Mount Hood Wilderness #321; **Permit:** None; **Contact:** Hood River Ranger District, MHNF; **Notes:** Do not park in front of the dam gate; **GPS:** N 45°27.486', W 121°39.432'

This trail was supposed to be a loop, primarily for mountain bikers. But when more designated wilderness was added to the area in 2009, this trail project was abandoned, leaving this switchbacking ascent and wooded ridge walk as a simple out-and-back route from the foot of Laurance Lake dam. The payoff for this workout is some pretty impressive views over the lake and up Mount Hood's rugged north face, where you can get a look at several of the peak's long ridges and large glaciers.

GETTING THERE

From Interstate 84 in Hood River, take exit 64 for Mount Hood Highway (OR 35). Turn south for Mount Hood and Government Camp and drive approximately 13 miles, then veer right (southwest) on Cooper Spur Road (OR 281) for 1.8 miles toward the town of Parkdale. Turn right (west) on Baseline Road and proceed 0.5 mile through town, then left (south) on Clear Creek Road for 2.8 miles. At the fork, veer right (southwest) on Laurance Lake Drive and continue 3.6 miles, then left (west) at the next fork onto Laurance Lake Road (FR 2810) for 0.3 mile. Find parking on the road shoulder near the dam; don't block the dam road gate.

ON THE TRAIL

Start with an easy walk across the Laurance Lake dam, constructed on the Clear Branch in 1969. As you're crossing, throw a look back over your shoulder for some good views of Mount Hood. From the opposite (north) end of the dam, you can easily identify Pinnacle Ridge (Hike 8) and the Barrett Spur. The massive sheet of ice pouring down the mountain is Coe Glacier. Once you've finished your lake and mountain peeping, look northeast into the trees for an unsigned trail in a grove of alder, thimbleberry, pipsissewa, deer fern, and vine maple. Start up this trail, which plunges into the shady woods on nice, duffy tread, and begin ascending on a gentle grade. The path progresses along fairly easily to 0.5 mile, where it makes its first turn to proceed up the ridge.

Now climbing into a mature forest of tall Douglas fir, red cedar, sword fern, Oregon grape, and bear grass, the trail begins its upward plod through several switchbacks between two wide talus slopes. Outward views are minimal at first, with the trail mostly confined to the trees. Finally, at the crux of a switchback, at 0.8 mile, you get a nice, open view over the lake with Mount Hood in the distance. The spindly, silvered forest blanketing the slopes of the mountain show the extent of the 2011 Dollar Lake Fire. Continuing through several more

The best views of Laurance Lake and Mount Hood come before you reach the top of the ridge.

switchbacks, the trail passes a couple of massive ponderosa pines (notable for their scaly, orange bark and long needles) and reaches another viewpoint at 1.1 miles. Nearing the top, the switchbacks start stretching out, snaking upward, until the trail reaches the 3750-foot crest of the ridge at 1.8 miles.

Now enjoy an effortless, meandering stroll westward under shady hemlock, fir, and larch woods. Joining the floral surroundings on the ridgetop is an assortment of rhododendron, snowberry, huckleberry, penstemon, cow parsnip, and vanilla leaf. As the trail bends to the north side of the ridge, a few small breaks in the trees offer partial views over Bear Creek Canyon and File Butte, and you may be able to spot Mounts Adams and Rainier on the distant horizon. The trail then dips through a saddle on the ridge, where a number of sawed tree stumps indicate that this area was once logged. The path then climbs out of the saddle and proceeds easily through more woods full of manzanita and rhododendron to end abruptly at the old Bear Creek Road (FR 1612) at 2.9 miles.

Quite the anticlimactic finish, there is nothing to see here with the dense shrubbery obstructing any outward views. Since that's just not a suitable ending, take the left fork of Bear Creek Road and follow this old roadbed west for 0.4 mile. The way is overgrown with alder and bitter cherry and

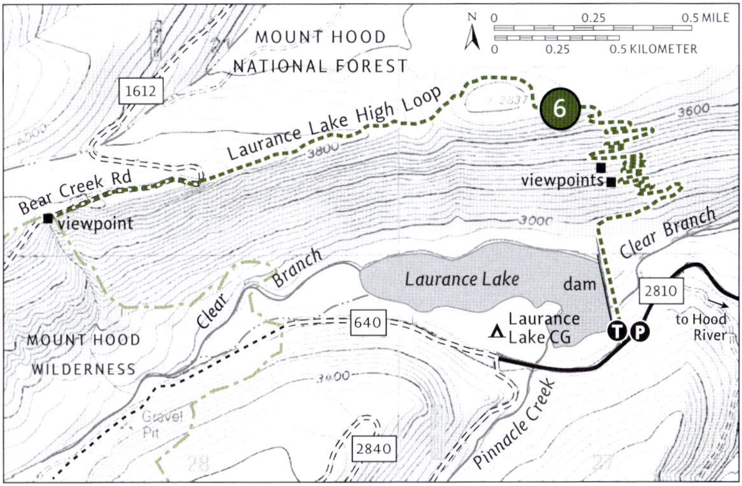

continues ascending along the ridgetop to the point where it collapsed off the hillside. At this point, you get one more nice view of Laurance Lake and Mount Hood. Return to your starting point by turning around and heading back the way you came.

7 Elk Cove

RATING/ DIFFICULTY	ROUNDTRIP	ELEV GAIN/ HIGH POINT	SEASON
****/5	9.4 miles	2970 feet/ 5460 feet	Aug–Oct

Map: Trails Illustrated Mount Hood Wilderness #321; **Permit:** Self-issue wilderness permit; **Contact:** Hood River Ranger District, MHNF; **Notes:** This is a mostly exposed hike through a wildfire burn area; minor route-finding and/or bushwhacking may be necessary; not recommended during periods of heavy wind or rain; **GPS:** N 45°26.820', W 121°40.662'

 *This challenging trail ascends a long ridge that was burned in the 2011 Dollar Lake Fire. Much of the route is exposed among charred and twisted forest, but in recent years it's been recovering nicely, and summer brings a bevy of wildflowers to the scorched hillsides. Your reward for this journey is a delightful cascading creek within a sprawling alpine meadow, along with impressive views of Barrett Spur, Coe Glacier, and Mount Hood's rugged north face.*

GETTING THERE

From Interstate 84 in Hood River, take exit 64 for Mount Hood Highway (OR 35). Turn south for Mount Hood and Government Camp and drive approximately 13 miles, then veer right (southwest) on Cooper Spur Road (OR 281) for 1.8 miles toward the town of Parkdale. Turn right (west) on Baseline Road and proceed 0.5 mile through town, then left (south) on Clear Creek Road for 2.8 miles. At

The hike to Elk Cove is a big climb to wide meadows and wider mountain views.

the fork, veer right (southwest) on Laurance Lake Drive and continue 3.6 miles, then left (west) at the next fork onto Laurance Lake Road (Forest Road 2810) for 0.7 mile. Past the dam and directly across from the campground, turn left (south) onto FR 2840 and proceed 1.1 miles up the mountain on good gravel. Just before the road makes a hairpin turn, turn left (south) on FR 650 for 75 yards to the trailhead and parking.

ON THE TRAIL

Before putting boots to trail, fill out your free wilderness permit and drop the slip in the slot. Then slather on some sunscreen and get to it. The hike starts by heading into a lively green forest of mossy fir, hemlock, and alder where you'll quickly cross Pinnacle Creek on a log bridge. This verdant gully is crowded with lady fern, vanilla leaf, and assorted berries. Look for showy little spotted knapweed, which resembles little bursts of purple fireworks. Enjoy this lush setting, as it doesn't last for long. The trail then exits forest cover and proceeds along an old logging road for the next mile. The path is wide and rocky for fairly easy walking on a gentle ascent. There aren't any views on this initial stretch, as the route remains confined to a wooded corridor, the upslope portion showing significant fire damage. The abundance of foxglove, fireweed, goldenrod, and pearly everlasting lining the way lends some color to the otherwise unimpressive roadway.

Proceed through a hairpin turn at 0.9 mile, where the trail contours back across the burned slope, still climbing. In summer months, look for clusters of purple penstemon on the rocky roadsides; to the west, you may spy Pinnacle Ridge (Hike 8) through wilted, matchstick trees. The way then turns south into greener woods where a large log and rock pile block the way at 1.2 miles. At this point, veer left (north) off the road and onto the duffy Elk Cove Trail, which switchbacks up into the trees. The path reaches the lower ridge crest near 1.4 miles, where it exits tree cover and proceeds southwest along the ridgeline on a steady, moderate incline. The way forward for the next few miles gets loose and dusty, and alternates between long stretches of burned forest and small "islands" of greener trees that escaped the fire. These offer a few good shade breaks. Looking ahead, Mount Hood starts to take center stage, giving you some impressive eye candy amid dense shrubs of pearly everlasting, huckleberry, Oregon grape, bear grass, and mountain ash.

Still steadily ascending, the trail traverses a narrow section of the ridgeline around 2.5 miles, where you can peer into the wide valleys to the west and east. Amid a stark sea of silvered forest, the Coe Branch and Compass Creek can be seen flowing down the latter. Don't forget to throw a look behind now and then to take in a wide panorama of the upper Hood River valley and Washington's big peaks on the horizon. At 3 miles, look for an obvious path that branches left (east) to the Coe overlook. From this vantage, you're given a striking view of Mount Hood and the surrounding ridges and valleys emanating from the mountain. Eagle-eyed viewers can peer up the Coe Valley to spot Wallalute and Kalakwhahtie Falls in the distance. Onward and upward, the trail dips through a charred saddle then climbs through overgrown huckleberry to a pleasant oasis at 3.7 miles. On warm summer days, this spot makes a good shade break before continuing into the next stretch.

The scenery starts to improve dramatically at 3.9 miles, where the trail crosses clear Cove Creek, which tumbles down a series of small steps in a verdant draw bordered by clusters of pink and yellow monkeyflower. From here, the grade eases as the trail heads up a shallow gully filled with aster and wild strawberry. Small campsites begin to appear near the trail around 4.3 miles. This signals that you are close to the Timberline Trail junction, which comes shortly past 4.6 miles. To visit Elk Cove, turn right (west) on the Timberline and proceed about 0.1 mile to another crossing of Cove Creek, where you'll end the hike at 4.7 miles with a stunning view of Mount Hood rising high above a sprawling meadow filled with aster, pasqueflower, and corn lily. A few more campsites can be found in the trees nearby. The giant, rocky ridge in the foreground is Barrett Spur; left (east) of that, the foot of Coe Glacier can be seen above its wide, barren valley. This gives indication of how far down the mountain this glacier extended long ago. This spot makes a good place to unpack your camp chair, dig out your lunch, and kick back for a while—or if you have any gas left in the tank, venture a little farther to Dollar Lake (see Extend Your Trip). Either way, when you've gotten your fill of the area, head down by the same route.

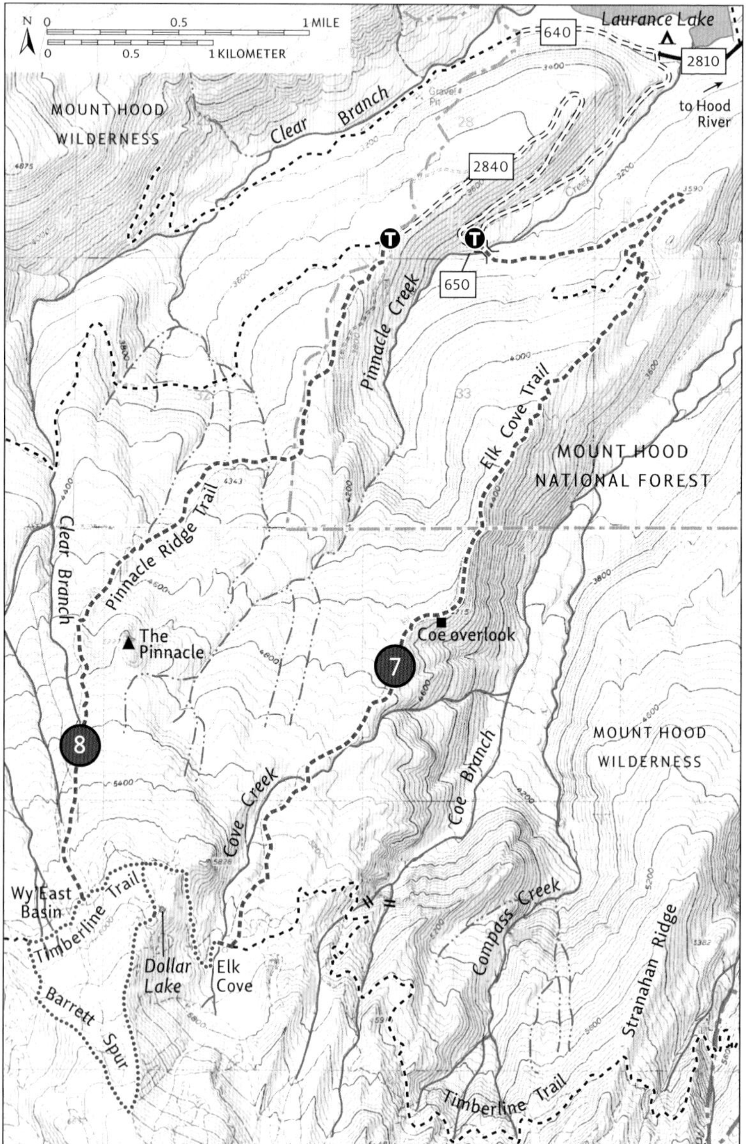
1 MILE
1 KILOMETER
Laurance Lake
640
2810
to Hood River
MOUNT HOOD WILDERNESS
Clear Branch
2840
650
Pinnacle Creek
Elk Cove Trail
MOUNT HOOD NATIONAL FOREST
Pinnacle Ridge Trail
Clear Branch
The Pinnacle
Coe overlook
7
8
MOUNT HOOD WILDERNESS
Coe Branch
Cove Creek
Wy'East Basin
Timberline Trail
Dollar Lake
Elk Cove
Barrett Spur
Compass Creek
Stranahan Ridge
Timberline Trail

DOLLAR LAKE FIRE

In the summer of 2011, lightning sparked a wildfire on the north flank of Mount Hood. Named for the small lake near its ignition point, it quickly spread to encompass a total of 6300 acres, stretching from the lower base of the mountain all the way up to the subalpine tree line. It wasn't fully extinguished until the fall rains came, months later. Classified as a "mosaic" fire, it burned some areas lightly, some areas heavily, and some areas not at all. While much of the charred forest still stands as a ghostly reminder of the fire, the area began quickly recovering within just a few years, mostly in the form of wildflowers, berry shrubs, and young conifers. Many of the trails in the burn area were damaged to varying degrees, but in the years since most have been restored and are open for hiking.

While the scenery may have changed and may be more desolate in some places than others, it gives visitors an opportunity to view the power of nature to recover itself. Hikers should exercise caution when venturing into burn areas, as they can continue to be hazardous even years after the event. Avoid hiking through these areas during periods of heavy wind and rain, which can topple trees and cause landslides and flooding, and watch for burned stumps and loose rocks that can dislodge easily.

EXTEND YOUR TRIP

For a bigger mountain view from the shore of a quiet little alpine lake basin, add 1.9 miles to your trek with a visit to Dollar Lake. From the Cove Creek crossing, continue west on the Timberline Trail. The way first proceeds alongside the Elk Cove meadow for 0.1 mile, then switches back, contouring upward, to traverse around the toe of Barrett Spur. Proceed across a couple of wide talus slopes, then make a short ascent into a grove of big, shady conifers. Near the edge of a small clearing, approximately 0.7 mile from the creek, look for a side trail left (south), often marked by a small cairn. Take this path for 0.2 mile up a wide, rocky gully filled with lupine, heather, and paintbrush to the shallow basin holding Dollar Lake, named for its nearly perfectly round shape. Here, you will find numerous campsites in the trees ringing the lake. For the best view of Mount Hood, climb the low ridge on the south side of the lake. When it's time to go, just backtrack down by the same route.

8 Pinnacle Ridge

RATING/ DIFFICULTY	ROUNDTRIP	ELEV GAIN/ HIGH POINT	SEASON
***/5	6.6 miles	2500 feet/ 5820 feet	Aug–Oct

Map: Trails Illustrated Mount Hood Wilderness #321; **Permit:** Self-issue wilderness permit; **Contact:** Hood River Ranger District, MHNF; **Notes:** This is a strenuous, mostly exposed hike through a wildfire burn area; minor routefinding and/or bushwhacking may be necessary; not recommended during periods of heavy wind or rain; **GPS:** N 45°26.820', W 121°40.662'

This demanding trail on the north flank of Mount Hood is all about working for your reward. Similar to its neighbor, the Elk Cove Trail (Hike 7), the Pinnacle Ridge Trail climbs through the 2011 Dollar Lake Fire burn area to connect

with the Timberline Trail high on Mount Hood. The majority of the route is steep, dry, and dusty through recovering forest, but the higher you go, the better the views. And if you really want to push yourself, you can add a trip up Barrett Spur for an in-your-face look at Mount Hood's Coe and Ladd Glaciers.

GETTING THERE

From Interstate 84 in Hood River, take exit 64 for Mount Hood Highway (OR 35). Turn south for Mount Hood and Government Camp and drive approximately 13 miles, then veer right (southwest) on Cooper Spur Road (OR 281) for 1.8 miles toward the town of Parkdale. Turn right (west) on Baseline Road and proceed 0.5 mile through town, then left (south) on Clear Creek Road for 2.8 miles. At the fork, veer right (southwest) on Laurance Lake Drive and continue 3.6 miles, then left (west) at the next fork onto Laurance Lake Road (Forest Road 2810) for 0.7 mile. Past the dam and directly across from the campground, turn left (south) onto FR 2840 and proceed 3 miles on good gravel up the mountain to the trailhead at the end of the road.

ON THE TRAIL

With such a great view of Mount Hood right from the trailhead, it almost makes you reconsider committing to this challenging hike. It will be work, for sure, but the spectacular panoramas to be had from this lesser-seen side of the mountain will (hopefully) make your efforts worth it. Don't be fooled by the initial start in mossy Douglas fir and hemlock forest, filled with Oregon grape, rhododendron, huckleberry, and bear grass. This is just a sliver of the forest that wasn't engulfed in the fire. Just before entering the burn area, at 0.1 mile, stop at the wilderness permit kiosk, fill out your form, and drop the slip in the slot. You might also want to apply some sunscreen, as the way forward is mostly dry and exposed, where in midsummer it can get quite sunny and warm.

The trail gets down to the business of climbing straightaway, heading right up the ridge on soft, dusty tread, amid a ghostly stand of wilted trees and charred snags. The scene is not total desolation, however, as underneath the phantom forest, an abundance of wildflowers, ferns, green shrubs, and young hemlocks and noble firs have taken hold. Fireweed and pearly everlasting are two of the most prolific occupants of this burned ridge. The former blooms with stalks of pretty pink flowers, the latter with clusters of small white blossoms. Following the short, initial climb, the grade eases for a stretch as the trail parallels greener woods to the right (west), and passes an old wilderness boundary signpost near 0.6 mile. Then it's back out into the open to ascend the next step in the ridge.

The trail then bends west and you're granted a short reprieve from the climbing as the trail dives into a wooded gully at 1.1 miles to cross a clear creek on a log bridge. The way continues westward, undulating gently to cross a few more seasonal springs, then contours around a large rock pile at 1.3 miles. Look and listen for cute little pikas scurrying and chirping among the rocks. Rounding the rock pile, the trail starts climbing again on rough, uneven tread to cut across a wide, rocky wash adorned with huckleberry, vanilla leaf, and goldenrod. It then mounts the opposite side and continues its stair-stepping ascent southwestward

Channel your inner mountain goat with a climb up Barrett Spur, high above Pinnacle Ridge.

through more burned forest. Soon, the trail's namesake pinnacle comes into view as the trail curves around its western side. Close up, you won't get much of a view of this rocky spire, but from higher up it's quite prominent.

Approaching 2.3 miles, shortly past the pinnacle, enter a grove of small trees, where heather, aster, and wood strawberry thrive under dense huckleberry bushes. The upside to all this huckleberry is that if you hike at the right time, there are plenty of tasty berries to snack on. The downside is that these bushes get quite overgrown, so you'll likely be bushwhacking through. Next, at 2.4 miles, where the trail crosses a small stream, veer left (south) at what looks like an unsigned fork. The trail continues south, climbing through more huckleberry to reach the Pinnacle meadows at 2.6 miles, where it crosses a few more creeks. The trail continues up the west side of the grassy slope, where it can be quite muddy and difficult to follow in some places. In summer, this meadow is full of wildflowers, and when you reach the top, the view northward is pretty stunning.

Almost there, continue your upward trajectory, where the forest starts getting livelier, and the trail angles across a wide heather meadow between stands of green trees. Passing 3 miles, the trail crosses a few more small creeks, then follows the drainage upward under mossy, shady trees to end at the Timberline Trail at 3.3 miles. This viewless trail junction hardly makes a worthwhile destination for all your hard work to get here, so you have a few options for where to go. Two of them are easy. One is hard. For the easy, take the Timberline Trail right (west) for 0.3 mile to Wy'East Basin's sprawling wildflower meadows, or left (east) for 0.5 mile to Dollar Lake. Either of these makes a great place to have lunch, take in the views, and recharge for the grinding descent you have in store. Or, if you're a glutton for punishment, take on the challenging loop up and over Barrett Spur (see Extend Your Trip). This supplement adds another 2.5 miles and 1300 feet of elevation gain but rewards with some eye-popping views—in addition to netting both Wy'East Basin and Dollar Lake.

EXTEND YOUR TRIP

To bag Barrett Spur, take a deep breath and turn right (west) from the Pinnacle Ridge junction onto the Timberline Trail. Now on pleasant, duffy trail, amble 0.3 mile though mature, subalpine forest to Wy'East Basin. Along the way, the trail crosses a couple of small, rocky gullies before arriving at a sprawling, grassy meadow where an idyllic creek meanders through and a kaleidoscope of wildflowers bloom in summer. You'll find several inviting campsites in the area. Turn left (south) on an obvious path and follow the creek upstream, alongside the meadow. The grade starts easy but steadily increases. Mounting a small bluff, a few more campsites can be found at 0.4 mile. From this point, the trail gets increasingly steep and difficult, and snow may linger in the upper basin long into the summer. If you're confident in your mountain goat skills, put your game face on and keep climbing.

The trail curves upward and along the wall of the basin on increasingly loose, sandy tread, to reach the crest at 0.6 mile. Continue up the narrow ridge, with views getting increasingly bigger and better the higher you go. The patches of rich, green succulent with pretty white flowers are saxifrage. As you get nearer the top, the route gets progressively rocky and harder to follow; stay to the east side of the ridge and watch for small cairns marking the way. At 1.1 miles, the ridge converges with the one to the east and you'll find the faint trail that heads down to Dollar Lake. At this point, the rocky mass of Barrett Spur divides Coe and Ladd Glaciers. The view is pretty stellar. You can continue up the spine of the spur for even bigger views, but the route gets steeper and more challenging and treacherous. Proceed with caution.

To continue the loop, head down the next ridge toward Dollar Lake. The trail fades here and there, but with the lake in clear view, just make that your target. Below to the east is the wide, barren valley that once contained a much larger Coe Glacier; below that are the wide meadows of Elk Cove. At 1.9 miles, reach the shallow basin that holds Dollar Lake, where you'll find a few campsites in the trees ringing the little pool. Pick up the more obvious trail now and descend a rocky wash filled with heather and lupine to reconnect with the Timberline Trail at 2.2 miles. Close the loop by turning left (west) and traipse easily along the Timberline for 0.3 mile back to the Pinnacle Ridge Trail junction. Now you just have to descend the 3.3 steep miles back to your starting point.

9 Owl Point

RATING/ DIFFICULTY	ROUNDTRIP	ELEV GAIN/ HIGH POINT	SEASON
****/3	4.2 miles	970 feet/ 4940 feet	July–Oct

Map: Trails Illustrated Mount Hood Wilderness #321; **Permit:** Self-issue wilderness permit; **Contact:** Hood River Ranger District, MHNF; **Notes:** Google Maps directions are incorrect; follow the directions below; narrow, winding forest roads; use turnouts for oncoming vehicles. **GPS:** N 45°26.574', W 121°43.752'

Abandoned by the Forest Service in the 1960s, the northern portion of the Vista Ridge Trail spent decades in disrepair. It wasn't until late 2007 that volunteers with Trailkeepers of Oregon began restoring this old ridgetop route. Despite this, the trail remained "unofficial" until it was formally recognized again by the Forest Service in 2018. The upside is that hikers have another view trail to enjoy on the quieter north side of Mount Hood. The downside is that this trail originates from the most remote trailhead on the mountain, requiring a little more time and effort to get to it. Conversely, you're likely to have less company on-trail.

GETTING THERE

From Sandy, drive Mount Hood Highway (US Highway 26) east for approximately

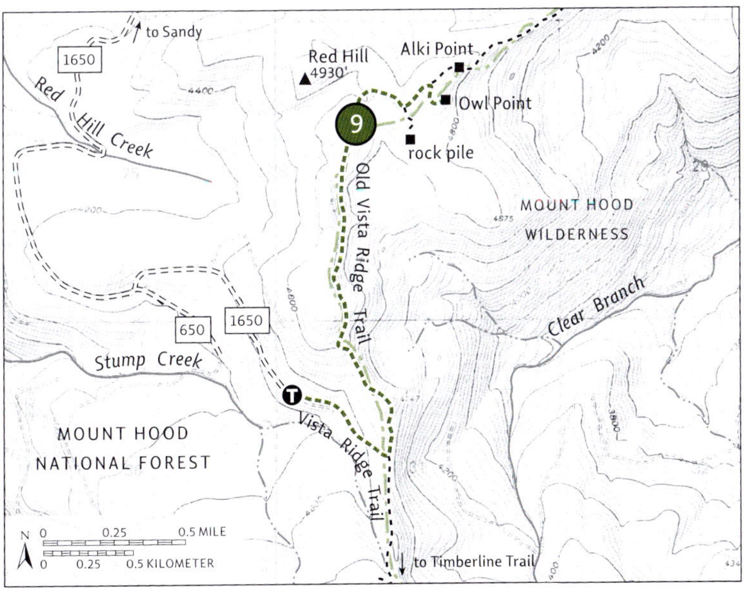

You're more likely to enjoy the sweeping vistas of Mount Hood from Owl Point with pikas rather than other hikers.

17 miles to Welches. Turn left (north) on East Lolo Pass Road and drive 10.5 miles to Lolo Pass. Turn right (southeast) on Forest Road 18 for 10.5 miles; the first 5.5 miles are on good gravel, then the road turns to pavement again. Make a sharp right (south) U-turn onto paved FR 16 and zigzag up the hillside for 5.4 miles, then make another sharp right (south) U-turn onto gravel FR 1650 for 3.6 miles, veering left at an unsigned fork for the last mile to the trailhead. FR 18 and the trailhead can also be accessed from the north via Lost Lake Road.

ON THE TRAIL

Shake off your white-knuckled drive to the trailhead with a mildly ascending contour along the forested slope above Stump Creek. To start, the trail is rough and rocky amid young hemlock and silver fir woods. Keep your eyes peeled for trilliums, violets, and glacier lilies mixed into the mountain carpet of bear grass and huckleberry. Passing through 0.2 mile, the trail enters shady, more mature woods, where it becomes more duffy and comfortable for easy rambling to the Vista Ridge junction at 0.4 mile. To the right (south), the Vista Ridge Trail makes a steady, 2.4-mile climb through burned forest to the Timberline Trail; to the left (north), the Old Vista Ridge Trail makes an undulating ascent to Owl Point.

Turn left (north) onto the old trail and walk briefly along the edge of the 2011 Dollar Lake Fire burn area. The trail then

plunges into greener woods and quickly begins a steady, fairly steep, winding ascent. Scanning the trailsides, you'll get a look at the extensive number of trees that had to be cut and cleared from the trail to get it reopened. The trail eventually levels along the ridgetop near the 1-mile mark, and the hiking forward becomes pretty effortless through abundant huckleberry and wild strawberry. A few well-worn user paths break off to the right (east) to viewpoints overlooking the upper Clear Branch valley. From these windows along the ridge, it's easy to pick out Pinnacle Ridge (Hike 8), vaguely resembling an old ship among a stormy sea of silvered forest.

At 1.3 miles, the trail crests beside a rocky prominence, then dips into a wide huckleberry-filled meadow. Unseen to the east is 4930-foot Red Hill. Continue across the meadow, where the trail ducks back into the trees and begins a gently ascending bend eastward to the rock pile junction at 1.9 miles. At this point, the main route turns left (east), however, if you're up for a short detour, the path straight ahead (south) proceeds through a heather and huckleberry meadow to an impressive viewpoint atop a wide scree slope. This is a good place to watch and listen for cute little pikas. To continue to Owl Point, veer left and ascend another 0.1 mile to the next junction. Now turn right (south) and follow this path briefly through the trees, then out into the open as it curves around the slope of Owl Point at about 2.1 miles.

Here, amid blooms of bear grass and mats of juniper, you're presented with a wide panorama of Mount Hood to the north and the Clear Branch valley, all the way to Laurance Lake, to the east. With plenty of rocks to sit on, find your perfect seat and enjoy the view for a while. The large ridge on the mountain, above the tree line, is Barrett Spur (Hike 8). The glaciers to either side of the spur are Ladd (right, or west) and Coe (left, or east); directly above the spur, below Hood's summit, is Pulpit Rock. Before departing, look for the Owl Point register in an old ammo can. You can sign the logbook inside and leave any comments for fellow hikers. Once you've signed, make sure the can is completely closed before departing. Then just traipse your way back the way you came.

EXTEND YOUR TRIP

If the day is clear and you want a few more mountains, you can bag one more viewpoint with minimal effort. From Owl Point, return to Old Vista Ridge Trail, turn right (northeast), and proceed just 0.1 mile to the scree slope on Alki Point. The foreground is marred by clearcut slopes, but on bluebird days you can gaze across the Columbia River Gorge and pick out Washington's Mounts St. Helens, Rainier, and Adams lining up on the horizon. If you venture out onto the scree slope for the best views, watch your footing on the loose rocks. When you're satisfied with your mountain peeping for the day, return by the same route.

Opposite: *They don't call it "Paradise Park" for nothing. This hike boasts some of the most stunning scenery on Mount Hood (Hike 25).*

mount hood west

I go to nature to be soothed and healed,
and to have my senses put in order.
—John Burroughs

The west side of Mount Hood offers some of the closest access to the mountain from the Portland metro area. Yet despite these trails' proximity to the city, as well as the many small towns in between, it's still possible to find pockets of solitude—and without having to go too far. Take your pick from casual river rambles to strenuous ridge climbs right within the Mount Hood Highway corridor. Or get off the main highway and get into the Mount Hood or Salmon–Huckleberry Wilderness backcountry. Here, you can wander an ancient forest, frolic in an alpine meadow, explore a dramatic river canyon, or summit any of a number of subpeaks. Do one, or, better yet, do them all. Then do them all again in different seasons for a completely new experience. Keep in mind, however, that while many of these trails start relatively low on the mountain, they head up high. It's entirely possible that you may run into a wall of snow if you attempt some of these trails too early in the season. Check trail and road conditions online, or call the local ranger station, before you head out. And a word to the wise: be prepared for mosquitoes—*a lot of them*—soon after the snow melts.

From Bald Mountain, you don't have to choose between flowers and views—you get both!

10 Bald Mountain

RATING/ DIFFICULTY	ROUNDTRIP	ELEV GAIN/ HIGH POINT	SEASON
****/2	2.2 miles	890 feet/ 4440 feet	June–Oct

Map: Green Trails Maps Mount Hood #462S; **Permits:** NW Forest Pass for trailhead parking; self-issue wilderness permit; **Contact:** Zigzag Ranger District, MHNF; **Notes:** High-use trail; **GPS:** N 45°22.338', W 121°49.356'

Bald Mountain, once the site of a Forest Service fire lookout, is a 4591-foot prominence on the northwest side of Mount Hood. Instead of being an isolated peak, Bald Mountain is actually one of many high points along a lengthy ridgeline that emanates from high on Hood and stretches all the way to Lolo Pass. While the trail to the summit is no longer maintained, the short loop trail around the mountain offers spectacular views of Oregon's tallest peak from a delightful rock and flower garden high above the Muddy Fork Canyon. There are two options for enjoying this trail: a shorter, less strenuous approach from the Top Spur Trailhead, or a longer excursion via the Lolo Pass Trailhead. Hike this loop counterclockwise so you're walking into the views.

GETTING THERE

Top Spur: From Sandy, drive Mount Hood Highway (US Highway 26) east for approximately 17 miles to Welches. Turn left (north) on East Lolo Pass Road and proceed alongside the Sandy River for 4.2 miles, then veer right (east) onto Muddy Fork Road (Forest Road 1828) for 0.7 mile. At the next fork, continue straight (north) on FR 1828 and drive another 5.6 miles. Where the road forks yet again, veer right (southeast) onto gravel FR 118 for 1.5 miles. Find parking on the side of the road, opposite the trailhead. *For the Extend Your Trip option that begins at Lolo Pass:* From Welches, turn onto East Lolo Pass Road and drive 10.5 miles to the trailhead.

ON THE TRAIL

Begin with a short hike up the Top Spur Trail to a junction with the Pacific Crest Trail (PCT). This route climbs steadily on rocky, rooty ground under dense conifer forest and is surrounded by an assortment of berry shrubs, lady fern, inside-out flower (duckfoot), and vanilla leaf. Look for clusters of bugbane, which resemble little fireworks bursts, and pretty white queen's cups. Just as you find your stride, the Top Spur Trail ends at its junction with the PCT at 0.5 mile. Turn right (east) and proceed about 50 yards to a large trail junction with a map board, wilderness permit kiosk, and a campsite in the trees nearby. Obtain your free permit, drop the slip in the slot, then bear right (south) onto the Timberline Trail.

The loop around Bald Mountain begins by contouring the forested west slope of the peak. Cruise through the trees on duffy, gently ascending trail. As the path turns east along the southern flank, it exits the tree cover onto Bald Mountain's namesake open slopeside near 0.8 mile. Here, Mount Hood comes into full and striking view, rising high above the rugged crags and rocky spires at the head of the Muddy Fork Canyon. A visit here in early to midsummer showcases a kaleidoscope of multicolored wildflowers decorating the open hillside: Indian paintbrush, penstemon, larkspur, aster, lupine,

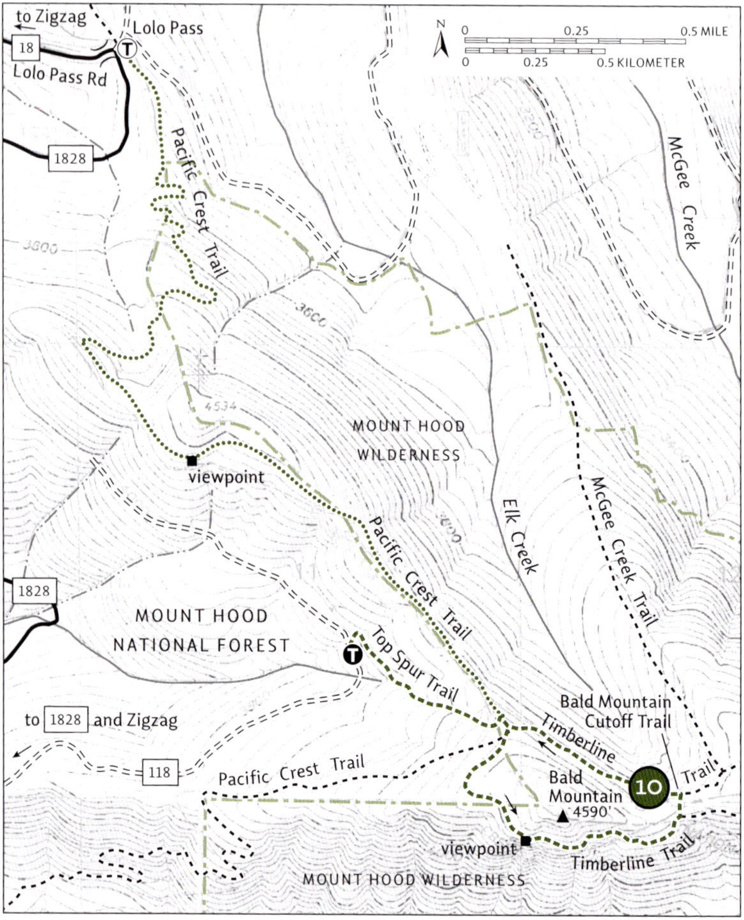

mariposa lily, and arnica, to name just a few. A few large rocks alongside the trail offer nice places to sit and contemplate the scene for a while.

Continue heading downslope through more gardens, with more views, until the trail reenters forest cover. Following a minor ascent, look for the Bald Mountain Cutoff Trail around 1.3 miles. Turn left (north) off the Timberline and take this short spur through the trees to reconnect with the Timberline on the opposite side of the peak. Turn left again (west) to make a short descent through a draw above Elk Creek, then close the loop with an easy ascent back to the main junction. Along the way, you may spy some of Washington's distant peaks to the north through gaps in the trees. Complete your hike by retracing your steps back down the PCT, then down the Top Spur Trail to your starting point.

EXTEND YOUR TRIP

For a longer, 6.5-mile outing with more of a workout, hike the Pacific Crest Trail to the Bald Mountain loop from the Lolo Pass Trailhead. This option adds a few more miles and another 1000 feet of elevation gain. The additional effort nets you another viewpoint and some pretty summer rhododendron gardens—in addition to a quad-burning ascent.

From the trailhead, head south on the PCT, first through a short stretch of shady fir and hemlock forest, then across a brushy section of alder, rhododendron, and fireweed. The trail reenters shady forest and the work begins with a steady ascent toward Peak 4534. Work your way up over rough, rocky, rooty tread through a series of tight switchbacks before curving west through a draw, where the trail returns to a smoother, duffy surface. At 1.6 miles, skirt the edge of a clear-cut, where the scene opens up and you're granted a tantalizing view of Mount Hood. Having just gained a quick 1000 feet, the climbing is over and the route forward undulates along the ridgeline for mostly easy walking amid dense salmonberry and cow parsnip. At 2.6 miles, the PCT passes the Top Spur Trail junction; follow the preceding directions from this point.

11 Bald–Ramona Loop

RATING/ DIFFICULTY	ROUNDTRIP	ELEV GAIN/ HIGH POINT	SEASON
*****/5	10.4 miles	3470 feet/ 4440 feet	June–Oct

Map: Green Trails Maps Mount Hood #462S; **Permits:** NW Forest Pass for trailhead parking; self-issue wilderness permit; **Contact:** Zigzag Ranger District, MHNF; **Notes:** This route traverses high, narrow ridges and requires multiple challenging river crossings; **GPS:** N 45°22.338', W 121°49.356'

Day-hikeable loops on Mount Hood are few and far between, largely due to the extended distances required to connect multiple trails. That makes this loop, which incorporates portions of both the Pacific Crest Trail (PCT) and the Timberline Trail, a real treat. The route begins with a lively jaunt through verdant forest on the PCT, which is followed by a pleasant walk up Ramona Creek to the fantastic Ramona Falls. From there, transition to the Timberline for a fantastic and rugged journey high into the Muddy Fork Canyon, and finish with a walk through Bald Mountain's delightful slopeside meadows. Pack a lunch and plenty of snacks for this hearty, full-day journey.

GETTING THERE

From Sandy, drive Mount Hood Highway (US Highway 26) east for approximately 17 miles to Welches. Turn left (north) on East Lolo Pass Road and proceed alongside the Sandy River for 4.2 miles, then veer right (east) onto Muddy Fork Road (Forest Road 1828) for 0.7 mile. At the next fork, continue

The upper Muddy Fork can be a challenging water crossing in early summer.

straight (north) on FR 1828 and drive another 5.6 miles. Where the road forks yet again, veer right (southeast) onto gravel FR 118 for 1.5 miles to the Top Spur Trailhead. Find parking on the side of the road, opposite the trailhead.

ON THE TRAIL

Begin with a hike up the Top Spur Trail to connect with the PCT. This 0.5-mile path climbs steadily on uneven terrain under lush fir, cedar, and hemlock forest, amid plenty of forest berries, ferns, and wildflowers. Where the trail ends at the PCT, turn right (east) and proceed about 50 yards to a large trail junction. Here you will find a large map board, a wilderness permit kiosk, and a small campsite in the trees nearby. Collect your free permit, drop the slip in the slot, then turn right (west) and follow the PCT (southbound) toward the Sandy River.

The route descends the west flank of Bald Mountain on a fairly moderate grade. The path is shady and forested, with ample amounts of thimbleberry, sword fern, bear grass, rhododendron, and wild ginger along the trailsides. At 1.2 miles, turn south and continue downward through a series of switchbacks toward the Muddy Fork River. Partway down, at 1.7 miles, the trail contours through a rocky drainage, where a seasonal spring cascades across the path. The descent finally bottoms out at 2.7 miles, where the trail passes through a section of overgrown hedge nettle, crosses another small spring, and comes to the edge of the churning Muddy Fork. Now you get to exercise your balance beam skills and carefully cross the downed log that bridges the rushing brown water below. A parallel log with a rope attached acts as a handrail and is helpful for balancing.

Once across, head up the bank and past a large campsite to the junction with the Ramona Falls Trail at 2.8 miles. Turn left (southeast) through the stock control gate and proceed on flat, duffy trail under a canopy of tall conifers. The surrounding forest changes briefly, turning thin, dry, and scraggly as the trail crosses a section of ancient floodplain. This is short-lived, and things get green and lively again as the trail pulls alongside Ramona Creek. The way forward is verdant with rich, mossy groundcover dotted with delicate wildflowers; look for rare fairy slippers through here. The trail crisscrosses the creek a few times on good bridges, then at 4.6 miles passes a junction with the Timberline Trail, which climbs away to the left. Continue a few more paces around the bend to the sturdy wooden bridge at the base of Ramona Falls. Across the bridge is plenty of room for sitting and admiring the wispy curtain of water that cascades down a wall of broken columnar basalt.

After enjoying lunch or a break at the falls, return to the Timberline Trail junction and veer right (northwest), uphill and away from Ramona Creek. The trail steadily ascends the forested slope to crest the nose of Yocum Ridge at 5.3 miles. From here, the Yocum Ridge Trail heads 5.2 steep miles up the ridgeline into Mount Hood's alpine zone. Continue on the Timberline, now on the north side of the ridge, and contour the slope through numerous drainages, where seasonal springs cascade down the hillside and splash across the trail. In some places, the path may get loose and narrow, as this unconsolidated slope is susceptible to washouts and landslides. At 7.4 miles, drop into the wide upper floodplain of the Muddy Fork, where you have three crossings directly ahead. The first two are usually easy rock-hops and fairly inconsequential. The third, crossing the main branch, may require a little more effort and routefinding. Depending on the water level, scout up- and downstream for a safe crossing location.

Once across, pull away from the Muddy Fork and begin a gradual ascent of Bald

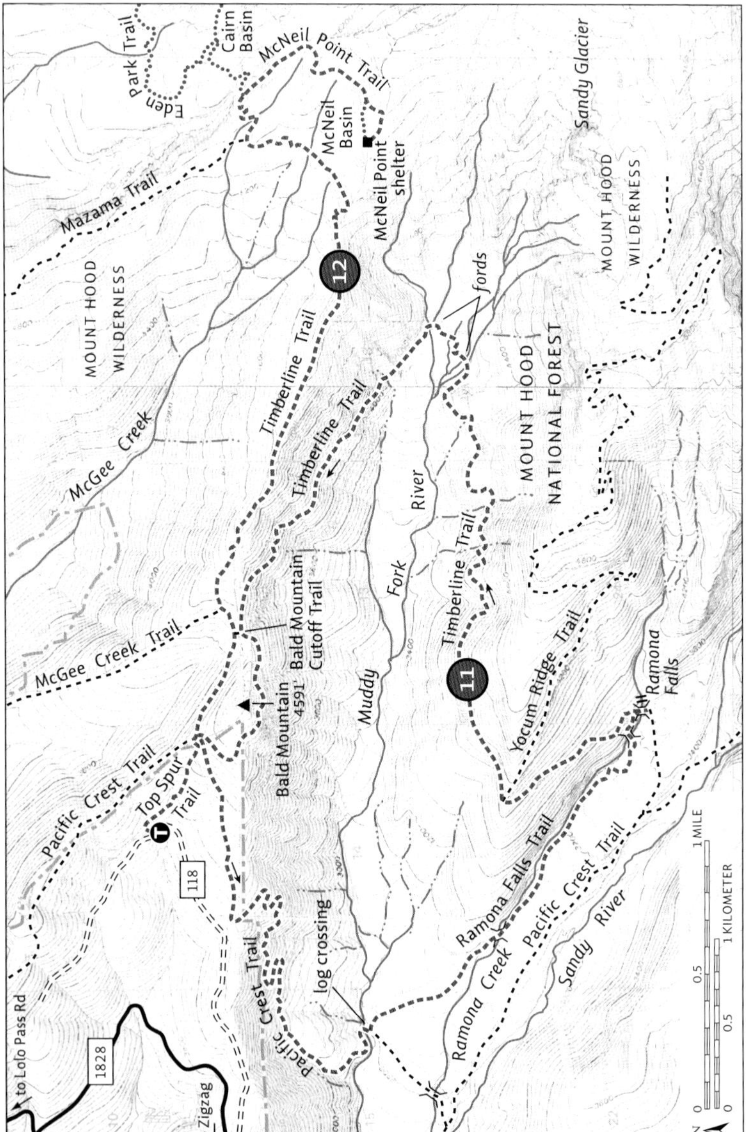

Eden Park Trail
Cairn Basin
McNeil Point Trail
McNeil Basin
McNeil Point shelter
Sandy Glacier
Mazama Trail
MOUNT HOOD WILDERNESS
12
fords
MOUNT HOOD WILDERNESS
Timberline Trail
Timberline Trail
Timberline Trail
McGee Creek
MOUNT HOOD NATIONAL FOREST
Muddy Fork River
Timberline Trail
Bald Mountain Cutoff Trail
McGee Creek Trail
Bald Mountain 4591'
11
Yocum Ridge Trail
Ramona Falls
Pacific Crest Trail
Top Spur Trail
118
Ramona Falls Trail
Pacific Crest Trail
log crossing
Pacific Crest Trail
Ramona Creek
Sandy River
to Lolo Pass Rd
1828
to Zigzag
0 0.5 1 MILE
0 0.5 1 KILOMETER
N

Mountain's southeastern flank. The trail remains mostly under the cover of trees, popping out only now and then to cross a few narrow drainages. Bright yellow monkeyflower is usually prolific in these spots. Nearing the top of the ridge, the grade eases and passes the Bald Mountain Cutoff Trail at 9.1 miles. Just 0.2 mile farther, exit the tree cover and proceed across Bald Mountain's slopeside meadows. In summer months, this flourishing rock garden is usually adorned with cheerful Indian paintbrush, penstemon, aster, and other specimens. Near the western edge of the meadows, at 9.5 miles, a rocky outcrop provides a perfect perch for taking in a wide panorama of the entire Muddy Fork Canyon with Mount Hood rising high above—and for giving some perspective over the circuitous route you've just hiked. Complete the loop with a final 0.4 mile back to the large junction where you began. Now just retrace your steps back down the Top Spur Trail to finish a great day on Mount Hood.

12 McNeil Point

RATING/ DIFFICULTY	ROUNDTRIP	ELEV GAIN/ HIGH POINT	SEASON
*****/5	9.2 miles	3210 feet/ 6180 feet	July–Oct

Map: Green Trails Maps Mount Hood #462S; **Permits:** NW Forest Pass for trailhead parking; self-issue wilderness permit; **Contact:** Zigzag Ranger District, MHNF; **Notes:** High-use trail; this hike may require traversing a steep snowfield; **GPS:** N 45°22.338', W 121°49.356'

Climb high above the Timberline Trail to one of the few remaining stone shelters in Mount Hood's alpine zone. Your work will be rewarded with cascading creeks, flower-filled meadows, and plenty of big mountain views. An early start is recommended, as you'll want plenty of time to enjoy this one.

GETTING THERE

From Sandy, drive Mount Hood Highway (US Highway 26) east for approximately 17 miles to Welches. Turn left (north) on East Lolo Pass Road and proceed alongside the Sandy River for 4.2 miles, then veer right (east) onto Muddy Fork Road (Forest Road 1828) for 0.7 mile. At the next fork, continue straight (north) on FR 1828 and drive another 5.6 miles. Where the road forks yet again, veer right (southeast) onto gravel FR 118 for 1.5 miles. Find parking on the side of the road, opposite the trailhead.

ON THE TRAIL

Begin your hike on the Top Spur Trail, which climbs 0.5 mile to a junction with the Pacific Crest Trail (PCT). This short connector climbs steadily on rocky, rooty ground under dense conifer forest, surrounded by an assortment of berry shrubs, lady fern, and wildflowers. Turn right (east) and proceed about 50 yards to a large trail junction with a Mount Hood map board and wilderness permit kiosk. Obtain your free self-issue permit, drop the slip in the slot, then fork left (east) onto the Timberline Trail.

The route forward contours the wooded north slope of Bald Mountain on nice, duffy tread, dipping gently through the draw above the head of Elk Creek. The surrounding forest is lush and lively and keeps the trail mostly shady. As the path begins a gentle ascent, pass the Bald Mountain Cutoff Trail at 0.9 mile. This short spur hops over to the south side of the ridge and connects with

Traipse through sprawling heather meadows on your way to the McNeil Point shelter.

another portion of the Timberline Trail. This is great to use as an alternate return route or to make a loop around Bald Mountain (Hike 10). At 1 mile, pass the McGee Creek Trail, which climbs steeply from a trailhead off Lolo Pass Road, and continue ascending the ridgeline that divides the McGee Creek and Muddy Fork drainages.

After climbing through a viewless tree tunnel for a while, the trail pops out into the open amid a ridgetop flower garden at 2.1 miles. Here, look for paintbrush, penstemon, Columbia lily, mariposa lily, and pearly everlasting. You're also presented with an impressive view of Mount Hood, Sandy Glacier, and the jagged head of the Muddy Fork Canyon. The ridgeline extending left (north) of the mountain is where you're headed. Continue forward, back into the trees, where bear grass, lupine, and corn lily become common, and summer brings Columbia windflowers to the trailside. The path dips to traverse a shallow saddle, then commences climbing more earnestly through a few switchbacks to an unmarked trail junction at 2.8 miles. (If you're channeling your inner mountain goat, you can break off here for a very steep 0.3-mile scramble directly up to McNeil Point.)

Continue on the Timberline Trail, which now leaves the ridgeline and begins contouring the forested northwest flank of Mount Hood, where avalanche lilies are profuse in early summer. Proceed across a few small creeks around 2.9 miles, then across larger McGee Creek at 3 miles. All of these are easy rock-hops and often decorated with spiraea, aster, monkeyflower, and bog gentian. Shortly past, cross an open meadow carpeted with pink heather at the base of a high talus slope, then climb through a couple of switchbacks to a large pond in a grassy basin. When the bear grass is blooming and the sun is shining, this meadow looks like it's illuminated with millions of flowery bulbs. Just beyond the pond, at 3.2 miles, keep right at an unmarked junction; the trail left goes to another small pond and a few campsites, then connects with the Mazama Trail; just a little farther, at 3.4 miles, the top of the Mazama Trail connects directly with the Timberline.

Continue east across another meadow with more flowers and views, then arrive at the McNeil Point Trail at 3.7 miles. Now veer right (south) off the Timberline and begin ascending a heather- and paintbrush-covered ridgeline. The higher you go, the more impressive the views become. Look for Washington's big peaks in your rearview. The path then turns off the ridge to contour a steep talus slope, where snow often lingers long into the summer months. The final stretch ascends through more meadows and flowers, then mounts the plateau of McNeil Point. Where the trail forks, at 4.4 miles, choose the high route to the left (southwest), or the rim route to the right (west) and complete your journey at the McNeil Point shelter at 4.6 miles. Now, all you have to do is soak it all in—it's almost overwhelming. Stay and enjoy the view for a while, then return by the same route.

EXTEND YOUR TRIP

Beyond the McNeil Point Trail, the Timberline continues around Mount Hood and connects to numerous other trails. Most of these extend beyond reasonable day-hikeability. If you've got the legs for it, two of the closest options are Cairn Basin and Eden Park. The former is a wooded camp area with an old stone shelter, while the latter is a large, flowery meadow below the Timberline. Unfortunately, large portions of this area burned in the 2011 Dollar Lake Fire, which charred the hillsides. The area has been recovering, and wildflowers are usually profuse in summertime, which helps enhance the stark scenery.

To visit the Cairn Basin shelter, continue about 0.4 mile east on the Timberline Trail. The route dips through a rocky gorge to cross Ladd Creek, then traverses a couple of wildflower meadows. To visit Eden Park, veer left (northwest) off the Timberline, just west of the Cairn Basin shelter. This 2.6-mile loop steeply descends a partially burned hillside to circuit Eden Park's meadows. This is followed by several creek crossings and a steep climb to the Vista Ridge Trail. Turn right (south) to reconnect with the Timberline, then right (west) one more time through more spotty burned forest to return to the basin.

ORIGIN STORIES: MCNEIL POINT

Located at an elevation of 6034 feet, the McNeil Point shelter stands at the edge of an alpine plateau on the northwest slope of Mount Hood. This stone structure was built in the 1930s by the Civilian Conservation Corps and named in honor of Fred McNeil, who migrated to Oregon in 1912. McNeil was a journalist for the *Oregon Journal*, an active member of the Mazamas, and a founder of the Pacific Northwest Ski Association.

This is one of many stone and wood shelters built around Mount Hood that were intended to provide a resting place for mountaineers and climbers. The commanding view from this high prominence is one of the best on the mountain.

13 Ramona Falls

RATING/ DIFFICULTY	ROUNDTRIP	ELEV GAIN/ HIGH POINT	SEASON
****/4	7 miles	1230 feet/ 3470 feet	Apr–Nov

Map: Green Trails Maps Mount Hood #462S; **Permits:** NW Forest Pass for trailhead parking; self-issue wilderness permit; **Contact:** Zigzag Ranger District, MHNF; **Notes:** High-use trail; requires challenging river crossing; road closed Dec. 1–Apr. 1; **GPS:** N 45°23.202', W 121°49.920'

Oregon is known for its spectacular waterfalls. Many of them can be viewed directly from highways and short trails (such as in the Columbia River Gorge), but some of them require a little work to see—which makes them all the better. And while the hike to Ramona Falls is not difficult, when you finally stand near the base of this misty, 100-foot curtain of falling water, hidden away in its lush, mossy grotto, you'll wonder when you left Oregon and entered Middle Earth.

GETTING THERE

From Sandy, drive Mount Hood Highway (US Highway 26) east for approximately 17 miles to the town of Welches. Turn left (north) on East Lolo Pass Road for 4.2 miles. Where the road forks, veer right (east) onto Muddy Fork Road (Forest Road 1828) for 0.7 mile, then turn right again to cross the Sandy River onto FR 1825 for 1.7 miles, then fork left (east) on FR 100; proceed a bumpy 0.3 mile to the large trailhead parking area.

ON THE TRAIL

Start your journey on the Sandy River Trail, located on Old Maid Flats, just south of 3934-foot Last Chance Mountain. Find the

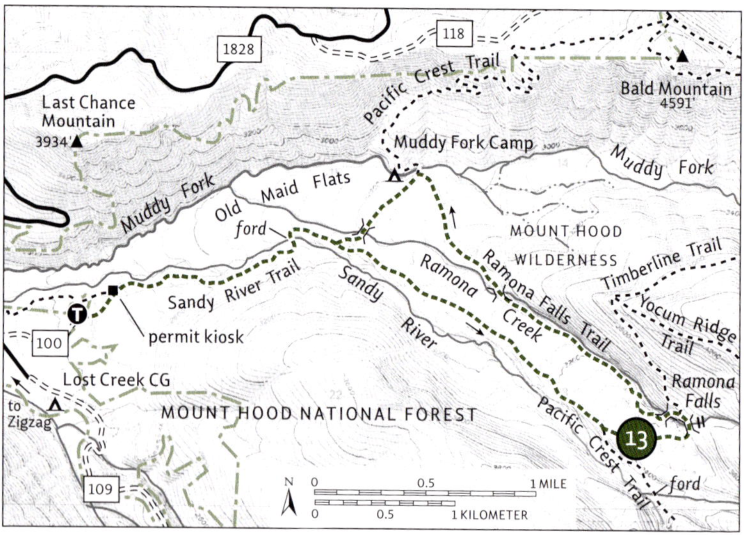

Ramona Falls is so fantastical, you may sense faeries and pixies nearby.

trailhead in the southeast corner of the parking area, where the path dives into open forest adorned with mountain rhododendron and vine maple. The way forward is wide and sandy and proceeds at a very slight incline. In less than 0.2 mile, the western portion of the Sandy River Trail branches off to the left (north). Proceed through the junction to the wilderness area kiosk and obtain your backcountry permit.

Continue ahead (east) and come to the high bank of the Sandy River near 0.3 mile, where you'll enjoy a nice view of Mount Hood. As one of Oregon's Wild and Scenic Rivers, the Sandy flows for 56 miles from Reid Glacier on Mount Hood to the Columbia River. When the Marmot and Little Sandy dams were demolished in 2007 and 2008, the Sandy was once again permitted to flow freely after almost a century of containment. The trail, now adorned with an assortment of fireweed, pearly everlasting, penstemon, thimbleberry, and mountain ash, continues up through the forest, paralleling the river. The way is easy and pleasant, and you'll be happy for the shade on warm, sunny afternoons.

At 1.2 miles, exit the trees and drop onto the rocky floodplain of the Sandy. The bridge that crossed the river here was washed out in 2014 and the Forest Service has not since replaced it due to the challenges posed by the river's ever-changing course and loose, rocky banks. In spring and early summer, during peak runoff periods, the river may be too high and impassable. If it looks dangerous, it probably is—don't risk it. If the river flow is moderate to low, look for a safe crossing area; you may need to scout a little ways up- or downstream to find a good passage. Before crossing, take note of where the trail continues on the opposite side so you can get back on track.

Once across, ascend the bank to a sandy bench and proceed through a swath of mountain ash to what looks like an unsigned junction. Turn left (north) for the proper trail and make a wide curve eastward, dipping through a gully, then plunging back under the cover of trees. At 1.4 miles, the path forks where you meet the Pacific Crest Trail (PCT). This begins the loop portion of your hike. Veer right (southeast) to begin a counterclockwise loop; you will return via the left branch. The trail, now on the north bank of the Sandy and lined with more rhododendron, begins climbing a steady, moderate grade and gaining good elevation above the river.

The next junction comes at 2.9 miles, where the PCT veers off to the right (south) and the Timberline Trail to the left (east). Take the left fork onto the Timberline and continue ascending through mixed forest. Here, you may notice the forest alternates through stretches of healthy, green, shrubby sections and dry, sandy, debris-laden sections. This is due to how different flood events on Mount Hood have impacted the river basins and surrounding forest. The trail, now adorned with huckleberry, twists and turns upward, and the sound of falling water can be heard ahead. At 3.3 miles, proceed through a stock control gate, then descend into a lush, shady grotto where Ramona Falls cascades down a wall of broken, columnar basalt. Drop your pack and take a moment to admire the falling curtain of water, which looks as though it were taken right out of the pages of a Tolkien book.

When you're ready to move on, cross the double-rail bridge below the falls and veer left (west) onto the Ramona Falls Trail; the Timberline continues to the right. Now follow Ramona Creek downstream through verdant, green forest. The path crosses the creek on a good bridge at 3.4 miles then proceeds on soft, duffy tread, where the forest is brimming with ferns, berries, devil's club, vanilla leaf, pipsissewa, lily of the valley, and more; the high wall opposite the creek is the lower extent of Yocum Ridge. Near 4.4 miles, the trail veers away from the creek and passes through another stretch of dry lodgepole forest, then it's back under greener trees before reconnecting with the PCT at 5.1 miles.

Turn left (southwest) on the PCT and meander through the forest on nearly level trail to a good bridge over Ramona Creek at 5.4 miles; just 0.2 mile farther you're back at the junction where you started the loop. Turn right (west), back onto the Sandy River Trail and start to backtrack the way you came. Recross the Sandy—where you may need to find a different crossing location if the river level has risen in the afternoon—then make the easy stroll back to your waiting vehicle.

ORIGIN STORIES: RAMONA FALLS

Ramona Falls was supposedly named after a popular romantic song of the 1930s. It was designated as such by John Mills, who discovered the falls while building trails for the USFS—and thinking of his fiancée.

14 Sandy River

RATING/ DIFFICULTY	ROUNDTRIP	ELEV GAIN/ HIGH POINT	SEASON
**/1	3.6 miles	360 feet/ 2440 feet	Apr–Nov

Map: Trails Illustrated Mount Hood Wilderness #321; **Permit:** NW Forest Pass for trailhead parking; **Contact:** Zigzag Ranger District, MHNF; **Notes:** Road closed Dec. 1–Apr. 1; **GPS:** N 45°23.028', W 121°51.756'

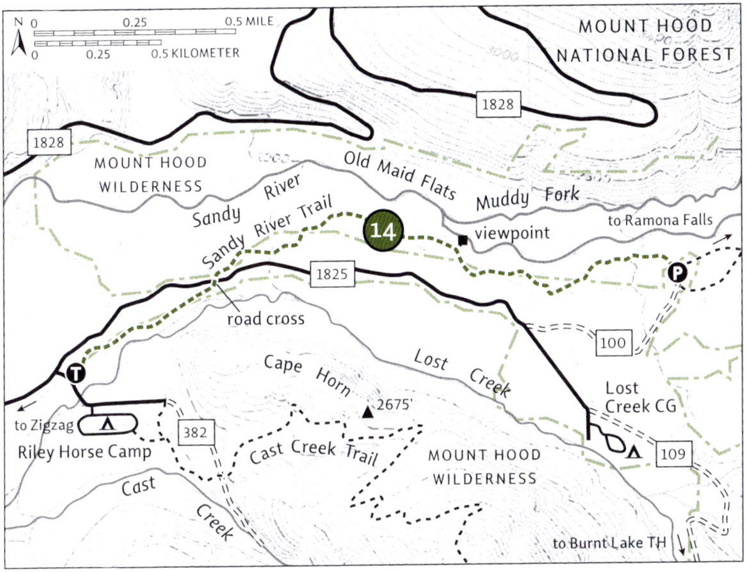

The Sandy River is one of the largest drainages on Mount Hood. It begins as runoff from Reid Glacier and flows more than 56 miles west and north to drain into the Columbia River. This is where the Sandy derives its name, as when encountered by William Clark (of the famed Lewis and Clark Expedition), who proclaimed the river "a quick sand, and impassible." On the mountain, the Sandy cascades down a deep, glaciated canyon, cutting into multiple layers of pyroclastic deposits and debris flows. This mostly flat segment of trail gives you the opportunity to casually explore a portion of the valley bottom where the Sandy has buried an ancient forest and cut a wide river channel.

GETTING THERE

From Sandy, drive Mount Hood Highway (US Highway 26) east for approximately 17 miles to the town of Welches. Turn left (north) on East Lolo Pass Road for 4.2 miles. Where the road forks, veer right (east) onto Muddy Fork Road (Forest Road 1828) for 0.7 mile, then right again to cross the Sandy River onto FR 1825. Proceed 0.5 mile to the next fork, signed for various trailheads and the Riley Horse Camp. Veer right and find the trailhead on the east side of the road; park on the road shoulder.

ON THE TRAIL

Begin on a wide, sandy path that heads east onto Old Maid Flats, an airy Douglas fir and lodgepole pine forest, where wispy witch's hair adorns the boughs, and manzanita and mosses carpet the ground. This is where centuries of debris flows have piled up on the valley floor—most notable by its hummocky terrain and rocky, sandy surface. To the right (south), you'll hear Lost Creek gurgling down its tree-shrouded channel. Along the way, there will be numerous user paths that branch off to creek views or hidden campsites. Just stick with the wide, sandy path to stay on track—and watch out for landmines (horse droppings), as this trail is frequented by equestrians.

After strolling along for about 0.4 mile, cross a paved road (FR 1825), then plunge back under cover of trees to continue along an easy, meandering course. You'll soon hear the sound of rushing water again, this time to the left (north), where the Sandy River comes within earshot. Around the 1-mile mark, the scene changes dramatically. The

An easy stroll along the banks of the Sandy River is a pleasant way to get a quick outdoor fix.

larger trees become skeletal and barren, and the trail gets overgrown with mixed shrubs, alder, big-leaf maple, and pearly everlasting. This stretch doesn't last long, and soon enough, you're back under mossy forest on duffy tread. Just when you start wondering when the Sandy River will become visible, you're presented with your first viewing opportunity.

Just past 1.1 miles, where the trail forks, veer left on a well-trod user path through more overgrown brush and onto a wide, sandy bench with a viewpoint. Take note of where you exited the brush to find your way back. Here in the wide open, the large, forested peak directly north is 3934-foot Last Chance Mountain; to the east, Mount Hood looms large in the near distance. Proceed to the edge of the bench—but not too close—for a look at the Sandy River pouring down its deeply incised channel. In spring and early summer, the Sandy can be a wide, raging torrent of silty floodwater. By autumn, it often dwindles to a murmuring, meandering stream. Once you've explored the area, proceed back to the main trail.

Continue eastward, winding through more mossy forest. Around 1.3 miles, the trail bends to skirt alongside the river channel. Nearby, large rhododendron shrubs bloom with clusters of vibrant pink flowers in the spring and early summer. Take in another look at the debris-laden channel and imagine the amount and force of water it takes to transport the massive logs and rocks strewn about the floor. Again, exercise caution near the channel's edge, as these loose slopes can easily and unexpectedly collapse. The trail then pulls away from the riverside to continue its winding course through the trees.

Around 1.7 miles, side trails veer off to a couple of campsites, partially hidden in the trees. The way then dips across a shallow gully, peaks on the other side, and drops into the large parking area for the Ramona Falls Trailhead. Here, at 1.8 miles, you have two options. If you're satisfied with your casual river romp, do an about-face and return by the same route. Or, if you're up for more exploration, continue on the Sandy River Trail to Ramona Falls (Hike 13). This will add another 7 miles (and 1100 feet of elevation) to your hike, for a total 10.6-mile journey that nets you more river views and one of Mount Hood's most stunning waterfalls.

15 Cast Lake

RATING/ DIFFICULTY	ROUNDTRIP	ELEV GAIN/ HIGH POINT	SEASON
***/5	11.2 miles	3590 feet/ 4610 feet	June–Oct

Map: Trails Illustrated Mount Hood Wilderness #321; **Permits:** NW Forest Pass for trailhead parking; self-issue wilderness permit; **Contact:** Zigzag Ranger District, MHNF; **Notes:** You can start this trail from three different trailheads; parking is limited at each; if one is full, try one of the others; road closed Dec. 1–Apr. 1; **GPS:** N 45°22.932', W 121°51.564'

Cast Lake is a quiet, forested pool high on the north flank of Zigzag Mountain. There are several routes you can take to get there, via a variety of trails in the area, but—even at 11.2 miles roundtrip—this ridgeline route is the shortest. The tradeoff is you'll do a lot of climbing to get there. And while much of the route remains confined to the trees, you'll be rewarded with

Secluded Cast Lake is a quiet destination for picnics and overnight camping.

an amazing viewpoint along the way before arriving at this secluded, tree-ringed tarn in an ancient glacial cirque. Tackle this one as a full-day round-trip, or pack your gear and enjoy an overnight in the woods.

GETTING THERE

From Sandy, drive Mount Hood Highway (US Highway 26) east for approximately 17 miles to the town of Welches. Turn left (north) on East Lolo Pass Road for 4.2 miles.

Where the road forks, veer right (east) onto Muddy Fork Road (Forest Road 1828) for 0.7 mile, then right again to cross the Sandy River onto FR 1825. Proceed 0.5 mile to the next fork, signed for various trailheads and the Riley Horse Camp, and veer right. For the main trailhead, turn right into the horse camp and proceed to the back of the camp loop. For the alternate trailheads, continue on good gravel FR 380 to the trailhead beside the road, or at the end of the road.

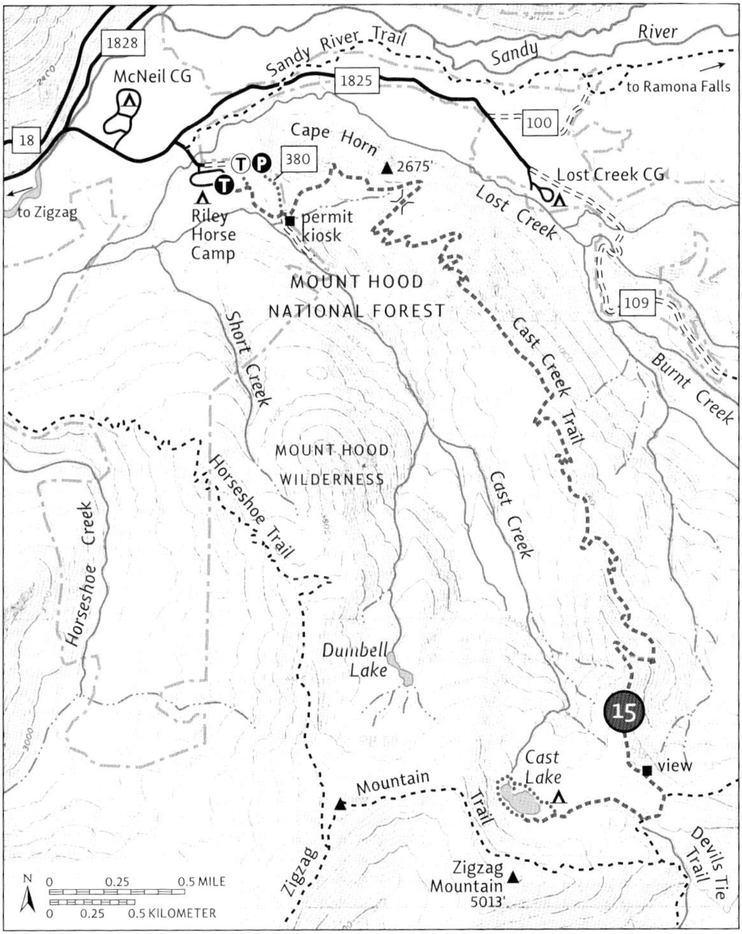

ON THE TRAIL

From the main Cast Creek Trailhead in the Riley Horse Camp at the foot of the Cape Horn ridge, proceed 0.3 mile through mossy hemlock and vine maple forest, on soft, sandy tread, to the wilderness permit kiosk on the south end of a small clearing. If you're starting from the roadside trailhead, walk the short, sandy path to connect with this route midway, or from the road's end trailhead, walk the 0.1-mile spur across a shallow gully to the clearing. However you come to the kiosk, fill out your wilderness permit, drop it in the slot, and get ready to get your climb on.

Begin your ascent into shady, green forest, where the slopes are adorned with a variety of ferns, salal, Oregon grape, thimbleberry, and inside-out flower (duckfoot). The trail tread here, and through much of the hike, is wide and duffy, with few obstacles to negotiate, which adds a little extra comfort to compensate for its length and elevation gain. As you get underway, you may spy a very brief peek at Cast Creek in the draw below; this will be your only look. Near the 1-mile mark, circuit a lush spring basin filled with mossy rocks, fern, and a wide carpet of sorrel. On the opposite side of the basin, the switchbacks begin and up, up, up you go.

The view along the way remains confined to the surrounding forest, with no windows to the wider world, but there is plenty to observe along the way to help ease the endless ascent. The trail crosses a small bridge over a trickling spring; it skirts a wide draw filled with huge, prehistoric-looking devil's club; and it passes the giant exposed rootball of a fallen hemlock. (Take a look at the size of the rootball in comparison to the diameter of the tree.) At this point, about 2.2 miles along, you're given a brief respite from the climbing to descend across a shallow, shaded saddle on the ridgeline. But with only half of your ascent completed, it's time to get busy again.

Continue climbing along the ridgeline, at times on very narrow track, where dense salal and rhododendron occasionally line the trailsides. You may begin to notice an occasional burned-out tree or stump, each standing like a charred monument on the hillside. These are the remnants of a wildfire that burned through this forest nearly a century ago. After proceeding through another series of switchbacks, and past a few large, rocky mounds, the trees begin parting to offer glimpses outward. Finally, the trail reaches the 4610-foot crest of the ridge at 4.8 miles and you're presented with a grand panorama of the Sandy River valley, East Zigzag Mountain, and the glacier-draped western face of Mount Hood. This view alone makes all the climbing worth the effort.

The route now makes a steep descent to a junction with the Zigzag Mountain Trail at 5 miles. Fork right and continue descending another 0.1 mile to another junction. At this unsigned fork, veer right again and traipse along a narrow, rocky, up-and-down track through dense huckleberry and lupine to crest a minor ridge before descending toward the lake. Almost there, at 5.5 miles, a side trail branches off to a few campsites around the north side of the lake. Continue a final 0.1 mile, crossing a muddy inlet creek, to the south shore of Cast Lake at 5.6 miles. Find a dry spot near the shore and watch the fish jump, the crawfish scurry, and dragonflies dart around while you enjoy a well-deserved lunch break. When you're ready (deep breath), return by the same route.

16 Burnt Lake

RATING/ DIFFICULTY	ROUNDTRIP	ELEV GAIN/ HIGH POINT	SEASON
****/3	6.6 miles	1560 feet/ 4140 feet	June–Oct

Map: Trails Illustrated Mount Hood Wilderness #321; **Permit:** Self-issue wilderness permit; **Contact:** Zigzag Ranger District, MHNF; **Notes:** High-use trail; road closed Dec. 1–Apr. 1; **GPS:** N 45°22.338', W 121°49.356'

Nestled in a beautiful forested basin between Zigzag Mountain and Mount Hood, Burnt Lake is a pleasant backcountry setting for picnics and paddling around a pretty mountain pool. On the hike to get there, you'll see the ghosts of an ancient cedar forest that used to occupy the area prior to the early 1900s wildfire that gives the area its name. This is a popular destination on warm summer days, so expect a lot of company on the trail and around the lake. There are even a few designated campsites nearby for extending your visit and exploring more of the area.

GETTING THERE

From Sandy, drive Mount Hood Highway (US Highway 26) east for approximately 17 miles to the town of Welches. Turn left (north) on East Lolo Pass Road for 4.2 miles. Where the road forks, veer right (east) onto Muddy Fork Road (Forest Road 1828) for 0.7 mile, then right again to cross the Sandy River onto

Pack a small inflatable with you and enjoy some summer paddling around scenic Burnt Lake.

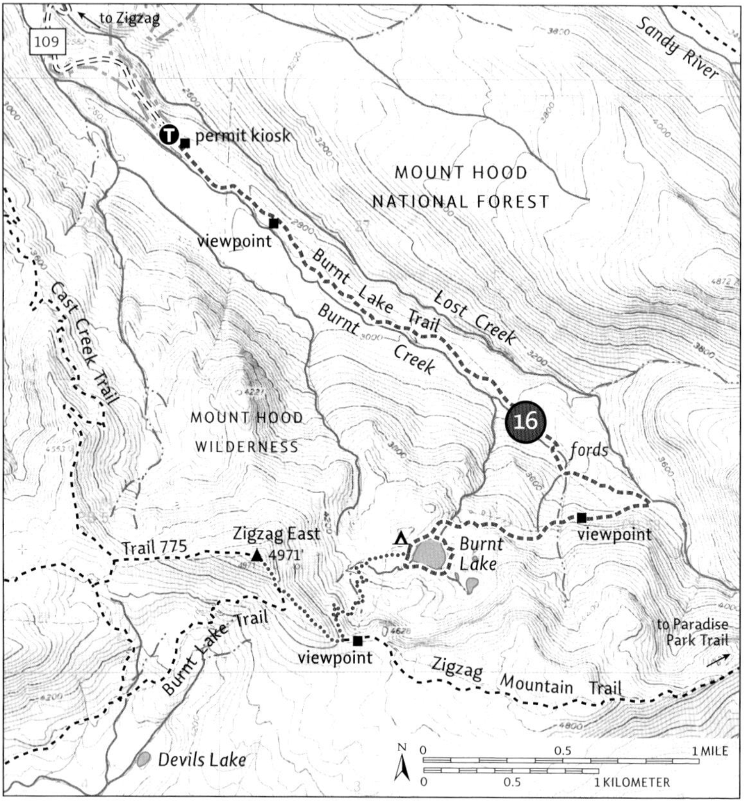

FR 1825. Proceed 2 miles to the Lost Creek Campground. Just before the campground entrance, veer left (southeast) onto narrow FR 109 and drive 1.4 miles on good gravel to the trailhead at the end of the road.

ON THE TRAIL

Start your hike to Burnt Lake under a canopy of vine maple, western hemlock, and silver fir, where bunchberry, wild strawberry, lady and sword fern, Oregon grape, sorrel, and starry Solomon's seal carpet the forest floor. In season, look for tasty thimbleberries along the trail. Shortly after getting underway, about 100 yards up the trail, you'll come to the wilderness entry kiosk, with a picnic table nearby. Collect your permit and continue up the wide, duffy path, which parallels Burnt Creek to the right (west), which remains mostly heard but not seen. You'll soon begin to see the moss-covered remains of charred, old-growth cedars in the forest mix. These are the enduring remains of the wildfire that scorched this area more than one hundred years ago.

The trail proceeds upward on a gentle grade, where large Douglas firs begin to join the forest mix, keeping the path mostly shady. Around the 0.6-mile mark, as you pass an immense uprooted tree trunk, a short path left (north) leads to a viewpoint over the wooded Lost Creek Canyon; at 0.7 mile, a short path right (south) descends through ferns and huckleberry to the side of Burnt Creek. The way forward is lush and pleasant, with the trail remaining mostly wide and even for effortless walking through the faerie-like woodland. Near 1.2 miles, skirt the mossy hulk of a massive, burned-out cedar, then begin ascending a little more earnestly until the trail comes right alongside the creek, where several large hemlocks in the shape of tuning forks reach for the sky with double trunks.

Now it's time to get your feet wet. First, at 1.9 miles, cross a wide, shallow creek in a rocky bed. Then cross it again at 2 miles, where it pours across the trail in several places amid thickets of fern, salmonberry, and devil's club—watch out for thorns! The trail then begins contouring up the hillside on a moderate grade, making a sharp switchback at 2.4 miles to continue upward and westward. Right before this switchback, a short side trail left (northeast) descends to Lost Creek. A little farther, at 2.6 miles, the trail briefly pops out of the trees to traverse a clearing below a rocky slope where several seeps and springs spill across the path. Here, you can catch a view of Mount Hood to the east, then it's back into the trees.

The ascent finally eases as you pass through 3 miles and, near the top, proceed through an area choked with alder and a variety of forest flora. Hop across the lake's outlet on large rocks, then follow the path as it levels out in dense rhododendron to a fork at 3.3 miles to complete the hike. From here, you can explore the brushy shore of Burnt Lake on a 0.4-mile loop. A map board nearby shows designated sites around the lake good for picnics and day-use (lettered) and overnight camping (numbered). For the best views of Mount Hood across the deep blue, tree-ringed pool, fork right and follow the trail to the sites on the west side of the lake. If you're up for a little more adventure, you can continue up to the Zigzag East Lookout (see Extend Your Trip), otherwise, once you've finished your visit to the lake, return by the same route.

EXTEND YOUR TRIP

If you're up for a healthy climb to a great viewpoint, you can continue up the Burnt Lake Trail to Zigzag East Lookout. From the west side of the lake's loop trail, veer right (west) and proceed past a few campsites and skirt the marshes above Burnt Lake. The trail crosses a small creek 0.2 mile from the lake, then proceeds up a series of switchbacks to a trail junction atop the ridge, 0.7 mile from the lake. To the left (east), the Zigzag Mountain Trail goes for 2.8 miles along the viewless ridgetop through overgrown huckleberry to end at the Paradise Park Trail (Hike 25). There is a good viewpoint atop a rocky bluff about 50 yards down this path. To the right (west), the trail climbs 0.5 mile to the 4971-foot crown of Zigzag East. About halfway up, veer right (northwest) at the fork with the Burnt Lake Trail. The lookout tower is long gone, but the panoramic views of Mount Hood remain.

17 Zigzag Mountain Lookout

RATING/ DIFFICULTY	ROUNDTRIP	ELEV GAIN/ HIGH POINT	SEASON
****/5	11.3 miles	4400 feet/ 4520 feet	May–Oct

Map: Trails Illustrated Mount Hood Wilderness #321; **Permit:** Self-issue wilderness permit; **Contact:** Zigzag Ranger District, MHNF; **Notes:** This is a steep, challenging trail with narrow ridges and sheer cliffs; not recommended for small children or the acrophobic; **GPS:** N 45°20.364', W 121°55.050'

All together now: "I love switchbacks." Again: "I love switchbacks." Once more with gusto: "I looooooovve switchbacks!" Put your game face on because persistence pays on this steep route to an old fire lookout site on the western flanks of Mount Hood. The visual rewards come incrementally along the way, with a final grand panorama that spans the central Cascades to Oregon's coast ranges.

GETTING THERE

East trailhead: From Sandy, drive Mount Hood Highway (US Highway 26) east for approximately 19 miles, through Zigzag, to Rhododendron. Turn left on East Arlie Mitchell Road for 0.3 mile, then left on gravel Zigzag River Road (signed Barlow Road Route) for 0.3 mile to the trailhead at the end of the road. *West trailhead:* From Zigzag, turn left onto East Lolo Pass Road (Forest Road 18) for 0.4 mile, then right on East Mountain Drive for 0.7 mile to its end.

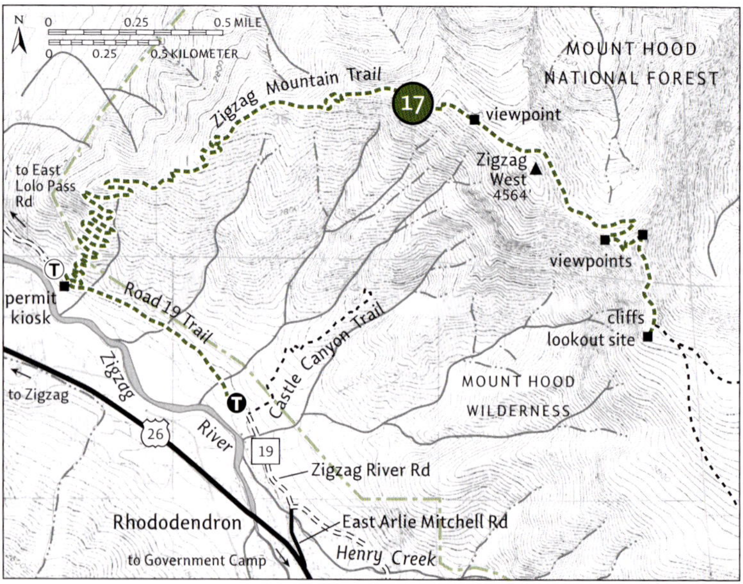

ON THE TRAIL

Starting at the east Barlow Road Route Trailhead is a good way to warm up your legs for the coming climb, then a good way to cool off and stay limber following your subsequent descent. (If you'd rather just get to it and cut out 1.6 miles, start at the west trailhead.) The hike begins with a pleasant walk along a section of the historic Barlow Road (Road 19 Trail). Look around at the mossy forest of Douglas firs and big-leaf maples as well as the dense fern and berry shrubs, and imagine being an 1840s emigrant trying to make passage through this Northwest jungle. A little farther up the old road, wagons actually had to be lowered by rope to keep them from running off the steep slope. After about 0.8 mile of comfortable walking, reach the Zigzag Mountain Trailhead, just upslope from the Zigzag River. Now it's time to get to work.

Start up the trail and quickly come to the Mount Hood Wilderness permit kiosk. Fill out your permit, drop the slip in the box, and check the map and info board for any local notices. Take a deep breath and begin a steady, 1200-foot ascent over the next 1.5 miles in a series of sixteen sweeping east–west switchbacks. Fortunately, the trail surface is mostly smooth, on a carpet of soft forest duff, and there's plenty to distract you from the ongoing climb, largely in the form of a vibrant and lovely forest. Sunlight filters through the canopy of towering firs and hemlocks to illuminate vine and big-leaf maples and get dispersed upon a slopeside mantle of salal, sword and lady fern, Oregon grape, and vanilla leaf. Look for a variety of strange and colorful fungi along the way, from various mushrooms to alien-like freckle pelts. At the top of the last switchback, at 2.8 miles, the easy part is over.

The trail now turns east and the grade increases to a more moderate degree to trace the ridgeline upward. The trail starts to get a little rougher, with more rocks and roots to navigate, and a little narrower, with dense salal and rhododendron encroaching on the path. Proceed through a few more switchbacks—yes, there's more—to keep trending along the ridgeline; the view remains isolated to the surrounding brushy forest. Soon, interesting oddities start breaking up the tedium: a curious bare patch of forest at 3.4 miles, a giant block of mossy rock at 3.5 miles, and a narrow, slightly harrowing ridge traverse at 3.7 miles. Finally, at 4.2 miles, following a few more switchbacks, you're treated to your first view of the wider world. Look south and find the peak of Mount Jefferson rising above a horizon of endless wooded ridgelines.

At this point, your climbing is mostly done—*mostly*—and the trail rolls along the ridge for a spell before beginning a moderate descent to circuit a heavily wooded prominence; around 4.4 miles, look for a window in the trees that offers a view of glacier-capped Mount Rainier far to the north. Now on the cooler, shadier north side of the ridge, contour under a wall of mossy rocks. On one outcrop stands a sharp pinnacle that points to the sky. (Take note of this, as you will see it again later.) The trail then loops through a wide switchback to crest an exposed section of the ridge at 5.1 miles that opens up a wide panorama over the forested valley far below. Climb another 0.2 mile through a few more switchbacks and the big view of Mount Hood you've been waiting for is suddenly and spectacularly before you. Very thoughtfully, nature placed a convenient cluster of rocks at this location, giving you an ideal place to have a seat and enjoy the view.

Watch your footing as you traverse the cliffs atop Zigzag West—then enjoy the views.

You may be tempted to call it good at this point, but the lookout site is just a short distance away. Follow the ridgeline south where clusters of bear grass line the way, and make a steep descent, then an equally steep ascent to mount an exposed, rocky outcrop. At 5.5 miles, skirt a precipitous edge along a seemingly bottomless abyss; across the void is a deep crack in the rock that reveals a harrowing look down to the valley floor. Continue through the brush the last few paces to a small clearing near the edge of the rocky plateau, just past 5.6 miles. The view is expansive and gives one of those on-top-of-the-world impressions. From 1929 to 1966, this was the site of a Forest Service fire lookout. Now, all that remains are the concrete footings it was once mounted on. From here, the Zigzag Mountain Trail continues on to junctions with various other area trails, but this makes an ideal turnaround point for a day's endeavor. When you're ready, turn around and head down by the same route.

18 Castle Canyon

RATING/ DIFFICULTY	ROUNDTRIP	ELEV GAIN/ HIGH POINT	SEASON
***/4	1.8 miles	970 feet/ 2490 feet	Apr–Nov

Map: Trails Illustrated Mount Hood Wilderness #321; **Permit:** Self-issue wilderness permit; **Contact:** Zigzag Ranger District, MHNF; **Notes:** This is an especially steep, narrow trail with sharp drops that requires some minor scrambling; not recommended for small children or dogs; **GPS:** N 45°20.274', W 121°54.942'

Ready for some cardio in Middle Earth? This short, wooded trail vaults you nearly 1000 feet up a sylvan hillside to a cluster of hidden volcanic pinnacles that conjure images of crumbling fortresses and otherworldly giants. Actually, these are the remains of ancient lava flows, exposed and sculpted over centuries of erosion. You'll work to get there, and the last few hundred yards will require the use of your hands to ascend a series of steep steps to mount this otherworldly precipice.

GETTING THERE

From Sandy, drive Mount Hood Highway (US Highway 26) east for approximately 19 miles to Rhododendron. Turn left on East Arlie Mitchell Road for 0.3 mile, then left on gravel Zigzag River Road (signed Barlow Road Route) for 0.2 mile to the trailhead. There are a few shoulder turnouts for parking nearby; do not block or park in residential driveways.

ON THE TRAIL

The Castle Canyon Trail begins deceptively easy. From the nondescript trailhead beside the road, plunge into mossy Douglas fir and western hemlock forest, interspersed with vine and big-leaf maple. In the spring and summer months, these latter two seem to illuminate the forest with filtered sunlight. In the fall months, they turn vibrant shades of yellow, orange, and red to create a dramatic and vibrant contrast against the dark green conifers. The way is lined with a lush assortment of deer and sword fern, inside-out flower (duckfoot) and thimbleberry, among other forest shrubs and flowers. Several user paths cross the trail in the first few hundred yards. Ignore these and proceed to the wilderness permit kiosk and trail map board at 0.1 mile. Fill out your form, deposit the slip in the slot, and move along.

A mossy volcanic monolith in Castle Canyon

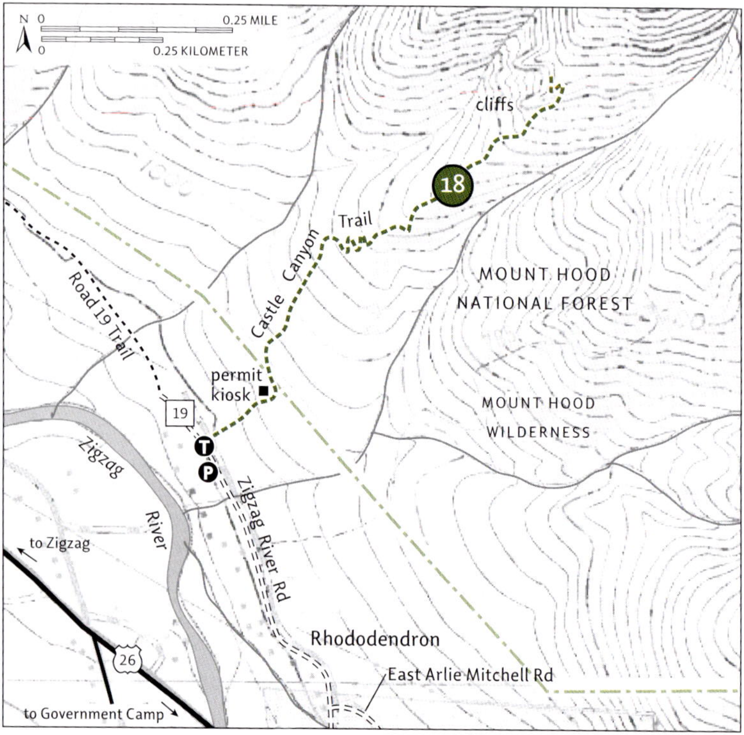

In short order, the trail gets down to business by commencing a fairly moderate ascent of the shady hillside, steeply switching back several times to quickly gain elevation. As it climbs, Oregon grape and rhododendron are added to the forest mix, offering more cover for the elves and faeries sure to inhabit this verdant copse. At approximately 0.5 mile, a small clearing beside the trail provides an opportunity to pull over and take a breath. It only gets steeper from here. Keep huffing up the narrow ridgeline, where rocky outcrops are blanketed in swathes of fern and rich, green moss. At 0.6 mile, it's time to get your hands dirty by ascending a short, rocky chute, then continuing past a large boulder sitting atop a fern- and salal-draped pedestal.

The first of the pinnacle formations appears beside the trail as a gnarly finger of mossy rock jutting more than 20 feet high. The trail continues getting steeper as it circuits the base of this spire and continues upward. Then, out of the shadows of the trees, appears what seems to be a cluster of sleeping giants—three more pinnacles, even larger than the first. Could these be Bilbo's stone trolls? (We're going to say yes.)

Continue around the base of the easternmost troll—er, pinnacle—and scramble up a couple of short, steep switchbacks on the side of this bizarre formation to mount a rocky knife-edge on its back side at 0.9 mile. From atop this crest, you're presented with a decent panorama over the forested valley below.

There are numerous narrow user paths that venture farther out onto the rocky ridges, some requiring bushwhacking or moderate scrambling. These are not for the acrophobic, and a fall from one of these ledges could be severe, so use extreme caution. When you're ready to return, head down the same way you came. Take it slow and use your hands to steady yourself on the steep slopes and steps to keep from slipping. As you descend, throw a glance back over your shoulder to ensure you haven't woken the trolls, then ramble back down into the safety of more peaceful, enchanted forest on your way back to your waiting vehicle.

19 Pioneer Bridal Trail

RATING/ DIFFICULTY	ONE-WAY	ELEV GAIN/ HIGH POINT	SEASON
**/1–2	7.7 miles	2270 feet (west to east)/ 3630 feet	All year

Map: Trails Illustrated Mount Hood Wilderness #321; **Permit:** NW Forest Pass for trailhead parking; **Contact:** Zigzag Ranger District, MHNF; **Notes:** Multiuse trail; be courteous and exercise proper right-of-way; **GPS:** N 45°19.194', W 121°54.222'

The Pioneer Bridle Trail stretches all the way from the town of Rhododendron, on the lower western flank of Mount Hood, to the town of Government Camp, high on its south side. The trail follows a portion of the historic Barlow Road, part of the original Oregon Trail wagon road. The upper (eastern) portion skirts Laurel Hill, considered by many emigrants to be the most difficult portion of the trail, while the lower (western) portion traces the banks of Camp Creek and the Zigzag River. Accessible year-round, you can choose from four trailheads to hike, ride, or snowshoe as near or far as you like.

GETTING THERE

West trailhead: From Sandy, drive Mount Hood Highway (US Highway 26) east for approximately 20 miles, through Rhododendron. Just past the Tollgate Campground, turn right (south) into the Tollgate/Pioneer Bridle Trail parking area. *East Trailhead:* Continue on Mount Hood Highway, past Rhododendron and the west trailhead, another 7 miles to the Glacier View Sno-Park; turn left for 0.2 mile to the trailhead. You can also access the trail from the Camp Creek Campground and the Zigzag Falls Trailhead.

ON THE TRAIL

For an easy, relatively flat walk or winter stroll, start at the Tollgate (west) Trailhead, just east of the town of Rhododendron. The trail starts at a replica tollgate in the same location where pioneers of bygone days once had to stop and pay a five-dollar fee for using Barlow Road. That's just the price of a latte today but no small chunk of change in the 1840s. The trail proceeds on a mix of gravel and duffy tread, on a very gentle upward grade, passing under mossy fir, hemlock, alder, and big-leaf maple woods as it heads eastward, between US 26 and the

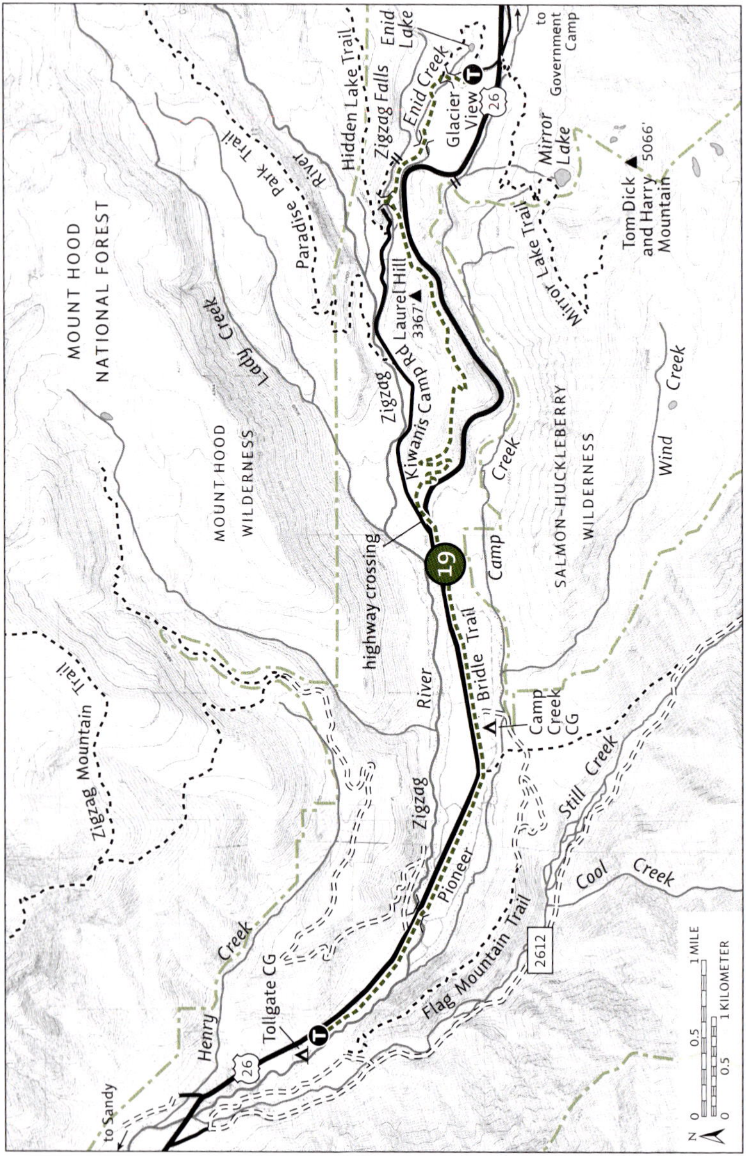
MOUNT HOOD
NATIONAL FOREST
MOUNT HOOD
WILDERNESS
SALMON-HUCKLEBERRY
WILDERNESS
Lady Creek
Paradise Park Trail
Zigzag River
Hidden Lake Trail
Zigzag Falls
Enid Lake
Enid Creek
Glacier View
26
to Government Camp
Mirror Lake
Mirror Lake Trail
Tom Dick and Harry Mountain
5066'
Laurel Hill
3367'
Zigzag
Kiwanis Camp Rd
Camp Creek
Wind Creek
highway crossing
19
Bridle Trail
River
Camp Creek CG
Still Creek
Zigzag Mountain Trail
Zigzag
Pioneer
Cool Creek
Flag Mountain Trail
2612
Henry Creek
Tollgate CG
26
to Sandy
0
0.5
1 MILE
0
0.5
1 KILOMETER
N

Zigzag River. Alongside the trail are plenty of fern, salal, Oregon grape, and trillium to keep things interesting and distract from the nearby highway noise.

In the first mile of walking, you'll cross a couple of access roads, and pass a few old cabins and service buildings. At 1 mile, cross the Zigzag River on a nice wooden bridge. This makes a good turnaround point if you're just out for a quick fix. From here, the trail continues gently uphill through the woods, paralleling the highway. In the near distance to the right (south), Camp Creek flows downhill but remains out of sight. Around the 2-mile mark, the trail reaches the outskirts of the Camp Creek Campground. Look for a side trail that breaks off right; this leads to the Still Creek Trailhead inside the campground (Hike 24). Just beyond, near 2.2 miles, is the campground access road.

Walk the wagon route used by some of Oregon's earliest settlers on the Pioneer Bridle Trail.

This makes a good turnaround point for a 4.4-mile round-trip. If you choose to go on, the trail crosses the highway a little farther ahead, then starts climbing Laurel Hill.

For more of a rambling hike on the Pioneer Bridle Trail around Laurel Hill, begin at the Glacier View (east) Trailhead, just west of Government Camp. Start by heading north, descending into mossy hemlock and fir forest, with dense thickets of rhododendron, fern, and huckleberry. The trail briefly levels out and crosses a small bridge over Enid Creek, then comes to a wide junction with the Enid Lake Loop at 0.3 mile. Turn left (west) and start an easy descent alongside Enid Creek, crossing again on another bridge, and passing some impressively large Douglas firs. Shortly past 0.7 mile, a short side trail breaks off left (south) to the Glacier View snow trail. Continue descending, briefly skirting US 26, then pass through a stone tunnel under the old highway. You can climb up to and take this old road 0.1 mile north to the Zigzag Falls Trailhead (Hike 27).

Continue westward, contouring along the south slope of 3367-foot Laurel Hill. This hill was considered the most treacherous portion of the old Barlow Road traverse, where pioneers had to lower their wagons by rope down the steep slope. A few gaps in the trees offer glimpses of the valley, but otherwise the trail stays confined to the woods. Following a few dips and rises, begin a steady descent, which finishes with a handful of switchbacks to unceremoniously drop onto the shoulder of the highway, 4 miles from where you started. Depending on your transportation situation, you can turn around here and start huffing your way back up the hill, or cross the highway and continue downhill, up to another 3.7 miles, to the end of the line at the Tollgate Trailhead.

20 Flag Mountain

RATING/ DIFFICULTY	ROUNDTRIP	ELEV GAIN/ HIGH POINT	SEASON
**/4	3.7 miles	1570 feet/ 2540 feet	Apr–Nov

Map: Trails Illustrated Mount Hood Wilderness #321; **Permit:** None; **Contact:** Zigzag Ranger District, MHNF; **Notes:** Multiuse trail; be courteous and yield the right-of-way; **GPS:** N 45°19.062', W 121°54.372'

Looking for a good pre- or postseason workout? While many of Mount Hood's higher trails may be buried under snow, try this moderately strenuous trail that roller coasters along a forested ridgeline between the Still Creek and Camp Creek valleys. There's only one notable viewpoint along the way, but the lush forest is pleasant, with a lot of rhododendrons and mushrooms, which bloom profusely in summer and fall, respectively.

GETTING THERE

From Sandy, drive Mount Hood Highway (US Highway 26) east for approximately 19 miles to Rhododendron. Just past the Dairy Queen, turn right (south) on Road 20 and continue 0.8 mile to a fork. Veer left (east) on gravel Road 20 East for about 100 yards to a small parking turnout on the left (north) side of the road. The trailhead is located on the opposite (south) side of the road a few yards back. Do not park in or block residential driveways.

ON THE TRAIL

The trail begins deceptively flat and inviting under a mossy canopy of big-leaf maple, Douglas fir, cedar, and hemlock, where

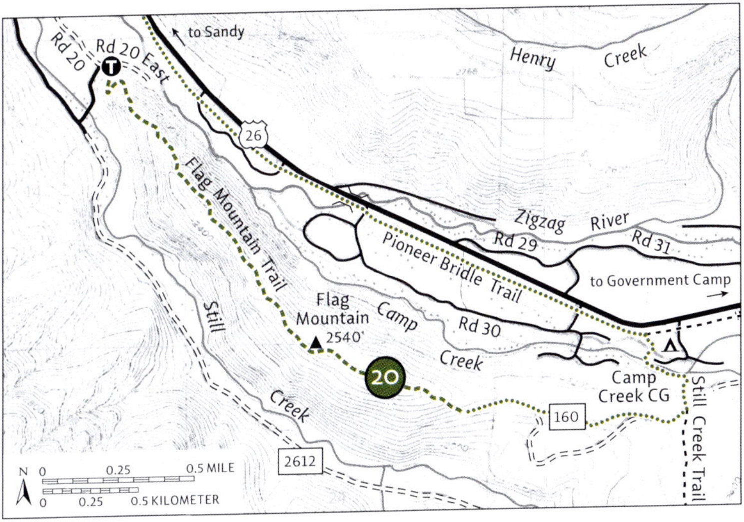

sword fern and salal carpet much of the ground. Pass a couple of old cabins then get your climb on. The trail quickly commences upward through a series of increasingly steep switchbacks on initially duffy tread. As you gain elevation, Oregon grape and inside-out flower (duckfoot) begin to appear along the trail. About 0.2 mile up, the path starts getting rough and bends around a large, rocky knob covered with mosses and ferns. Just a little ways farther, reach the crest of the ridge beside another mossy outcrop. Here, you can catch a partial view over the side of the ridge into Still Creek Canyon; the high point to the southwest is 4033-foot Hunchback Mountain.

Now proceed along the spine of the ridge, southeastward, through dense shrubs of salal, Oregon grape, and sword and lady fern, with a smattering of snowberry, salmonberry, and false Solomon's seal mixed in. The grade eases for a short stretch, then it's back to heading up. The way forward repeats this pattern of short, flat stretches between short, moderate ascents. Passing through 0.4 mile, clamber up a section of rocky, rooty steps to the next crest on the ridge, where the surrounding woods become more open and airy, and rhododendron appears here and there. By the time you reach 0.6 mile, the majority of the strenuous climbing is over and the rest of the trail continues rolling gently along the ridgetop on mostly duffy tread.

As you casually stroll along the wooded crest, notice that the surrounding woods become more prominently silver fir and hemlock, with a few clusters of cedar, and rhododendrons become more prolific. A few gaps in the trees offer the sparest of glimpses of Mount Hood to the east. The big—and only—viewpoint comes near 0.9 mile, where the trail skirts an opening on the ridgeline. Here, there's a nice look at

Get an early-season peek at Mount Hood's summit from atop Flag Mountain.

Mount Hood rising beyond forested Zigzag Mountain and Laurel Hill. Continuing along, the trail dips through a couple of saddles filled with vine maple and alder, then climbs to reach Flag Mountain's viewless and anticlimactic summit at 1.4 miles. The next 0.2 mile of the trail continues on pleasant, mild terrain before descending steeply to end at old Forest Road 160 at about 1.8 miles. At this point, just make an about-face and head back the way you came.

EXTEND YOUR TRIP

It's possible to turn the Flag Mountain hike into a 6.5-mile loop utilizing the Pioneer Bridle Trail (Hike 19) along Camp Creek as the return route. It requires some road walking for a couple of stretches, but it offers a change of scenery on the way back, while adding a little more mileage to your outing. From the east end of the Flag Mountain Trail, walk gravel FR 160 east (which turns into Road 32) for 0.8 mile to the Still Creek Trail (Hike 24). Veer left (north) and descend through a sea of sword fern to the bank of Camp Creek. Follow this path downstream under some impressively large conifers, then cross the creek on a good bridge to the trailhead in the Camp Creek Campground.

Cross the camp road turnaround and continue another 0.1 mile to connect with the Pioneer Bridle Trail, now 3 miles from your starting point. Turn left (west) and begin a gentle descent along this forested route, which once served as a portion of the historic Barlow Road. At 4.1 miles, the trail crosses the Zigzag River on a good bridge, then comes to an old tollgate at the Pioneer Bridle Trailhead at 5.1 miles. Cross the parking area and continue west for another 0.5

mile, passing the Tollgate Campground, to paved Road 20 at 5.6 miles. Now just walk the road you came in on for the last 0.9 mile back to your starting point at the Flag Mountain Trailhead.

21 Old Salmon River

RATING/ DIFFICULTY	ROUNDTRIP	ELEV GAIN/ HIGH POINT	SEASON
***/1	4.9 miles	470 feet/ 1600 feet	Apr–Nov

Map: Trails Illustrated Mount Hood Wilderness #321; **Permit:** NW Forest Pass for trailhead parking; **Contact:** Zigzag Ranger District, MHNF; **Notes:** There's a lot to discover on this trail; bring a nature guide to help you identify many of the plants and animals you may see; **GPS:** N 45°18.504', W 121°56.580'

The Old Salmon River Trail explores a stretch of the—you guessed it—Salmon River. The trail is easy to get to and is often accessible earlier in the season than many other trails on Mount Hood due to its lower elevation. The trail itself is an adventure through a primeval river bottom, replete with towering, old-growth forest and abundant wildflowers, mosses, and fungi. The only thing missing is dinosaurs, so just use your imagination. The following description highlights a north-to-south hike, but it can be hiked just as easily south-to-north, or from any of the intermediate access points.

GETTING THERE

From Sandy, drive Mount Hood Highway (US Highway 26) east for approximately 17 miles to Welches. Turn right (south) on East Salmon River Road and proceed 2.6 miles to

A stroll along the wild and scenic Salmon River is an enjoyable spring outing.

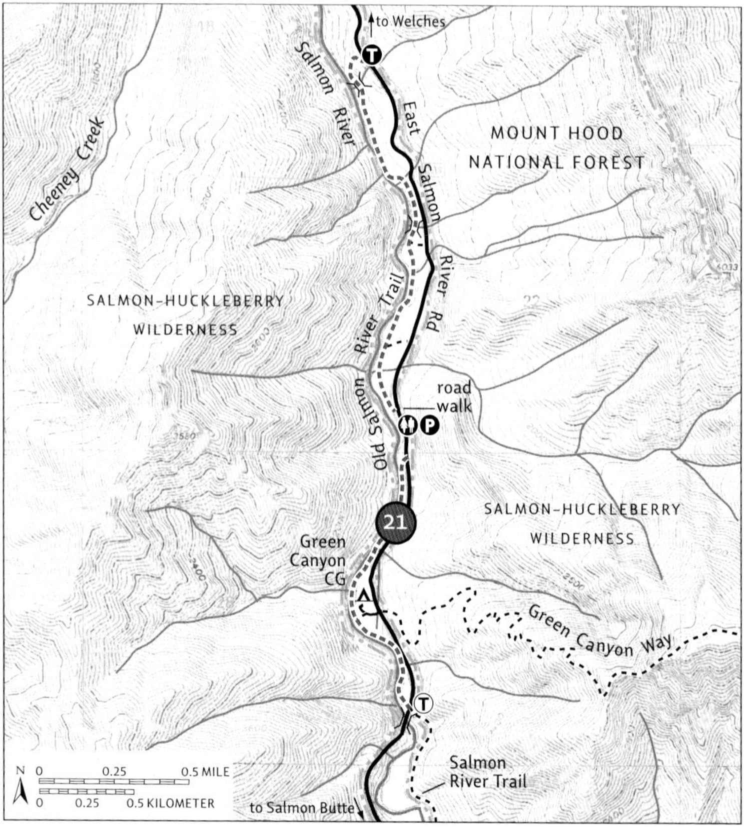

the north trailhead, or 5 miles to the south trailhead.

ON THE TRAIL

Starting at the northernmost trailhead, descend into a jungle of giant mossy hemlock, cedar, fir, and big-leaf maple, where abundant vine maple fills the understory and sword ferns, thimbleberry, sorrel, Solomon's seal, inside-out flower (duckfoot), fairy bells, and fringe cup carpet the forest floor. Following rain showers, when everything is damp and dripping, the scene is positively primordial; on bluebird days, scant sunlight is filtered through curtains of witch's hair, which gives the forest an illuminated, enchanted appearance. Following the quick descent, cross a sturdy bridge over a feeder creek, and traipse along the riverside, where the trail is nearly flat and mostly duffy. It's

SALMON RIVER

Oregon's Salmon River has the rare distinction of being the only National Wild and Scenic River in the contiguous United States for its entire length. From its headwaters high on Mount Hood to its confluence with the Sandy River, the Salmon River flows freely for nearly 34 miles through alpine environments, basalt canyons, wetland meadows, and a portion of the Salmon–Huckleberry Wilderness. In addition to providing a habitat for diverse wildlife, the river is home to a variety of salmon, steelhead, and trout, as well as rare and unique types of native flora. By combining numerous trails, it's possible to hike almost the entire length of the Salmon River—however, that would likely take several days. Fortunately, you can explore some of the most scenic portions of the Salmon River as day hikes. Flip to the following hikes for more options:

21. Old Salmon River
22. Salmon River
70. Little Crater Camp to Wapinitia Pass
72. Barlow Pass to Timberline Lodge

easy walking, allowing you to admire the multiple layers of the lush forest around you.

Near the half-mile mark, cross another creek and proceed up a winding series of steps to come beside a massive Douglas fir that's had its base blown out by a lightning strike. The trail then undulates forward, crosses yet another creek, and enters a wide area on the riverbank where, nearing 0.8 mile, a side trail climbs left (east) to the road, and an old camp area can be found on the right (west). Camping on the river is not permitted within a quarter mile of the road, but this location makes a nice picnic spot with good river access. If you're interested in a chilly dip, there's a deep, calm spot in the river here, between two riffles.

As you continue rolling along upstream, another side trail breaks off left (east) to the road at 1 mile. Just beyond, the trail crosses a wide, rocky creek bed. If there's water flowing, there are plenty of larger rocks to hop across on. The path then bends upward through copious berry shrubs and pops out of the trees to the side of the road at 1.3 miles; on the opposite side of the road is a large parking area and outhouse. Carefully walk the side of the road, right beside the river, for the next 0.1 mile, then pick up the trail again by veering right (southeast) back into the woods. At 1.5 miles, notice the giant, moss-covered nurse log that's been cut through. This is a signature feature of ancient forests, where fallen trees nurture new trees.

The trail crosses another bridged creek at 1.8 miles, after which the tread gets more rugged, with frequent rocks and roots to trip you up, so watch your footing. It then skirts the large Green Canyon Campground, sticking to the riverside through abundant mixed ferns, blackberry, salmonberry, and salal. The final stretch of the trail once again pops out onto the roadside to hug a bend in the river, ducks back into the trees for the last 0.2 mile, then ends at the south trailhead at the Salmon River bridge at about 2.4 miles. Now all you have to do is walk back the way you came and enjoy it all over again—or if you want a longer, more rugged Salmon River adventure, continue into Hike 22.

22 Salmon River

RATING/ DIFFICULTY	ROUNDTRIP	ELEV GAIN/ HIGH POINT	SEASON
***/4	11.6 miles	3340 feet/ 2740 feet	May–Nov

Map: Trails Illustrated Mount Hood Wilderness #321; **Permits:** NW Forest Pass for trailhead parking; self-issue wilderness permit; **Contact:** Zigzag Ranger District, MHNF; **Notes:** Many of the trails above the Salmon River are not regularly maintained; if you're thinking of venturing farther, be prepared for possible bushwhacking and routefinding; **GPS:** N 45°16.674', W 121°56.388'

You don't have to hike all 14 miles of the Salmon River Trail to enjoy some of the best it has to offer. The first few miles are a pleasant walk along the river in a mossy, primeval forest. Continuing farther up, the trail traverses several high ridges that offer wide views over the rugged river canyon. This trail also makes a great destination for entry-level backpackers, with an abundance of campsites along the river over a fairly easy section of trail, where you can go as near or far as you like.

GETTING THERE

From Sandy, drive Mount Hood Highway (US Highway 26) east for approximately 17 miles to Welches. Turn right (south) on East Salmon River Road and proceed 5 miles to the trailhead on the left (east) side of the road at the Salmon River bridge.

ON THE TRAIL

Before getting underway, take a moment to check out the interpretive signs near the trailhead. These offer some insights and background about the river and wilderness you are about to explore. Then, armed with your enhanced appreciation for the preservation of wild areas, step onto the trail and get moving. Start with a quick ascent under overhanging vine and big-leaf maple to gain the hillside along the Salmon River. The rough, rocky path crosses several springs and seeps that dribble down the canyon wall, which is shrouded in a lush assortment of hanging mosses, sword and maidenhair ferns, salal, salmonberry, pathfinder, stonecrop, and wood violets. To the right (south), the river basin is filled with more ferns, large rocks, and hemlock, fir, and maple, all enveloped in luxuriant mosses and festooned with curtains of wispy witch's hair. All of this gives the area a very prehistoric ambience.

At 0.3 mile, curve around a rocky escarpment, where you get a nice view over the river, then it's back into the trees, where the trail rolls along on wide, duffy tread for a delightful walk in the primordial woods. More forest flora join the verdant setting, including thimbleberry, trillium, sorrel, Solomon's seal, fringe cup, bleeding heart, and devil's club. As you stroll effortlessly along for the next 1.5 miles, the trail crosses a couple of bridges over cascading creeks, and passes several inviting campsites. At 1.7 miles, enter the Salmon–Huckleberry Wilderness, where you'll find a map board and permit kiosk. Collect your permit, drop the slip in the slot, and keep on going.

Heading farther up the canyon, pass a few more campsites, then start climbing away from the river around the 2-mile mark. The ascent begins on a gentle grade, which quickly increases as the trail contours up the hillside, steadily gaining elevation as it dips in and out of small side drainages. At 3 miles, fork right (south) at an unsigned junction to

Venture through primeval forest on a hike up the rugged Salmon River Canyon.

stay on the main trail as it wraps around a ridge and briefly escapes the trees to traverse an open, rocky slope where you'll get a wide view over the wooded canyon. (The path left [east] loops over the crest of the ridge to a large campsite.) Back in the trees, proceed up to a T junction at 3.3 miles and turn right (east) to keep heading up the canyon; left (north) leads back to the campsite. The path now rolls along on nice, duffy tread. The tall, mossy hemlocks keep the trail shady, and abundant vanilla leaf, thimbleberry, and Oregon grape keep the hillside green and lively.

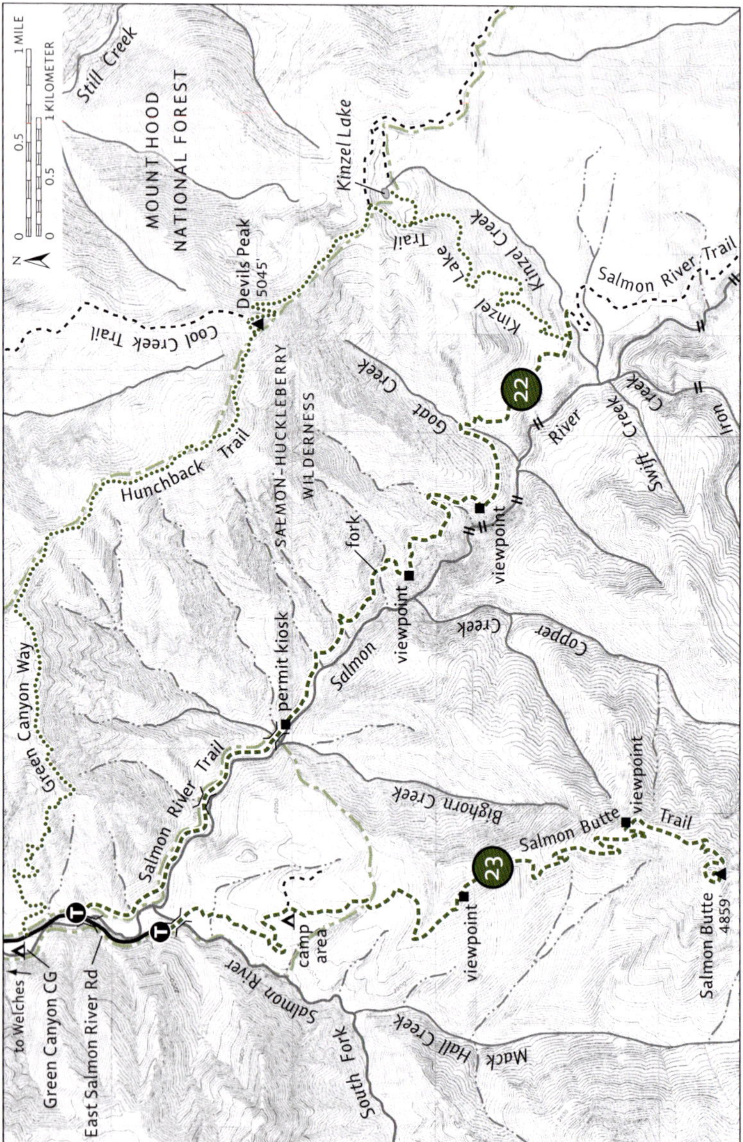
MOUNT HOOD
NATIONAL FOREST
SALMON-HUCKLEBERRY
WILDERNESS
Still Creek
Devils Peak
5045'
Cool Creek Trail
Hunchback Trail
Kinzel Lake
Kinzel Lake Trail
Kinzel Creek
Salmon River Trail
Goat Creek
River
Swift Creek
Iron Creek
Green Canyon Way
fork
viewpoint
permit kiosk
Salmon
Copper Creek
Bighorn Creek
Salmon Butte Trail
Salmon Butte
4859'
camp area
Salmon River
South Fork
Mack Hall Creek
to Welches
Green Canyon CG
East Salmon River Rd
22
23
0 0.5 1 MILE
0 0.5 1 KILOMETER
N

At 3.6 miles, the trail veers into another side drainage. Pass a narrow, overgrown path that descends steeply right (east) to the creek. Just ahead, at 3.8 miles, you can make an easy rock-hop across, then proceed out of the drainage, where the trail pops out of the trees at 4.1 miles. Here, at the edge of a high bluff, you get another good view over the Salmon River Canyon. Continue contouring around this wooded ridge into the next drainage, Goat Creek, and hop across this one at 4.7 miles. From here, resume ascending, passing another campsite, crossing another creek, then proceed through dense thickets of salal, rhododendron, and snowberry to the junction with the Kinzel Lake Trail at 5.5 miles. This narrow, brushy trail climbs 2.1 steep miles to the small lake below Devils Peak (see Extend Your Trip).

This viewless junction is a bit anticlimactic. Instead of ending here, proceed another 0.3 mile to the Kinzel Creek crossing, where the water tumbles down a series of slick rocky steps and chutes. The banks of the creek are covered with ferns, vine maple, and waterleaf, but there are a few good spots to sit and enjoy a snack before starting the return journey.

EXTEND YOUR TRIP

There are a few opportunities to go "higher, further, faster," but all are long and difficult. A visit to Kinzel Lake adds 4.2 miles and 1600 feet of elevation gain to your round-trip. From the junction at 5.5 miles, the Kinzel Lake Trail zigs and zags upward through more brushy woods, then across a recovering burn area. After climbing for 1.8 miles, veer right (east) at an unsigned junction and drop sharply down into the lake basin. The small lake is surrounded by alder, willows, and a variety of wetland wildflowers.

To bag 5045-foot Devils Peak, veer left (north) at the Kinzel Lake junction and climb another 0.3 mile to the Hunchback Trail. Turn left (west) and ascend the ridge for 1.2 miles to the Cool Creek Trail junction. Turn left (west) for about 100 yards, then left (south) again for a short ascent to the lookout tower on the summit. After tagging the top, continue west on the Hunchback Trail for 2.3 miles, then drop 3 steep miles down the primitive Green Canyon Way to Salmon River Road. Then just walk the road 0.4 mile back to the trailhead you started from.

23 Salmon Butte

RATING/ DIFFICULTY	ROUNDTRIP	ELEV GAIN/ HIGH POINT	SEASON
****/4	10.8 miles	4160 feet/ 4860 feet	June–Oct

Map: Trails Illustrated Mount Hood Wilderness #321; **Permit:** NW Forest Pass for trailhead parking; **Contact:** Zigzag Ranger District, MHNF; **Notes:** For those with creaky knees, trekking poles are highly recommended; **GPS:** N 45°16.278', W 121°56.472'

One of the more popular subpeaks to bag near Mount Hood, 4859-foot Salmon Butte is favored for its early season accessibility, diverse forest cover, showy wildflowers, and the spectacular view from its summit. The hike is a steady grind the entire way, but you probably won't be thinking much about that as you marvel instead at the way the scenery frequently changes the higher you go.

GETTING THERE

From Sandy, drive Mount Hood Highway (US Highway 26) east for approximately 17

From Salmon Butte, Mount Hood hides in the clouds.

miles to Welches. Turn right (south) on East Salmon River Road and proceed 5.5 miles to the trailhead at the end of the road.

ON THE TRAIL

Begin your trek to Salmon Butte with a flat, easy walk up an old gravel road. The way is lined with big-leaf maple, alder, cedar, and hemlock; on the shoulders are a mix of sword fern, vanilla leaf, and low grasses and shrubs. Very shortly after starting, pass a pretty creek that cascades out of a mossy grotto, then cross a wide, paved bridge. Nearby, a short path descends to a day-use area on the creek. After this, start meandering easily upward into a lively canyon of ferns, mixed berries, herb Robert, penstemon, and bleeding heart. To the right (west), the South Fork Salmon River can be heard but remains mostly unseen in the trees. The grade begins to increase slightly as the gravel road narrows and begins contouring up the hillside; several springs and small creeks tumble down the left (east) side of the canyon and spill across the trail.

Near the 1-mile mark, make a sharp turn where a massive tree has toppled over, leaving a gaping crater. The path then proceeds through a stretch of overgrown alder, horsetail, giant devil's club, and foxglove, after which it ducks into shady woods, where a large campsite can be found right (west) of the trail at 1.2 miles. The old roadway diminishes as it passes a grassy clearing where it turns into duffy trail tread and enters the Salmon–Huckleberry Wilderness. Now in

SALMON-HUCKLEBERRY WILDERNESS

Established in 1984, and expanded in 2009, the Salmon-Huckleberry Wilderness protects more than 62,000 acres of forests, mountains, and ridges. It is named for the proliferation of wild huckleberries within the region, as well as the Wild and Scenic Salmon River that runs right through the area. Within the wilderness, including in the rugged river canyon, are numerous volcanic plugs, pinnacles, cliffs, and peaks that have been worn and sculpted by millions of years of erosion. Long ago, Salmon Butte and Devils Peak were once prominent volcanoes, but time, gravity, and glaciation have reduced them to subordinate crests among the higher, younger Cascade Mountains. With more than 70 miles of hiking trails available for roaming the valleys, lakes, and ridges, the Salmon-Huckleberry makes an attractive—and less crowded—destination than the neighboring Mount Hood Wilderness.

lively forest, you'll find an abundance of lush greenery covering the hillside, including trillium, wild strawberry, sorrel, Solomon's seal, twinflower, Oregon grape, wild ginger, and various spreading mosses. Keep ascending on a moderate grade as the trail zigs and zags through sweeping turns up Salmon Butte's northern ridgeline. As you gain elevation, large, old-growth cedars and Douglas firs begin to appear, and deer and sword ferns, huckleberry and salal begin covering the hillside.

Your first viewpoint comes at 2.5 miles, where the trail skirts around a rocky outcrop in a small clearing. Below is the Mack Hall Creek valley; directly west is 4484-foot Sheepshead Rock. At this point, you're about halfway to the butte and have done about one-third of your total elevation gain—so there's still a lot of climbing ahead. The trail continues steadily upward, snaking and switchbacking along the west side of the ridge. Along the way, cross a couple of small springs that spill across the way at 3 and 3.6 miles. At 4.5 miles the trail finally mounts the ridgeline and a break in the trees grants a wide view east of long, forested ridges dividing the Copper Creek, Iron Creek, and Salmon River valleys. Proceed along the narrow ridgeline through dense rhododendron and bear grass until, at 4.8 miles, the trail slides off the ridge and proceeds through a few steep, narrow switchbacks to an abandoned road at 5.1 miles—the home stretch!

For the final push, turn right (north) and follow the old road as it makes a lazy spiral up and around the west side of the butte. In summer months, the roadside is decorated with a rainbow of lupine, aster, penstemon, paintbrush, and heather. The road finally peters out on the south side, just shy of the summit. Now just climb a few rocky switchbacks through overgrown manzanita and huckleberry to claim the 4859-foot peak at 5.4 miles. From this perch, your efforts are rewarded with a sweeping panorama to the north, east, and south; west is blocked by a grove of noble firs. Mount Hood looms large to the north, with Washington's Mounts St. Helens, Adams, and Rainier beyond; to the south, Mount Jefferson dominates the horizon, followed by the Three Sisters. Take some time to soak it all in before making the long trek back down.

24 Still Creek

RATING/ DIFFICULTY	ROUNDTRIP	ELEV GAIN/ HIGH POINT	SEASON
**/2	3.1 miles	910 feet/ 2380 feet	Apr–Nov

Map: Trails Illustrated Mount Hood Wilderness #321; **Permit:** None; **Contact:** Zigzag Ranger District, MHNF; **Notes:** This trail can also be used to access Flag Mountain (Hike 20); **GPS:** N 45°18.216', W 121°52.164'

Often overlooked, this quiet, pretty trail through berry-filled woods makes an easy outing for youngsters or taking Fido for a stroll. There's a lot of Northwest flora to admire along the way, including towering old-growth trees, carpets of lush ferns, and plenty of colorful wildflowers.

GETTING THERE

From Sandy, drive Mount Hood Highway (US Highway 26) east for approximately 22 miles to the Camp Creek Campground. Turn right (south) into the campground to a fork, then right (west) for 0.2 mile to the trailhead at the road turnaround. There are a few parking spaces nearby; do not park in campground spaces.

ON THE TRAIL

Start this easy walk in the woods by crossing the bridge over Camp Creek, signed for the Still Creek Trail. On the opposite (south) side

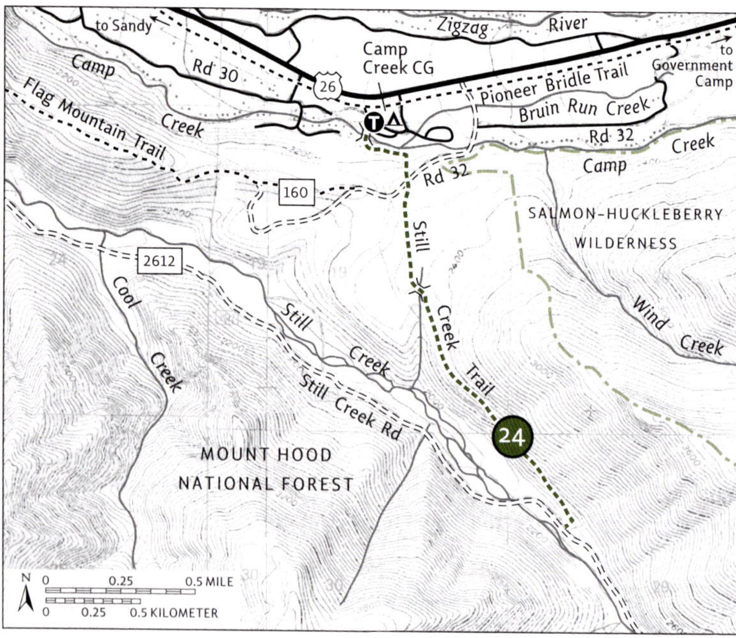

Still Creek Trail offers a pleasant walk under towering cedars among fern and Oregon grape.

of the bridge, turn left and start walking the flat path upstream amid plentiful lady and sword fern, wood sorrel, bunchberry, and thimbleberry. There are good views of the creek below, where the water cascades over rocks and a lot of woody debris. Some of the larger logs and tangles in the creek bed indicate the power of the floods that can surge down this forested channel. Before turning away from the creek, the trail passes a few impressively large old-growth cedars and hemlocks with mossy branches reaching for the sky.

Bending southward, scramble up a rocky slab—watch your footing—and proceed into lush forest where sword fern dominates the understory. Add in some trillium, wood violet, and devil's club and the forest brandishes an almost primeval appearance. Returning to duffy tread, the grade eases and the path crosses paved Road 32 at 0.3 mile. Turning right (west) on this road leads to the east trailhead for Flag Mountain (Hike 20). Angle right across the road to continue into mossy forest, where ferns give way to Oregon grape and a splash of salal, snowberry, twinflower, and deer fern. The walking is pleasant and effortless. Keep your ears perked for woodpeckers in the trees.

Passing through 0.5 mile, cross an old logging road lined with large rhododendron shrubs, then dip into a woody draw to descend a series of short puncheons and turnpikes where several seasonal springs converge and dribble down the arroyo toward Still Creek. The trail then commences another gentle ascent, contouring a slopeside covered with scattered rhododendron and bear grass. Around the 1-mile mark, reach a low crest where the sound of running water rises from the valley below. An abundance of new shrubbery begins to appear along the trail in the form of wild ginger, pipsissewa, and salmonberry, while silver firs become more prominent. The trail then descends on rough, rooty tread, and a small gap in the trees offers your only view of the wider world: a rocky escarpment on the flank of 5045-foot Devils Peak.

The trail then abruptly ends shortly past 1.5 miles, at the side of Still Creek Road (Forest Road 2612). For a look at the trail's namesake waterway, cross the road and mount a low berm, then descend a rocky path to an old campsite at the side of the creek. A bend in the channel here creates a small pool between little riffles and large debris snags and logjams; a few ancient fir and cedar trees tower overhead. Camping is no longer permitted here, but there's enough room on the rocky banks, with several larger rocks suitable for sitting, for having a picnic lunch or enjoying a riverside snack. When you're ready, head back the way you came.

25 Paradise Park Trail

RATING/ DIFFICULTY	ROUNDTRIP	ELEV GAIN/ HIGH POINT	SEASON
*****/5	13.9 miles	3670 feet/ 6310 feet	July–Oct

Map: Trails Illustrated Mount Hood Wilderness #321; **Permit:** Self-issue wilderness permit; **Contact:** Zigzag Ranger District, MHNF; **Notes:** If you don't want to drive the rough road to the trailhead in the campground, there are parking spaces on the road shoulder outside of the campground; **GPS:** N 45°18.864', W 121°48.954'

With an incredible view like this, what are you waiting for?

Paradise Park is one of the premier hiking destinations on Mount Hood. The common approach to this wonderland of alpine meadows and mountain vistas is via the PCT/Timberline Trail from Timberline Lodge (Hike 32). Yet, while shorter, Hike 32 is often a crowded thoroughfare on any sunny summer day. Instead, try this backdoor trail to Paradise Park. You'll get a good workout en route, gaining nearly two-thirds of a vertical mile, but along the way you'll enjoy a pleasant romp, sans crowds, featuring splendid, mossy forest, cool creeks, and a few extra viewpoints.

GETTING THERE

From Sandy, drive Mount Hood Highway (US Highway 26) east for approximately 23 miles. At the sign for Kiwanis Camp, turn left (northeast) on Kiwanis Camp Road (Road 39) and continue 1.2 miles to the Twin Bridges Campground. Turn left again, across the Zigzag River, to the small parking area near the trailhead. The last 100 yards to the trailhead are rough and rocky, and may not be suitable for low-clearance vehicles.

ON THE TRAIL

The Paradise Park Trail begins in the primitive Twin Bridges Campground on flat, wide, duffy trail. Overhead, a canopy of mossy hemlock, Douglas fir, and red cedar filters the sunlight on the primeval setting. Covering the gently rolling terrain is an abundance of vine maple, sword and deer fern, Solomon's seal, rhododendron, pipsissewa, huckleberry, and salal. Where there isn't shrubbery or flowers, the ground and rocks are carpeted with lush mosses. Nearby, the sound of the gurgling Zigzag River sings a happy tune. As you amble along the first half mile, it's easy to get lulled into a blissful state of tranquility. This is short-lived. When you arrive at the

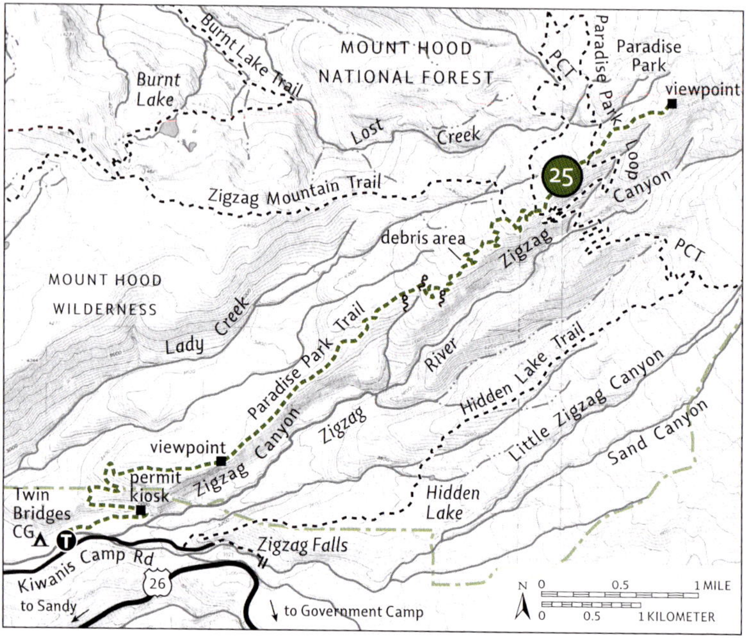

wilderness permit kiosk, it's time to wake up and get down to business.

Collect your self-issue permit, drop the slip in the slot, and get your grind on. The trail makes a sharp switchback and starts a steady, contouring ascent of the wooded slopeside. The sound of the river soon fades into the distance as you quickly gain elevation and crest the high ridge that divides Zigzag Canyon from Lady Creek Canyon. Proceed through a few more winding switchbacks, then commence your generally northeast trajectory up the ridgeline. While the grade is steadily upward, the trail remains duffy and pleasant to walk on, and the shady forest is green and lively. In season, the rhododendron and bear grass lining the trail bloom in bursts of pink and white flowers.

You're given a brief respite from the climbing just prior to a nice viewpoint at 2.3 miles. Here, you can hop off the trail at a rocky outcrop and take in a wide view across the valley to 5066-foot Tom Dick and Harry Mountain directly south (Hike 28), and 4656-foot Multorpor Mountain to the southeast. After your peek, the climbing continues, with the ridgeline getting increasingly narrower, and the slopes falling sharply away to both sides. Cedars and silver firs start to become more prolific, as well as the berries: huckleberry, salmonberry, bunchberry, and wild strawberry. Ever upward, hop across a couple of small springs at 3.9 and 4.1 miles, then begin a series of zigzagging switchbacks into an area that was devastated by a windstorm that leveled a huge swath of the forest in 2017.

The trail winds upward through the debris, where fallen trees lay stacked four and five high. It took trail crews three seasons to clear the extensive damage here and get the trail reopened. And they did all this using only hand tools! At 4.9 miles, you're through the tangle and back on good trail in stately forest. The trail then swings over to the north side of the ridge and passes the east end of the Zigzag Mountain Trail at 5.4 miles. Continue up through a few more switchbacks and cross the Pacific Crest Trail at 5.8 miles. Now approaching the timberline, the forest begins to open up, revealing parklike meadows bursting with summer paintbrush, lupine, aster, and bistort. Continue climbing to the Paradise Park Loop junction at 6.3 miles, at the edge of a sprawling meadow of bear grass, arnica, and mariposa lily—as well as an eye-popping view of Mount Hood. If you're satisfied with your endeavor, this is a good spot to do an about-face and head down for fries and a milkshake.

More likely, you'll be drawn to the user path that continues upward through the meadows. You've gone this far, so what's a little more? Keep heading uphill, leaving the forest behind and entering an alpine zone of wide meadows with even wider views. Mount Hood looms large straight ahead, beckoning you to get just a little closer. The sandy trail bends to contour up a high mound swathed with paintbrush and aster. To the right (south), the yawning chasm of Zigzag Canyon opens up beneath the basalt cliffs of Mississippi Head; to the left, the wide basin of Lost Creek merges into the sprawling meadows of Paradise Park. The scene is at once impressive and otherworldly. The path finally crests the 6310-foot mound at a rocky clearing surrounded by carpets of heather at about 6.9 miles. Various user paths continue onward from this point into the basin below, and farther up the mountain, but this makes an ideal ending point to just have a sit and take it all in. When you're eventually able to tear yourself away, head back down the way you came.

26 Hidden Lake

RATING/ DIFFICULTY	ROUNDTRIP	ELEV GAIN/ HIGH POINT	SEASON
**/3	3.8 miles	990 feet/ 3870 feet	June–Oct

Map: Trails Illustrated Mount Hood Wilderness #321; **Permits:** NW Forest Pass for trailhead parking, self-issue wilderness permit; **Contact:** Zigzag Ranger District,

The flowers along Hidden Lake Trail are a pleasant forest treat.

MHNF; **Notes:** Mosquitoes can be especially bad in early summer; **GPS:** N 45°18.816', W 121°47.988'

Whoever decided to name this small, marshy pool a "lake" was feeling quite generous. It's actually more of a large, grassy pond. The trail to get here is fairly steep in sections, views are limited, and the lake is inaccessible, but displays of summer wildflowers and berries help redeem this lesser-used trail for taking a quiet hike in pleasant woods.

GETTING THERE

From Sandy, drive Mount Hood Highway (US Highway 26) east for approximately 23 miles. At the sign for Kiwanis Camp, turn left (northeast) on Kiwanis Camp Road (Road 39) and continue 2 miles to the large trailhead area.

ON THE TRAIL

Start the Hidden Lake Trail from the west side of the parking area and pause at a small clearing with a picnic table, wilderness info sign, and permit kiosk. Fill out your free permit and drop the slip in the slot. An interpretive board nearby details the origin of the Mazamas. Founded in 1894, they are the third-oldest mountaineering club in the US. From here, the trail proceeds into mossy conifer forest laden with lady fern, salal, huckleberry, and rhododendron. In early summer, these large and abundant rhododendron bushes burst with colorful displays of vibrant pink and white flowers. Adding to the fireworks display along the way are an assortment of pipsissewa, twinflower, and bunchberry to give you plenty to admire in the otherwise closed-in and viewless forest.

Following a short ascent, wind your way through a handful of switchbacks to gain the crest of the wooded ridge. At the top of the switchbacks, a little past 0.2 mile, catch a partial view over the forested valley below. The trail then eases for a casual stroll among more rhododendrons, as well as tall firs, hemlocks, and cedars draped with wispy witch's hair. At 0.5 mile, enter the Mount Hood Wilderness, where the grade increases again for the next ascent. The moderately steep climb is short and the trail levels again around 0.7 mile, where the ridgetop widens into gentle terrain. Enjoy another easy ramble through sun-dappled forest, where huckleberry and bear grass start to become more prolific; listen for a variety of songbirds and woodpeckers in the trees.

The path continues to meander easily through the woods for the next mile before it turns and dips to the lake's outlet creek at 1.8 miles. Hop across the creek and look for the unsigned spur trail that forks right (east) to Hidden Lake. Take this short path through more rhododendrons and dense huckleberry bushes to a modest campsite tucked away in the trees, then just a few more paces to a view of Hidden Lake. Surrounded by tall marsh grasses and horsetail plants, with no easily accessible lakeshore, you have to enjoy your view from a distance. Without much to do here, gather some huckleberries to munch on as you make your way back down the mountain.

EXTEND YOUR TRIP

If you want a little more mileage, and a lot more climbing (1900 feet!), continue another 2.3 miles up the Hidden Lake Trail to Mount Hood's Timberline Trail. The trail remains confined to the woods and proceeds up a few more successive ridgelines. For the

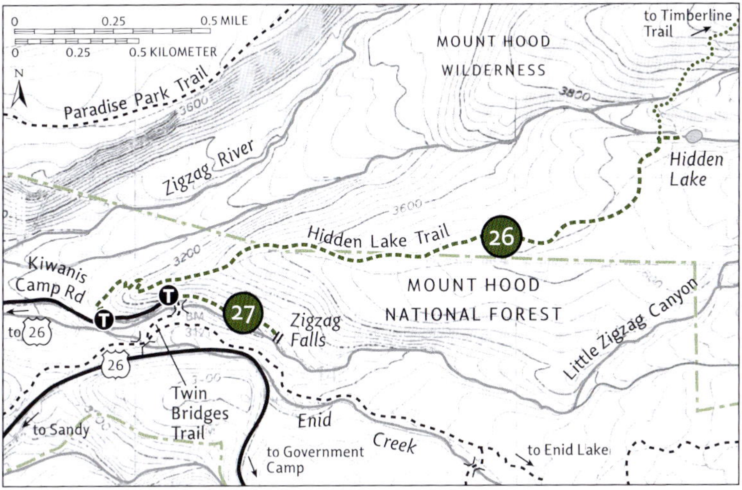

best view for your effort, turn left (west) on the Timberline for 0.8 mile to the edge of the yawning Zigzag Canyon. Along the way, the trail crosses several meadowy slopes carpeted with aster, paintbrush, lupine, and mariposa lily, and grants a few more impressive views. Altogether, this makes a 10-mile round-trip with 3350 feet of elevation gain.

27 Zigzag Falls

RATING/ DIFFICULTY	ROUNDTRIP	ELEV GAIN/ HIGH POINT	SEASON
***/1	0.6 mile	250 feet/ 3220 feet	Apr–Nov

Map: Trails Illustrated Mount Hood Wilderness #321; **Permit:** NW Forest Pass for trailhead parking; **Contact:** Zigzag Ranger District, MHNF; **Notes:** You can also use this trailhead for access to the Pioneer Bridle Trail (Hike 19); **GPS:** N 45°18.846', W 121°47.760'

This short interpretive trail makes an effortless outing to a pretty cascade in a wooded grotto and is a good place to look for unique and rare wildflowers.

GETTING THERE

From Sandy, drive Mount Hood Highway (US Highway 26) east for approximately 23 miles. At the sign for Kiwanis Camp, turn left (northeast) on Kiwanis Camp Road (Road 39) and continue 2.2 miles to the trailhead at the end of the road.

ON THE TRAIL

Begin at the trailhead on the north side of the stone bridge that crosses Little Zigzag River. This bridge is a relic of the original Mount Hood Highway that replaced the old Barlow Road in 1926. An interpretive sign nearby gives more information on this historic roadway. Get underway by heading east among an abundance of vine maple, salmonberry,

Misty Zigzag Falls tumbles down a lush, fern-filled grotto.

and wild strawberry to a small riverside picnic area. A second interpretive sign details the health benefits of nature—and specifically waterfalls—in their production of negative ions. Among other benefits, negative ions can improve moods and relieve stress—a good reason to hike more!

The easy trail proceeds along the north side of the river, where plenty of rhododendron and huckleberry adorn the steep slope rising to the left, and tall Douglas firs and western red cedars keep the path mostly cool and shady. Look for an assortment of moisture-loving wildflowers along the mossy riverbank, including Columbia lilies, fairy slippers, and spotted coralroot; watch out for giant, thorny devil's club. Before you know it, you're standing in front of Zigzag Falls, which is spilling over a mossy, rocky escarpment. Take a seat on the rocks nearby and enjoy the tranquil setting while you soak up all of those nourishing negative ions.

Opposite: *Trillium Lake is a summer mountain playground that offers hiking, biking, paddling, picnicking, and camping (Hike 36).*

mount hood south

Of all the paths you take in life,
make sure a few of them are dirt.
—John Muir

The south side of Mount Hood offers some of the quickest and easiest access to many of the most spectacular hiking trails in the Mount Hood Wilderness. The trailheads for many of these are conveniently located right off Mount Hood Highway or within some of the mountain's ski areas. You may initially scoff at the idea of hiking around ski resorts, but they offer great access to high-elevation trails—and the ski slopes often become sprawling wildflower meadows in summer months. The epicenter of this mountain playground is the small village of Government Camp. Here, you can roam or ride the village's own network of year-round, multiuse trails, or you can head out in any direction and be at a trailhead in mere minutes. Of course, if you're visiting this side of the mountain, a visit to the historic Timberline Lodge is in order. Located high on Mount Hood, the Timberline—and the aptly named Timberline Trail—can be used as your launch point to visit gaping canyons, raging rivers, and some of the largest alpine meadows on the mountain. Word to the wise, however: don't expect much summer solitude on these terrific trails. If you want to go frolic in the flowers, you'd better be ready for company!

Postcard-perfect views of Mount Hood reflected in Mirror Lake make this hike a favorite.

28 Mirror Lake

RATING/ DIFFICULTY	ROUNDTRIP	ELEV GAIN/ HIGH POINT	SEASON
****/3	4.1 miles	970 feet/ 4140 feet	June–Oct

Map: Trails Illustrated Mount Hood Wilderness #321; **Permit:** NW Forest Pass for trailhead parking; **Contact:** Zigzag Ranger District, MHNF; **Notes:** High-use trail; avoid holidays and weekends; section of barrier-free path; **GPS:** N 45°18.156', W 121°46.638'

If there's one hike on Mount Hood that draws locals and visitors alike it's Mirror Lake. With the opening of the rerouted trail in the fall of 2018, access is safer and easier, with the new trailhead now off the shoulder of the highway. The new route is a little longer than the old one, as the path meanders through the trees and over a series of rustic bridges to connect with the old trail about halfway up the hillside. Once at the lakeshore, the payoff is pretty huge: a spectacular view of Mount Hood from across the far side of the lake, which (in the right conditions) perfectly mirrors Oregon's highest peak—thus earning its name. Of course, you will likely be sharing the trail and views with a lot of visitors, so put on your smiley face.

GETTING THERE

From Sandy, drive Mount Hood Highway (US Highway 26) east for approximately 27 miles to the Mirror Lake Trailhead, just west of Government Camp. Turn right (south) into the new parking area at the entrance to Skibowl West.

ON THE TRAIL

Begin the Mirror Lake Trail from the west end of the new parking area, near the restroom and information board. The trail begins as a paved, barrier-free path that gently snakes down toward Camp Creek into fir, hemlock, and cedar forest. Along the trailside are sparse bunches of rhododendron, bear grass, and lady fern. At 0.2 mile, the paved section ends and the path crosses the creek on a nice wooden bridge. Now on wide, duffy tread, meander westward on a gently undulating course of slight dips and rises, crossing numerous bridges over small gullies and dribbling creeks. Eventually, more shrubbery begins to adorn the trailsides, mostly in the form of mountain rhododendron, which blooms with vibrant clusters of pink and white flowers in early summer.

At 0.9 mile, cross another rustic bridge, this one over Mirror Lake's outlet stream, where the water cascades down the hill in a series of steps. Here you may find patches of inside-out flower (duckfoot), wild ginger, and snowberry along the trail. Then, at 1.1 miles, the easy walking is over and it's time to head up, beginning with a fairly steep, curving ascent to connect with the original Mirror Lake Trail at 1.2 miles. Now climb into denser forest through a series of short switchbacks that eventually ease alongside the outlet creek again. At 1.8 miles, the trail forks at the beginning of the 0.5-mile lake loop. Veer right (southwest) and continue a short distance through the trees to the lake, which fills a wide, tree-ringed basin. The high, rocky ridgeline above the lake is 5066-foot Tom Dick and Harry Mountain.

Now you can explore the lake area, beginning with the small beach to the left (east), which grants access to the lake for

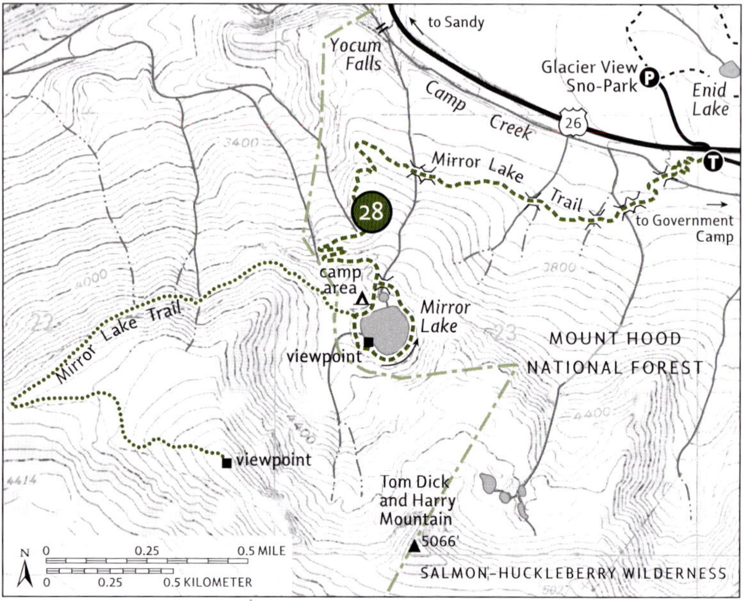

wading; a few short side trails right (west) lead to secluded campsites. The lakeside loop then forks again at 1.9 miles, where the trail to Tom Dick and Harry (see Extend Your Trip) branches off to the right (west). The trail then loops around the backside of the lake on planked boardwalk through boggy rose spiraea and fireweed. Look for the planked walkway leading left (north) to the water's edge. This is where you get the picture-perfect view that you came for: Mount Hood reflected in Mirror Lake. Take a moment to enjoy the scene. Photographers, if you're looking for that postcard-worthy shot, plan your visit for early morning or evening, when the lake water is at its calmest.

The trail continues around the lake and back under the cover of trees, where a few more campsites can be found. Views are then limited to the closed-in, forested surroundings, with just the slightest view of the lake through the trees. Along the way, look for salmonberries, monkeyflowers, and big, white Washington lilies with their notably freckled petals. Close the lake loop by crossing the outlet on a log bridge, where thorny devil's club fills the gully. Then it's just a few more paces to return to the junction where you started the loop. Turn right (north) and make quick work of the return trip, retracing your route back to the parking area.

EXTEND YOUR TRIP

For an even bigger view, consider adding a side trip to the top of Tom Dick and Harry Mountain. The round-trip adds 3.1 miles to your hike, and another 850 feet of elevation gain on a fairly moderate grade—but the additional work is worth it. Start by veering off the lake loop and proceed into the Salmon–Huckleberry Wilderness on easy trail through lady fern, bunchberry, and more rhododendron. The path proceeds to contour the open, northwest slope of the mountain that bursts with summer color in the form of paintbrush, penstemon, pokeweed, lupine, thimbleberry, and Columbia lily, among other vibrant blossoms. A few spots along the way offer views west over the Zigzag Valley below.

Continue heading up to the top of the ridge at 1 mile, where the trail makes an abrupt U-turn at a large rock pile and continues on level ground through scrubby pine forest decorated with bunches of bear grass, pipsissewa, and huckleberry. The grade eventually increases again, winding upward over increasingly rocky, rooty terrain, then mounts the ridgetop at 1.6 miles. From this 4930-foot perch, the view is all-encompassing in every direction. To the north, the wide profile of Mount Hood takes center stage; Mirror Lake can be seen far below. To the south, look for central Oregon's Cascade peaks all lined up on the horizon: Mount Jefferson, Mount Washington, and the Three Sisters. Once you've soaked in the view, retrace your steps back to the Mirror Lake Loop and continue your journey.

29 Multorpor Fen

RATING/ DIFFICULTY	ROUNDTRIP	ELEV GAIN/ HIGH POINT	SEASON
**/1	2.3 miles	330 feet/ 3840 feet	May–Oct

Map: Government Camp Recreational Trails (see appendix II); **Permit:** Sno-Park Permit for parking Nov. 1–Apr. 30; **Contact:** Zigzag Ranger District, MHNF; **Notes:** Portions of this trail are multiuse; for winter directions, see Hike 80; **GPS:** N 45°18.132', W 121°46.170'

A great trek for kids of all ages, this easy trail winds through fern- and berry-laced woods to a mountain bog at the edge of a wide wetland meadow on the doorstep of Mount Hood. It's located near the Skibowl East base area, so after you explore the bog, you can check out the adventure park's climbing wall, alpine slide, disc golf course, and other outdoor attractions.

GETTING THERE

From Sandy, drive Mount Hood Highway (US Highway 26) east for approximately 27 miles to Government Camp. Opposite the left turn into town, turn right into the Skibowl Sno-Park. Proceed 100 yards to the parking area; find the trailhead on the east side of the road, near the Camp Creek bridge.

ON THE TRAIL

Begin your journey to the Multorpor Fen on the Summit Trail by plunging into dense fir and hemlock forest. The path starts out wide and duffy for easy walking. Alongside the trail and filling the woods, you'll find an assortment of rhododendron, bunchberry, deer fern, salal, and pearly everlasting. Shortly after starting, cross a couple of branches of Camp Creek on wide bridges, where the creek bottoms are choked with vine maple and skunk cabbage. The path then narrows and starts snaking easily upward through a boggy area over a series of turnpikes and boardwalks. Following this short climb, the trail levels again for easy walking through copious huckleberry thickets.

Before you know it, the trail pops out of the woods at 0.9 mile into the Skibowl East base area. Veer left (northeast) to pass a chairlift station and follow a gravel road into a grove of trees. Look for the signed entrance to the fen on the left (north) side of the road at 1 mile. Turn into the fen on a narrow trail and proceed about 60 yards, passing both side trails, to its end at a fenced viewpoint. Here you can enjoy a great view of Mount Hood over a wide, wet meadow and a large pond. This rare mountain wetland is home to a variety of local and migratory birds, so see how many you can spot. When you've finished your bird and mountain peeping, turn around and head back to the fen's side trails.

To do a figure-eight loop through the fen, start with the trail on the east side. Follow this narrow path through the dark, gnarled bog, which may conjure visions of exploring the murky swamps of Dagobah. Be careful to stay on the narrow trail and boardwalks so as not to trample the sensitive ecosystem. As you're exploring, look for a variety of unusual mosses, fungi, plants, flowers, frogs, and newts. The path exits the bog onto a gravel road beside the putt-putt golf course; turn right (south) and follow the road back to the fen entrance. Dive back in, and take the west side trail to continue your exploration by winding through the other half of the bog. When you exit to the road again, turn right (west) and retrace your steps back to your starting point.

EXTEND YOUR TRIP

You can extend your hike beyond the fen area by adding in the east portion of the Summit Trail. The path traverses the base of the ski area, which, in summer months, offers a variety of outdoor activities. Opposite the ski area, the trail continues on an old forest road at the base of Multorpor Mountain. There aren't any views, but

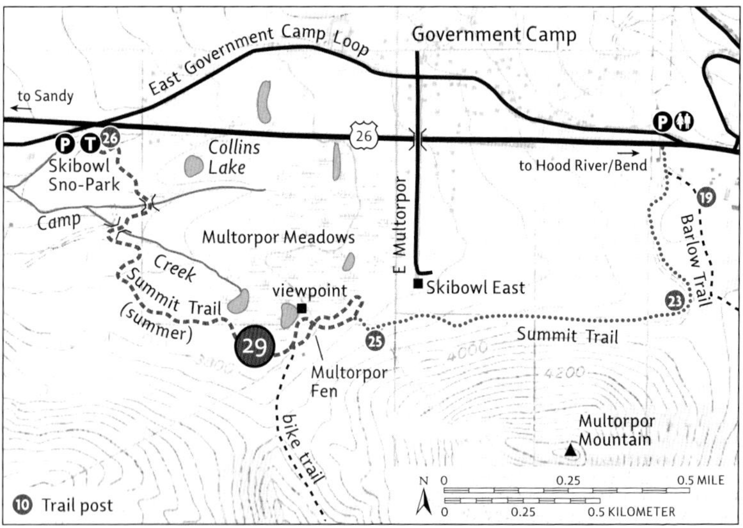

Multorpor Fen is a unique mountain wetland and home to various waterfowl and songbirds.

the wooded corridor is mostly flat and the walking is fairly pleasant. The path is lined with an assortment of berry shrubs, devil's club, inside-out flower (duckfoot), alder, sorrel, corn lily, deer and lady fern, and Pacific waterleaf. The old road eventually snakes north, passes an old clear-cut, then ends beside a fenced-in generator building. Here, the Barlow Trail continues east, so this makes a good turnaround point for a 4.1-mile round-trip. The full Summit Trail also makes a nice snowshoe romp in the winter (Hike 80).

ORIGIN STORIES: MULTORPOR
The name "Multorpor," as in Multorpor Mountain and Multorpor Fen, was created by combining the first parts of Multnomah, Oregon, and Portland.

30 Enid Lake

RATING/ DIFFICULTY	ROUNDTRIP	ELEV GAIN/ HIGH POINT	SEASON
**/2	1.2 miles	210 feet/ 3700 feet	All year

Map: Government Camp Recreational Trails (see appendix II); **Permit:** Sno-Park Permit for parking Nov 1–Apr. 30; **Contact:** Zigzag Ranger District, MHNF; **Notes:** Multiuse trail; be courteous and exercise proper right-of-way; hikeable in winter; **GPS:** N 45°18.318', W 121°46.770'

The village of Government Camp on Mount Hood offers an extensive network of trails for roaming the local forest year-round. You won't find stunning views in alpine environs, but you will find short, peaceful

routes where a summer stroll showcases an abundance of wildflowers, birds, and small critters, and winter offers opportunities to strap on some snowshoes and tromp around a quiet, winter woodland. This short loop on the west end of town visits a small lake and explores a pretty section of lush forest that is ideal for a quick outdoor fix, getting the kids out, or walking the dog.

GETTING THERE

From Sandy, drive Mount Hood Highway (US Highway 26) east for approximately 27 miles to Government Camp. Just before town, turn left (north) into the Glacier View Sno-Park, opposite the Mirror Lake Trailhead; park on the road shoulder.

ON THE TRAIL

Begin the short Enid Lake loop at the large Glacier View Trailhead, where you'll find a large interpretive sign that shares the story of Mount Hood's sister mountain, Lushan (Mount Lu) in China, and where the local communities have pledged to support conservation, protect the ecosystem, promote sustainable tourism, and honor cultural legacies. There's also a picnic table here and an outhouse nearby.

Get moving at trail post 1 by heading east on the Crosstown Trail and making a gentle ascent into shady forest of mixed fir and hemlock. You're likely to hear some highway noise, being in such close proximity, but as you progress around the loop it will eventually fade away. After walking for just a few minutes, at 0.1 mile, veer left (east) on an obvious user path which proceeds about 40 yards through brushy willow and spiraea shrubs to the marshy edge of Enid Lake, which lies quietly in a wide, grassy clearing. Lily pads often decorate the lake's surface, dragonflies flit here and there, and little salamanders can be seen swimming in

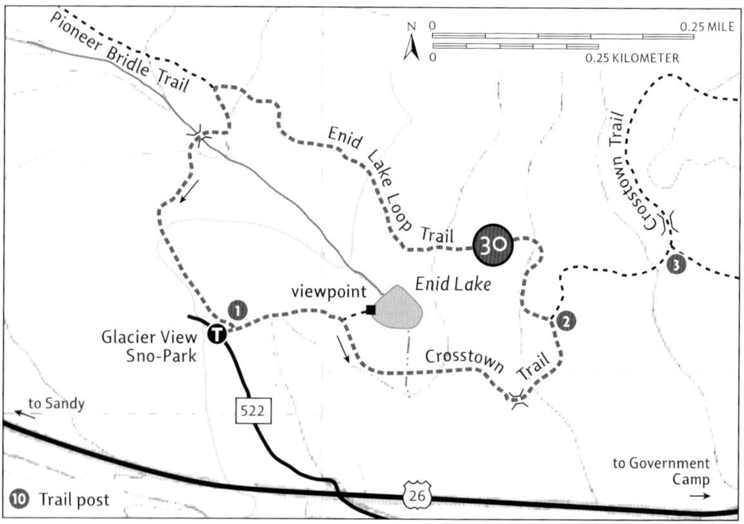

The short Enid Lake loop trail is a pleasant walk in the woods at any time of year.

the cloudy water. Unfortunately, there's not really anywhere to sit and admire the scene, so enjoy the view for a few moments, then return to the main trail.

Continue your circuit by crossing a small bridge over a trickling creek, then make a short ascent, passing a notably large red cedar, to the loop's high point at 0.4 mile. Here, at trail post 2, turn left (west) onto the Enid Lake Loop Trail and continue on a narrow path that plunges through dense thickets of huckleberry and rhododendron. Now on a gentle descent, cross a couple of seeping springs where giant skunk cabbage abounds in the boggy setting. The descent increases slightly as the trail dives deeper into the forest, where deer fern, bunchberry, vanilla leaf, and wild ginger thrive under the mixed canopy. The path eventually bends and comes alongside a clear, cold spring trickling down a woody gully. A few paces farther, cross the spring on a makeshift bridge of small logs.

After a few more twists and turns, the loop trail ends at its low point at 0.9 mile, where it meets the Pioneer Bridle Trail (Hike 19). Turn left (south) onto wide, duffy trail and cross a small bridge over a salmonberry-choked gulley where Enid Lake's outlet creek flows west to eventually merge with the Zigzag River. Take note of the blue diamond markers high on the trees indicating this as a winter route—maybe worth revisiting in the snowy season. Finish the loop with a short, moderate ascent before easing again for a nice, casual cruise back to your starting point.

31 Crosstown Loop

RATING/ DIFFICULTY	ROUNDTRIP	ELEV GAIN/ HIGH POINT	SEASON
**/2	2.4 miles	390 feet/ 4070 feet	All year

Map: Government Camp Recreational Trails (see appendix II); **Permit:** Sno-Park Permit for parking Nov. 1–Apr. 30; **Contact:** Zigzag Ranger District, MHNF; **Notes:** Multiuse trail; be courteous and exercise proper right-of-way; hikeable in winter; **GPS:** N 45°18.282', W 121°45.786'

Oregon goldenrod along the Crosstown Trail

This pleasant walk in the woods links several of the trails in the Government Camp Recreational Trails system. Signed for year-round use, hike it on duffy forest paths in summer or snowshoe it in winter. With all the branching spurs and connectors in the area, it's a good idea to carry a trail map to help you stay on track.

GETTING THERE

From Sandy, drive Mount Hood Highway (US Highway 26) east for approximately 27 miles to Government Camp. Turn left (north) onto the East Government Camp Loop road for 0.3 mile and park on the shoulder near East Collins Lake Road. Find the trailhead on the north side of the road beside the Thunderhead Lodge.

ON THE TRAIL

Start by heading up an old logging road lined with pearly everlasting, spiraea, aster, and white alder to a wide fork signed for the Thunderhead Trailhead. Here you'll find a large map board displaying the surrounding trail network. Begin the loop by forking left (northwest) on Maggie's Trail and making a gentle descent into dry hemlock forest crowded with huckleberry, bear grass, and rhododendron. Look for the distinctively papery bark of cedar trees here and there. Continue right (northwest), passing Lucy's Trail at 0.3 mile (trail post 4), and continue another 0.2 mile through mossy fir forest to the next junction (trail post 3).

Now fork right (north) onto the Crosstown Trail and cross a wide bridge over a boggy creek gully filled with skunk cabbage. After this, begin a gentle ascent on a trillium-, lupine-, and bunchberry-lined

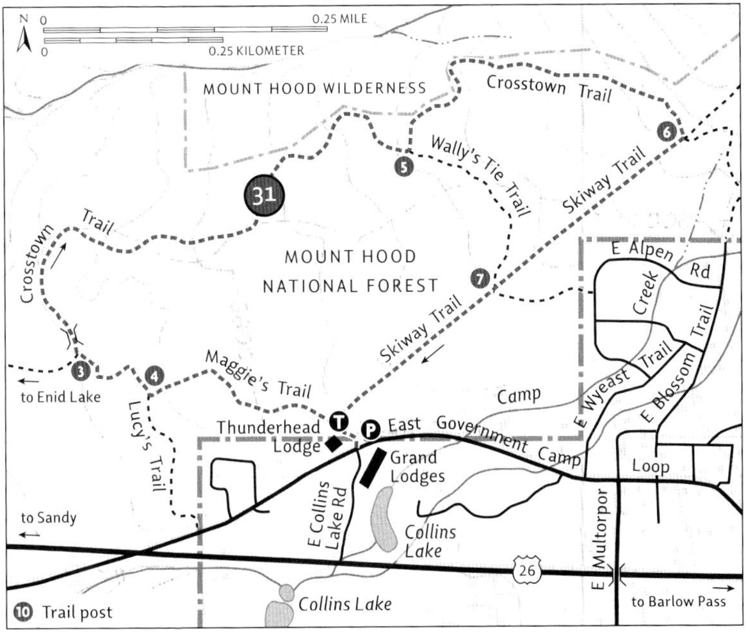

path. Stay alert for mountain bikers who might be out for a fun ride. The grade picks up for a little more climbing and you'll pass a moss-covered boulder looking entirely out of place in the otherwise wooded setting. At the next junction (trail post 5), shortly past 1.2 miles, Wally's Tie Trail veers off to the right (south). This 0.3-mile spur shortcuts the larger loop—an option if Fido or the little ones start getting antsy. Stay left (northeast) and continue ascending on sandy tread lined with manzanita, now in open forest, until the loop peaks at the next junction (trail post 6), at 1.7 miles.

This well-signed junction in a wide clearing is about the midpoint for the larger trail network, with several routes accessible to the east. To continue the loop, turn right (southwest) and begin descending the Skiway Trail, an old service road alongside a line of telephone poles. The wide trail corridor heads down the slope in a generally straight line, where you're able to glimpse the rocky ridgeline of Tom Dick and Harry Mountain (Hike 28) in the distance. The route then gets rough and rocky for a short distance to one more junction (trail post 7), at 2.1 miles, at the south end of Wally's Tie Trail. Continue heading down the hill for the final stretch, where tall goldenrod stalks bloom in brilliant yellow flowers in summer months. When you reach the Thunderhead Trailhead where you started, make a final left (south) turn and descend back to your starting point.

MOUNT HOOD WILDERNESS

The Mount Hood Wilderness is more than 67,000 acres of protected land within the larger Mount Hood National Forest. The centerpiece of the wilderness is Oregon's tallest peak, Mount Hood, at 11,240 feet. Designated in 1964 and expanded in 2009, the area protects a diverse assortment of landscapes and ecosystems, from old-growth rainforests to volcanic ridges to alpine glaciers. The wilderness area encompasses almost the entire mountain, with the exception of the ski areas on the south and east sides, and is the source of many of northwest Oregon's rivers. With hundreds of miles of hiking trails, including the Timberline and Pacific Crest Trails, Mount Hood is a magnet for hikers, backpackers, and mountain climbers—yet it's not difficult to find a secluded path to escape for a while.

32 Paradise Park Loop

RATING/ DIFFICULTY	ROUNDTRIP	ELEV GAIN/ HIGH POINT	SEASON
*****/5	12.2 miles	3470 feet/ 6090 feet	July–Oct

Map: Green Trails Maps Mount Hood #462S; **Permit:** Self-issue wilderness permit; **Contact:** Zigzag Ranger District, MHNF; **Notes:** High-use trail; requires a potentially challenging river crossing; **GPS:** N 45°19.842', W 121°42.630'

The hike up to Paradise Park is arguably one of the best on Mount Hood. It is also one of the most strenuous, as there is no easy way to get there. Of the three approaches you can take to reach these sprawling wildflower meadows, cascading streams, and in-your-face views of Mount Hood, all of them are long and possess a significant amount of elevation gain and loss. But once you get there, it makes all the work worth it.

GETTING THERE

From Sandy, drive Mount Hood Highway (US Highway 26) east for approximately 29 miles, past the village of Government Camp. Turn left (north) on the Timberline Highway and head 5.5 miles up the mountain to the Timberline Lodge and ski area; park in the main parking area.

ON THE TRAIL

Starting on the east side of Timberline Lodge, walk 0.2 mile up the service road to the Pacific Crest Trail/Timberline Trail junction, turn left (west) and get underway. Ramble through the ski area among plenty of summer wildflowers, and pass the junction with the Mountaineer Trail (Hike 33) at 0.9 mile. Just a little farther, collect your wilderness permit at the backcountry kiosk, then drop into the rocky gully containing the Little Zigzag River. Hop across, crest the other side, and continue downward into mixed forest, where huckleberries are abundant. Pass the Hidden Lake Trail (Hike 26) at 1.6 miles, then make an easy contour through a wide, flower-laden basin. The trail

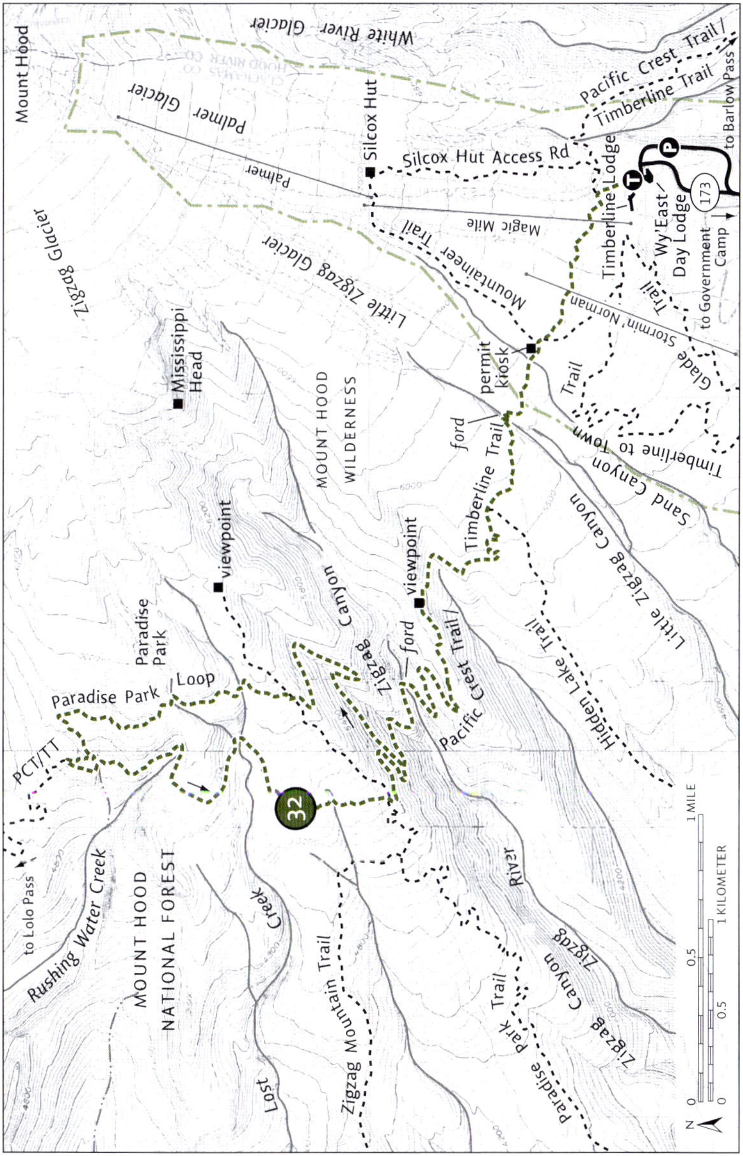
Mount Hood
White River Glacier
Palmer Glacier
Palmer
Silcox Hut
Silcox Hut Access Rd
Pacific Crest Trail /
Timberline Trail
to Barlow Pass
Timberline Lodge
Wy'East Day Lodge
173
to Government Camp
Magic Mile
Mountaineer Trail
Stormin' Norman
Glade Trail
Zigzag Glacier
Little Zigzag Glacier
Mississippi Head
MOUNT HOOD WILDERNESS
permit kiosk
ford
Timberline Trail
Trail
Timberline to Town
Sand Canyon
Little Zigzag Canyon
Hidden Lake Trail
viewpoint
viewpoint
Paradise Park
Zigzag Canyon
ford
Pacific Crest Trail /
Paradise Park Loop
PCT/TT
32
to Lolo Pass
Rushing Water Creek
MOUNT HOOD NATIONAL FOREST
Lost Creek
Zigzag Mountain Trail
Zigzag River
Paradise Park Trail
Zigzag Canyon
N
0
0.5
1 MILE
0
0.5
1 KILOMETER

Prepare to be wowed on the hike to Paradise Park.

then curves up to the brink of the imposing Zigzag Canyon at 2.3 miles. Here, you're treated to an impressive view of the Zigzag River—nearly 700 feet below—cascading down from Mississippi Head and Zigzag Glacier. Cast your gaze across the canyon to the high meadows beyond—that's where you're headed. Game face.

Now begin the big descent into the canyon, switchbacking down the lush, forested south wall. Several springs tumble down the hillside and across the trail, which nourish an abundance of shrubs, berries, and wildflowers. Sooner than you think, you reach the bottom of the canyon, where the trail spills out onto the rocky floor at 3.3 miles. Now you have to find your way across the roiling Zigzag River. Depending on the season and amount of runoff, this could be a challenging crossing. Use your best judgment and save it for another day if it looks too risky. Otherwise, scout up- and downstream for a safe crossing, then pick up the trail on the other side. The route now starts climbing steadily up the canyon's drier north side, where you will notice a difference in the flowers and shrubbery.

Following a few switchbacks, veer right (northeast) off the Pacific Crest Trail (PCT) onto the Paradise Park Loop at 3.7 miles. Continue climbing into a forested drainage. The higher you get, the more the forest peels away until you wind up in a narrow canyon. Hop across a pretty creek at 4.1 miles, where wildflowers are everywhere, and make a circuiting ascent of the opposite ridge. Where the trail turns back, cross the creek again, and make a final ascent into the lower reaches of Paradise Park. Now that you've done the work, it's time to play—but don't linger too long in one place, as you still have a lot of miles to cover.

Proceed onward to a four-way junction with the Paradise Park Trail at 4.8 miles, an alternate method for reaching Paradise Park (Hike 25). If you have the time and energy, turn right (northeast) onto the Paradise Park Trail and ascend 1 mile through wide wildflower meadows to a ridgetop viewpoint, an unparalleled look at Mount Hood, and an endless view in all directions. Otherwise, continue forward on a gentle, meandering contour of Mount Hood's western flank, where wildflowers carpet the slopes in white, pink, red, yellow, blue, and purple. Splash across Lost Creek, then observe a house-size boulder just off-trail and wonder how it came to its curious resting place.

Just when you're about to go into scenery overload, the trail turns west and descends out of the meadows and back into the trees. Drop through a few switchbacks and connect with PCT again at 6.2 miles. Now turn left (south) to begin your return journey. After a short distance, descend into the barren Rushing Water Creek Canyon, where you get to splash across the base of a wispy waterfall before climbing back out the other side. From here, continue on a fairly effortless course through the woods, cross Lost Creek, and proceed straight (south) through the lower junction with the Paradise Park Trail at 8 miles. When you reach 8.5 miles, you're back where you started the Paradise Park Loop. Now you just have to backtrack to your original starting point—back down into the Zigzag Canyon and a steady climb back up to the Timberline Lodge.

ORIGIN STORIES: ZIGZAG CANYON

It is believed that Zigzag Canyon received its name from a journal entry belonging to Joel Palmer, a pioneer who crossed the river canyon in the fall of 1845. He describes his descent as "turn directly to the right, go zigzag . . . then turn short around, and go zigzag . . . until you come under the place where you started from . . . and so on . . ." Could this have been the origin of the switchback?

33 Mountaineer Loop

RATING/ DIFFICULTY	ROUNDTRIP	ELEV GAIN/ HIGH POINT	SEASON
***/4	2.8 miles	1170 feet/ 6950 feet	Aug–Sept

Map: Green Trails Maps Mount Hood #462S; **Permit:** None; **Contact:** Zigzag Ranger District, MHNF; **Notes:** This high-elevation trail is fully exposed; sun and wind protection are highly recommended; trekking poles advised; **GPS:** N 45°19.842', W 121°42.630'

Of the few trails on Mount Hood that travel above the timberline for big mountain panoramas, the Mountaineer Loop to Silcox Hut is the shortest and easiest to get to. But the hike is hard work. The trail is steep, and dry, and mostly exposed to the sun and wind. Before taking on this grinder, fuel up at the fantastic breakfast buffet at Timberline Lodge—a meal of legend according to many Pacific Crest Trail hikers.

GETTING THERE

From Sandy, drive Mount Hood Highway (US Highway 26) east for approximately 29 miles, past the village of Government Camp. Turn left (north) on the Timberline Highway and head 5.5 miles up the mountain to the Timberline Lodge and ski area; park in the main parking area.

ON THE TRAIL

Start the Mountaineer Loop on the paved service road on the east side of Timberline Lodge. Walk this road 0.2 mile up the mountain to a signed junction with the Pacific Crest Trail/Timberline Trail. While the view

Colorful buckwheat and aster decorate the view-packed trailsides along Mountaineer Loop.

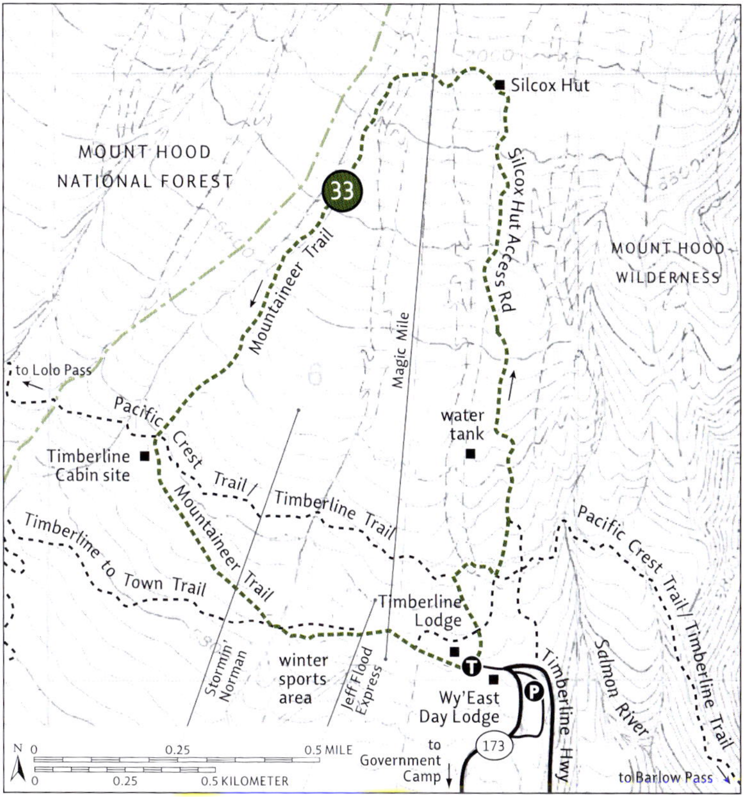

looking straight up at Mount Hood is impressive, the wider scene is fairly desolate. Above the tree line, the mountainside is mostly gray sand and rock—after all, this is a volcano. By midsummer, though, the scene is enriched with plentiful patches of alpine wildflowers that add brilliant splashes of color to the drab terrain. Look for dwarf lupine, penstemon, buckwheat, monkeyflower, and phlox. Turn right (east) onto the Pacific Crest Trail (PCT) and dip through a shallow gully to a junction at 0.3 mile, at the edge of a

WANNA CHEAT?

Purchase a ticket and take a ride up the Magic Mile Chairlift to Silcox Hut. This will cut out the big grind uphill, so all you have to do is frolic down the mountainside back to Timberline Lodge. You can purchase summer lift tickets at the lodge's front desk or at the bottom of the chairlift.

TIMBERLINE LODGE

Opened to the public in 1938, Timberline Lodge was constructed as a Depression-era Works Progress Administration project, built from local timber and stone. It was dedicated by President Franklin D. Roosevelt, who declared, "Those who will follow us to Timberline Lodge on their holidays and vacations will represent the enjoyment of new opportunities for play in every season of the year."

The lodge enjoyed a period of recreation through the 1940s but eventually fell into disrepute and disrepair and was closed by the US Forest Service in 1955. The closure didn't last long, as Richard L. Kohnstamm began renovating the establishment and reopened it to the public. After extensive renovation and additions, Timberline Lodge was designated a National Historic Landmark in 1977. It has since become one of the Northwest's most popular year-round vacation destinations, most notably for its Magic Mile chairlift, which whisks skiers and snowboarders high onto Mount Hood for epic year-round snowplay.

The interior of Timberline Lodge is adorned with hand-carved ornamentation, mosaic artwork, and stone arches, as well as a small museum displaying photos and relics from the lodge's early years. In addition to a variety of charming, well-appointed rooms, Timberline offers its guests several dining options, including an upscale restaurant and a basement pizza parlor. The Ram's Head Bar on the top floor offers a variety snacks and beverages that can be enjoyed while taking in a fantastic view of Mount Hood, and it's a great place to end any day of hiking on the mountain.

cluster of weather-beaten hemlocks and noble firs. To the right are a couple of small campsites commonly used by PCT hikers.

Now turn left (north) on the Mountaineer Trail and start huffing straight up the ridgeline. The route upward is lined with lupine and juniper and is fairly steep and sandy, making the ascent a bit of a slog. Enjoy the shade while you can, because it won't last for long. Approaching 0.4 mile, the trail exits tree cover and merges with Silcox Hut Access Road. Now in the big, wide open, just start walking the dirt and gravel road upward. As you gain elevation and pause for breath, throw a look over your shoulder. On bluebird days, you can see as far south as Diamond Peak, more than 100 miles distant. The ascent eventually becomes a bit easier on sturdier ground, until you're standing at the doorstep of Silcox Hut at 1.1 miles. The wood-and-stone hut, built in 1939, originally served as a warming shelter for skiers. It eventually fell into disrepair and the Forest Service considered demolishing the hut in the 1980s. It was saved and renovated by the Friends of Silcox Hut and reopened in 1993 as a premiere lodging destination. Even though the hut isn't open for visiting, the perch at nearly 7000 feet on the flank of Mount Hood offers an impressive panoramic view of Trillium Lake (Hike 36) and most of Oregon's Cascade peaks lined up on the horizon.

From the top of the loop at Silcox Hut, the rest of the trail is mostly downhill. Depending on your knees, that could be a good thing or a bad thing—it's just as steep going down as it was coming up. Here, in the summer ski area, watch out for skiers and snowboarders whizzing by. Proceed west across a gully, then past the bottom of the Palmer chairlift and under the Magic Mile chairlift. Ignore the service road that veers off to the left (south) and cross another (possibly snowy) gully to follow the Mountaineer Trail downward along the boundary of the ski area, where it twists down a steep, sandy ridge decorated with pretty purple aster. The trail then drops into a grove of pine and hemlock before arriving at a junction with the PCT at 2.1 miles.

From this junction, the walk back to Timberline Lodge is pleasant and mostly level—a nice way to cool off after the steep ascent and descent. Cross the PCT, sticking with the Mountaineer Trail, and pass the Timberline Cabin site, where a few pieces of foundation debris are all that remain. Veer left (south) at an unsigned fork to stay on track and traipse through airy forest and flowery slopes (ski runs), where vibrant magenta paintbrush bursts in colorful blooms. At 2.5 miles, veer left (east) at the junction with the Timberline to Town Trail, make a slight ascent through another grove of trees, then go straight through a junction with the Glade Trail at 2.7 miles. Watch for mountain bikers through this section. The final stretch turns into a wide gravel road through the ski base area and ends at the lodge's upper parking lot. When you're finished, reward yourself with a tasty snack or beverage from the Ram's Head Bar. You deserve it!

34 Buried Forest Overlook

RATING/ DIFFICULTY	ROUNDTRIP	ELEV GAIN/ HIGH POINT	SEASON
****/3	3.1 miles	920 feet/ 6050 feet	July–Oct

Map: Green Trails Maps Mount Hood #462S; **Permit:** None; **Contact:** Zigzag Ranger District, MHNF; **Notes:** This high-elevation trail is fully exposed; sun and wind protection are highly recommended; trekking poles advised; **GPS:** N 45°19.842', W 121°42.630'

While the crowds are all heading west on the Timberline Trail to enjoy the wildflowers at Paradise Park, head east instead along this volcanic ridgeline. Along the way, you can take in impressive views over a windswept alpine plain and peep over the vast White River Canyon, where a centuries-old eruption buried an ancient forest.

GETTING THERE

From Sandy, drive Mount Hood Highway (US Highway 26) east for approximately 29 miles, past the village of Government Camp. Turn left (north) on the Timberline Highway and head 5.5 miles up the mountain to the Timberline Lodge and ski area; park in the main parking area.

ON THE TRAIL

Begin this moderate out-and-back at the service road trailhead on the east side of Timberline Lodge. Before you get moving,

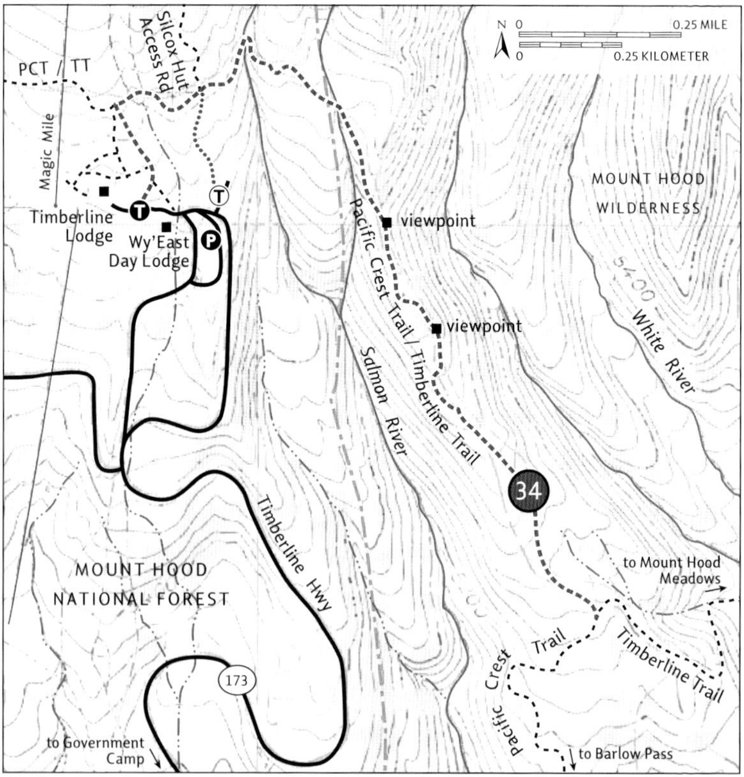

The White River cuts a wide scar down the south flank of Mount Hood.

slather on some sunscreen (there's little shade on this journey), then start walking the paved path upward (north) into an ashen landscape of volcanic sand and boulders strewn with low, patchy shrubs. In summer months, lupine, penstemon, and buckwheat blossom with vibrant patches of blue, purple, and yellow flowers. In autumn, low mats of huckleberry turn into a patchwork of vivid yellow, orange, and red leaves. At 0.2 mile, where the Pacific Crest Trail/Timberline Trail crosses the road at a signed junction, you've reached the high point of your hike. It's all downhill from here—at least until the return trip.

Turn right (east) off the road and onto sandy trail to follow the Pacific Crest Trail (PCT) through a shallow gully, then through a grove of windblown hemlocks. At 0.3 mile, pass through a junction with the Silcox Hut Access Road. (You can also use this trail to start from the east side of the parking area.) Proceed across a larger gully where the Salmon River begins its journey down the mountain; crossing is usually an easy rock-hop. The grade of the descent now increases moderately and the trail turns soft and sandy as it bears southward to head down the ridgeline that divides the Salmon River and White River Canyons. The first big view comes at 0.8 mile, where the trail skirts the precipitous edge of White River Canyon. Enjoy the look, but use caution near the loose and sandy edge. Proceed a little farther to a narrow section of the ridge where you can look over both canyons to the west and east.

Continue on, curving through another grove of alpine conifers and mountain ash, then enter a broad, open plain where the views are all-encompassing. Clusters of mangled white pines hunch over a carpet of tall grasses, lupine, aster, buckwheat, paintbrush, and mariposa lily. As the trail continues downward, the view of White River Canyon comes to span almost 180 degrees, from its origin high on Mount Hood, below

White River Glacier, and down into the wide valley between Barlow and Bonney Buttes. A large cascade can be seen pouring over a rocky escarpment, and if you look closely into the canyon you can spot the partially revealed remains of the ancient hemlock forest that was buried by a volcanic eruption more than 250 years ago.

At 1.5 miles, the trail reaches the tree line, where little pocket meadows bloom with goldenrod and white rhododendron. Just a little farther, at about 1.6 miles, the Pacific Crest and Timberline Trails veer apart at a signed junction. The Timberline heads east to dive into White River Canyon and continue its journey around Mount Hood; the PCT continues south to Barlow Pass, Twin Lakes (Hike 42), Timothy Lake (Hike 49), and beyond. Without committing to a much longer hike, this makes a good turnaround point. On the way back, you'll have Mount Hood looming large right in your face as you retrace your steps back up through the flowery plains, then back up the sandy slopes to return to your starting point. When you finish, you can spend the rest of your day kicking back in the historic Timberline Lodge.

35 Timberline Gardens

RATING/ DIFFICULTY	ROUNDTRIP	ELEV GAIN/ HIGH POINT	SEASON
***/1–2	Up to 3 miles	Up to 350 feet/Up to 6090 feet	July–Oct

Map: Trails Illustrated Mount Hood Wilderness #321; **Permit:** None; **Contact:** Zigzag Ranger District, MHNF; **Notes:** These high-elevation trails are fully exposed; sun and wind protection are highly recommended; **GPS:** N 45°19.842', W 121°42.630'

You don't have to commit to a big hike to enjoy some spectacular wildflowers and Mount Hood scenery. Throw on your trail shoes, slather on some sunscreen, grab a bottle of water, and explore some of the short nature trails around Timberline Lodge. With 3 miles of interconnected trail segments—including portions of the Pacific Crest Trail (PCT) and Mountaineer Trail, you can stroll as near or far as you like without packing for a whole day on the mountain. This is a great option for strolling with little ones, taking Fido for a walk, or showing off the mountain to visiting friends and family.

GETTING THERE

From Sandy, drive Mount Hood Highway (US Highway 26) east for approximately 29 miles, past the village of Government Camp. Turn left (north) on the Timberline Highway and head 5.5 miles up the mountain to the Timberline Lodge and ski area; park in the main parking area.

ON THE TRAIL

There is no one way to go, so you can just wander these short trails at will. Since you'll be above the tree line with minimal shade and a lot of exposure to sun and wind, it's a good idea to apply sunscreen, wear a hat and light jacket, and carry water to stay hydrated. You can start at any of the trailheads in the area: the east parking lot, near the east side of the lodge, the west end of the lodge parking loop, or the patio at the back (north) side of the lodge.

Once you set foot to trail, you'll plunge into a volcanic alpine environment. Clusters of stunted trees—mountain hemlock, alpine fir, and whitebark pine—eke out a harsh existence on the sandy ridges.

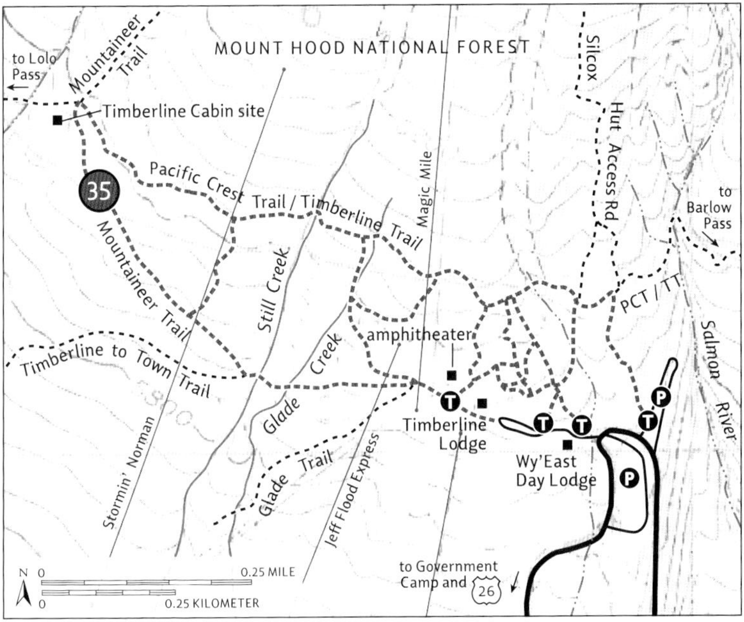

Rock gardens of flowering shrubs—dwarf lupine, tundra aster, penstemon, heather, phlox, buckwheat, and fleeceflower—add splashes of vibrant color here and there. And ever-present is the jagged peak of Mount Hood looming above, flanked by the glistening Zigzag, Palmer, and White River Glaciers. The rocky prominence to the west of the peak is Illumination Rock, which received its name from the 1887 Independence Day event when climbers hauled up and ignited one hundred pounds of red fire (strontium salt) to light up the mountain.

For a short, 0.3-mile walk with great views and little elevation gain, try this loop that starts and finishes at the lodge patio. Set out from the east side of the patio area on a path that ascends a low ridge between a service road and a shallow gully. The route meanders easily into increasingly exposed terrain, with big views of Mount Hood straight ahead. A little over 0.1 mile up, connect with the PCT and turn left (east). Walk the PCT about 25 yards, then turn left again (south) on a marked path. As you begin descending, look south to pick out Olallie Butte, Mount Jefferson, Mount Washington, and the Three Sisters lined up on the horizon. Reach the bottom of the loop shortly past 0.2 mile, beside the lodge amphitheater. Make one more left turn (east) and walk the last stretch back to the lodge.

To stretch your legs on a longer jaunt, sporting more views and more flowers, try this 1.5-mile loop that gains a few hundred feet of elevation along the way. Start at the

Pretty purple aster carpets the ski slopes around Timberline Lodge in summer.

trailhead/service road on the east side of the lodge and walk 0.2 mile up this paved path to the signed junction with the PCT. Turn left (west) onto gravelly tread and ascend a low ridge where you have Mount Hood large on your right and a vast panorama of Oregon's northern and central Cascades on your left. Make an easy contour through a couple of gullies and under a few ski chairlifts to a four-way junction at 0.8 mile. Now turn left onto the Mountaineer Trail and pass the site of the old Timberline Cabin. Continue descending as the trail proceeds though stretches of hemlock forest and across open ski slopes where summer wildflowers are often profuse. At 1.2 miles, near the bottom of the loop, turn left (east) on the Timberline to Town Trail and dip through a shallow gully containing Still Creek. Close the loop by making a short, quick ascent back into the trees, then past a chairlift building to finish at the west end of the lodge parking loop.

36 Trillium Lake

RATING/ DIFFICULTY	ROUNDTRIP	ELEV GAIN/ HIGH POINT	SEASON
***/1	1.9 miles	110 feet/ 3620 feet	June–Oct

Map: Trails Illustrated Mount Hood Wilderness #321; **Permit:** NW Forest Pass for trailhead parking; **Contact:** Zigzag Ranger District, MHNF; **Notes:** High-use trail; avoid holidays and weekends; for the winter route, see Hike 81; **GPS:** N 45°15.996', W 121°44.484'

Formed in 1960 after the damming of Mud Creek, Trillium Lake is a popular outdoor destination just south of Mount Hood that offers hiking, biking, camping, picnicking, and paddling. In summer months, the 2-mile, barrier-free trail around the lake offers plenty of views, berries, wildflowers, and bird-watching. Look for the lake's namesake flower in the shadier, wooded portions of the trail.

GETTING THERE

From Sandy, drive Mount Hood Highway (US Highway 26) east for approximately 30 miles. Turn right (south) on Trillium Lake Road (Forest Road 2656) and drive 1.8 miles to the fork with FR 2612; veer right (west) and continue 0.2 mile to the day-use parking area; find the trailhead near the dam.

ON THE TRAIL

Start your counterclockwise stroll around the lake near the east end of the dam and picnic area. The path begins by heading northeast under a canopy of hemlock, cedar, and fir as it traces the lake's southern shoreline. After about 0.2 mile, take the short path left (north) to a small pier for a picture-perfect view of Trillium Lake and Mount Hood. Return to the trail, cross the boat ramp, and continue back into the trees. The path turns north, crosses another boat ramp at 0.3 mile, and continues between the lakeshore and the campground for the next half mile. The lakeside amphitheater at 0.6 mile makes a nice place to pause and enjoy another view. Forest naturalists and rangers offer interpretive programs here on summer weekends. The mountain across the lake to the west is 4880-foot Eureka Peak.

Trillium Lake is a perfect destination for summer picnics and paddling.

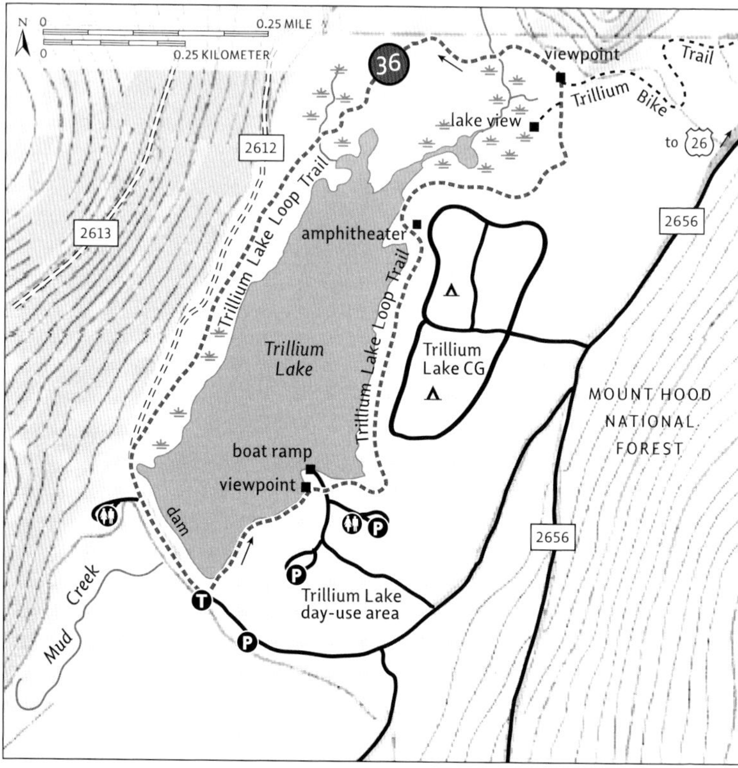

Leave the campground behind, and meander through a grove of cedars, salmonberry, and bunchberry and into Trillium Lake's northern wetlands area. Fork left (west) at the Trillium Bike Trail junction at 0.9 mile, then look for a boardwalk path left (south) to another viewpoint. Follow this short path through dense shrubs of spiraea to the edge of a sprawling, grassy meadow. After your look, back on the loop trail, continue through alternating stretches of shady hemlock and spruce forest, and open wetland areas of willow and alder, with patches of huge, prehistoric-looking skunk cabbage. In the open areas, watch for small songbirds, ducks, ospreys, and bald eagles. Around 1.2 miles, the lake comes back into view from across another meadow area before reentering forest.

Now on the west side of Trillium Lake, the path continues through airy woods above the shoreline. Look for a variety of wildflowers through here, including lupine, hedge nettle, columbine, cow parsnip, monkeyflower, aster, and willow herb, as well as several dense thickets of thimbleberry and vine maple. The forest then closes in, the lush green groundcover is replaced with woody debris, and a few primitive campsites can be found on the slope above the trail. Unfortunately, these camps are often strewn with trash left by careless campers. At 1.7 miles, the path ends at a paved road (FR 2612); turn left (south) and walk the road shoulder for the final stretch to cross the lake's dam. Below the trail, a narrow strip of sand and rocks serves as the lake's "beach," and as you close the loop, you'll be treated to another nice view of the lake and Mount Hood.

37 Veda Lake

RATING/ DIFFICULTY	ROUNDTRIP	ELEV GAIN/ HIGH POINT	SEASON
***/3	2.8 miles	950 feet/ 4720 feet	July–Oct

Map: Trails Illustrated Mount Hood Wilderness #321; **Permit:** None; **Contact:** Zigzag Ranger District, MHNF; **Notes:** Road to trailhead is very rough; high-clearance vehicle recommended; **GPS:** N 45°14.886', W 121°47.268'

Enjoy views of Still Creek valley, Multorpor Mountain, and Mount Hood en route to Veda Lake.

The hardest part of the hike to Veda Lake is just getting to the trailhead. Once you've made the drive on the rough and bumpy road, the short hike to this secluded lake is rather smooth and pleasant. Along the way, you'll get a nice view of the Still Creek valley and Mount Hood before descending to this quiet forest pool. With its abundance of berry shrubs and vine maple, this trail is particularly colorful in the autumn.

GETTING THERE

From Sandy, drive Mount Hood Highway (US Highway 26) east for approximately 30 miles. Turn right (south) on Trillium Lake Road (Forest Road 2656) and drive 1.8 miles to the fork with FR 2612; veer right (west) and continue another 1.4 miles around the west side of the lake. At the four-way junction, make a hairpin left (south) turn onto Sherar Burn Road (FR 2613) and slowly take this rough, rocky road 3.7 miles to the trailhead; find parking in the primitive camp area nearby.

ON THE TRAIL

Begin the Veda Lake Trail by climbing steeply up a rocky, uneven path away from the road and into a forest of mossy Douglas fir and hemlock. The slopes and trailsides

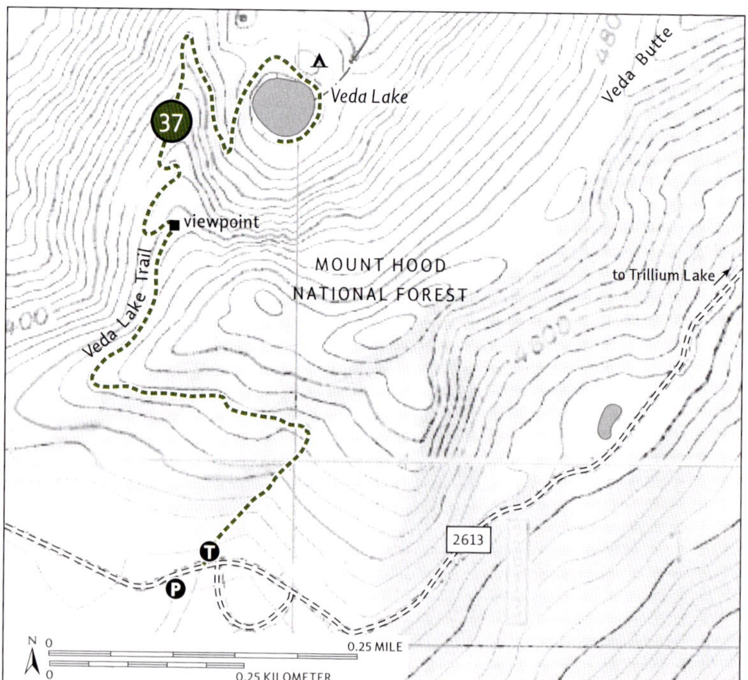

are adorned with an abundant mix of huckleberry, bear grass, vanilla leaf, and deer fern. After 0.2 mile, the path turns and levels for a nice walk on smoother trail to contour the wooded hillside. As you stroll along, you will find the tree canopy transition to more silver fir forest, with sparse patches of mountain strawberry and bunchberry adding greenery to the hillside. Approaching 0.5 mile, the trail hooks around the western extension of 4974-foot Veda Butte, where you'll commence a steady descent into closed-in forest.

At 0.7 mile, the trail skirts the edge of the bluff where an opening in the trees offers a wide view over the Still Creek valley. In the distance, Mount Hood dominates the horizon, with Multorpor Mountain at the head of the valley and Veda Lake in the forested basin below. At this point, the trail begins descending the ridge on the west side of the lake basin, jogging through a few loose switchbacks. The way is girdled by mountain rhododendron, which blooms with brilliant pink flowers in summer, and vine maple, which turns colorful shades of yellow, orange, and red in fall. Nearing 1.1 miles, the trail turns off the ridgeline and into the basin, where it passes a jumble of mossy rocks then proceeds toward Veda Lake's brushy shore.

The opaque green lake comes into view at 1.3 miles, where a steep, loose bootpath descends toward the water. This is one of the lake's few access points, as most of this quiet pool is bordered by dense alder, rhododendron, and berry shrubs. Continue another 0.1 mile to an obvious fork just before the lake's inlet stream. The path to the left (northeast) proceeds a short distance to a couple of nice campsites. The path right (east) crosses the inlet and narrows through overgrown thimbleberry and alder to another campsite uphill from the lakeshore. At 1.4 miles, the path finally peters out on the south side of the lake, at the swampy shoreline, where you actually get the nicest view. After a snack or lunch break, return by the same route.

38 Grave Trail

RATING/ DIFFICULTY	ROUNDTRIP	ELEV GAIN/ HIGH POINT	SEASON
**/2	1.9 miles	480 feet/ 4160 feet	All year

Map: Trails Illustrated Mount Hood Wilderness #321; **Permit:** NW Forest Pass for trailhead parking; **Contact:** Hood River Ranger District, MHNF; **Notes:** For winter directions, see Hike 83; **GPS:** N 45°16.950', W 121°41.118'

Between the 1840s and the 1860s, more than 300,000 pioneers attempted the 2000-mile wagon journey from Missouri to the Pacific Northwest on what became known as the Oregon Trail. The more disturbing name for this wild, cross-country route is America's Longest Graveyard. It is estimated that up to 10 percent of emigrants died along the way—perhaps as many as 30,000 people. Many of them were buried in unmarked graves or just abandoned along the trailside. During the construction of US Highway 26 over Barlow Pass, workers discovered the grave of an unknown pioneer woman, estimated to have died along the route sometime in the 1840s. Today, a small monument and stone grave marks the site, which can be visited by hiking a short stretch of the old wagon road.

GETTING THERE

From Sandy, drive Mount Hood Highway (US Highway 26) east for approximately 30 miles. Merge right onto OR 35 north toward Hood River and continue another 2.3 miles to the Barlow Pass Sno-Park and trailheads; turn right (south) and drive for 0.2 mile to the large parking area.

ON THE TRAIL

The Grave Trail starts on the west side of the large Barlow Pass parking area. It is a remnant of the old Barlow Road, as noted by the easy-to-miss "Original Wagon Route" sign attached to an aged fir tree. The wide route begins by heading downhill into dense and dark hemlock and fir forest, where the hillside is covered with a mix of woody debris and meager patches of huckleberry, bunchberry, bear grass, wild ginger, and fringe cup, all only partially illuminated by filtered sunlight. Shortly after beginning, come to a fork, also signed "Original Wagon Route." The original route heads straight down the hillside but has been obstructed by fallen trees. Veer left and follow the old roadbed instead.

As the path snakes its way downhill, the surface becomes rough and rocky for some awkward stepping. More groundcover starts to appear in the form of deer fern, vanilla leaf, devil's club, and kinnikinnick, lending to greener and more pleasant surroundings. There are also some notably large old-growth cedars and Douglas firs standing out among the smaller hemlocks, indicating the multigenerational nature of this portion of forest. About 0.4 mile along, the grade eases onto smoother tread and you're given tantalizing peeks of Mount Hood through the trees to the north. The full view comes just a little farther. After proceeding through another S-turn, look for a path right (north) at 0.6 mile that leads to a small clearing at the edge of the hillside with an unobstructed

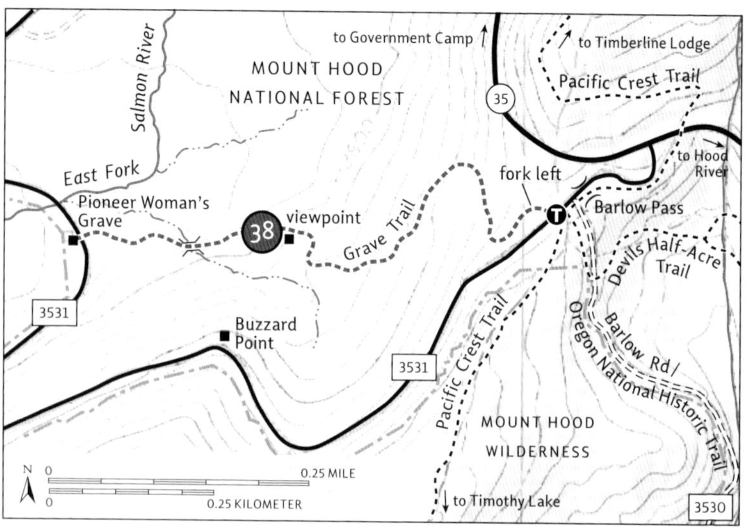

Venture though dark woods on an old wagon road to the gravesite of an unknown pioneer.

view of Mount Hood rising from a sea of trees.

The path/road continues downhill, the grade temporarily increasing a little more and the surface becoming rough once again. Large rhododendron shrubs start to fill the understory of the forest, and multiple smaller paths appear to branch off the main route. Stick with the wider path to stay on course. At 0.8 mile, dip through a boggy drainage and cross a seasonal creek on a rotting bridge, then take an easy walk along the final stretch to end at Forest Road 3531, next to a large clearing, at about 1 mile. Cross the road to the Pioneer Woman's Grave monument, a large stone with a memorial plaque. Nearby, a large mound of stones and sticks, often adorned with small trinkets and offerings, marks the unknown woman's final resting place.

39 Barlow Butte

RATING/ DIFFICULTY	ROUNDTRIP	ELEV GAIN/ HIGH POINT	SEASON
**/3	2.9 miles	1340 feet/ 5050 feet	July–Oct

Map: Trails Illustrated Mount Hood Wilderness #321; **Permit:** NW Forest Pass for trailhead parking; **Contact:** Hood River Ranger District, MHNF; **GPS:** N 45°16.974', W 121°41.008'

The Barlow Butte Trail spans the entire length of the forested ridge that divides the Barlow Creek valley to the west and the larger White River valley to the east. Fortunately, you don't have to hike the entire ridge to bag the butte, the former site of a fire lookout. That said, you'll still work to earn this summit, as it climbs rather steeply for the majority of this short trail segment. That makes this a great conditioning hike if you're planning bigger things on the Timberline or Pacific Crest Trails.

GETTING THERE

From Sandy, drive Mount Hood Highway (US Highway 26) east for approximately 30 miles. Merge right onto OR 35 north toward Hood River and continue another 2.3 miles to the Barlow Pass Sno-Park and trailheads; turn right (south) and drive for 0.2 mile to the large parking area.

ON THE TRAIL

Start the Barlow Butte Trail on the east side of the parking area, where the Pacific Crest Trail cuts across at a large junction. Follow the wide trail (a former wagon route) as it curves southeast to merge with the historic Barlow Road. Watch for vehicles as you cross the road and pick up the butte trail about 50 yards down, at 0.1 mile, where it drops off the road to the left (east). Follow this curving path down into dense hemlock, fir, and spruce forest. The shady woods here are carpeted with salmonberry, lady fern, and mountain strawberry; look for splashes of red columbine, white trillium, and pink pyrola. The path crosses a few seasonal springs as it enters a marshy creek bottom—watch out for thorny devil's club near the trail—then comes to a junction a little past 0.3 mile.

Here, the Devils Half-Acre Trail (see Extend Your Trip) branches off to the right (southeast). Fork left (northeast) to cross Barlow Creek on a sturdy bridge, then start ascending on a gentle grade. The next junction comes quickly at 0.6 mile. Turn right (south) to stay on the butte trail. The path straight ahead is the Mineral Jane Ski Trail, part of the Mount Hood Nordic trail network, which heads east to the White River area. The butte trail now enters the Mount Hood Wilderness, still on a fairly gentle incline but one that increases quickly as it turns southeast to begin steeply ascending the butte's northwest flank. (Some older topo maps show the trail turning south to ascend the butte's west flank; these are no longer accurate directions.)

The way up is steep and fairly rooty, on tight switchbacks under cover of large

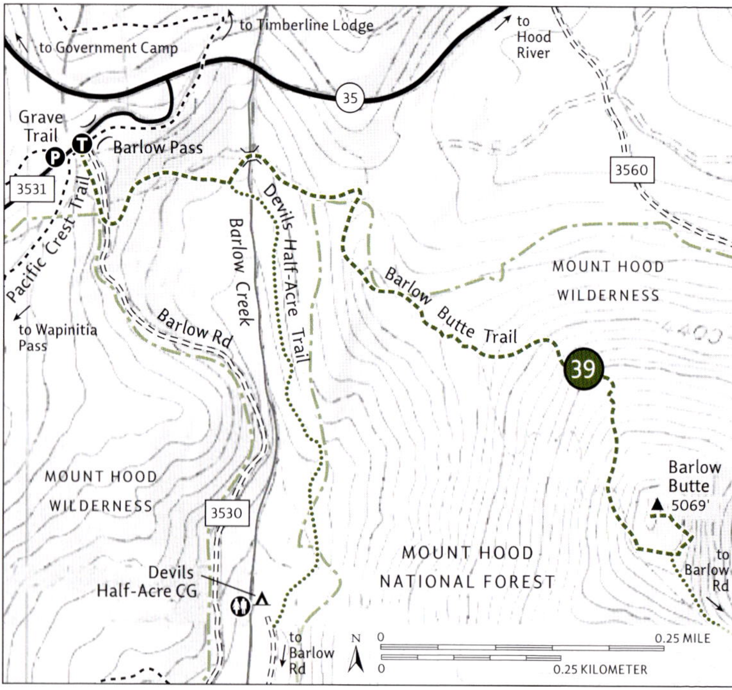

Unusual volcanic rocks cap the summit of Barlow Butte.

hemlocks and Douglas firs. Groundcover thins to a mix of sparse huckleberry and bear grass, with more woody debris than greenery. This improves with elevation, where vanilla leaf, inside-out flower (duck-foot), and avalanche lily start dressing the higher slopeside. Around 1.1 miles, the grade eases temporarily, allowing you to catch your breath. It then increases again for the final stretch to the crest of the ridge at 1.4 miles. A large cairn at this point marks the junction where the Barlow Butte Trail continues south along the ridgeline (see Extend Your Trip), and the path to the summit continues straight ahead (east).

Follow this spur about 0.1 mile as it curves north through patches of heather and manzanita and skirts the edge of the butte, where you get a nice view over the wide White River valley and south to Frog Lake Buttes (Hike 43) and Bonney Butte (Hike 45). It then ducks back under tree cover and bends west to reach the summit area of Barlow Butte—a rather anticlimactic finish in a small clearing ringed with huckleberry and only a partial view west over the Barlow Valley. Patches of rock penstemon and stonecrop adorn some large, craggy rocks that offer a place to sit for a drink and a snack before heading back down the way you came.

EXTEND YOUR TRIP

If you're looking for more mileage after bagging the butte, consider adding an easy side trip to Devils Half-Acre (Hike 40) as an alternate return route, or a more challenging trek farther along the Barlow Butte Trail. For the former, head back down the way you came. When you get to the Devils Half-Acre Trail junction, turn left (south) and take a pleasant walk along Barlow Creek to the camp area and a large valley meadow; return via Barlow Road. For the latter, continue heading south from the ridgetop junction. This unmaintained portion of the trail undulates along the overgrown ridgetop for a couple of miles, crosses a few small meadows with mountain views, then makes a steep descent to Barlow Road (Forest Road 3530) near the White River. Hiking the entire butte trail is a 10.4-mile round-trip with nearly 4500 feet of elevation gain.

40 Devils Half-Acre

RATING/ DIFFICULTY	ROUNDTRIP	ELEV GAIN/ HIGH POINT	SEASON
**/2	2.2 miles	480 feet/ 4160 feet	All year

Map: Trails Illustrated Mount Hood Wilderness #321; **Permit:** NW Forest Pass for trailhead parking; Sno-Park Permit for parking Nov. 1–Apr. 30; **Contact:** Hood River Ranger District, MHNF; **Notes:** This hike uses a portion of the old Barlow Road, which is open to vehicles; be alert, and maintain control of dogs and small children; **GPS:** N 45°16.974', W 121°41.008'

Imagine trying to cross the Cascade Mountains with no roads. A walk to Devils Half-Acre will give you an idea of how it was done nearly two centuries ago. In 1845, Sam Barlow set out from The Dalles to find a way through the mountains as an alternative to taking the treacherous barges down the raging Columbia River (prior to all the dams that exist today). The following year, he opened the 80-mile Barlow Road as Oregon's first official roadway. As for the origin of Devils Half-Acre, it's not quite known. Some theorize that it's the location of a wildfire that cleared this section of the forest, referred to as the Big Deadening. Others believe it might be the site of Barlow's Fort Deposit, where the road-building pioneers stashed their tools and wagons over winter.

GETTING THERE

From Sandy, drive Mount Hood Highway (US Highway 26) east for approximately 30 miles. Merge right onto OR 35 north toward Hood River and continue another 2.3 miles to the Barlow Pass Sno-Park and trailheads; turn right (south) for 0.2 mile to the large parking area.

An old wagon route post along the historic Barlow Road to Devils Half-Acre.

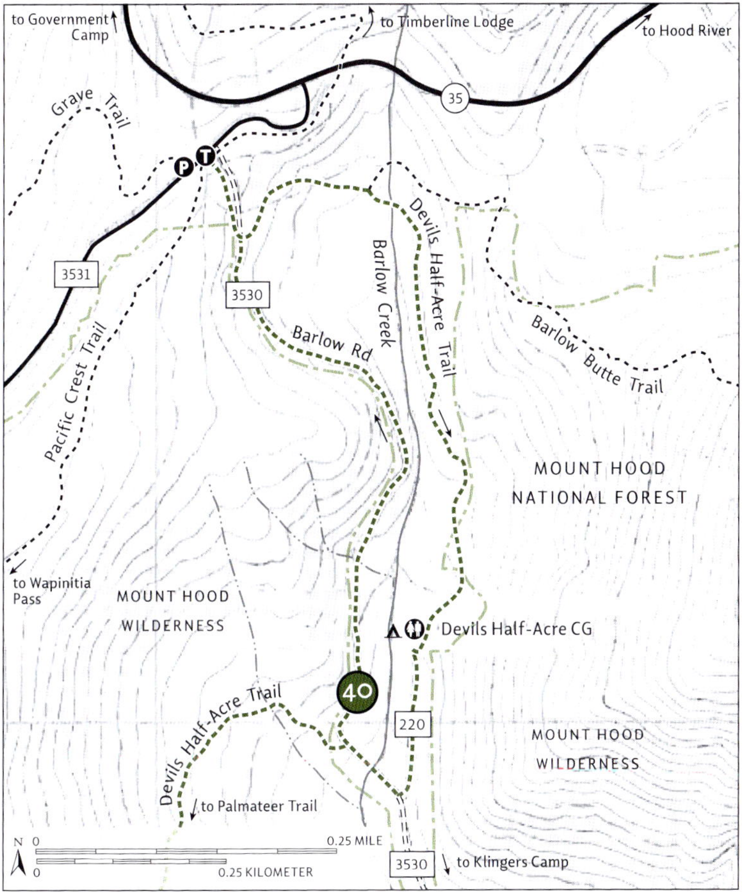

ON THE TRAIL

Begin at a large trail junction on the east side of the parking area, where the Pacific Crest Trail heads off north and south, and the Barlow Butte Trail heads off east. Take the latter path, a wide former wagon road that curves 0.5 mile southeast to merge with the historic Barlow Road. Watch for vehicles as you cross the road and head about 50 yards down, to continue on the butte trail where it drops off the road to the left (east) at 0.1 mile. Follow this trail down into dense hemlock, fir, and spruce forest, where lady fern, vanilla leaf, mountain strawberry, salmonberry, and inside-out flower (duckfoot) are abundant. Hop across a few seasonal springs and enter

SNOWSHOE ROUTE

The Devils Half-Acre Trail can be hiked in winter months for a pleasant and fairly easy snowshoe outing. The route is the same as the summer directions, with a portion of the trail marked with blue diamonds high on the trees. Take note, however, that the stretch between the Barlow Creek junction, near the top of the loop, and the Devils Half-Acre Campground is not as well marked and gets narrow and brushy in sections—bring a map and compass to stay on track.

a marshy creek bottom—watch out for thorny devil's club encroaching on the trail. A little past 0.3 mile, veer right (southeast) onto the Devils Half-Acre Trail.

Now head south, crossing Barlow Creek, where you'll find some impressively large hemlocks and red cedars. Look for a small sign that indicates this as the "Original Wagon Route," precursor to Barlow Road, and imagine trying to navigate a horse-drawn wagon through this dense and tangled jungle. Continue on flat trail, now paralleling the creek, where alder, bunchberry, false Solomon's seal, and aster line the way. The path crosses a couple of seasonal creeks, then a small, brushy meadow, and then comes to the Devils Half-Acre Campground at 1 mile. Here you'll find a ramshackle privy and a couple of small campsites—usually strewn with trash. Continue south, now on a gravel road, across a grassy clearing, then back under tree cover for a short distance to meet Barlow Road at 1.2 miles.

Now walk the rough-and-tumble route of the old wagon trains by turning right (northwest) to begin ascending the second half of the loop. The road crosses Barlow Creek, which flows under by way of a wide culvert, then skirts the edge of a sprawling meadow. At the north end of the meadow, at 1.3 miles, the Devils Half-Acre Trail branches left (west) off the road to continue south to connect with the Palmateer Trail (Hike 41). Continue up the rutted road corridor, now paralleling the creek on the west side, which is lined with pearly everlasting, hedge nettle, and abundant thimbleberry. At 1.7 miles, notice the remains of a weathered post indicting the old wagon route, after which the road bends west then north again for the final stretch back to your starting point.

41 Palmateer Point

RATING/ DIFFICULTY	ROUNDTRIP	ELEV GAIN/ HIGH POINT	SEASON
***/3	5.4 miles	1160 feet/ 4560 feet	July–Oct

Map: Trails Illustrated Mount Hood Wilderness #321; **Permit:** NW Forest Pass for trailhead parking; **Contact:** Hood River Ranger District, MHNF; **Notes:** There are several options for extending this hike; see Hikes 42 and 43 for more info; **GPS:** N 45°16.974', W 121°41.008'

Palmateer Point is a 4400-foot-high escarpment near the head of the Barlow Creek valley. From the exposed summit point, you can enjoy a sweeping panoramic view that takes in Mount Hood, Barlow Butte, and the Frog Lake Buttes. As summer turns to fall, the valley's slopesides

often display a patchwork of autumn-hued vine maple and huckleberry in a vibrant medley of greens, yellows, and reds for a pleasant, seasonal scene when the temps are cooler and the trail traffic is lighter. Of the many ways to access the point, this route is the most direct.

GETTING THERE

From Sandy, drive Mount Hood Highway (US Highway 26) east for approximately 30 miles. Merge right onto OR 35 north toward Hood River and continue another 2.3 miles to the Barlow Pass Sno-Park and trailheads; turn right (south) for 0.2 mile to the large parking area.

ON THE TRAIL

Begin on the Pacific Crest Trail (PCT) near a picnic table and a large, weathered sign showing the Barlow Pass–Twin Lakes Trail area. Head south into mixed forest of Douglas fir, western hemlock, and lodgepole pine, where a collage of huckleberry, vanilla leaf, deer fern, and pipsissewa carpet the terrain. The way proceeds on a fairly moderate ascent along the northern ridge of an unnamed mount between the Barlow Creek and Salmon River valleys. Views are restricted to the surrounding forest, but the path is wide and duffy for comfortable walking, and summer months often showcase a variety of wildflowers along the trailsides, including avalanche lily, columbine, trillium, and coralroot. At 1.1 miles, the trail leaves the ridgeline and veers southeast to make a gentle, contouring descent around the unseen summit of the crest.

Just as you start picking up steam, arrive at the upper junction with the Palmateer Trail

Autumn vine maple adds a splash of color to the Palmateer Trail.

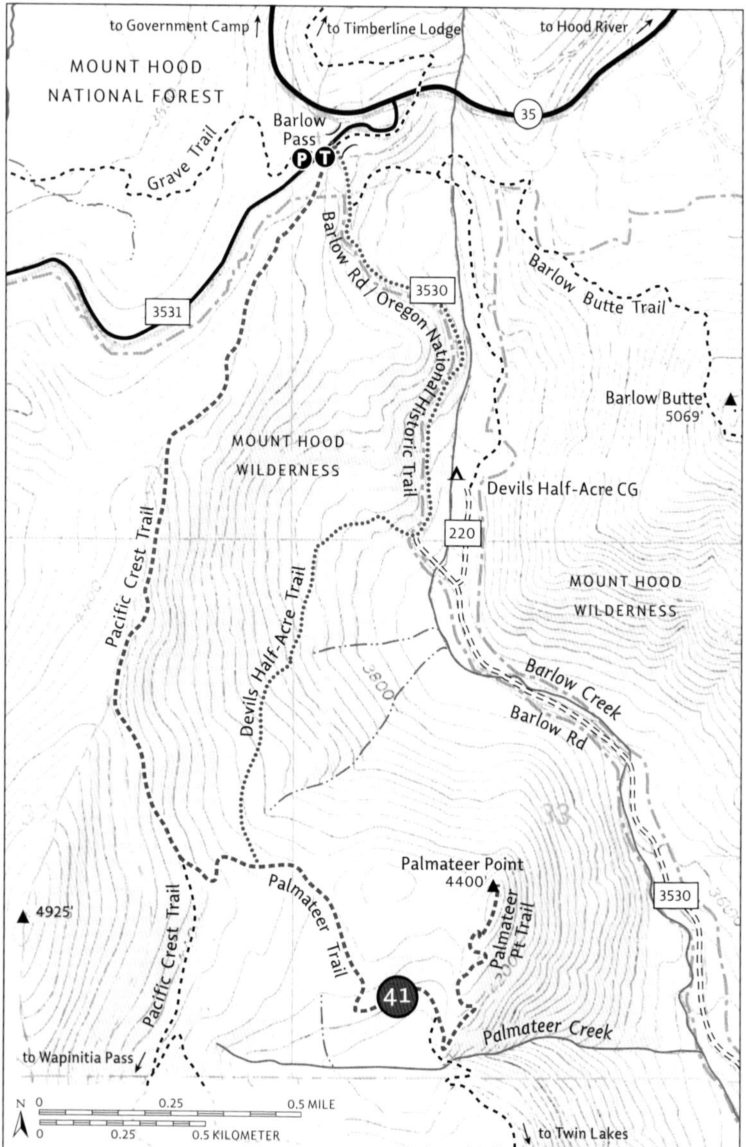
to Government Camp
to Timberline Lodge
to Hood River
MOUNT HOOD
NATIONAL FOREST
35
Barlow
Pass
Grave Trail
3531
3530
Barlow Rd / Oregon National Historic Trail
Barlow Butte Trail
Barlow Butte
5069'
MOUNT HOOD
WILDERNESS
Devils Half-Acre CG
220
Pacific Crest Trail
Devils Half-Acre Trail
3800
MOUNT HOOD
WILDERNESS
Barlow Creek
Barlow Rd
Palmateer Point
4400'
Palmateer Trail
Palmateer Pt Trail
3530
4925'
Pacific Crest Trail
41
Palmateer Creek
to Wapinitia Pass
to Twin Lakes
N
0 0.25 0.5 MILE
0 0.25 0.5 KILOMETER

at 1.5 miles. Veer left (east) off the PCT and descend a short, somewhat steep slope onto a forested plateau. The surroundings are still closed in by trees, but the scene is rich with berry shrubs, ferns, and Oregon grape. Breeze past the Devils Half-Acre Trail at 1.7 miles, where the grade eases to an easy walk through the woods, and a variety of summer wildflowers speckle the ground with purples, reds, pinks, yellows, and whites. Continue winding southeast toward Palmateer Creek when you'll come to the junction with the Palmateer Point Trail at 2.3 miles. To the right (west) of the junction, a nice campsite can be found in the trees; the creek is just 0.1 mile farther.

Now veer left (south) on the Palmateer Point Trail and start a winding, switchbacking ascent. The trail circuits several outcrops of weather-worn volcanic rock draped with heather and manzanita. At 2.6 miles, the trail exits tree cover and proceeds up the spine of the ridge, dotted here and there with mats of juniper. Proceed the final 0.1 mile to the summit at the end of the trail and enjoy the view. To the north, Mount Hood takes center stage, flanked by Barlow Butte in the nearer distance; to the east, the wide Barlow Creek valley stretches from the foot of Mount Hood southward to intersect the White River valley. From this vantage, imagine being a nineteenth-century pioneer navigating up this valley along the rugged and historic Barlow Road, out of sight in the trees below (see Alternate Route). When you're ready to return, head back by the same route, or consider the alternate route for a change of scenery.

Alternate Route

After getting a look over the wide valley that emigrants traversed on their journey to Oregon's Willamette Valley, take this alternate route back to walk some of the old road itself. The distance and elevation gain/loss are fairly comparable. Return the way you came, but when you get back to the junction with the Devils Half-Acre Trail, veer right (north) on this path and commence a steady descent toward the valley floor. As you near the bottom, the path curves east and crosses several streams then meets Barlow Road at 4.6 miles, at the edge of a sprawling meadow. Turn left (north) and start walking the rocky, rutted road 1 mile uphill through a forested corridor, back to your starting point. As you're walking along, you can contemplate life as an 1840s pioneer. Despite its rough condition, Barlow Road is open to vehicles, so stay alert.

42 Twin Lakes

RATING/ DIFFICULTY	ROUNDTRIP	ELEV GAIN/ HIGH POINT	SEASON
***/3	7.3 miles	1160 feet/ 4520 feet	All year

Map: Trails Illustrated Mount Hood Wilderness #321; **Permits:** NW Forest Pass for trailhead parking; Sno-Park Permit for parking Nov. 1–Apr. 30; **Contact:** Clackamas River Ranger District, MHNF; **Notes:** High-use trail; the lower portion is marked for winter use; **GPS:** N 45°16.974', W 121°41.008'

The Twin Lakes are a couple of forest-ringed pools, south of Mount Hood, where you'll find year-round opportunities to go romp in the woods. In summer months, the lakes are a pleasant destination for a swim or picnic lunch. The lower of the two lakes even has a nice camp area for spending the night in the

backcountry without having to hike too far. In fall, the lakes trails are one of the better places to admire autumn color, with abundant huckleberry and vine maple turning vibrant hues of red, orange, and yellow. In the winter and spring, you can even snowshoe to the Lower Lake, thanks to the wide, well-marked trail and fairly easy grades.

GETTING THERE

From Sandy, drive Mount Hood Highway (US Highway 26) east for approximately 35 miles; stay left at the OR 35 junction to continue on US 26 south toward Bend. At the top of Wapinitia Pass, turn left (east) into the Frog Lake Sno-Park; the trailhead is located on the north side of the parking area.

ON THE TRAIL

Begin the hike to the Twin Lakes by walking about 20 yards from the parking area to a well-signed junction with the Pacific Crest Trail (PCT). Along this short spur are a large info board (with a reminder to display your NW Forest Pass), a picnic table, a restroom, and a trash can. Turn right (east) on the PCT and commence a comfortable stroll on wide, duffy trail under tall hemlock forest adorned with huckleberry, rhododendron, and mountain strawberry. After a few minutes of easy walking, the trail starts gaining elevation on a moderate incline as it curves to the southeast. Take note of the blue diamond markers high on the trees. These indicate the route for winter snow travel. At 0.6 mile, the trail makes an abrupt switchback and continues gaining elevation, now on a northeasterly bearing.

The grade finally eases where it comes to a wide junction at the boundary of the Mount Hood Wilderness, at 1.4 miles. Turn right (east) off the PCT onto the Twin Lakes Trail and proceed through a saddle between 4767-foot Bird Butte to the north and an

Mount Hood peeks above the forest surrounding Upper Twin Lake.

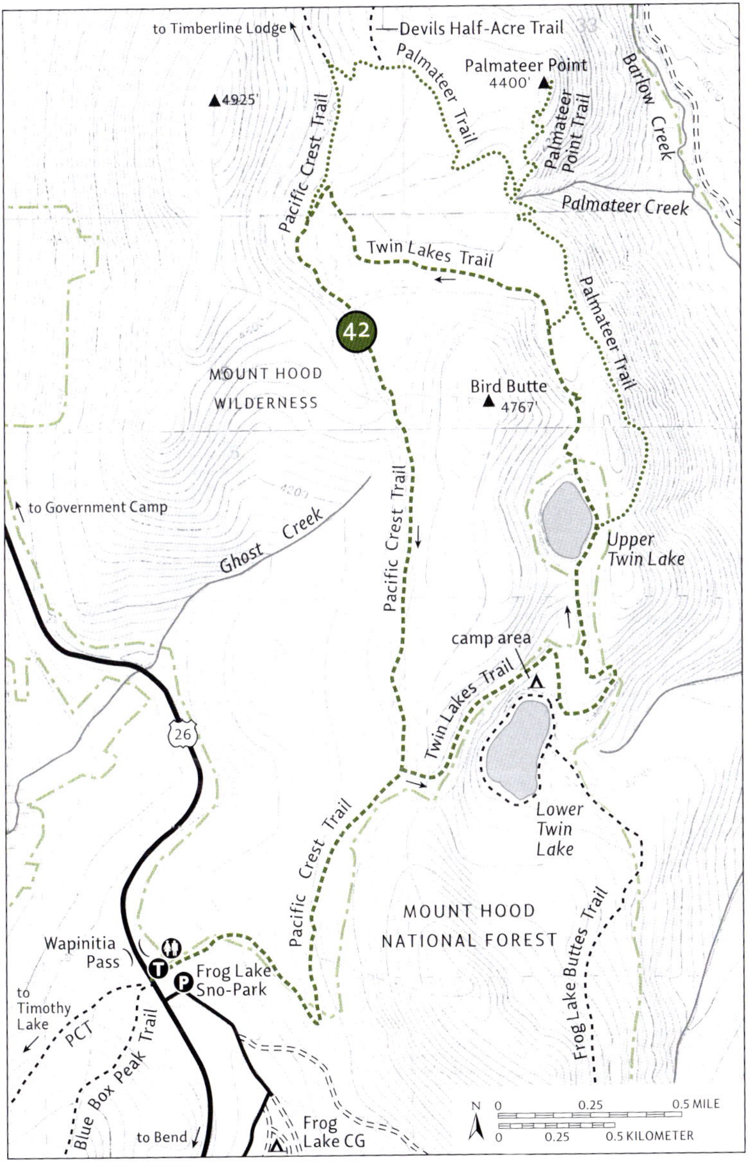
to Timberline Lodge
Devils Half-Acre Trail
Palmateer Trail
Palmateer Point
4400'
Barlow Creek
4925'
Pacific Crest Trail
Palmateer Point Trail
Palmateer Creek
Twin Lakes Trail
Palmateer Trail
42
MOUNT HOOD
WILDERNESS
Bird Butte
4767'
Pacific Crest Trail
to Government Camp
Ghost Creek
Upper
Twin Lake
camp area
Twin Lakes Trail
26
Lower
Twin
Lake
Pacific Crest Trail
MOUNT HOOD
NATIONAL FOREST
Frog Lake Buttes Trail
Wapinitia
Pass
Frog Lake
Sno-Park
to
Timothy
Lake
PCT
Blue Box Peak Trail
to Bend
Frog
Lake CG
N
0
0.25
0.5 MILE
0
0.25
0.5 KILOMETER

unnamed peak to the south, after which you'll make a gentle, curving descent into the lower lake basin. Catch a few scant peeks of the lake on the way down, then cross a seasonal spring around 1.9 miles. Just beyond, as the trail levels for nice, easy walking, look for a side trail on the right (south) at 2.1 miles. Turn onto the short spur and proceed to the shore of Lower Twin Lake. Nearby, you'll find several campsite pads and plenty of logs near the lakeshore for sitting to have a snack and admire the scene. Lake access is easy for taking a refreshing dip. There is a 0.7-mile path that circuits the lake for more exploring, as well as the Frog Lake Buttes Trail (Hike 43), which starts from here.

When you're ready for the next lake, return to the main trail, turn right (south) and begin a short, curving ascent to climb into the upper basin. The route remains confined to the trees, mostly Douglas fir and hemlock, with Oregon grape and lupine lining the trailsides. At 2.7 miles, reach the southern shore of Upper Twin Lake. From this point, you get a nice view across the lake, with Mount Hood peeking above the trees. A few hidden campsites can be found in the trees around the lake, accessible by a narrow loop path. Proceed along the east side of the lake through a lot of huckleberry and bear grass, passing the Palmateer Trail (see Extend Your Trip) at 2.8 miles, then go left to pass a spur to the Palmateer Trail a little farther along. Now gain a little elevation through a forested saddle, followed by a curving descent west around the north flank of Bird Butte, and finally a short climb to reconnect with the PCT at 4.3 miles.

You're now on the home stretch. Turn left (south) on the PCT and commence a gradual ascent along the west slope of Bird Butte. The trail, confined to the trees, is wide and duffy for comfortable walking under shady conifers. Ferns, bear grass, and berries line the way, and little Douglas squirrels are commonly seen darting here and there. In the canopy overhead, watch for Canada jays and listen for woodpeckers. Once you reach the Lake junction again at 5.9 miles, continue south on the PCT to retrace your steps back to your starting point.

EXTEND YOUR TRIP

While you're in the neighborhood, make it a larger, 9.1-mile loop by incorporating Palmateer Point into your outing (Hike 41). This adds several flowery meadows, some nice views of Barlow Creek valley, and a fantastic panorama of Mount Hood and Barlow Butte. Follow the directions above to Upper Twin Lake. At the junction with the Palmateer Trail at 2.8 miles, veer right (northeast) and climb away from the lake on narrow, brushy trail. The path contours the top of the slope above Barlow Creek, then makes a steady decent to cross Palmateer Creek at 4 miles. Just beyond, at 4.1 miles, veer right (southeast) on the Palmateer Point Trail.

This 0.5-mile spur makes a winding, switchbacking ascent of a rocky slope adorned with heather, manzanita, and juniper. From the exposed, 4400-foot point, take in a sweeping 360-degree panorama. After another snack break to enjoy the view, return to the Palmateer Trail and turn right (north). The path curves west through the trees on a gentle ascent among more huckleberry and deer fern, where lupine and Indian paintbrush add splashes of color to the wooded surroundings. At 5.6 miles, pass the Devils Half-Acre Trail, then make a short, moderate ascent to meet the PCT at 5.8 miles. Turn left (south) and follow the PCT 3.3 miles back to your starting point.

43 Frog Lake Buttes

RATING/ DIFFICULTY	ROUNDTRIP	ELEV GAIN/ HIGH POINT	SEASON
**/4	3.8 miles	1430 feet/ 5300 feet	July–Oct

Map: Trails Illustrated Mount Hood Wilderness #321; **Permit:** NW Forest Pass for trailhead parking; **Contact:** Clackamas River Ranger District, MHNF; **Notes:** For winter directions, see Hike 82; **GPS:** N 45°13.332', W 121°41.550'

The steep hike to this viewless summit may not have a big payoff at the end, but is ideal for training for bigger trails, checking local high points off your list, or just taking a quiet hike in the woods.

GETTING THERE

From Sandy, drive Mount Hood Highway (US Highway 26) east for approximately 35 miles; stay left at the OR 35 junction to continue on US 26 south toward Bend. At the top of Wapinitia Pass, turn left (east) into Frog Lake Sno-Park, then right (south) to Frog Lake Campground. At the second fork, veer left onto gravel Forest Road 2610 for 0.2 mile to a small parking area on the right (west) side of the road.

ON THE TRAIL

Find the trailhead to Frog Lake Buttes about 25 yards south of the small parking turnout, on the opposite side of the road. The trail immediately starts climbing into silver fir woods, which quickly turns to larger hemlock and Douglas fir forest. The trail tread is good and mostly duffy for easy hiking; groundcover is mossy with patches of bear grass, pearly everlasting, and huckleberry here and there. After just 0.2 mile, the trail exits shady tree cover and contours across a recovering clear-cut overgrown with huckleberry, chinquapin, bear grass, fireweed, and small lodgepole pines and silver fir. Directly

The trail to Frog Lake Buttes is not long, but it's steep.

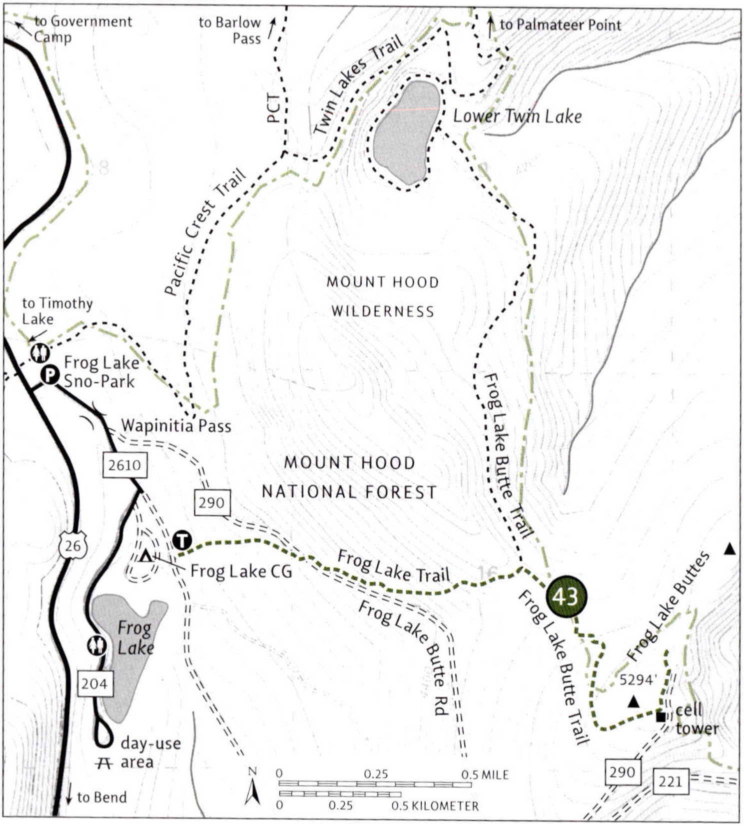

west, you can trace the ridgeline of Blue Box Peak (Hike 44); to the south, you may be able to spy Mount Jefferson on the horizon. At the opposite end of the clear-cut, the trail angles across gravel Frog Lake Butte Road (FR 290) and begins climbing, back under the cover of shady forest.

Now start contouring steeply up the hillside under airy, pleasant forest. Wide gaps in the canopy overhead allow plenty of sunlight to illuminate the abundant display of witch's hair dangling from trunks and limbs. Flora remains fairly scarce, with just a smattering of green on the otherwise woody slope. Around halfway up the hill, at 0.8 mile, the trail bends slightly east and proceeds straight up the steep slope to a signed junction in a wide saddle at 1 mile. Turn right (southeast) onto the Frog Lake Buttes Trail, and quickly resume your climbing as the trail vaults straight up the northwest flank of the lower butte. When you pause to catch your breath, throw a glance in your rearview for a fleeting view down into Barlow Creek valley. About halfway up this next slope, the grade eases and the trail proceeds through a few tight switchbacks before swinging southward and exiting the forest at 1.5 miles.

Now with most of your climbing finished, veer right (southeast) at what appears to be a wide fork and follow a rocky old roadbed into young noble and silver fir woods where abundant lupine, huckleberry, bear grass, and manzanita cover the ground. At 1.6 miles, pass an abandoned jeep road that meets the trail on the right and proceed another 0.2 mile to Frog Lake Butte Road beside a fenced cellular tower. There's nothing to see here, so to make your effort worthwhile, turn left (north) and walk a short distance to a wide, three-way fork in the road. Take the middle fork and continue a little more than 0.1 mile to a roadside campsite (likely strewn with abandoned trash), at 1.9 miles, which offers a decent view of Mount Hood through a gap in the trees. It's not the best panorama, but hey, you sure gave your quads a great workout. Return by the same route, or give your knees a break and walk the curving gravel road back down the hill.

44 Blue Box Peak

RATING/ DIFFICULTY	ROUNDTRIP	ELEV GAIN/ HIGH POINT	SEASON
**/3	7.8 miles	1900 feet/ 4610 feet	June–Oct

Map: Trails Illustrated Mount Hood Wilderness #321; **Permit:** NW Forest Pass for trailhead parking; **Contact:** Clackamas River Ranger District, MHNF; **Notes:** Multiuse trail; be courteous and exercise proper right-of-way; trail is not maintained regularly, so portions may be overgrown; **GPS:** N 45°16.974', W 121°41.008'

In the timeless words of Gandalf the Gray, "There are older and fouler things in the deep places of the world." There is no history or evidence to suggest that Blue Box Peak is haunted, but that is the feeling that seems to emanate from this ridgeline of quiet, old-growth forest, and it may have you jumping at every creak and crack in its shadowy woods.

GETTING THERE

From Sandy, drive Mount Hood Highway (US Highway 26) east for approximately 35 miles; stay left at the OR 35 junction to continue on US 26 south toward Bend. At the top of Wapinitia Pass, turn left (east) into the Frog Lake Sno-Park; the trailhead is located on the north side of the parking area.

ON THE TRAIL

Start at the trailhead at the north end of the parking area, near the outhouse building, and walk the short path to a signed T junction with the Pacific Crest Trail (PCT). You'll find a picnic table and garbage can nearby. Turn left (west) on the PCT and walk on flat, duffy tread under shady mixed conifers among an assortment of ferns and berries. In about 100 yards, the trail spills out onto the shoulder of US 26. Look both ways and cross quickly, picking up the PCT again directly on the other side. The trail plunges into dark hemlock and silver fir woods and proceeds about another 100 yards to a faint junction near a tall signpost. Turn left (south) on the narrow Blue Box Trail to begin your ridgeline traverse.

The trail starts on a gentle grade on woody, rocky, rooty tread that blends easily

Hike the Blue Box Peak trail in autumn when the western larches are glowing gold.

with the sparse groundcover. This requires you to pay a little more attention to your passage in order to stay on course; look for chiseled notches in the trees marking the way. What vegetation you may find is mostly in the form of scrubby huckleberry, rhododendron, pipsissewa, bear grass, and salal; shaggy peat moss cloaks many of the rocks alongside the trail. Start a steady ascent, twisting and turning up the ridgeline. As you're climbing, the trail slides over to the west side of the ridge, where noise from the highway fades away and you can proceed along on a quiet path through the woods. As the grade eventually eases, large sword ferns begin to occupy the hillside, under the cover of big Douglas firs. The walking is easy and the forest is mostly pleasant, though it has the potential of being eerily quiet on windless days. The rare bird or chipmunk chirp can elicit easy starts.

At 0.9 mile, cross a gravel road (Forest Road 220) and begin turning lazily through the woods on soft, duffy tread. The path is confined to the immediate forest, with no outward views to give any impression of where you are, and the surrounding groundcover continues to be a mix of rhododendron, sparse shrubbery, and large tangles of woody debris. Nearing 1.3 miles, dip into a shallow draw filled with jumbles of mossy volcanic boulders. Keep your eyes peeled for goblins lurking in the caves and crevices. Finally, at 1.6 miles, you're given a welcome view of the sky as the trail exits the shadows to cross an old clear-cut on the crest of 4610-foot Blue Box Peak. Proceed across, where overgrown bear grass obscures the rocky trail. While still viewless, this traverse is especially colorful in autumn when the huckleberry is bright red and western larches glow in golden hues.

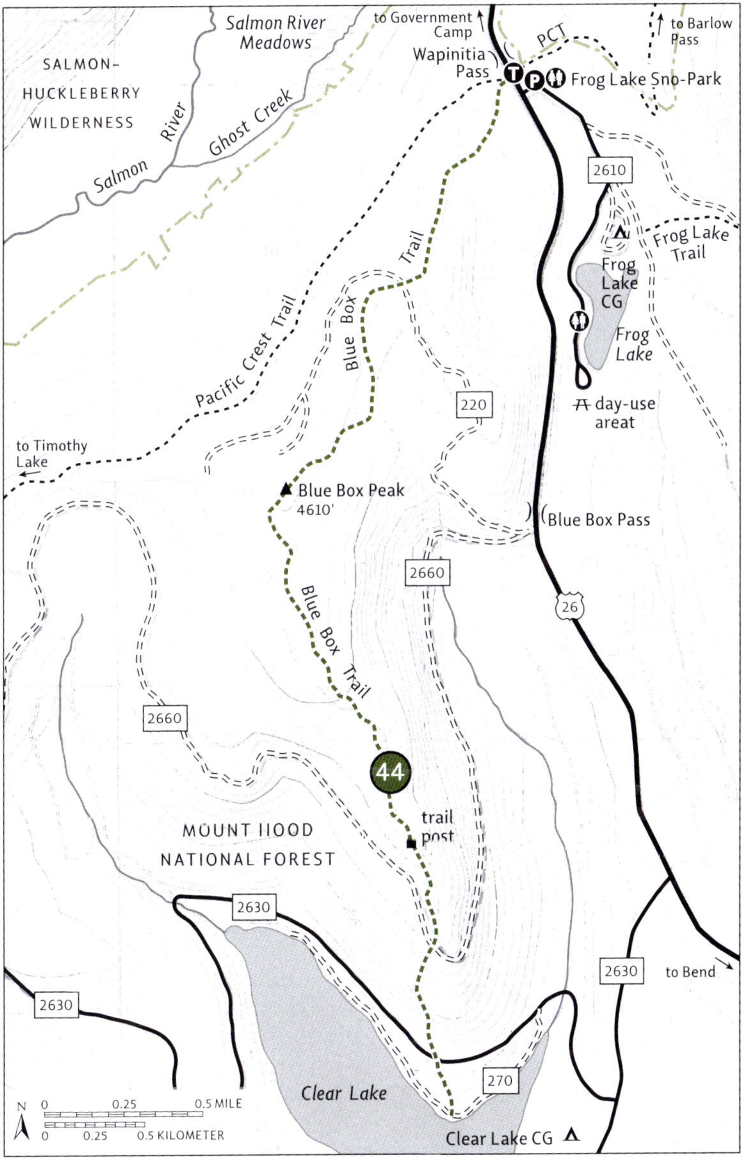
Salmon River Meadows
to Government Camp
to Barlow Pass
SALMON-HUCKLEBERRY WILDERNESS
Wapinitia Pass
PCT
Frog Lake Sno-Park
Salmon River
Ghost Creek
2610
Frog Lake Trail
Frog Lake CG
Frog Lake
Pacific Crest Trail
Blue Box Trail
220
day-use area
to Timothy Lake
Blue Box Peak
4610'
Blue Box Pass
2660
26
Blue Box Trail
2660
44
trail post
MOUNT HOOD NATIONAL FOREST
2630
2630
to Bend
2630
270
Clear Lake
Clear Lake CG
0 0.25 0.5 MILE
0 0.25 0.5 KILOMETER
N

From here, it's all downhill—at least until the return trip. The trail reenters shady forest, now mixed with Douglas firs, vine maple, and gobs of huckleberries. Pay close attention to the trail, as markings are few and the path becomes faint in places. The farther down you go, the more the grade increases. At 3 miles, look for a wooden post marking where the trail descends a rocky chute, after which it twists down through a tunnel-like passage of overgrown vine maple, then crosses another gravel road (FR 2660) at 3.3 miles. The trail now commences a steep descent toward Clear Lake, which you may get a slight glimpse of through some impressively large Douglas firs. The descent eases a bit at 3.7 miles, where you cross a worn paved road (FR 2630), then continue down past a couple of primitive campsites to end at a rough dirt road at 3.9 miles.

To access the lakeshore, turn left (east) for about 20 yards to another dirt road that descends right (south) to the lake, which is now in clear view. Take note of where you're exiting the woods to find your way back, then proceed out onto the rocky plain. A small cluster of trees near the shoreline makes a nice place to drop your gear and break for a snack or lunch. The view across the lake is fairly nice and serene, with 4092-foot Basin Point to the west and 4454-foot Clear Lake Butte to the south. If you're thinking about a refreshing dip in the lake, walk the shoreline north a little ways to where it's less mucky. When you're ready for the return trip, just retrace your steps back to the trail and repeat your trek over Blue Box Peak in reverse.

ORIGIN STORIES: BLUE BOX PASS
According to the book *Oregon Geographic Names*, Blue Box Pass was named for a blue box located on this hill between Frog Lake and Clear Lake. The box contained a USFS telephone, and it was used as a reference to mark the location of the old Clackamas Lake Road.

45 Bonney Butte

RATING/ DIFFICULTY	ROUNDTRIP	ELEV GAIN/ HIGH POINT	SEASON
****/3	5.2 miles	1840 feet/ 5580 feet	July–Oct

Map: Trails Illustrated Mount Hood Wilderness #321; **Permit:** None; **Contact:** Hood River Ranger District, MHNF; **Notes:** Bring binoculars for bird watching from the summit; **GPS:** N 45°14.748', W 121°36.174'

Bonney Butte is a subsummit of a long glacial ridge southeast of Mount Hood. Named after a local rancher in the late 1800s, it was the site of a Forest Service fire lookout in the early 1900s for its sweeping vista of Oregon's Cascade Range. More recently, however, Bonney Butte has become an observation site for researchers to monitor birds of prey on their winter migration route. Visit this location in late summer and early fall to spy a variety of hawks, eagles, falcons, merlins, and ospreys making their passage south.

GETTING THERE

From Sandy, drive Mount Hood Highway (US Highway 26) east for approximately 30 miles. Merge right onto OR 35 north toward Hood River and continue another 4.5 miles to White River Sno-Park East. Turn right (south) onto Forest Road 48 for 6.8 miles, then left (east) onto Forest Road 4890 for 0.9 mile to a crossroads with a worn gravel road (Forest Road 220). Park on the shoulder of this crossroads; the trailhead is located on the southeast corner.

ON THE TRAIL

Find the northbound portion of the Bonney Meadows Trail on the northeast corner of the forest road junction, just east of FR 4890 and tucked behind a thicket of alder. The path immediately dives into shady hemlock and fir forest where Oregon grape, bunchberry, pipsissewa, and vanilla leaf sprout here and there. The trail passes a signboard, proceeds through a few short switchbacks, and begins its moderate ascent in a generally northeast direction to contour up the Bonney Creek drainage. At 0.3 mile, the path enters the Badger Creek Wilderness and patches of alder, vine maple, bear grass, and huckleberry join the assortment of mountain flora.

As the trail ascends, views are limited to the surrounding forest, which is pretty, mossy, and green. The trail tread is nice and duffy for mostly easy walking, with just a few short stretches that cross rocky or rooty sections. About a mile up, you may begin to hear the sound of running water. This is Bonney Creek, still well below the trail. Continue upward, where the trail comes alongside the creek channel near 1.5 miles, and little grouse whortleberry lines the trailsides. Just a little farther, at 1.6 miles, exit the woods onto a rough, rocky road (FR 4891). Across the road, the trail continues to Bonney Meadows (see Alternate Route). For the Butte, turn left (north), cross the creek, and start walking the road; stay to the side and be alert for off-road vehicles.

A pleasant stroll around Bonney Meadows is a nice side trip after bagging the butte.

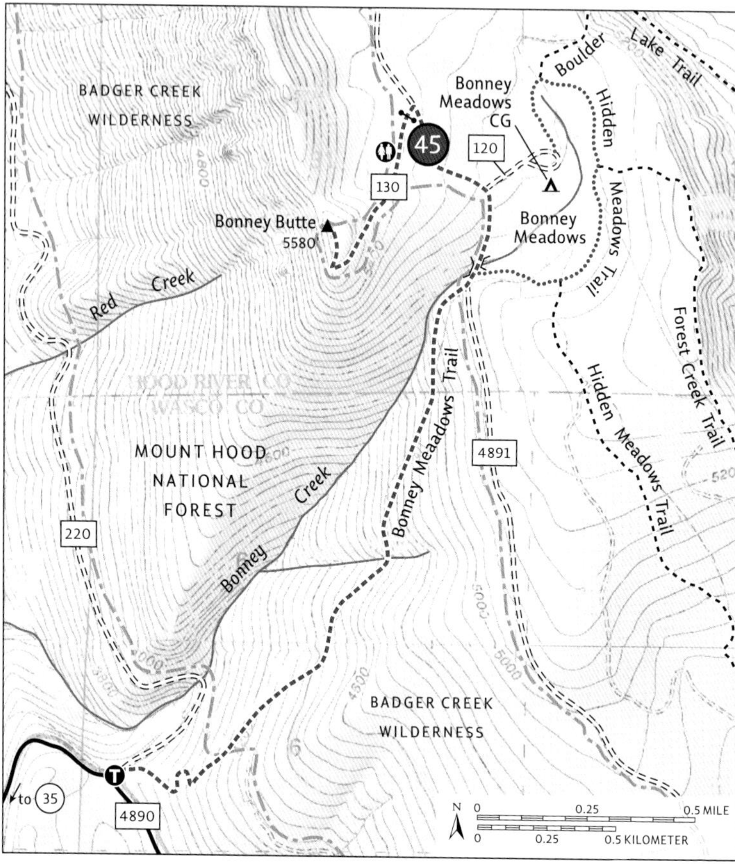

The road continues upward on a moderate grade where lodgepole pines line the way, with large patches of lupine and manzanita underneath. At 1.8 miles, the road to Bonney Meadows Camp forks off to the right (east). Continue heading up the road another 0.3 mile to a fork in the road; turn left (southwest) for the butte. Proceed past the gate (if it's closed, just go around) and start up the flat, uneven road; at 2.2 miles, a vault toilet can be found just right (west) of the trail. The road grade then increases significantly and begins curving around to reach the top. Just before the summit, the views begin to open up, first with a wide look south to central Oregon's high peaks. At 2.6 miles, the road/path ends at the 5580-foot summit of Bonney Butte and you're treated to an all-encompassing 360-degee view.

HAWKWATCH INTERNATIONAL

Since 1994, volunteer teams with Hawkwatch International have taken up temporary residence on Bonney Butte to survey and record the migration habits of hawks and other birds of prey on this portion of the Pacific Coast Flyway. Volunteers are typically on site daily—rain or shine—during the months of September and October, and welcome visitors to hike to the top of the butte and join them in scanning for birds. Some of the species most often observed are sharp-shinned, red-tailed, and Cooper's hawks; bald and golden eagles; merlins; and turkey vultures. Team members are happy to offer environmental education programs that demonstrate how they monitor bird migration trends. Before heading up to Bonney Butte, visit https://hawkwatch.org for more information.

While on top of the butte, check out the site of the fire lookout that used to occupy the summit from 1933 to 1964. There is also a set of interpretive signs that provide information about the types of raptors known to the area and their migration habits. In the months of September and October, you may be able to meet the Hawkwatch International volunteers who monitor raptor migration patterns. They can help you spot and identify birds passing by and sometimes demonstrate tagging and measuring methods. It's a great opportunity to get an up-close look at some beautiful birds of prey. When you're ready, head down the same way you came up, or take the alternate route back (see below) for a change of scenery and a few more views.

Alternate Route

Instead of taking the direct route back, proceed back down FR 4891 to the Bonney Meadows Camp junction; turn left (east) and head for the campground. Where the campground loop begins, veer left to the Boulder Lake Trailhead. Start down the easy path, which gently ascends through a wooded swale and crosses the head of Bonney Creek. Just beyond, turn right (east) on the Hidden Meadows Trail, proceed 0.2 mile through a dark, wooded tunnel, then fork right again. The path circuits the eastern edge of

Bonney Meadows, where gaps in the trees offer views over the sprawling meadows, with Mount Hood rising above the opposite tree line. After another 0.3 mile, make one more right turn onto the Bonney Meadows Trail and descend to the road. Cross over and head down the same way you came up.

46 Catalpa Lake

RATING/ DIFFICULTY	ROUNDTRIP	ELEV GAIN/ HIGH POINT	SEASON
***/1	1.7 miles	290 feet/ 4140 feet	June–Oct

Map: Trails Illustrated Mount Hood Wilderness #321; **Permit:** None; **Contact:** Hood River Ranger District, MHNF; **Notes:** Please pack out your litter, and consider picking up any other you may find to help keep this location clean; **GPS:** N 45°13.116', W 121°37.944'

Named in the 1950s for a type of flowering tree native to the southern and eastern US—but not to the Northwest—Catalpa Lake is a small, forested tarn on the east flank of the Frog Lake Buttes. Visit this secluded pool for plenty of summer flowers and berries, or later in the year for vibrant fall colors.

GETTING THERE

From Sandy, drive Mount Hood Highway (US Highway 26) east for approximately 41 miles; stay left at the OR 35 junction to continue on US 26 south toward Bend. Turn left (northeast) on Cedar Burn Road (Forest Road 43) for 3 miles, then turn left (north) on FR 2610

Ditch the crowds at the more popular destinations with a short hike to secluded Catalpa Lake.

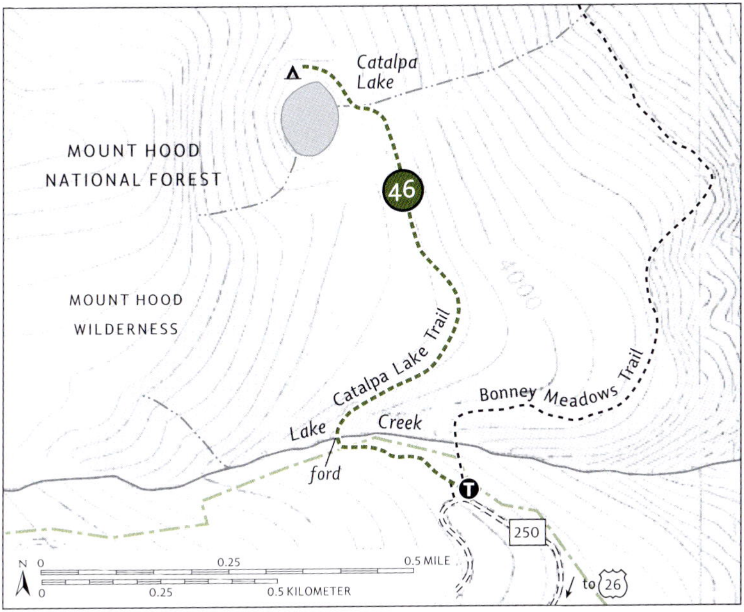

for 0.7 mile. Stay right at a fork to continue straight ahead on gravel FR 250 for 1 more mile, then veer right on an unsigned turnout to the trailhead.

ON THE TRAIL

From the signboard at the trailhead at the back of the narrow parking area, choose the unsigned left fork, which heads west on old gravel roadbed. The right fork that drops into the trees is the west end of the Bonney Meadows Trail, which climbs 5.5 miles to the Bonney Meadows and campground (Hike 45). Proceed along a wide, rocky path lined with silver firs, huckleberry, bear grass, and rhododendron for a short spell. The path eventually narrows to regular trail, enters the Mount Hood Wilderness, and drops down to Green Lake Creek. There's no bridge here, so splash or rock-hop across and begin contouring up out of the drainage on the other side, now on nice, duffy trail lined with plenty of Oregon grape.

The trail curves north and levels to a gently undulating track in pleasant, mossy forest, where large shrubs of mountain rhododendron bloom with clusters of vibrant pink flowers in early summer. Where the trail reaches a slight crest, near 0.5 mile, a cluster of large western white pines drop their big cones on and around the trail—watch your head! Continue meandering easily forward under big western hemlocks and Douglas firs, with plenty of huckleberry covering the ground. In fall months, you can easily pick out the western larches for their brilliant golden needles. The trail then dips through the lake's shallow drainage channel, passes a twisted pile of downed trees, and comes to the lakeside at about 0.8 mile.

For better lake views and a good place to kick back and enjoy a snack or lunch, continue another 0.1 mile around to the north shore. The trail passes through more dense huckleberry, followed by a wide scree slope where you may hear the "Eeeeepp!" of little pikas. The path ends at a large camp area with a giant fire ring and several log benches. The lake bottom is quite mucky, with a lot of woody debris, so not especially ideal for wading, but you may be able to spot some of the resident rough-skinned newts swimming around the shallow waters. When it's time to go, just retrace your steps back the way you came.

47 Jackpot Meadows

RATING/ DIFFICULTY	ROUNDTRIP	ELEV GAIN/ HIGH POINT	SEASON
*/1	2.6 miles	240 feet/ 3970 feet	June–Oct

Map: Trails Illustrated Mount Hood Wilderness #321; **Permit:** None; **Contact:** Zigzag Ranger District, MHNF; **Notes:** Mosquitoes can be voracious here in early summer; **GPS:** N 45°11.256', W 121°46.056'

The Jackpot Meadows Trail is a remote stretch of forested path that links the Pacific Crest Trail with the Salmon River Trail. Due to its location and

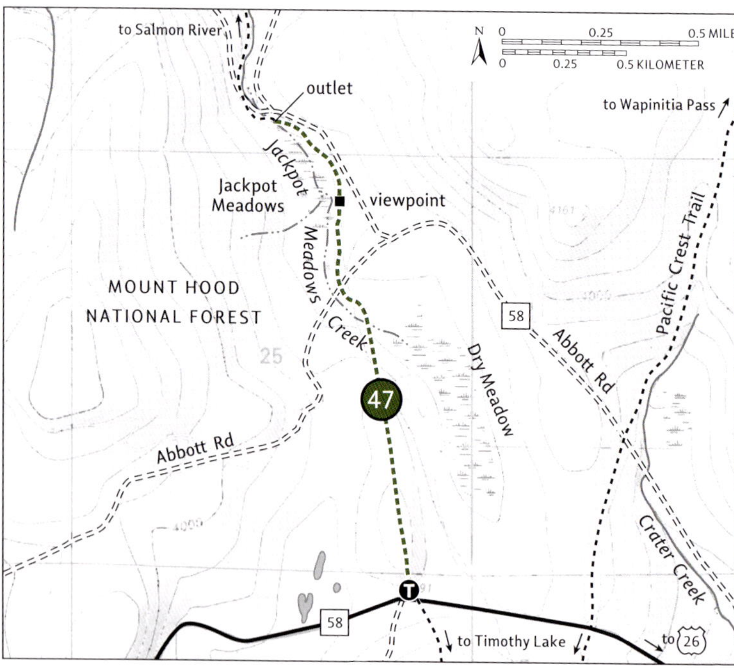

distance, it's more suited to backpackers seeking a secluded journey between Timothy Lake and destinations along the upper Salmon River. This short segment of the trail, accessible by a decent paved road, offers a pleasant walk in quiet woods among summer flowers and berries to the view of a wide mountain meadow.

GETTING THERE

From Sandy, drive Mount Hood Highway (US Highway 26) east for approximately 39 miles; stay left at the OR 35 junction to continue south toward Bend. Turn right on Oregon Skyline Road (Forest Road 42) for 4.1 miles, then right again on paved FR 58 toward Little Crater Lake. Continue 6 miles, staying right

Jackpot Meadows is a remote clearing once used to graze the stock of early Oregon emigrants.

at an unsigned fork after 0.9 mile. Keep your eyes peeled for the Pacific Crest Trail crossing, then proceed another 0.4 mile west to the signed trailhead; find parking nearby on the road shoulder.

ON THE TRAIL

From the roadside trailhead, head north into shady fir and hemlock forest. The local groundcover starts as a mix of woody debris with sparse clumps of huckleberry, whortleberry, and bear grass. The trail proceeds on fairly level grade for easy walking on wide, mostly duffy tread; however, be prepared to scramble over or around fallen trees, as this remote section of trail sees little maintenance. The neighboring clear-cut with its big slash piles can be seen through the trees to the east, so it's best to stay focused straight ahead, or admire your close-in surroundings, which start to include some large rhododendron shrubs.

As you stroll along, the forest starts to get a bit livelier, with sprays of purple lupine, pink pipsissewa, and Oregon grape, which blooms in bright yellow flowers in spring that then turn into tart little berries in summer. More walking, as the trail begins a gentle descent, reveals wild strawberry, bunchberry, and salal as you head deeper into the forest and away from the old logging operation. Shortly past 0.6 mile, a well-worn bootpath leads right (east) to a large campsite. The path then dips through a shallow gully that was once an old logging road and has since been "restored" with woody fill-in. The trail then levels again and exits the forest to cross gravel Abbott Road (FR 58) at 0.8 mile.

Jog a few paces right (east) and pick up the trail again on the north side of the road, following the arrow markers. The path is once again wide and duffy, with a lot of deer and lady fern along the way. At 0.9 mile, cross a wide clearing, which may have been an old road junction at one time and now shows evidence of a camp area; look for another arrow marker pointing the correct way forward (north). As you near the 1-mile mark, the forest starts to brighten to the northeast, suggesting a break in the trees. Look for a bootpath left (west) that leads to the edge of the south end of Jackpot Meadows. The sunny meadow is wide and filled with tall grasses, summer flowers, and shrubs. There aren't any trails into the meadows, so this is about the best view you're going to get.

The path continues along the edge of the meadow, but views are spare through the dense brush and snags. The trail thins as huckleberry and vanilla leaf encroach on the path as it bends west and comes to the rocky outlet channel of Jackpot Meadow Creek, surrounded by thickets of rosy spiraea, at 1.3 miles. To keep the walk short and easy, turn around here as the path forward dives deep into the remote reaches of the Salmon River Canyon. Head back the way you came, enjoying the birdsong and any other flowers you may have missed along the way.

48 Little Crater Lake

RATING/ DIFFICULTY	ROUNDTRIP	ELEV GAIN/ HIGH POINT	SEASON
***/1	0.3 mile	None/ 3240 feet	May–Nov

Map: Trails Illustrated Mount Hood Wilderness #321; **Permit:** NW Forest Pass for trailhead parking; **Contact:** Zigzag Ranger District, MHNF; **Notes:** Swimming is not permitted in Little Crater Lake; in order to preserve the pristine nature of this unique feature, please view the lake from the

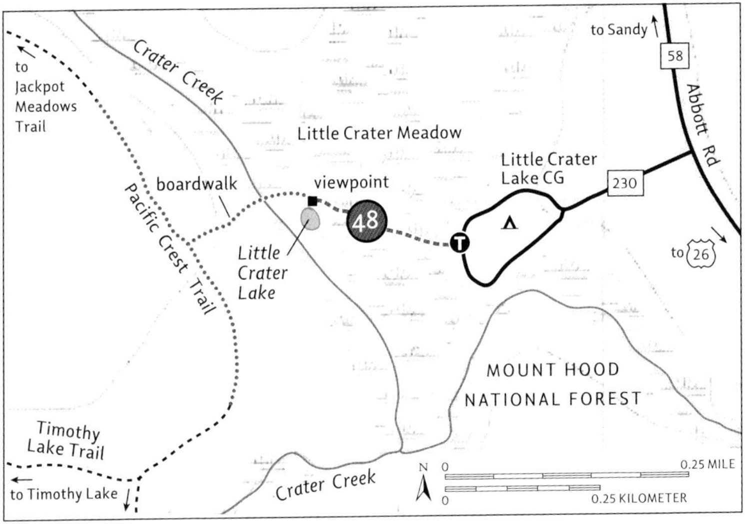

platform, and avoid trampling and degrading the fragile lake edges; do not throw anything into the lake, natural or otherwise; **GPS:** N 45°08.868', W 121°44.862'

More a casual walk than a hike, this short, barrier-free path leads to a viewing platform that lets you peer down into the 45-foot cerulean depths of a unique forest pool. Because the lake is fed from underground springs, it maintains its clarity and a constant thirty-four degrees year-round. The lake is otherwise mostly ringed by shrubbery and mixed conifers. It's definitely worth checking out, or for showing off one of Mount Hood's unique natural features to visiting friends or family.

GETTING THERE

From Sandy, drive Mount Hood Highway (US Highway 26) east for approximately 39 miles; stay left at the OR 35 junction to continue south toward Bend. Turn right on Oregon Skyline Road (Forest Road 42) for 4.1 miles, then right again on Abbott Road (FR 58) for 2.4 miles; stay right at the fork after 0.9 mile. Turn left onto FR 230 into Little Crater Lake Campground, and drive around the camp loop to the parking area and trailhead.

ON THE TRAIL

Start at the well marked trailhead on the west end of the Little Crater Lake Campground loop. The short, flat, paved path heads west for about 800 feet through Little Crater Meadow, a wide clearing of tall grasses and wildflowers. In summer, look for splashes of lupine, arrowleaf groundsel, and extremely poisonous corn lily. The trail ducks through a grove of shady lodgepole pine and spruce, then comes to a sturdy wooden viewing platform at the edge of the sapphire pool. An interpretive sign nearby

Little Crater Lake is a deep blue spring named for its larger national park cousin.

illustrates how the lake formed. The still lake water often perfectly mirrors the surrounding forest, creating dramatic and vivid photographs. After your look, just retrace your steps back to the parking area, or consider a longer outing by continuing onward.

EXTEND YOUR TRIP

With such a short distance to go to look at Little Crater Lake, you'll probably be in the mood to do a little more exploring in the area. This trail is also an access point to the Pacific Crest Trail (PCT), just 0.2 mile farther over a wooden boardwalk and through a wet meadow choked with skunk cabbage. From the PCT junction, you can head north to connect with the Jackpot Meadows Trail (Hike 47) for a 10-mile out-and-back, or south to Timothy Lake, where you can roam either the east or west shorelines or make a day of hiking the entire 12-mile lake loop (Hike 49).

LITTLE CRATER LAKE

Little Crater Lake is not so much a "lake" as it is a deep spring-fed pool. Its water is so pure that its rich, azure color rivals that of its big sister in southern Oregon, thus the complimentary name. Unlike other bodies of water in the Northwest's volcanic Cascades that fill basins and glacial depressions with rain and snowmelt, this pool formed when underground springs forced their way to the surface along a fault line. As the water continued to jet its way upward, it dissolved the surrounding siltstone and enlarged its opening on the surface until it eventually formed this 100-foot-wide pool.

49 Timothy Lake Loop

RATING/ DIFFICULTY	ROUNDTRIP	ELEV GAIN/ HIGH POINT	SEASON
****/3	12.4 miles	660 feet/ 3340 feet	May–Nov

Map: Trails Illustrated Mount Hood Wilderness #321; **Permit:** NW Forest Pass for trailhead parking; **Contact:** Zigzag Ranger District, MHNF; **Notes:** A portion of this loop is open for multiuse; be courteous and exercise proper right-of-way; the Southshore Trail segment can be confusing with its many junctions; for more info on this section, see Hike 51; **GPS:** N 45°08.868', W 121°44.862'

Timothy Lake is the largest lake in the Mount Hood area and offers plenty of outdoor opportunities for hikers, backpackers, campers, paddlers, and more. This loop can be started from several trailheads nearer the lake, but this backdoor approach helps you avoid some of the busy summer crowds. With ample primitive and established campsites all around the lake, you can turn this moderate day hike into an easy overnight backpack.

GETTING THERE

From Sandy, drive Mount Hood Highway (US Highway 26) east for approximately 39 miles; stay left at the OR 35 junction to continue

There are plenty of small coves and beaches to discover on a hike around Timothy Lake.

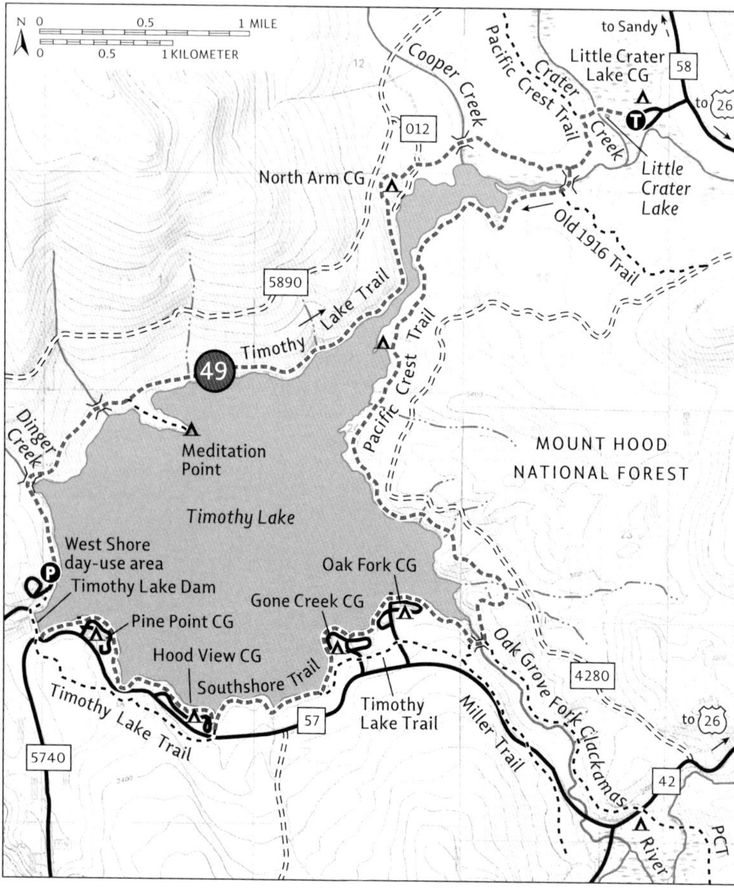

south toward Bend. Turn right on Oregon Skyline Road (Forest Road 42) for 4.1 miles, then right again on Abbott Road (FR 58) for 2.4 miles; for Little Crater Lake, stay right at the fork after 0.9 mile. Turn left onto FR 230 into Little Crater Lake Campground, and drive around the camp loop to the parking area and trailhead.

ON THE TRAIL

From the trailhead at Little Crater Meadow, head west on paved path for 800 feet to the Little Crater Lake viewpoint. Take in the sight of the deep sapphire pool, then continue onward through a marshy area surrounded by skunk cabbage to a wide junction with the Pacific Crest Trail (PCT) at 0.3 mile. Turn left (south) on the PCT and amble along wide, duffy trail under a shady conifer canopy, where large Douglas firs and ponderosa pines display Swiss-cheese-like patterns of woodpecker holes in their bark. Along the trailsides are a lush medley of huckleberry, Oregon grape, vanilla leaf, inside-out flower (duckfoot), wild ginger, mountain strawberry, and bunchberry. At 0.6 mile, the trail forks at a well-signed junction, with the PCT veering off to the left (south) and the Timothy Lake Trail heading off to the right (west). For a counterclockwise loop, take the right fork, saving the PCT for the return.

Heading west on the Timothy Lake Trail, proceed over a short boardwalk through another boggy area, then cross a small bridge over Cooper Creek near 1.2 miles. Just beyond, a side trail branches off left (south) to a view over a large wetlands meadow where the creek empties into the upper branch of Timothy Lake. Continuing onward, the groundcover starts to show pipsissewa, lupine, trillium, and large rhododendron shrubs. Enter the North Arm Campground area at 1.4 miles, where the trail proceeds through; a vault toilet can be found here in case of need. Turning southward, pass a few more campsites and contour the slope above the North Arm channel, where you can access the lake for water and views at a narrow, rocky beach. The trail merges with an old lakeside route at 2.1 miles and proceeds along the west shore of the main portion of Timothy Lake.

The next 1.5 miles are a pleasant walk on gently undulating trail under a mix of hemlock, fir, and vine maple. Numerous side trails branch off on the lake side to designated campsites, many with nice lake views. At 3.6 miles, pass the side trail to Meditation Point (Hike 50), a small wooded peninsula with a handful of nice campsites. The trail then pulls away from the lake for a stretch, contouring the wooded slopeside through a series of dips and rises, then crosses the rocky bed of Dinger Creek on a good bridge at 4.3 miles. After this, the lake comes into view again and the trail levels out for easy walking past several more campsites to the West Shore day-use area trailhead near 4.8 miles. From here, walk the paved shoreline path south, past another restroom and parking area, to the dam road (FR 57) at 5 miles, then turn left (south) and cross the dam.

Once you reach the opposite side of the dam, veer left (east) onto the Southshore Trail. The next few miles are where you're likely to have the most company, as this trail passes the many large, developed campgrounds and day-use areas along the south shore—but also offers plenty of nice gravelly beaches with lake views. Through this segment, you'll also have access to picnic tables, restrooms, water, and trash receptacles. At 6.4 miles, veer left (north) onto the Timothy Lake Trail for a short stretch to keep along the lakeshore, then left (north) again, back onto the Southshore Trail. Near 7.9 miles, the trail passes one more nice beach then turns into the inlet of the Oak Grove Fork Clackamas River. Pass one more junction with the Timothy Lake Trail to cross the river, then climb a rocky slope to connect with the Pacific Crest Trail at 8.3 miles.

Back on the PCT, turn left (north) to leave the crowds behind and head into fir and hemlock forest adorned with a mix of woody debris and bunches of huckleberry, bear grass, vine maple, and rhododendron. Soon you will find numerous side trails breaking off the PCT to secluded campsites near the lakeshore or on the hillside above. At 10.2 miles pass a small, half-moon-shaped bay with a nice campsite, then climb away from the lakeshore to proceed along the east side of the North Arm, where the corridor gets closed in amid scraggly forest for a spell. The trail then crosses several springs and skirts the wide, wet meadow at the head of Timothy Lake before passing the Old 1916 Trail (mountain biking route) and crossing Crater Creek on a wide bridge at 11.7 miles. Continue 0.1 mile farther to close the loop at the big junction where you started, then backtrack the last 0.6 mile back past Little Crater Lake to your starting point at the Little Crater Meadow trailhead.

50 Meditation Point

RATING/ DIFFICULTY	ROUNDTRIP	ELEV GAIN/ HIGH POINT	SEASON
***/1	2.8 miles	290 feet/ 3320 feet	May–Nov

Map: Trails Illustrated Mount Hood Wilderness #321; **Permit:** NW Forest Pass or Timothy Lake day-use fee for trailhead parking; **Contact:** Zigzag Ranger District, MHNF; **Notes:** Multiuse trail; be courteous and exercise proper right-of-way; **GPS:** N 45°07.032', W 121°48.264'

This bite-size portion of the Timothy Lake Loop (Hike 49) leads to a remote camp area on a forested peninsula. Here, you can enjoy nice lake views and easy water access, away from the more crowded south shore locations. With the relatively short mileage and minimal elevation gain, this is an ideal hike for taking Fido for a walk or for those with little ones in tow.

GETTING THERE

From Sandy, drive Mount Hood Highway (US Highway 26) east for approximately 39 miles; stay left at the OR 35 junction to continue south toward Bend. Turn right on Oregon Skyline Road (Forest Road 42) for 8.3 miles, then right on FR 57 for 3.6 miles to the Timothy Lake Dam. Cross the dam and turn right into the West Shore day-use area; proceed 0.2 mile to the parking area and trailhead.

ON THE TRAIL

Start from the trailhead at the north end of the West Shore day-use area. Here you'll find a large map board and a permit kiosk for backcountry camping at any of the designated sites along the lakeshore. Nearby is a small gravelly beach with picnic tables and good lake access. The trail plunges into mixed conifer woods, where an abundance of berry shrubs, rhododendrons, and ferns accompany a selection of forest wildflowers. Here and there you're offered peeks of the lake through the leafy canopy as you stroll along on wide, duffy trail. Along the way, you'll pass several designated campsites near the lakeshore. These are a nice alternative to the busy, crowded campgrounds—with more solitude—if you're willing to pack your gear in a little ways.

At 0.5 mile, cross the rocky gully of Dinger Creek on a long wooden bridge. The banks of the creek are overflowing with vine maple, thimbleberry, and lady fern. In fall months, all this vine maple turns vibrant shades of red, orange, and yellow, which creates a striking contrast against the surrounding greenery. Just below, the creek empties into Timothy Lake in a shallow cove. Once across the bridge, veer away from the lake and make a short, gentle incline that

Pack along your yoga mat and relax under big, scenic skies at Meditation Point.

contours over a minor ridge. Look for bright white trilliums and pink rhododendrons through here in early summer. Later in the season, you're likely to find columbines, wood violets, Columbia windflowers, and bunchberries. At 0.7 mile, you've reached the crest to begin the gentle descent into the next drainage.

Cross another bridge at 1 mile over a seasonal creek, then go through an unmarked junction where a side trail breaks off left (west) to an old logging road. Shortly past, come to the signed junction with the Meditation Point Trail at 1.1 miles. Turn right (east) on this spur and proceed out onto the wooded peninsula. After a short distance, you'll come to the first of the campsites, then to a vault outhouse. At the end of the peninsula, at 1.4 miles, is the largest campsite. Here you can head down to the water for a look at the lake or a refreshing dip. If the campsite is occupied, be courteous of its residents and use discretion when making your way down to the lakeshore. Once you've enjoyed your time by the lake, just turn around and retrace your steps back to your starting point.

EXTEND YOUR TRIP

Of course, you don't have to stop at Meditation Point if you've got the itch to keep going. Continuing north on the Timothy Lake Trail leads to more backcountry camps, more lake views, and eventually up Timothy Lake's North Arm, which continues on to a junction with the Pacific Crest Trail for a total of 4.1 miles (one way). Some other points of interest along the way are the North Arm Campground at 3.4 miles, and the Cooper Creek wetland meadows at 3.6 miles.

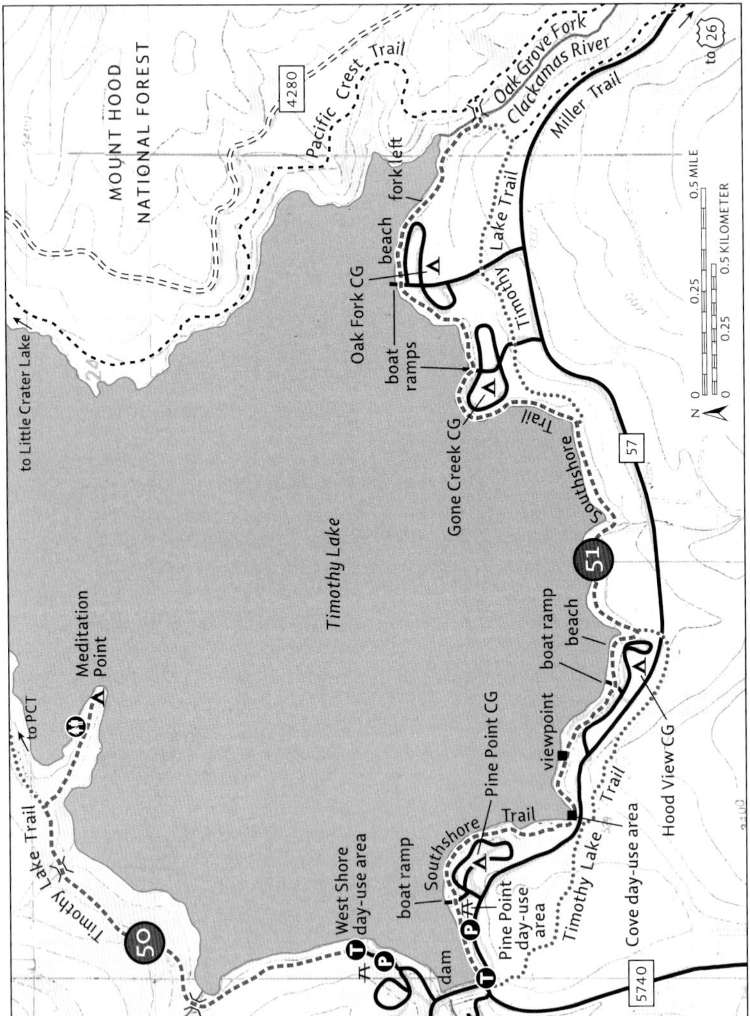
MOUNT HOOD
NATIONAL FOREST
Timothy Lake
to Little Crater Lake
Meditation Point
to PCT
Timothy Lake Trail
Dinger Creek
Pacific Crest Trail
4280
Oak Grove Fork
Clackamas River
Miller Trail
to 26
fork left
beach
Oak Fork CG
boat ramps
Timothy Lake Trail
Gone Creek CG
Southshore Trail
57
boat ramp
beach
viewpoint
Hood View CG
Pine Point CG
Southshore Trail
Timothy Lake Trail
Cove day-use area
boat ramp
West Shore day-use area
Pine Point day-use area
dam
5740
5810
Oak Grove Fork
Clackamas River
0
0.25
0.5 MILE
0.5 KILOMETER
N
50
51

51 Southshore Trail

RATING/ DIFFICULTY	ROUNDTRIP	ELEV GAIN/ HIGH POINT	SEASON
***/2	6 miles	250 feet/ 3250 feet	May–Nov

Map: Trails Illustrated Mount Hood Wilderness #321; **Permit:** NW Forest Pass or Timothy Lake day-use fee for trailhead parking; **Contact:** Zigzag Ranger District, MHNF; **Notes:** Multiuse trail; be courteous and exercise proper right-of-way etiquette; **GPS:** N 45°06.780', W 121°48.300'

Take a walk along the scenic shoreline of Mount Hood's largest lake. Mixing paved walkways, graded paths, and dirt trails, this nearly flat stroll offers plenty of lake and mountain views, in addition to summer flowers, berries, and opportunities to dip your feet in the water. The best way to enjoy is to pack a picnic lunch and kick back at one of the lakeside picnic areas or rocky beaches. Just don't expect quiet solitude in the summer months when Timothy Lake is bustling with campers, boaters, and outdoor aficionados. If crowds aren't your thing, consider exploring the lake in fall, after the campgrounds have closed and when the lakeside shrubbery and berry bushes are tinted in autumn hues.

GETTING THERE

From Sandy, drive Mount Hood Highway (US Highway 26) east for approximately 39 miles; stay left at the OR 35 junction to continue south toward Bend. Turn right on

Pack a picnic, and maybe your swimsuit, and enjoy a day on the Southshore Trail.

Look and listen for cute little pikas in rocky areas and talus slopes. Photo by Brandon Fralic

Oregon Skyline Road (Forest Road 42) for 8.3 miles, then right on FR 57 for 3.6 miles to the Timothy Lake Dam. Find parking and the trailhead at the Pine Point day-use area, near the south side of the dam.

ON THE TRAIL

Start the Southshore Trail by plunging into a lakeside forest of small, dense conifers for 0.1 mile to the first picnic area and a small boat dock. After this, duck back under tree cover and cross a paved boat ramp at 0.2 mile. Just beyond, proceed through another picnic area with access to a nice beach. Continue around Pine Point, at the margin between the forest and the lakeshore, passing by the Pine Point Campground. Along the trailside you'll find an assortment of mountain strawberry, bunchberry, salmonberry, thimbleberry, rhododendron, and bear grass.

Continue walking on good path to the amphitheater at the Cove day-use area, after which the trail turns to dirt and crosses a small inlet creek as it hooks around the small bay. After bending eastward again, near 0.9 mile, catch your first view of Mount Hood's craggy peak beyond Basin Point and Mud Creek Ridge. Now proceed through the appropriately named Hood View campground, where the path crosses another boat ramp. Veer left to stay along the lakeshore, where the path skirts a small, gravelly beach and then comes to a junction with the Timothy Lake Trail at 1.2 miles. Turn left (north) to stick with the shoreline route. (For a change of scenery, consider this trail for your return trip; see Alternate Route.)

Proceed through a stretch of younger forest, and across another inlet creek in a small cove at 1.6 miles. At 1.8 miles, veer left (north), back onto the Southshore Trail, where you'll get another good view of Mount Hood, after which the path curves around the Gone Creek Campground, and crosses another boat ramp. Immediately following, proceed through the Oak Fork Campground, where a long stretch of narrow beach beckons you to the lakeshore. Near the east end of the beach, at 2.8 miles, veer left (southeast) at an unsigned fork into shady forest brimming with big Douglas firs and abundant bunchberry, vanilla leaf, huckleberry, and Oregon grape. The end of the line comes at the Timothy Lake Trail junction at 3 miles, next to the Oak Grove Fork Clackamas River. Retrace your steps back the way you came, or take the lake trail back for something different.

Alternate Route

Take a more secluded return route on the Timothy Lake Trail. This route is confined to the forest with no views, but it's much quieter than tromping through all the lakefront campgrounds. From the junction at the east end of the Southshore Trail, make a short, steady climb into the forest to a junction with the Miller Trail. Turn right (west) and make a gentle descent under shady conifers back to the Southshore Trail junction west of Gone Creek Campground. Turn left (west) and retrace your steps along the lakeside to pick up the Timothy Lake Trail again near the Hood View Campground. Turn left (south) into the forest and cross FR 57. The route turns westward and parallels the forest road until it descends to the road again near the east end of the dam.

52 Clackamas Lake and Oak Grove Fork

RATING/ DIFFICULTY	ROUNDTRIP	ELEV GAIN/ HIGH POINT	SEASON
***/2	4.4 miles	480 feet/ 3420 feet	May–Nov

Map: Trails Illustrated Mount Hood Wilderness #321; **Permit:** NW Forest Pass for trailhead parking; **Contact:** Zigzag Ranger District, MHNF; **Notes:** Multiuse trail; be courteous and exercise proper right-of-way; **GPS:** N 45°06.108', W 121°44.802'

Cross the Oak Grove Clackamas Fork on a sturdy bridge between Timothy Lake and the PCT.

This loop hike connects portions of the Pacific Crest and Miller Trails into an easy excursion around Clackamas Lake and along a stretch of the Oak Grove Fork Clackamas River. The route remains mostly isolated to the surrounding old- and second-growth forest, where rhododendrons burst with pink and white flowers in the early summer, and vine maples glow in yellows, oranges, and reds in the fall.

GETTING THERE

From Sandy, drive Mount Hood Highway (US Highway 26) east for approximately 39 miles; stay left at the OR 35 junction to continue on US 26 south toward Bend. Turn right on Oregon Skyline Road (Forest Road 42) and continue 8.2 miles to the large roadside parking area at the Pacific Crest Trail crossing.

ON THE TRAIL

Begin your hike under the tall, wooden archway denoting the Pacific Crest Trail (PCT). From this point, it's only 2073 miles south to Mexico and 580 miles north to Canada. This hike doesn't go quite as far. Head south on the PCT into moss-draped fir and hemlock forest on a wide, duffy trail lined with vanilla leaf, twinflower, bunchberry, and pipsissewa. In summer months, bunchberry blooms in pretty white four-petaled flowers, and pipsissewa blossoms with short stalks of little pink buds. At 0.2 mile, pass the Joe Graham Trail and continue south on the PCT to cross the Oak Grove Fork Clackamas River,

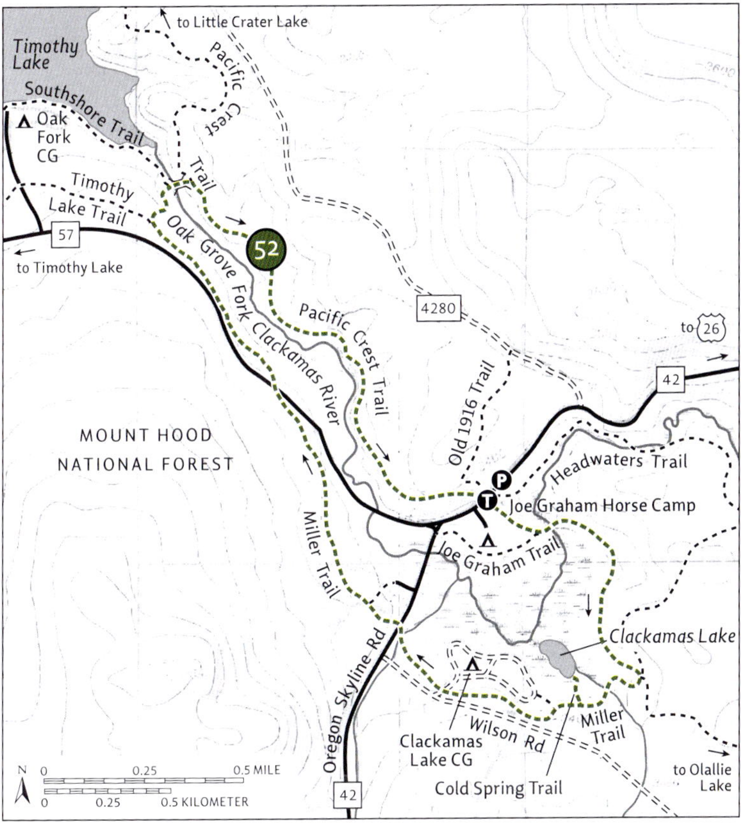

which dribbles through a mossy, grassy gap in the trees.

The trail then bends south and crosses a clearing, giving you a peek into the wide wetlands around Clackamas Lake. The view is brief, then you're back in the trees. Just past 0.7 mile, after bending eastward, come to a wide, well-signed junction. Turn right (south) off the PCT and onto the Miller Trail and follow this path westward, crossing a seasonal creek to the Cold Spring Trail near 0.9 mile. Turn right (north) and proceed 0.1 mile to the edge of the forest and a look at Clackamas Lake and its surrounding wetlands. Look for a variety of birds and waterfowl. After your look, head back to the Miller Trail, turn right (west) and continue your stroll through the forest, paralleling Wilson Road and passing the Clackamas Lake Campground.

When you reach Oregon Skyline Road (FR 42) at 1.7 miles, cross carefully and continue on a northwestward bearing. The trail skirts a white pine plantation, crosses FR 57 at 2.3 miles, and continues by contouring the wooded slope above the Oak Grove Fork. The walking is fairly effortless as the trail undulates along under large, shady old-growth conifers. At 2.9 miles, proceed through a series of trail junctions, turning right (north, east, and south, respectively) at each one. The first is the Timothy Lake Trail, followed just 0.1 mile farther by the Southshore Trail. For a nice look at Timothy Lake and Mount Hood, take this latter trail left (northwest) for 0.2 mile to a narrow, gravelly beach. Continue by descending to the Oak Grove Fork and crossing on a wide wooden bridge, then climb a few switchbacks up a rocky slope adorned with patchy vine maple to meet the PCT once again at 3.1 miles.

Now, closer to Canada but farther from Mexico, turn right (south) and descend to the soggy bank of the Oak Grove Fork Clackamas River, where you'll find gads of water-loving spiraea, hedge nettle, and monkeyflower bursting in pink and yellow summer blooms. The trail parallels the babbling creek for a spell, ascending easily through large swaths of lady fern and alder. Around the 4-mile mark, the trail pulls away from the creekside into drier forest, where vanilla leaf and bear grass take over the landscape once again, and the forest thins to expose more sky overhead. The home stretch comes with a short descent to the side of Oregon Skyline Road, across from the wooden arch where you started, 2073 miles from Mexico and 580 miles from Canada.

Opposite: *Journey high above the timberline into a region of rock and ice on Mount Hood's Cooper Spur Trail (Hike 63).*

mount hood east

Not all those who wander are lost.
—J. R. R. Tolkien

The east side of Mount Hood is where the Cascade Range meets the high plains of central Oregon. Here, in the rain shadow of Oregon's highest peak, among a series of long ridges and deep canyons, you'll find a dazzling combination of mountain scenery and greenery. Go wildflower frolicking in mountain meadows and high prairies, stroll under majestic ponderosas, and scale moraines above some of Oregon's largest glaciers. For leaf-peepers, this is where you'll find stands of oak, maple, and western larch putting on vibrant autumn displays; for bird-watchers, there are plenty of high points to scan for a variety of native and migratory raptors. Running right through the middle of all this is Mount Hood Highway (OR 35), between the city of Hood River in the Columbia River Gorge, and the village of Government Camp, high on Mount Hood. That makes it especially easy to access many of the trails in this region. Of course, all this awesomeness and easy access draws the summer visitors and hiking crowds, turning some of these trails into busy wilderness thoroughfares on holidays and weekends. Save your sanity and visit the most popular trails on weekdays, or in the shoulder seasons, when the air is cool and the trails are quiet. With two wilderness areas to explore—Mount Hood and Badger Creek—you're sure to find a path to get away from it all.

Part of the Mount Hood Meadows ski area, Heather Canyon isn't just for skiing. It's a great hike!

53 Heather Canyon

RATING DIFFICULTY	ROUNDTRIP	ELEV GAIN/ HIGH POINT	SEASON
*****/5	9.6 miles	2130 feet/ 5940 feet	July–Oct

Map: Trails Illustrated Mount Hood Wilderness #321; **Permits:** NW Forest Pass for trailhead parking; self-issue wilderness permit; **Contact:** Hood River Ranger District, MHNF; **GPS:** N 45°19.332', W 121°37.998'

With so many great trails crammed into this one section of Mount Hood, it's easy to overlook this short stretch of the Timberline Trail between the popular Elk Meadows and Umbrella Falls hikes. There are a few challenges along the way, but the payoff comes in the form of some impressive views from high on the mountain's rugged east flank.

GETTING THERE

From Sandy, drive Mount Hood Highway (US Highway 26) east for approximately 30 miles. Merge onto OR 35 north for Hood River and continue 7.8 miles to the Hood River Meadows ski area. Turn left and proceed 0.3 mile to the trailhead parking area.

ON THE TRAIL

Start your loop on the Sahale Falls Trail with a casual stroll north into mossy hemlock and fir forest loaded with huckleberry, lupine, and bear grass. Proceed through several clearings that resemble old, overgrown roads. These are paths within the Hood River Meadows Nordic Park that in the summer season are filled with wildflowers. In just 0.4 mile, the Umbrella Falls Trail branches off to the left (west). This route can be used as one of two options for completing your loop. Continue straight ahead (north), now on the Elk Meadows Trail, to Clark Creek at 0.5 mile, where a sturdy bridge crosses the churning water. Before crossing, collect your self-issue wilderness permit at the kiosk next to the bridge.

Continue cruising through the woods, where pearly everlasting and aster are common, sweet juicy huckleberries are prolific, and a small creek trickles down a wildflower-choked gully. At 1 mile, turn left (northwest) onto the Newton Creek Trail, just shy of where the path drops into the rocky Newton Creek channel (see Extend Your Trip). This begins the loop's big climb, which starts as a mild ascent following the creek upstream. There will be a few places where the trail comes right alongside the creek channel, which offer views all the way up to Mount Hood. When you reach a mucky spring at 2.1 miles, the climbing begins in earnest as the trail proceeds through a few switchbacks to mount an exposed ridgeline covered with manzanita and a few scraggly, weather-beaten pines; Newton Creek is now, suddenly, very far below. Take in the wide view but use caution near the loose, steep edges.

Nearing the top of your climb, the creek trail comes to its end where it meets the Timberline Trail at 2.8 miles. Veer left (northwest) and continue climbing just a little farther until the trail crests the next ridge at 3.3 miles. Now you get a reprieve as the Timberline exits the wilderness area and begins a contouring descent into the head of Heather Canyon. As you descend, the scene begins to open up dramatically, with Mount Hood now high overhead and a pretty, cascading waterfall spilling down the canyon. Keep this

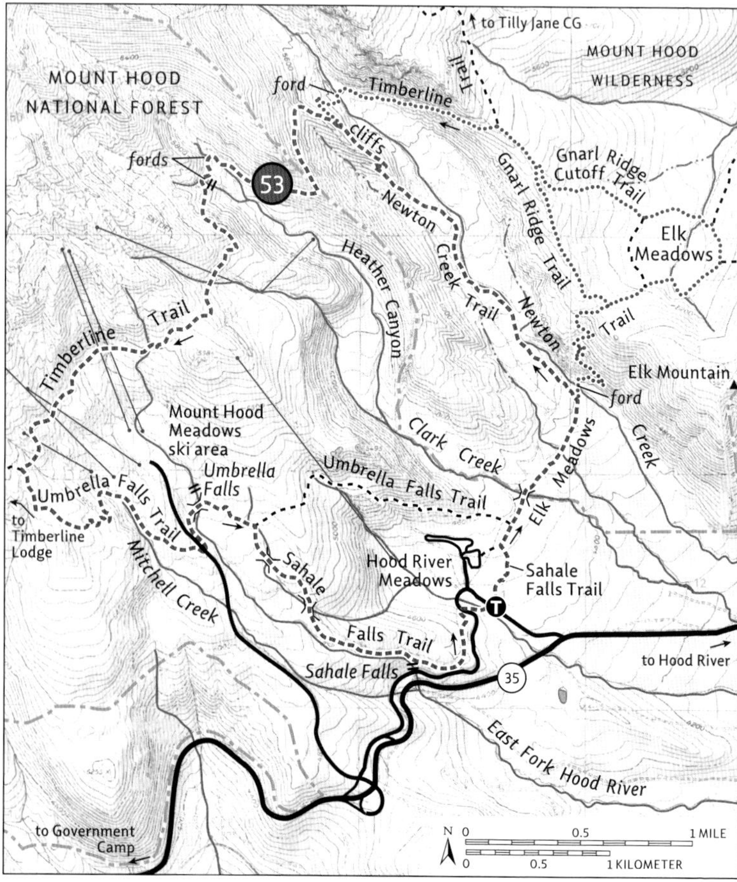

in mind, because soon you'll make a harrowing jump across the top of these falls. Before then, however, the trail bottoms out near the head of Clark Creek, at 3.8 miles, where you'll have to find a safe way across. Once safely across, zigzag up to the brink of the falls at 4.1 miles and do your best Jedi jump to the other side.

The trail then crests the ridge and enters the Mount Hood Meadows ski area, where it continues on a rolling path through alternating wildflower-strewn ski slopes and islands of shady trees. Along the way you'll hop across numerous creeks that feed into the East Fork Hood River, and enjoy plenty of big mountain views. Passing through 6 miles, the Timberline hops over Mitchell Creek, then crosses a gravel maintenance road. Just beyond, at 6.1 miles, turn left (south) onto the Umbrella Falls Trail to begin closing your loop. Follow this meandering path down through pocket meadows, and across Mitchell Creek one more time, until it spills out onto the ski area access road at 7.4 miles. Jog right (southeast) across the road to pick up the trail again on the other side and descend to the shady grotto containing Umbrella Falls.

Cross the bridge below the falls and walk on duffy trail through pleasant woods to the next junction just shy of the 8-mile mark. Now you get to choose how to finish your hike. To the right (south), the Sahale Falls trail descends 1.6 miles into berry- and rhododendron-filled woods, where it follows the upper East Fork Hood River for a spell, with an option to catch a look at pretty Sahale Falls before finishing at your starting point. To the left (northeast), the Umbrella Falls Trail contours back through the ski area for 1.8 miles, crossing several meadowy slopes and trickling creeks, before making a steep descent to the junction you passed shortly after starting your journey; from there, you just backtrack to the trailhead.

EXTEND YOUR TRIP

If you're up for a longer day hike, or even a moderate overnight backpack, you can combine several more trails in the area into an even larger loop, up to 12 miles. The first option comes when you reach the Newton Creek Trail at 1 mile. Instead of turning, continue straight ahead (north) and find a safe place to cross the creek, then switchback up to the next junction at 2 miles. Here you can choose to turn and head up Gnarl Ridge, or continue on a wider loop around Elk Meadows. See Hikes 54 and 55 for more details on these routes. When you reach the junction on the Timberline at the top of the Newton Creek Trail, continue onward using the directions above. Your additional mileage and elevation will vary depending on how much extra you add.

54 Umbrella Falls

RATING/ DIFFICULTY	ROUNDTRIP	ELEV GAIN/ HIGH POINT	SEASON
****/3	3.9 miles	940 feet/ 5270 feet	July–Oct

Map: Trails Illustrated Mount Hood Wilderness #321; **Permit:** NW Forest Pass for trailhead parking; **Contact:** Hood River Ranger District, MHNF; **Notes:** High-use trail; **GPS:** N 45°19.332', W 121°37.998'

Waterfalls are a rarity on Mount Hood. So the fact that you can net two waterfalls on this fairly easy loop hike is a real treat. Add some nice views and plenty of summer wildflowers and you've got the makings of a nice day on the mountain.

GETTING THERE

From Sandy, drive Mount Hood Highway (US Highway 26) east for approximately 30 miles. Merge onto OR 35 north for Hood River and continue 7.8 miles to the Hood River Meadows ski area. Turn left and proceed 0.3 mile to the trailhead parking area.

ON THE TRAIL

From the parking area, cross the road and head southeast into brushy woods on a narrow, 0.1-mile shortcut that dips through a shallow, berry-choked gully. The path rises

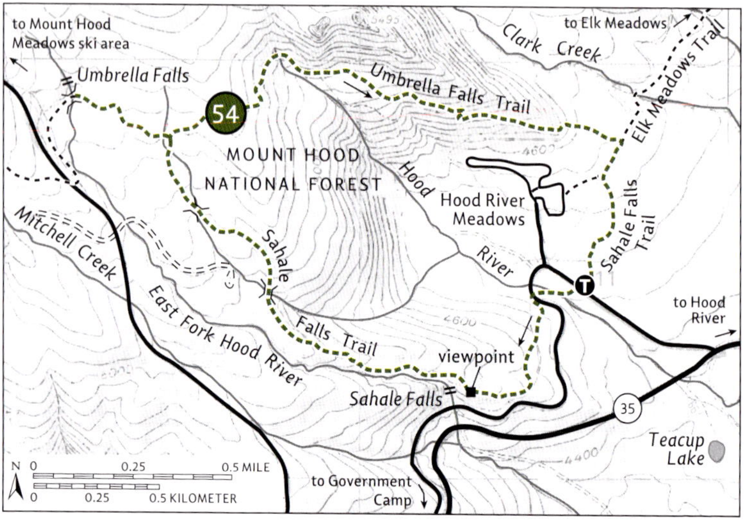

to meet the road again, where the Sahale Falls Trailhead can be found on the opposite side. Continue on a wider, more established trail, ascending a moderate grade under shady hemlock, silver fir, and Douglas fir forest, where ample huckleberry, bear grass, wild strawberry, and vanilla leaf adorn the hillsides. After a quick 0.5 mile, a signed spur trail branches off left (southwest) for a peek at cascading Sahale Falls. (*Sahale* is Chinook jargon for "high.") Take a quick stroll down to the viewpoint for a look at where the East Fork Hood River plunges 78 feet over a rocky precipice. Proceeding past the first viewpoint is not recommended, as the trail gets steep and loose. After your look, backtrack to the main trail.

Continue on the main trail alongside and above the East Fork for a ways, where the sound of cascading water provides a pleasant soundtrack for your hike. A few sparing glimpses of the forested valley below can be spied through the trees. The path eventually bends northward, still ascending, and pulls away from the riverside. In springtime, look for brilliant white trillium along the trail; in summer, these are replaced by pretty purple and blue lupine. At 1.1 and 1.4 miles, the trail crosses Meadows Creek on a couple of sturdy wooden bridges. Following the second bridge, a wide meadow can be spied to the left (west) of the trail. This is the first of many ski runs, where summer months carpet these open spaces with a fireworks show of wildflowers: lupine, paintbrush, aster, pearly everlasting, goldenrod, spiraea, and more.

At 1.6 miles, fork left (west) on the Umbrella Falls Trail and ramble along on a gentle grade through pleasant forest on wide, duffy tread. In no time, you'll begin to hear the sound of cascading water. Hop across one more small creek and arrive at Umbrella Falls at 1.9 miles. Here, the East

Hike through berry-laden woods to Umbrella Falls.

Fork Hood River cascades down a brilliant slope of red and green rock in a pretty, 60-foot curtain; the dense huckleberry and mountain ash shrubs surrounding the falls create a rich and dramatic contrast in colors. Around the falls are several places for sitting and enjoying the view with a snack or picnic lunch under big, shady hemlocks. Below the falls, a wide bridge crosses the river and the trail climbs to the ski resort's main parking area. When you've gotten your fill of the falls, backtrack to the Sahale–Umbrella Falls junction you came through earlier.

At this point, you can return the way you came on the Sahale Trail (what most visitors do), or you can continue on the Umbrella Falls Trail and go for a change of scenery on your way back. The distance is about equal either way you choose. Go for the change and veer left (northeast). The path forward is narrower and brushier than the way you came in—a good indicator that this is the lesser-traveled route—and proceeds across several open ski runs that display a bounty of summer berries and wildflowers. These open areas also offer a few big views of the meadows below and a look up at the impressive Newton Clark Glacier high on Mount Hood's southeast face. After hopping over a few springs and proceeding under the chairlifts, make a steady descent to the junction with the Elk Meadows Trail (Hike 55) at 3.5 miles. Turn right (south) and stroll the final 0.4 mile back to the parking area where you started.

55 Elk Meadows

RATING/ DIFFICULTY	ROUNDTRIP	ELEV GAIN/ HIGH POINT	SEASON
***/3	5.5 miles	1200 feet/ 5270 feet	July–Oct

Map: Trails Illustrated Mount Hood Wilderness #321; **Permits:** NW Forest Pass for trailhead parking; self-issue wilderness permit; **Contact:** Hood River Ranger District, MHNF; **Notes:** This hike requires a potentially challenging river crossing; high-use trail; avoid trampling in the meadows; **GPS:** N 45°19.332', W 121°37.998'

Scattered through the middle flanks of Mount Hood are several relics of a bygone era: backcountry shelters. They were built in the 1930s by the Civilian Conservation Corps and often constructed of local wood and stone. Today, some of these shelters still stand, defying nature and gravity, in various states of disrepair. Some have disappeared altogether. On the east side of Mount Hood, however, one still stands—albeit a bit off-kilter. There, on the edge of a sprawling meadow choked with summer aster, lupine, and gentian, the Elk Meadows backcountry shelter sits quietly under shady conifers, gazing upward at the east face of Oregon's tallest peak. It makes a delightful destination for a picnic on the mountain while you watch the clouds drift by.

GETTING THERE

From Sandy, drive Mount Hood Highway (US Highway 26) east for approximately 30 miles. Merge onto OR 35 north for Hood River and continue 7.8 miles to the Hood River Meadows ski area. Turn left and proceed 0.3 mile to the trailhead parking area.

ON THE TRAIL

Begin your hike on the Sahale Falls Trail by heading north into mossy forest on fairly mild terrain, where huckleberry, lupine, and bear grass line the trailsides. The trail crosses what appear to be old, brushy roads several times, but these are actually branches of the Hanel Loop Trail of the Hood River Meadows Nordic Park. In midsummer, these clearings are usually filled with wildflowers. After a quick 0.4 mile, the Umbrella Falls Trail branches off to the left (west). Continue straight ahead (north), now on the Elk Meadows Trail, to Clark Creek at 0.5 mile, where a sturdy bridge spans the drainage. Obtain your self-issue wilderness permit at the kiosk next to the bridge.

Cross the bridge, permit in pocket, and continue meandering easily through the forest, where summertime pearly everlasting and aster are common. The path circuits a shallow spring gully choked with wildflowers, crosses a small creek, and then comes to a junction with the Newton Creek Trail at 1 mile. Just beyond is Newton Creek, where the trail drops into the rocky drainage and you now have to find safe passage. In early summer, with heavy runoff, this may be more challenging. By late summer it's pretty effortless. Scan up- and downstream for a safe place to cross, then pick up the trail on the other side. Now it's time to gain some elevation.

Start up a series of moderate, sweeping switchbacks along the forested valley wall. In many places, it will be narrow and slick where seeping springs spill down the slope and across the path, nourishing an abundance of wildflowers, including penstemon, paintbrush, columbine, aster, and thimbleberry. As you get higher up the wall, you'll get a few sparing glances across Newton Creek's wide drainage below. Near the top, the grade eases and the trail turns east to a wide junction at 2 miles. Here, the Gnarl Ridge Trail (Hike 56) branches off to the left (west), and the Bluegrass Ridge Trail branches off to the right (east; see Extend Your Trip). Continue straight ahead (northeast), descending to the next junction at 2.2 miles. This begins the Elk Meadows Loop.

Turn right (east) to start a counterclockwise loop around the meadows. You'll be treated to a few peeks of the meadows through the trees to your left. You may also spy a couple of nice meadowside campsites along the way. On the far side of the meadow, veer left through the next two junctions—the first is the brushy Bluegrass Tie Trail; the second is the continuation of the Elk Meadows Trail to Polallie Campground. Stay on the Elk Meadows Loop to a fork at 2.8 miles (unsigned but obvious), veer left to cross a cool creek, then proceed 0.1 mile to the backcountry shelter at the edge of Elk Meadows. A few more campsites can be found in the trees nearby. Find a comfy place to drop your gear in the clearing in front of the shelter, get out your lunch, and enjoy the view of Mount Hood rising above the meadows and forest to the west.

When it's time to get moving again, backtrack to the unsigned junction and turn left (northwest) to continue the loop around the meadows. Back in the trees, there will be a few side trails that entice you to the edge of the meadows for more looks. In late summer, the meadows will often be filled with blue bog gentians. At 3.3 miles, pass the Gnarl Ridge Cutoff to continue curving around the west side of the meadow through berry-filled forest, and return to the beginning of the loop trail. Now turn right (west) and begin your return trip by retracing your steps back down the wall, back across Newton and Clark Creeks, and on to your waiting vehicle.

Views of Mount Hood and Elk Meadows from the Elk Meadows shelter

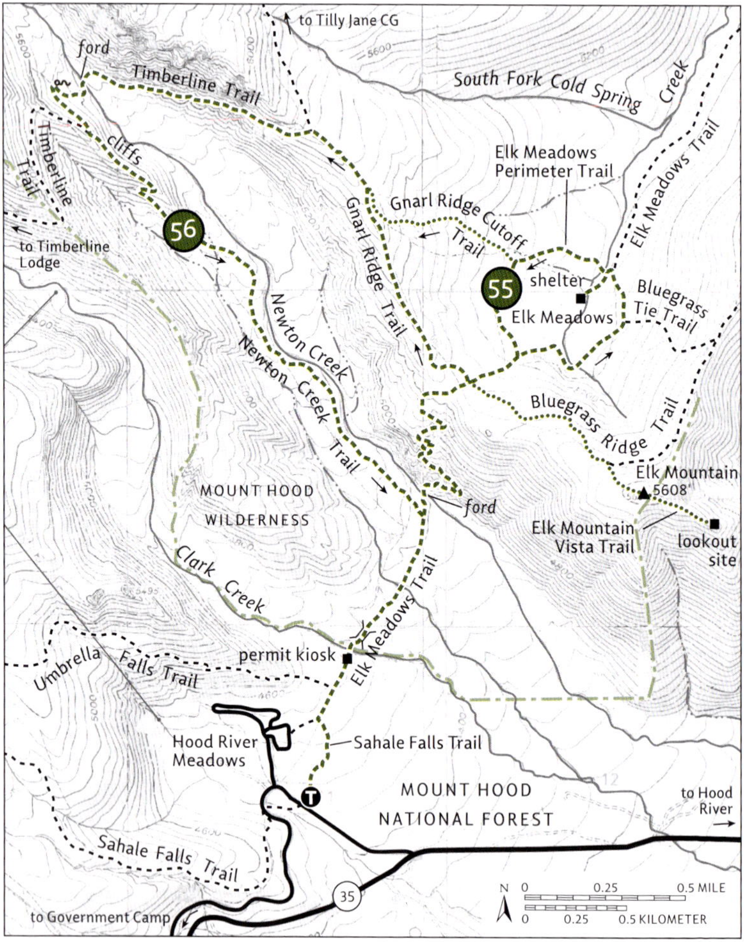

EXTEND YOUR TRIP

Want more? Add a 2-mile round-trip to Elk Mountain lookout. At the four-way junction with the Gnarl Ridge Trail, between the top of the switchbacks and the Elk Meadows Loop, turn east onto the Bluegrass Ridge Trail. The narrow path ascends on a fairly gentle grade through overgrown huckleberry and bear grass to a tree-ringed clearing at 0.7 mile. Just 0.1 mile farther, the Bluegrass Ridge Trail forks off to the left (north) at a signed junction. Proceed straight ahead (east) on the Elk Mountain Vista Trail for another 0.2 mile. The path makes a slight decent along an old, burned ridgeline; look for a view north to Mount Adams through gaps in the matchstick trees. The trail ends at the edge of a 5570-foot bluff, where a fire lookout used to stand on the precipice from the 1920s to the 1940s. The panoramic view takes in Lookout Mountain and Gunsight Butte to the east and as far as Bonney Butte (Hike 45), Mount Jefferson, and the Three Sisters to the south.

56 Gnarl Ridge

RATING/ DIFFICULTY	ROUNDTRIP	ELEV GAIN/ HIGH POINT	SEASON
****/4	6.8 miles	1600 feet/ 5650 feet	July–Oct

Map: Trails Illustrated Mount Hood Wilderness #321; **Permits:** NW Forest Pass for trailhead parking; self-issue wilderness permit; **Contact:** Hood River Ranger District, MHNF; **Notes:** This hike requires two potentially challenging river crossings; may not be suitable for young children; **GPS:** N 45°19.332', W 121°37.998'

Get off the Elk Meadows superhighway and take a hike on the wilder side of Mount Hood. This view-packed lollipop loop tests your trail mettle with two crossings of the rough and rocky Newton Creek basin before tracing a narrow path atop a lofty ridgeline.

GETTING THERE

From Sandy, drive Mount Hood Highway (US Highway 26) east for approximately 30 miles. Merge onto OR 35 north for Hood River and continue 7.8 miles to the Hood River Meadows ski area. Turn left and proceed 0.3 mile to the trailhead parking area.

ON THE TRAIL

This hike begins the same as the Elk Meadows hike (Hike 55). Start on the Sahale Falls Trail and head north into mossy forest on mild terrain amid ample huckleberry, lupine, and bear grass. Cross a few branches of the Hood River Meadows Nordic Park, where in midsummer the clearings are filled with wildflowers. At 0.4 mile, pass the Umbrella Falls Trail and continue to Clark Creek at 0.5 mile. Before crossing the bridge, fill out your self-issue wilderness permit at the kiosk. Cross the bridge and continue on an easy, meandering path through the forest, where summertime pearly everlasting and aster are common. Hop across a small creek, then come to the Newton Creek Trail junction at 1 mile. This is where you begin the loop portion of your hike, so continue ahead another 0.1 mile and drop into Newton Creek's rocky channel.

There is no bridge crossing here, so scout up and down the river for a safe crossing location. In spring and early summer this may be a challenging crossing—or not safe at all. If the water is too high, wide, or fast, consider revisiting this hike later in the season. By late summer it's usually pretty effortless. Pick up the trail on the opposite side and begin a series of moderate switchbacks up the forested valley wall where you're likely to see an abundance of summer penstemon, paintbrush, columbine, aster, and thimbleberry. Several seeping springs usually spill across the path, making it slick and muddy in sections. Near the top, the grade eases and the trail turns east to a wide junction at 2 miles. Turn left (west) onto the Gnarl Ridge Trail and begin a contouring ascent under shady firs and hemlocks.

Up for a challenge? Hike the rugged Gnarl Ridge route above Elk Meadows.

The next junction comes at 2.7 miles, where the Gnarl Ridge Cutoff Trail peels off to the south and descends steeply to the Elk Meadows Loop. Continue upward on soft, sandy trail another 0.2 mile to yet another junction—this one with the Timberline Trail. Now fork left (west) on the Timberline and begin descending the lower, forested flank of Gnarl Ridge. At a gap in the trees, look south for Mount Jefferson; just beyond, see Mount Hood and Newton Clark Glacier looming straight ahead. Continue descending, passing several large volcanic rock outcrops and a wide scree slope—the building blocks that make up Gnarl Ridge. Next, pass a small campsite beside the trail and drop into the wide, rocky upper channel of Newton Creek at 3.7 miles. With plenty of rocks to sit on (and a few more campsites nearby), this makes a fine place for a snack or lunch break with a pretty impressive view.

Now follow a series of cairns (stacked rocks) that lead the way across the channel and down to the water. Once again, you'll have to look for a safe crossing. Identify where the trail continues on the opposite side in case you need to scout up- or downstream so you can get back on track. Once across, follow the trail back up into the trees and cross a chilly spring; right around the bend, that spring bubbles right up out of the ground in a small clearing. The trail then switches back to contour up the ridge to the next junction at 4 miles. With all your climbing done for the day, turn left (southeast) on the Newton Creek Trail and begin cruising downhill. The path proceeds onto an exposed ridgeline, where Newton Creek is now suddenly very far below. Take in the wide view but use caution near the loose, steep edges.

The ridge then widens and continues downward, where manzanita covers the slopesides and a few skeletal, storm-twisted trees cast spindly shadows across the way. The path eventually switches back down the south side of the slope, reenters shady, lupine-filled forest, then dips through a rocky gully where it crosses a mucky spring near 4.7 miles. Here, the trail grade subsides for easy walking and bends to come alongside Newton Creek. Around 5.2 miles, skirt the edge of the channel, where you'll get a few good views up to Mount Hood. Before you know it, at 5.8 miles, you're back at the junction with the Elk Meadows Trail. Turn right (south) and retrace your steps back to your starting point.

EXTEND YOUR TRIP

While you're in the area, you can combine the trails from Hike 55 to take in a nice panorama from Elk Mountain or check out Elk Meadows. From the big junction at the 2-mile mark, start with a side trip to Elk Mountain. This 2-mile out-and-back climbs easily to an old fire lookout site with big views to the east and south.

For the meadows, and an additional 1.2 miles to your journey, continue 0.2 mile northeast to the T junction that begins the Elk Meadows Loop. Turn right to walk the easy path counterclockwise, passing several nice campsites along the way. At 2.8 miles, veer left for 0.1 mile to the Elk Meadows shelter and another nice view.

After your detour, continue around the perimeter trail to the Gnarl Ridge Cutoff Trail at 3.3 miles and veer right. The path climbs through the forest, somewhat steeply at times, to meet the Gnarl Ridge Trail at 3.9 miles. Now, fork right again and proceed on the Gnarl Ridge loop detailed above. (If taking this route, add 1.2 miles to all waypoints going forward.)

57 Gunsight Butte

RATING/ DIFFICULTY	ROUNDTRIP	ELEV GAIN/ HIGH POINT	SEASON
**/4	7.8 miles	2450 feet/ 5916 feet	July–Oct

Map: Trails Illustrated Mount Hood Wilderness #321; **Permit:** None; **Contact:** Hood River Ranger District, MHNF; **Notes:** Multiuse trail popular with mountain bikers; exercise courtesy and share the trail; **GPS:** N 45°20.388', W 121°34.212'

The Gunsight Butte Trail, at the edge of the Badger Creek Wilderness, traverses a high ridgeline east of Mount Hood, between Bennett Pass Road and the Gumjuwac Saddle. Although the butte is heavily forested, with no big views, there are a few points along the way that offer impressive panoramas, interesting rock formations, and plenty of huckleberries that make this a worthwhile outing. This hike description trades a long forest road approach for easy access and a big climb.

GETTING THERE

From Sandy, drive Mount Hood Highway (US Highway 26) east for approximately 30 miles. Merge onto OR 35 north for Hood River and continue for 11 miles. Park on the wide shoulder on the west side of the road, just south of the East Fork Hood River bridge. Find the trailhead across the bridge, on the east side of the road.

ON THE TRAIL

Carefully walk north on the shoulder of the road and cross the bridge over the East Fork Hood River, then cross the highway to the Gumjuwac Trailhead. The trail wastes no time getting down to business and immediately starts switchbacking up the hillside under cover of dense hemlock, fir, and cedar woods. For a few brief moments after

Strange rock formations resembling ancient, medieval ruins adorn the trail to Gunsight Butte.

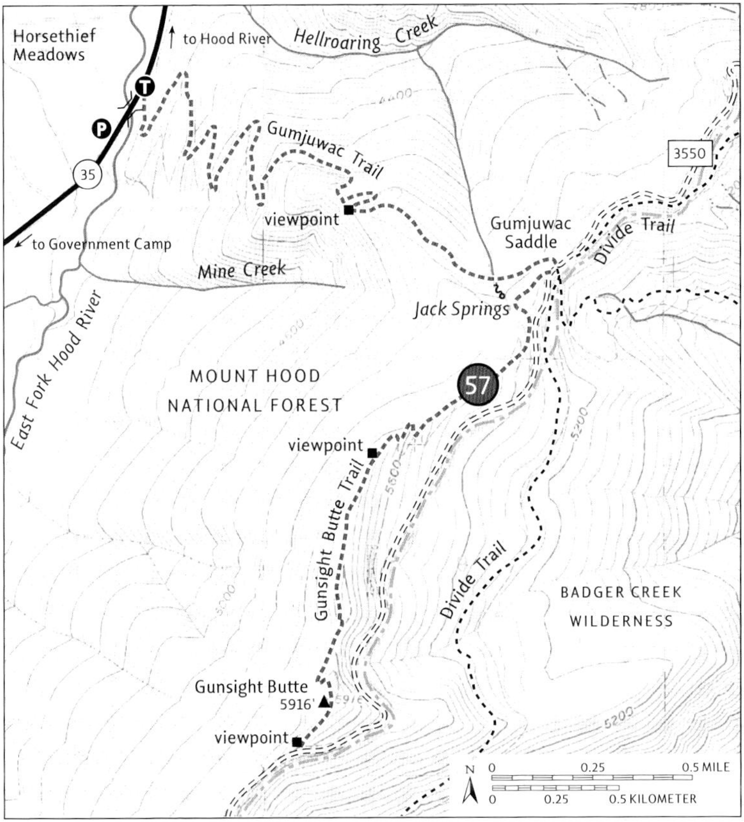

beginning, you'll get a glimpse of the East Fork Hood River below. (On your return, this will signal you're almost done.) The forest then closes in and your view is confined to the trees, the trail, and patches of vanilla leaf, Oregon grape, bunchberry, thimbleberry, twinflower, and pipsissewa here and there. As you gain elevation, look for some strikingly large Douglas firs, western red cedars, and an occasional ponderosa pine. These are the few relics of a much older forest, now mostly gone.

After 1.6 miles of steady switchbacking on comfortable duffy tread, the grade eases and passes a large, rocky pinnacle, which vaguely resembles the ruin of an ancient castle tower—not too dissimilar from those found near Parth Galen. (For *The Lord of the Rings* fans, this is the location of the ruins of Amon Hen, where Frodo and Sam parted ways with the rest of the Fellowship.) The route then exits the trees to circuit a high scree mound, switches back once again, and comes to an impressive viewpoint at 1.8 miles. The panorama takes in the entire east flank of Mount Hood. The silvered slope in the foreground is Huckleberry Ridge (burned in the 2006 Mount Hood Complex Fire); the massive glacier taking center stage on the mountain is Newton Clark; and the long, sloping ridge to the right (north) is Cooper Spur (Hike 63). With several good rocks for sitting, this makes a fine place to break for a snack and enjoy the view.

The route then proceeds east into shady silver fir woods on fairly level trail, where huckleberry and fern decorate the slopeside. At 2.2 miles, Jack Springs bubbles out of the ground into a small pool and streams down the hillside. Just beyond, at 2.3 miles, the trail turns out of the forest and deposits you on the side of Forest Road 3550 at 5520-foot Gumjuwac Saddle. Here, an old sign indicates distances to points north and south, as well as the origin of the name "Gumjuwac"—which is probably not what you would think. Nearby, there's a campsite in a small clearing beside the road, and numerous trails branch off in multiple directions. To the left (northeast), the Divide Trail heads for Lookout Mountain (Hike 58). A couple of others head into the Badger Creek Wilderness. To continue, turn right (south) and find the Gunsight Butte Trail on the right (west) side of the road.

Proceed along the ridgeline through more silver fir and huckleberry, with plenty of bear grass, pearly everlasting, and wild strawberry added to the mix. In fall months, the conifers with the brilliant yellow needles are western larch. The path continues along the ridgeline, through a few switchbacks, and into a section torched by the 2006 Mount Hood Complex Fire. Around 3.1 miles, a wide opening in the tree cover grants a big panorama that sweeps across the northern horizon, taking in Lookout Mountain, Mount Adams, and even Mount Rainier. Enjoy the view, then plunge back into the trees and proceed to the crest of Gunsight Butte at 3.8 miles. Disappointingly, there is no view from the 5916-foot summit, as it is completely forested. As a consolation, continue another 0.1 mile, beginning the descent on the south side, and look for a large scree mound on the right (west) side of the trail. Carefully scramble up the loose slope to the top and enjoy a view west to Mount Hood and south over the Badger Creek Wilderness and Badger Lake far below. When you're ready, return by the same route.

58 Lookout Mountain

RATING/ DIFFICULTY	ROUNDTRIP	ELEV GAIN/ HIGH POINT	SEASON
****/5	10.3 miles	3120 feet/ 6530 feet	July–Oct

Map: Trails Illustrated Mount Hood Wilderness #321; **Permit:** None; **Contact:** Hood River Ranger District, MHNF; **Notes:** For a shorter, less strenuous hike to Lookout Mountain, see Hike 59; **GPS:** N 45°20.388', W 121°34.212'

There are two ways to get to the big views from atop Lookout Mountain. This is the hard way. It starts from an easily accessible trailhead on Mount Hood Highway (OR 35) and makes a steady, 3100-foot ascent to reach the lofty summit. The payoff: more big trees, bright flowers, and sweeping views than you can shake a trekking pole at.

Volcanic pinnacles enhance the view of Mount Hood from the west slope of Lookout Mountain.

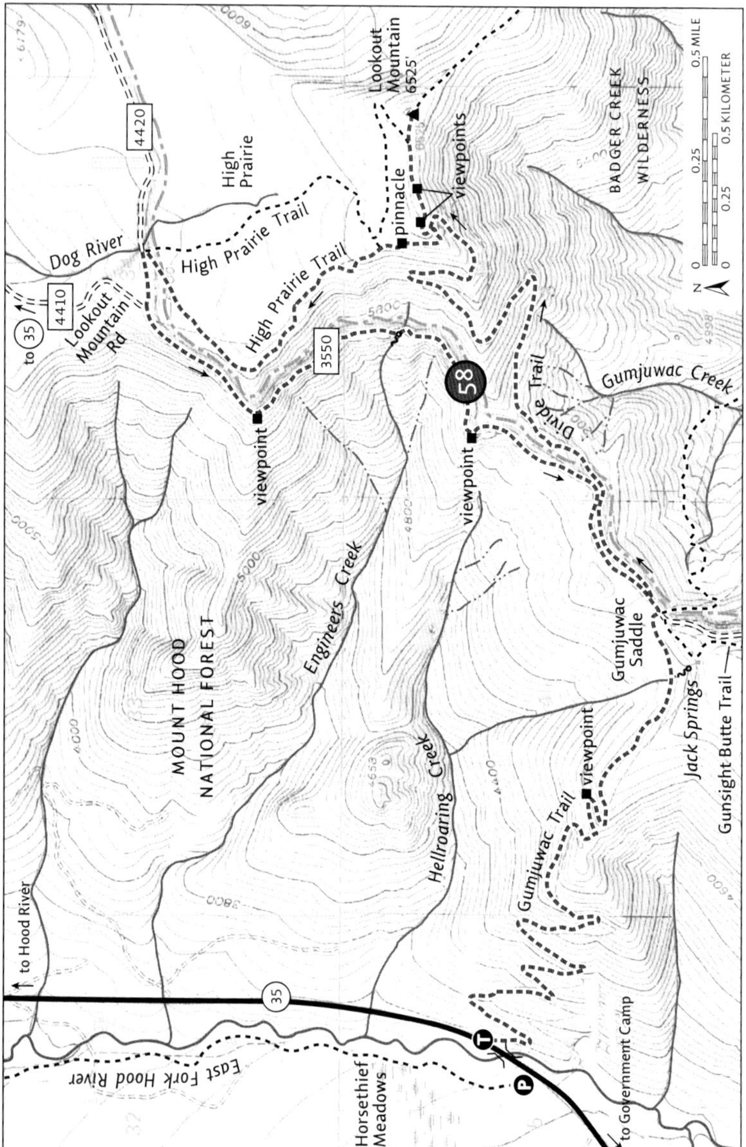

Lookout Mountain 6525'
High Prairie
4420
Dog River
High Prairie Trail
High Prairie Trail
pinnacle
viewpoints
BADGER CREEK WILDERNESS
0 0.25 0.5 MILE
0 0.25 0.5 KILOMETER
N
to 35
4410
Lookout Mountain Rd
3550
58
viewpoint
viewpoint
Divide Trail
Gumjuwac Creek
MOUNT HOOD NATIONAL FOREST
Engineers Creek
Hellroaring Creek
Gumjuwac Saddle
viewpoint
Jack Springs
Gunsight Butte Trail
Gumjuwac Trail
to Hood River
35
East Fork Hood River
Horsethief Meadows
to Government Camp

GETTING THERE

From Sandy, drive Mount Hood Highway (US Highway 26) east for approximately 30 miles. Merge onto OR 35 north for Hood River and continue for 11 miles. Park on the wide shoulder on the west side of the road, just south of the East Fork Hood River bridge. Find the trailhead across the bridge, on the east side of the road.

ON THE TRAIL

Start your workout at Gumjuwac Trailhead, with the same start as the Gunsight Butte hike (Hike 57). Switchback up the hillside amid dense hemlock, fir, and cedar, with plenty of vanilla leaf, Oregon grape, bunchberry, pipsissewa, and vine maple decorating the trailsides. As you gain elevation, look for some strikingly large Douglas firs, western red cedars, and an occasional ponderosa pine. After 1.6 miles of steady switchbacking, the trail grade eases and passes a large, rocky pinnacle. The route then exits the trees to circuit a high scree mound, switches back once again, and comes to an impressive viewpoint at 1.8 miles. The silvered slope in the foreground is Huckleberry Ridge; the massive glacier taking center stage on Mount Hood is Newton Clark; the long, sloping ridge on the right (north) of Hood is Cooper Spur (Hike 63).

Continue east into shady silver fir woods on fairly level trail that contours a fern- and huckleberry-covered slopeside. As the trail curves eastward, it passes Jack Springs at 2.2 miles, then turns out of the forest and comes to the side of Forest Road 3550 at 5520-foot Gumjuwac Saddle at 2.3 miles. Here, an old road sign indicates distances to points north and south, as well as the origin of the name "Gumjuwac." Nearby, there's a campsite in a small clearing beside the road, and numerous trails branch off in multiple directions. To the right (south), the Gunsight Butte Trail heads for its namesake summit and points beyond. A couple of others head into the Badger Creek Wilderness. To resume your ascent to Lookout Mountain, turn left (northeast) and veer off the road to start up the Divide Trail.

The path now begins traversing the lower flanks of Lookout Mountain, where open slopesides of manzanita, skyrocket, penstemon, and yarrow grant views over the Badger Creek Wilderness. Near 3.3 miles, following a wide, ascending contour, cross a small spring that feeds into Gumjuwac Creek, then begin a series of sweeping switchbacks across the crest of the ridge. In and out of the trees, occasionally brushy and overgrown, the trail continues scaling the hillside, where the twisted remains of burned trees mingle with newer forest. Following one more turn, at 4.1 miles, fork right onto the High Prairie Trail and crest the ridge at a dramatic viewpoint that sweeps across much of northern Oregon and southern Washington. Look for Mounts Adams, Rainier, and St. Helens to the north, and Mount Jefferson and the Three Sisters to the south; Mount Hood takes center stage to the west. To bag Lookout Mountain's 6525-foot summit, continue another 0.3 mile east past a few small campsites and more viewpoints, forking right (east) then left (north) to the top.

When you're ready to start the return journey, change up the scenery—and do your knees a favor—by taking a milder route down. Proceed back to the fork just below the summit crest and turn right (west) onto the High Prairie Trail. The path hooks around the west side of the mountain and traverses a gravelly slope of red cinders where a craggy volcanic pinnacle juts out

BADGER CREEK WILDERNESS

Designated in 1984, the Badger Creek Wilderness encompasses nearly 29,000 acres on the east side of the Cascade Range. Natural features range from glaciated valleys to ponderosa forests to oak grasslands. Of the 55 miles of hiking trails within the wilderness, only a handful of the trails make suitable day hikes. Many of the trails here are longer and more remote, requiring overnight backpacks that reach far into the area—ideal for escaping the crowds around Mount Hood.

of the hillside; another spot with a nice view. Then it's back into the trees for a gentle descent through shady woods until the trail turns northeast and crosses several pocket meadows adorned with summer aster, lupine, arnica, and daisies. When you reach the High Prairie Trail junction, at 6 miles, turn left (north), exit to a gravel road (FR 4420), and turn left (west) again. If needed, there's a vault toilet in the trailhead parking area. Now walk the road west to a fork at 6.1 miles and veer left (southwest) on old FR 3550. Follow this rugged road downhill as it contours the lower west flanks of Lookout Mountain. The walking is mostly easy and the old road passes several cool springs and nice viewpoints. At 8 miles, the road levels out at the familiar Gumjuwac Saddle. Now just turn right (west) and switchback back down to the highway to complete your hike.

59 High Prairie Loop

RATING/ DIFFICULTY	ROUNDTRIP	ELEV GAIN/ HIGH POINT	SEASON
****/2	2.5 miles	530 feet/ 6450 feet	July–Oct

Map: Trails Illustrated Mount Hood Wilderness #321; **Permit:** NW Forest Pass for trailhead parking; **Contact:** Hood River Ranger District, MHNF; **Notes:** For a longer, more strenuous hike to Lookout Mountain, see Hike 58; **GPS:** N 45°21.120', W 121°31.866'

There are two ways to reach the fantastic Mount Hood views from atop the Gumjuwac and Divide Trails. One is the grueling 3100-foot ascent from the trailhead on OR 35 via the Gumjuwac and Divide Trails (Hike 58). The other is this much gentler loop trail that starts high before making a casual ascent through flower-laden mountain meadows and pleasant hemlock and fir forest. Since the trail is not long or difficult, pack a picnic and plan to hang out a while.

GETTING THERE

From Sandy, drive Mount Hood Highway (US Highway 26) east for approximately 30 miles. Merge onto OR 35 north for Hood River and continue for 13 miles. Turn right (east) onto Brooks Meadow Road (Forest Road 44) for 3.8 miles, then right again (south) on Lookout Mountain Road (FR 4410). Take this good gravel road 4.6 miles to a fork, then turn left to the trailhead and parking area.

ON THE TRAIL

Start the High Prairie Trail on the south side of FR 4220, opposite the trailhead parking area, with an easy stroll into the Badger Creek Wilderness. Shortly after starting,

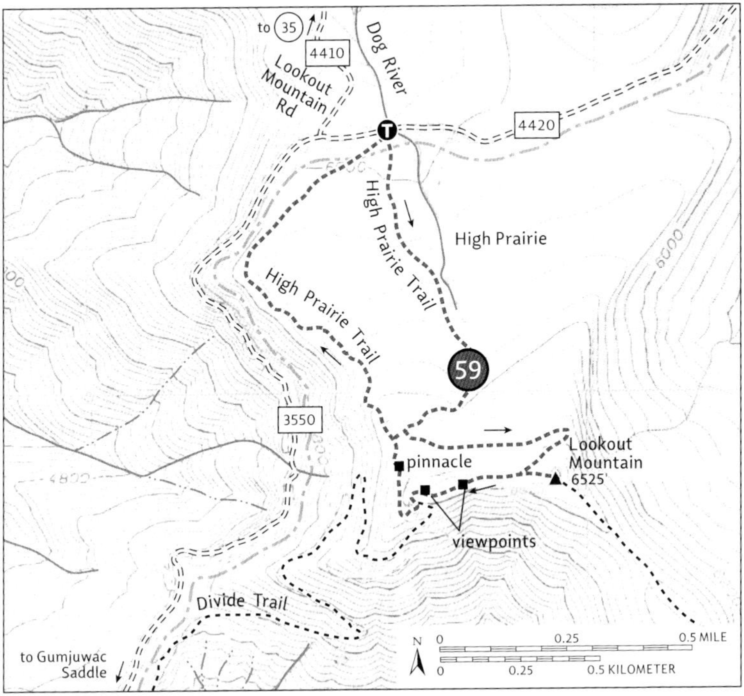

pass the loop junction and continue straight ahead on wide, old roadbed that gently ascends through open meadows of aster, arnica, camas, shooting star, and marsh marigold, where silver and noble firs line the trailsides. Just to the east, out of sight, a spring bubbles up to form the head of Dog River (Hike 64), which flows north and west to empty into the East Fork Hood River. At 0.5 mile, the trail turns and enters shady hemlock and fir forest and begins making a winding ascent of Lookout Mountain's north flank. Still on a fairly gentle grade, look for columbine, lupine, and wild strawberry alongside the trail.

Approaching 0.8 mile, exit the trees into a wide clearing where you make a U-turn to continue upward. Here you will find a well-trod user path that breaks off right (west) at the bend; this hops over a low rise to connect with the opposite side of the loop. Continue following the trail eastward and upward to another U-turn just below Lookout Mountain's summit, after which you'll come to another junction at 1.2 miles. If you're interested in bagging the 6525-foot summit, turn left (east) and proceed 0.1 mile to the tippy-top, where a fire lookout stood until the late 1960s. To continue the loop and score equally impressive views

Clusters of lupine decorate the trailsides on the High Prairie Loop.

without a detour, turn right (west) and walk the ridgeline 0.2 mile through a rock garden of Jacob's ladder, paintbrush, lupine, penstemon, and stonecrop among gnarled whitebark pines to a rocky outcrop and a grand panorama that sweeps across the horizon. Spy many of central Oregon's peaks to the south, Washington's peaks to the north, and a stellar look at Mount Hood directly west.

After a good, long break at the viewpoint, head a few paces down the south side of the ridge to a junction with the Divide Trail. Turn right (west) to continue the loop, which contours around the west side of the mountain. The path turns north and traverses a gravelly slope of red cinders where a craggy volcanic pinnacle juts out of the hillside; another spot with a nice view. Then it's back into the trees, where a truck-size lava boulder sits beside the trail at 1.6 miles; just past the rock, the cutoff path seen on the way up branches off to the right (east). Now commence a steady descent under shady Oregon grape and fern-filled woods until the grade eases and turns northeast to cross several pocket meadows adorned with more colorful summer wildflowers. When you reach the end of the loop, turn left (north) to exit back to the parking area.

60 Tamanawas Falls

RATING/ DIFFICULTY	ROUNDTRIP	ELEV GAIN/ HIGH POINT	SEASON
***/2	3.3 miles	820 feet/ 3470 feet	June–Nov

Map: Trails Illustrated Mount Hood Wilderness #321; **Permit:** NW Forest Pass for

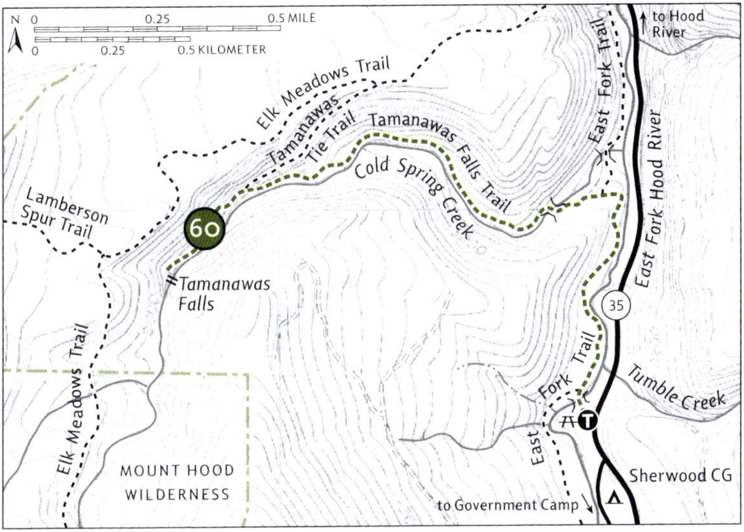

trailhead parking; **Contact:** Hood River Ranger District, MHNF; **Notes:** A new path through the rockfall area was opened in 2018; **GPS:** N 45°23.838', W 121°34.296'

What better way to spend a warm summer day than at a pretty waterfall with good friends? After all, Tamanawas is Chinook jargon for "friendly." Spilling over a precipice of crumbling volcanic basalt, this gushing waterfall fills the back of Cold Spring Creek Canyon with clouds of cool mist, making it an ideal destination for beating the heat. The hike up is equally captivating, through a jungle-like gorge of old-growth trees, thriving ferns, and prolific berry shrubs.

GETTING THERE

From Hood River (I-84, exit 64), drive Mount Hood Highway (OR 35) south for approximately 24 miles to the Tamanawas Trailhead. There is a large parking area on the west side of the road.

ON THE TRAIL

Start your ramble to the falls by dropping down into shady hemlock and Douglas fir forest. The trail proceeds through a picnic area, then crosses a long bridge over the churning East Fork Hood River. On the opposite side, back under shady trees, come to a T junction with the East Fork Trail (Hike 61). Turn right and follow this wide, dusty path as it winds through the trees on gently rolling terrain. Groundcover is a mix of woody debris and sparse patches of Oregon grape, salal, snowberry, and Solomon's seal. The grade then increases a bit as the trail bends north to contour the hillside above the river. At about 0.5 mile, the trail pops out of the trees atop a high bluff above the river and road. Looking east across the canyon is a high cliff of columnar basalt.

Tamanawas Falls fills the Cold Spring Creek Canyon with a curtain of mist.

Follow the trail through a sharp left (west) turn into the narrow canyon of Cold Spring Creek. As the path begins to descend, the East Fork Trail branches off to the right (north); continue straight ahead (west) on the Tamanawas Falls Trail, which continues descending to the creek, then crosses on a sturdy bridge. On the other side, turn left (west) and follow the creek upstream under big, shady, mossy trees. The trail tread is rough and uneven most of the way from here, with plenty of rocks and roots to navigate, so watch your footing. At 0.9 mile, look for a massive cedar along the riverbank that's had its entire root system exposed, likely from flooding and erosion. The canyon now becomes noticeably greener with an abundance of deer, lady and sword fern, thimbleberry, alder, and vanilla leaf. Just to the left, the creek tumbles down the canyon in pretty steps and small cascades.

The farther up you go, the narrower the canyon gets. Pass by some impressively large Douglas firs and a few ponderosa pines until, at 1.4 miles, the trail exits the trees at the base of a wide rockfall that's sluffed off the high cliff on the north side of the canyon. Follow the path that's been cleared through the jumble and pick the path back up on the other side, where the trail contours high above the river. After reaching a slight crest on the hillside, drop down into a mossy amphitheater, where the trail ends a little past 1.6 miles. At the back of the canyon, Tamanawas Falls plunges 100 feet over the rocky wall and fills the canyon with mist. The cliff walls behind the falls have been eroded away to create a wide cavern behind the falls. At this point, the trail gives way to numerous user paths. Wander at will, but beware going under the falls. There are a few good places near the creek for chilling out and having a snack or picnic. When you're sufficiently refreshed, head back the way you came.

61 East Fork Hood River

RATING/ DIFFICULTY	ONE-WAY	ELEV GAIN/ HIGH POINT	SEASON
**/2	6.2 miles	1270 feet/ 3570 feet	May–Oct

Map: Trails Illustrated Mount Hood Wilderness #321; **Permit:** NW Forest Pass for north trailhead parking; **Contact:** Hood River Ranger District, MHNF; **Notes:** The southern portion of this trail was rerouted in 2019; may not match current topo maps; **GPS:** N 45°25.038', W 121°34.224'

Admit it, there are some days you want to go for a hike, but you just don't want to work very hard. That's when a nice walk along a splashing mountain waterway just sings your tune. You can also use this casual river ramble as a backdoor approach to the popular Tamanawas Falls Trail (Hike 60). This hike describes a north-to-south route, but it can also be done vice versa. A full round-trip is 12.4 miles, but you only need to go as far as you're inclined.

GETTING THERE

From Hood River (I-84, exit 64), drive Mount Hood Highway (OR 35) south for approximately 22 miles to the north end Polallie Trailhead, just past Cooper Spur Road. Find parking on the east side of the road. For the south Robinhood Trailhead, continue another 5.6 miles south on OR 35, cross the East Fork bridge, and turn right (west) on a short dirt road to the trailhead and camp parking area.

ON THE TRAIL

Start the East Fork Trail on the west side of the highway and make a short ascent into shady evergreen and vine maple forest. In less than 0.1 mile, the Elk Meadows Trail branches off to the right (north). If you opt for the longer loop incorporating Tamanawas Falls, this is where you'll come out (see Extend Your Trip). Continue southward, paralleling the highway through a narrow, wooded cleft in the river canyon. With little to see beyond the trail, watch instead for birds and wildflowers as you roll along, contouring the hillside. Around 0.5 mile, the highway and the river switch sides within the canyon and you now get to walk along just upslope of the river.

Continue by contouring around the base of a steep bluff, then dip into a side canyon where Cold Spring Creek—the runoff of Tamanawas Falls—tumbles down to merge with the East Fork. Drop down into the cool, shady gorge, cross the creek, and make a short, steady climb back up the other side to the junction with the Tamanawas Falls Trail at 1 mile. For the longer loop, turn right (west; see Extend Your Trip), otherwise, turn left (east) and make a mild ascent to the edge of the bluff, where you get a decent view of the river, the canyon, and an unusual formation of columnar basalt on the opposite side of the canyon. Now start an easy descent into the trees where the rolling terrain is covered with a mix of woody debris and sparse patches of Oregon grape, rhododendron, salal, and snowberry.

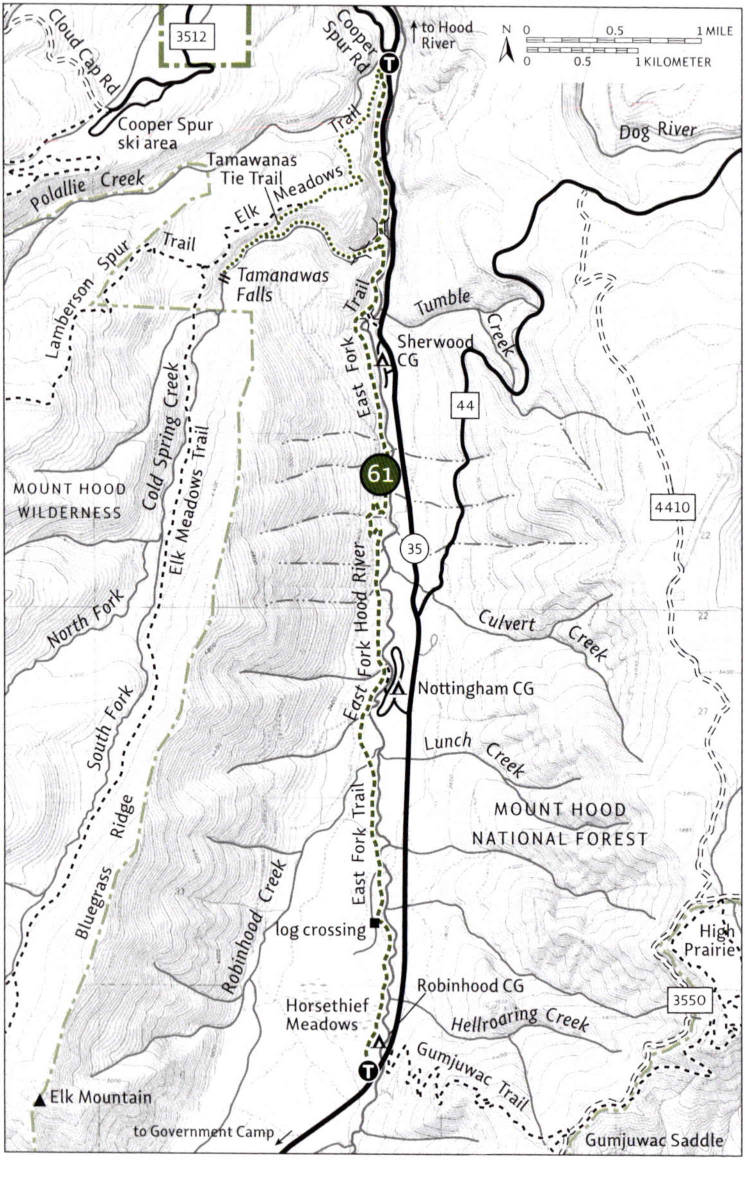
3512
Cloud Cap Rd
Cooper Spur Rd
to Hood River
N
0 0.5 1 MILE
0 0.5 1 KILOMETER
Cooper Spur ski area
Trail
Dog River
Polallie Creek
Tamawanas Tie Trail
Elk Meadows
Elk Trail
Lamberson Spur
Tamanawas Falls
Trail
Tumble Creek
Sherwood CG
East Fork
44
Cold Spring Creek
Elk Meadows Trail
MOUNT HOOD WILDERNESS
61
4410
35
North Fork
Culvert Creek
East Fork Hood River
Nottingham CG
South Fork
Lunch Creek
MOUNT HOOD NATIONAL FOREST
Bluegrass Ridge
East Fork Trail
Robinhood Creek
log crossing
High Prairie
Robinhood CG
3550
Horsethief Meadows
Hellroaring Creek
Gumjuwac Trail
Elk Mountain
to Government Camp
Gumjuwac Saddle

At 1.5 miles, a short spur trail branches off left (south) to cross the East Fork on a long bridge to the Tamanawas Trailhead and picnic area. Fork right (southwest) to continue following the river upstream. The trail contours up the slope, pulling away from the river into shady woods full of bunchberry and vanilla leaf. The walking is fairly effortless on duffy tread as the trail rolls along through pleasant forest. Here and there you'll spot the still-standing remains of ancient Douglas firs. You'll get a few river views as the trail proceeds through a roller-coaster-like series of small dips and climbs, crosses a couple of small creeks, then drops down into a brushy area near the river at 3.8 miles, opposite the Nottingham Campground.

The trail then continues south through a section that was repaired in 2019 following a significant washout. After this, the path flattens out to a barely perceptible incline and snakes easily through the trees, every now and then crossing a sandy plain or skirting the bank of the river. At 5.3 miles, cross a log over a rushing creek in a small gorge, then get a couple more decent river views before the trail winds back into the trees along the fringe of Horsethief Meadows. Cross several boardwalks and short bridges through a boggy area dense with skunk cabbage, waterleaf, and alder, then finish the trail at 6.2 miles where it crosses a small spring and empties into the Robinhood Camp parking area. At this point, just make an about-face and head back the way you came.

Take a casual ramble along the East Fork Hood River.

EXTEND YOUR TRIP

If you decide you're up for more of a challenge, turn onto the Tamanawas Falls Trail either on your way up the East Fork Trail, or back down, as described here. Follow this trail for 0.9 mile up the lush and narrow Cold Spring Canyon, where the creek tumbles down among mosses and giant cedars. At the edge of a large rockfall jumble, turn right (northeast) onto the Tamanawas Tie Trail and contour up the north wall of the gorge. At 1.4 miles, the trail reaches the crest of a wide, forested plateau. Turn right (east) on the Elk Meadows Trail and proceed over the ridgetop to begin a steady descent north on a narrow ridge extension. You may be able to spy a partial view up Polallie Creek Canyon and across to Polallie Ridge (Hike 62). At 2.9 miles, the trail bottoms out where it meets the East Fork Trail. Finish by turning left (north) and dropping back down to the trailhead where you started.

62 Polallie Ridge

RATING/ DIFFICULTY	ROUNDTRIP	ELEV GAIN/ HIGH POINT	SEASON
***/5	5.5 miles	2000 feet/ 5730 feet	July–Oct

Map: Trails Illustrated Mount Hood Wilderness #321; **Permit:** NW Forest Pass for trailhead parking; **Contact:** Hood River Ranger District, MHNF; **Notes:** This trail is not regularly maintained; some routefinding and bushwhacking may be necessary; **GPS:** N 45°24.870', W 121°36.204'

The Polallie Ridge and Tilly Jane trails are popular backcountry ski routes that are equally enjoyable in the summer and fall months for some spectacular mountain views. The trails cross a portion of the 2008 Gnarl Ridge Fire, where the silvered ghosts of a bygone forest still stand among the naturally recovering wilderness.

GETTING THERE

From Hood River (I-84, exit 64), drive Mount Hood Highway (OR 35) south for approximately 22 miles to Cooper Spur Road. Turn right (west) for 2.4 miles to the Cooper Spur Resort, then left (south) on Cloud Cap Road for another mile, following signs for Tilly Jane and Cloud Cap. At the fork for the Cooper Spur ski area, veer right; the trailhead and parking is 0.1 mile beyond the fork.

ON THE TRAIL

Begin your journey by heading up the Tilly Jane Ski Trail, opposite the parking area. The wide path proceeds up a fairly moderate grade under shady woods of hemlock, fir, and cedar. Decorating the trailside is an abundance of vanilla leaf and bunchberry, along with a smattering of deer fern, thimbleberry, wild strawberry, and pipsissewa; to the left (south) and below the trail, Doe Creek trickles down the canyon. The surrounding forest and underbrush are fairly dense, creating an almost imposing and primeval atmosphere. The path crosses a small tributary creek on a sturdy wooden bridge after 0.1 mile, then enters a wet, boggy area at 0.2 mile. Here, the trail proceeds through the muck over a series of old log turnpikes. Many of these boardwalks are in significant disrepair, but it's easy enough to navigate through and continue on.

At 0.7 mile, come to a somewhat confusingly signed junction. To continue on the Pollalie Ridge Trail, turn left (south), cross a shallow gully, and start contouring up the narrow canyon's opposite slope. Almost immediately after turning, veer right at an unmarked fork, following the blue diamond markers that indicate the ski trail. The path ascends easily along the hillside, covered in bear grass and twinflower, to reach the crest of the ridge at another junction at 1 mile. Turn right (west) and enjoy an easy stroll through pleasant woods for a short spell because it's going to get challenging soon enough. Where the forest thins, around 1.1 miles, among a loose cluster of ponderosa pines, the scene changes to a brushy ridgeline where the skeletons of charred trees now loom ahead. In the distance, you get your first look at Mount Hood's east face.

The path now proceeds straight up the ridgeline on moderate to steep grades through dense mountain ash. It may become necessary to bushwhack through some of the more overgrown sections. (This makes it

After your brushy scramble up Polallie Ridge, take a break at the Tilly Jane A-frame.

a good idea to wear long pants on this hike, and why you might want to leave Fido at home.) As you steadily gain elevation along the ridgeline, the scene around you begins to open up more and more. To the north, Mounts Adams and Rainier begin to show their sparkling, glacier-capped peaks; a little farther along, Mount St. Helens reveals its decapitated crown. To the south, the deep Polallie Creek Canyon reveals its wooded slopes marred with barren patches where landslides have occurred. As you're climbing, you're granted short reprieves where the trail reaches incremental crests on flat ridgeline, each showcasing more impressive views of Mount Hood directly ahead. At the third crest, at 2.3 miles, a jumble of rocks and cut tree stumps provide nice resting places to have a snack and enjoy the view. The massive wall of ice seen draped on Mount Hood's face from here is Eliot Glacier, the largest on the mountain.

From this 5490-foot high point, dip through a burned saddle littered with woody debris and carpeted with pearly everlasting. Due to the lack of maintenance on this route, there may be downed trees to navigate or scramble over. Make one more ascent to an unmarked junction at 2.7 miles, at the edge of the burn area, then turn right (northwest) and follow the blue diamond markers into greener, livelier woods. The path curves around the head of a draw and comes to another somewhat-confusing junction at 2.9 miles. At this junction, turn right (east) onto the Tilly Jane Ski Trail and head 0.1 mile to the Tilly Jane A-frame. Constructed in 1939, this structure serves as a ski and hiking

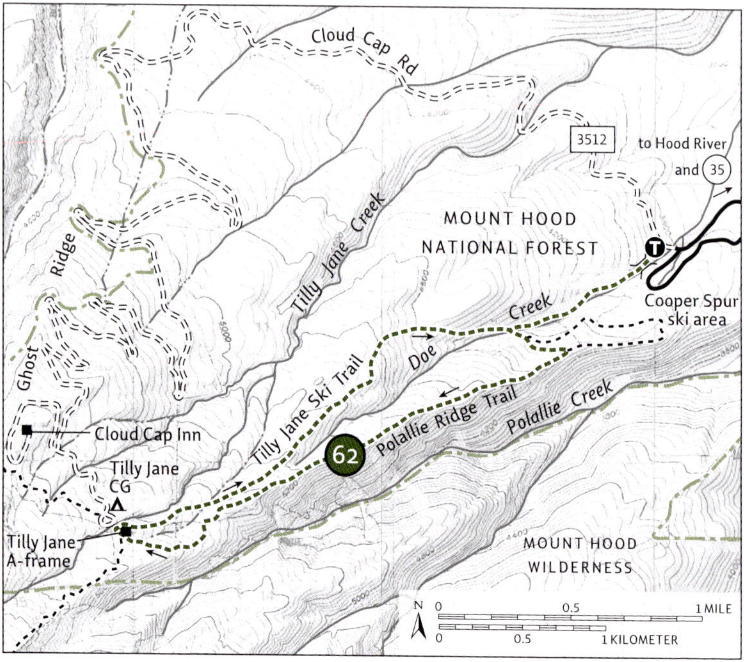

shelter and can be reserved for overnight stays (www.recreation.gov); near the shelter are a picnic area and community fire ring.

Now on the downward side of the loop, follow Tilly Jane's blue diamonds east. The trail descends back into the ghosted forest, where there are still plenty of impressive mountain views through the matchstick trees. Unlike the overgrown shrubbery that dominated Polallie Ridge, the Tilly Jane route is wider and clearer, making for easier, albeit steeper, passage. The recovering slopesides are adorned with an abundance of lupine, huckleberry, bear grass, and wild strawberry. The trail finally drops into greener forest at 4.5 miles, where you make a quick descent to a familiar junction at 4.8 miles. Complete your journey by turning left (east) and retracing your steps back down the hill.

ORIGIN STORIES: POLALLIE

There is some debate on the origin of the name Polallie. In Chinook jargon, *Polallie* means "sandy"—appropriate when describing both Polallie Ridge and Polallie Creek. Some, however, attribute Polallie to the French word *poudre*, translated as "powder." Either way, the meanings are similar and appropriate enough that you can take your pick.

63 Cooper Spur

RATING/ DIFFICULTY	ROUNDTRIP	ELEV GAIN/ HIGH POINT	SEASON
*****/5	6.6 miles	2680 feet/ 8490 feet	Aug–Oct

Map: Trails Illustrated Mount Hood Wilderness #321; **Permits:** NW Forest Pass for trailhead parking; self-issue wilderness permit; **Contact:** Hood River Ranger District, MHNF; **Notes:** This is a strenuous, high-elevation trail that has little water or shade; sun protection, wind jacket, and extra water are highly recommended; alternate trailhead available; **GPS:** N 45°24.150', W 121°39.300'

If you're ready to come face-to-face with Mount Hood, this is the trail you're looking for. Named in the 1880s for David Rose Cooper, who maintained a favorite campsite nearby, the Cooper Spur Trail tops out at nearly 8500 feet. This is the highest established trail on the mountain, reaching far into the alpine zone where there is little shelter from the elements. It's a strenuous slog up loose, sandy switchbacks, where snow may remain long into the summer, but the payoff is one of the most spectacular views you'll get without being a technical mountain climber.

GETTING THERE

From Hood River (I-84, exit 64), drive Mount Hood Highway (OR 35) south for approximately 22 miles to Cooper Spur Road. Turn right (west) for 2.4 miles to the Cooper Spur Resort, then left (south) on Cloud Cap Road for 8.5 miles, following signs for Tilly Jane Campground and Cloud Cap Inn (see sidebar). When you reach the fork at the top, turn right (west) and proceed 1 more mile to the Cloud Cap Trailhead and Campground. For the alternate Tilly Jane Trailhead, turn left (east) and proceed 1 mile to the Tilly Jane Campground at the end of the road.

The Cooper Spur shelter is your last respite before Mount Hood's rugged alpine zone.

CLOUD CAP ROAD AND INN

Cloud Cap Road (Forest Road 3512) is a 9.5-mile, high-elevation road that winds up the east side of Mount Hood, from the Cooper Spur Resort area to the historic Cloud Cap Inn. It also goes to Tilly Jane and Cloud Cap Campgrounds and Trailheads. The first mile of the road is paved, then it turns to narrow washboard dirt and gravel the remainder of the way. There are some rough stretches and several significant dips and potholes, but it is drivable by most passenger vehicles with moderate clearance—however, you may need an alignment job after driving this one. Just take it slow and easy.

Constructed in 1889, the **Cloud Cap Inn** sits atop a 6000-foot-high bluff on the northeast flank of Mount Hood. It was the first resort on the mountain, commissioned by Portland aristocrats William Ladd and Charles Wood and designed by architect William Whidden. The inn served as a luxury getaway for nearly fifty years. In the 1920s, there were even plans to expand the inn and install a tram between Mount Hood Highway and the crest. When the more elaborate Timberline Lodge opened in the 1930s, the inn was no longer able to draw the crowds. It eventually fell into disrepair and closed in 1946. In the 1950s, the Forest Service planned to demolish the inn, but the local Crag Rats rescue group was able to obtain the building to use as a base for rescues and survey operations. While closed to the public, it continues to serve this purpose today.

ON THE TRAIL

Begin your hike at the Cloud Cap Trailhead by proceeding through the camp area to the signed junction of the Timberline and Tilly Jane Trails. To the left (east), the Tilly Jane Trail descends to the Tilly Jane Campground and beyond (Hike 62). To the right (west), the Timberline Trail heads for the north side of Mount Hood, and straight ahead (south) for the east side of the mountain and the Cooper Spur Trail—your destination. It's all up from here, so take a deep breath and head up the Timberline into the Mount Hood Wilderness under a canopy of old-growth hemlock and Douglas and silver firs, where sparse vegetation grows in the sandy soil. In

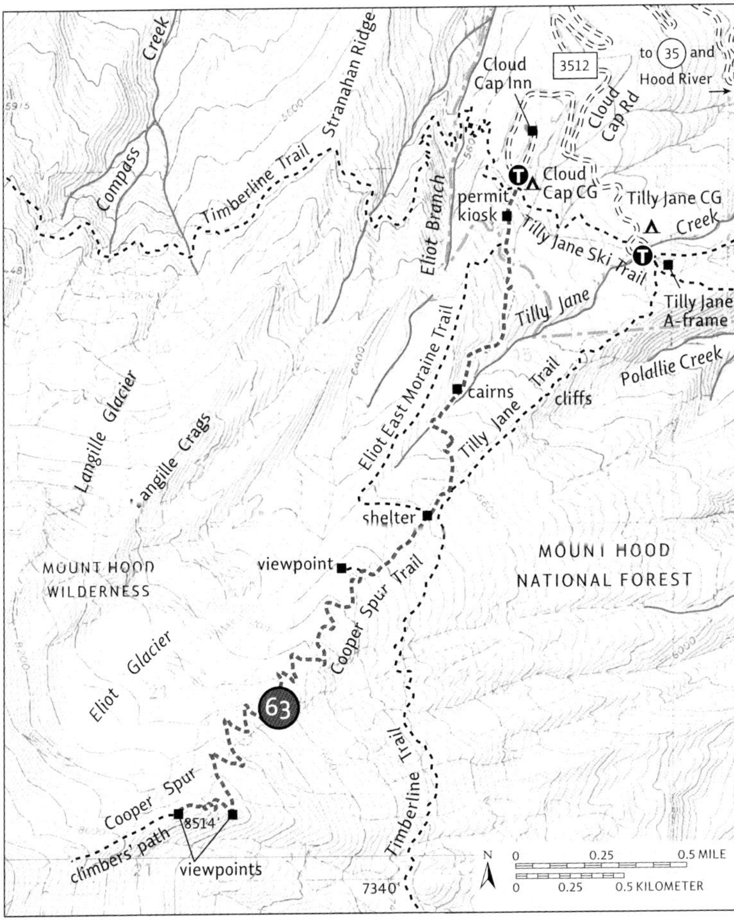

ELIOT GLACIER

Eliot Glacier, on the northeast flank of Mount Hood, is the largest glacier on the mountain. It was named in the late 1800s for Dr. Thomas L. Eliot, a mountaineer and pastor who lived in Portland. Scientists have been observing the Eliot since 1901. Recent measurements show the glacier covering nearly 1.6 square kilometers, with a thickness of up to 90 meters. According to the USGS, at its fullest extent Eliot Glacier may have reached up to 15 kilometers long and would have stretched from Mount Hood's summit all the way to its base. It is estimated that the Eliot has retreated nearly 600 meters in just the last century. The best way to view Eliot Glacier is on the Cooper Spur Trail (Hike 63). From high on this moraine between Eliot and Newton Clark Glaciers, you can get a bird's-eye view over this vast river of serrated, flowing ice. In early 2019, a small plane crashed into Eliot Glacier. The pilot's body was recovered, but pieces of the broken aircraft remain on the glacier.

just 0.1 mile, make a quick stop at the wilderness permit kiosk and fill out your form; drop the slip in the slot and move on.

The trail heads upward into the woods and quickly comes to a signed fork with the Eliot East Moraine Trail; veer left (south) to stay on the Timberline. Here and there you may spy small, primitive campsites tucked back in the trees. These are commonly used by backpackers hiking the full 43-mile Timberline loop. The trail then exits the trees and you cross a wide, sandy slope before bending to come alongside Tilly Jane Creek's wide, shallow gully. Here's your first view of Mount Hood's northeast face. The long, barren ridge leading right up to the mountain is Cooper Spur. From this vantage, it looks dauntingly high and far away. One step at a time. Continue upward, along and into the rocky gully. Cross a small, seasonal spring, after which the trail becomes a little challenging to follow, with numerous footpaths leading off in different directions. Look for large cairns with posts sticking out of them to help lead the way up and out of the channel and into a cluster of weather-beaten white pines on the opposite ridge.

Around the 1-mile mark, climb above the trees and take in a vast panorama over eastern Oregon and southern Washington. This is but a visual appetizer. Continue upward into a vast alpine environment where rocks dominate and a few hearty trees and shrubs cling to a meager existence. At 1.1 miles, the Timberline crosses paths with the Cooper Spur Trail and the Tilly Jane Trail. Turn right (southwest) onto the Cooper Spur Trail and climb another few hundred yards to the Cooper Spur shelter, which rests at an elevation of 6800 feet. Built in the 1930s by the Civilian Conservation Corps, this small stone shelter is one of the few remaining relics of Mount Hood's early mountaineering era. With its newer metal roof and heavy door flap, it can provide decent shelter to hikers caught out in the elements. For day hikers, it makes a nice scenic spot for a lunch stop.

After breaking at the shelter, it's time to put your game face on. The way forward is an unyielding climb up Eliot Glacier's east moraine—pretty much straight up the slope. The grade is only moderate, but the elevation and exposure will make it seem tougher. At 1.5 miles, the switchbacks begin. The first zigs right (west), where a well-worn side trail proceeds to the first of many Eliot Glacier viewpoints. Head on over for a look, but use caution on the loose edges of the moraine. Sprawled out before you is the massive channel that used to hold Eliot Glacier. Covering an area of more than four hundred acres, it is one of the largest glaciers in Oregon (see sidebar). After your look, commence zigging and zagging ever upward. At many of the zigs, you're given better and closer looks at the huge wall of ice cascading down the mountainside.

You may be tempted to call it good at any of these viewpoints on your way up, but your persistence will pay off as you reach the trail zag at 3 miles. Now you're presented with a new panorama southward, including another wall of ice on Hood's east face. If you haven't already, you may now start feeling very small on a very large mountain. Continue upward on increasingly tighter, rocky switchbacks just a little farther and crest the spur at 3.3 miles. Now, all you can do is gawk at the mountain before you. In every other direction, the view extends for hundreds of miles. To the north, look for Mounts St. Helens, Rainier, and Adams; to the south, Mount Jefferson, the Three Sisters, and Diamond Peak. From here, the path proceeds onward as a precarious climbers' route out onto the knife-edge between the two glacial basins, then up the face, so call it good here. Take some time to soak it all in and psyche your knees up for the coming decent.

Alternate Route

The Cooper Spur Trail can also be hiked via the Tilly Jane Trail. Start at the Tilly Jane Campground and hike 1.1 miles to the Timberline–Cooper Spur junction. This route skirts the vast Polallie Creek basin before climbing above the tree line. The distance and elevation gain from this trailhead is nearly identical to starting at Cloud Cap and offers a few more impressive mountain views.

64 Dog River

RATING/ DIFFICULTY	ROUNDTRIP	ELEV GAIN/ HIGH POINT	SEASON
***/3	6 miles	1700 feet/ 3330 feet	May–Nov

Map: Trails Illustrated Mount Hood Wilderness #321; **Permit:** NW Forest Pass for trailhead parking; **Contact:** Hood River Ranger District, MHNF; **Notes:** This trail is popular with mountain bikers; be courteous and share the trail; **GPS:** N 45°27.960', W 121°33.954'

Mount Hood is not really known for its fall color, but this trail on the lower northeast side of the mountain puts on a pretty fantastic autumn display when maples, oaks, and huckleberries are transforming from their summer greens to fall yellows, oranges, and reds. The entire trail

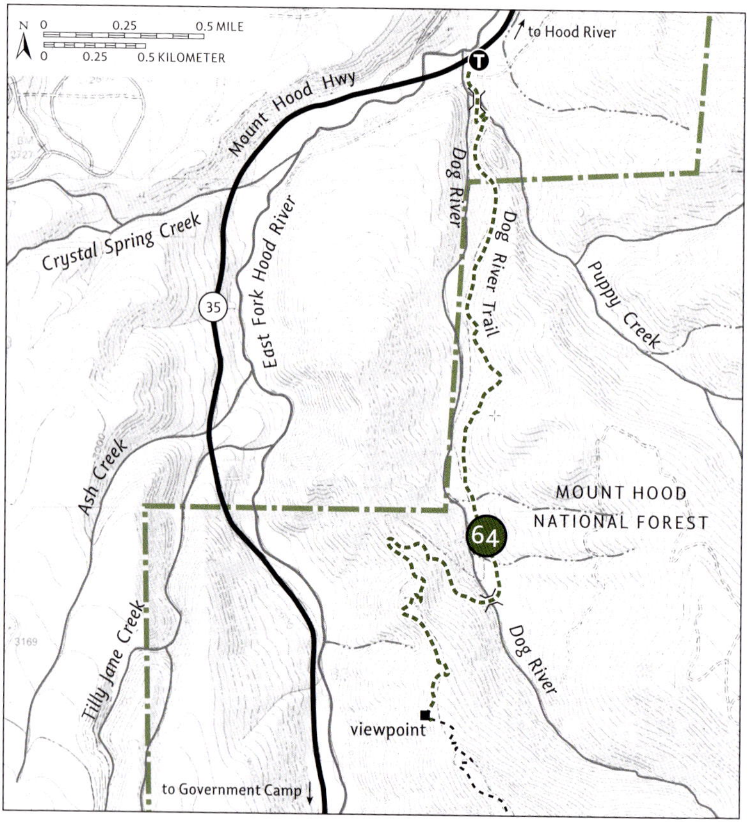

You will find plenty of fall color in season on the Dog River Trail.

stretches for nearly 6 miles (one way), but you only need to go about halfway to enjoy a nice stroll through seasonal forest to a great viewpoint of Mount Hood.

GETTING THERE

From Hood River (I-84, exit 64), drive Mount Hood Highway (OR 35) south for approximately 19 miles to the Dog River Trailhead, located on the left (east) side of the highway.

ON THE TRAIL

Dog River is one of the many waterways that feeds into the East Fork Hood River. It originates on the northern flanks of Lookout Mountain (Hike 58), where it meanders north through the high basins of the Dalles Watershed Management Unit before turning west and flowing down a series of steep, narrow canyons to eventually spill into the East Fork. Along the way, it picks up volume from several tributaries, including Blue Bucket Spring, Ward Creek, and, appropriately, Puppy Creek.

Start by walking around the wide gate at the trailhead area and proceeding up an old gravel road. The way briefly skirts the east bank of Dog River under a mixed canopy of vine and big-leaf maple, dogwood, alder, hemlock, and fir. Lining the old road is an equally mixed assortment of Oregon grape, thimbleberry, hedge nettle, and wild ginger. After just 0.1 mile, the path crosses a sturdy bridge over gurgling Puppy Creek, which, just west of the bridge, converges with Dog River. The path then narrows and pulls away from the river to begin ascending the wooded canyon.

As you climb on a fairly gentle grade, white oaks, red cedars, and ponderosa pines begin to join the mixed forest; wild strawberry, sword ferns, and vanilla leaf replace some of the shrubbery seen nearer the river. The path then contours through a couple of shallow culverts where seasonal creeks tumble down the hillside, after which the trail turns to cross Dog River on another good bridge at 1.9 miles. On the upstream side, the river is funneled into a chute by big, mossy logs; on the downstream side, it widens into a swirling pool shadowed by overhanging vine maple. Over the bridge, proceed through a stretch of overgrown thimbleberry where several seeping springs often turn the path mucky and muddy underneath.

Continue gaining elevation as the trail ascends the high ridge that separates Dog River canyon from the larger East Fork Hood River canyon. Look for cute little pink pipsissewa blossoms adorning the trailsides in summer months. Around 2.3 miles, reach the top of the ridge and begin tracing a fairly direct route south to follow the ridgeline. A few switchbacks help through the steeper sections, and a few gaps in the trees start to offer peeks at the wider world and suggest that big views are just ahead—and indeed they are. At 2.9 miles, look for a particularly large Douglas fir on the right (west) side of the trail. Here the trail makes a short, steep climb to a rocky outcrop at 3 miles, where you're presented with a wide panorama of Mount Hood.

With a few good rocks beside the trail, find a seat and take in an impressive view of the massive Eliot Glacier. To its left is the long ridge of Cooper Spur (Hike 63); to its right is the imposing, craggy wall of Barrett Spur (Hike 8). From this viewpoint, the Dog River Trail continues 2.3 miles south along the ridgeline, mostly in the trees, to end at the Zigzag–Surveyor's Ridge Trail junction. That makes this a good point to call it a day and head back down the way you came.

ORIGIN STORIES: DOG RIVER

Hood River was originally named Dog River. Its name was derived from a group of pioneers who came to the area and decided to eat their dogs rather than starve. Local residents objected to this name and changed it to Hood River in honor of the nearby mountain. The name Dog River was relegated to a tributary creek, which originates near Lookout Mountain and flows into the East Fork Hood River.

Opposite: *Take a journey around Mount Hood on the Timberline Trail, one day hike at a time (Hikes 65–68).*

timberline trail

Timberline Trail Overview

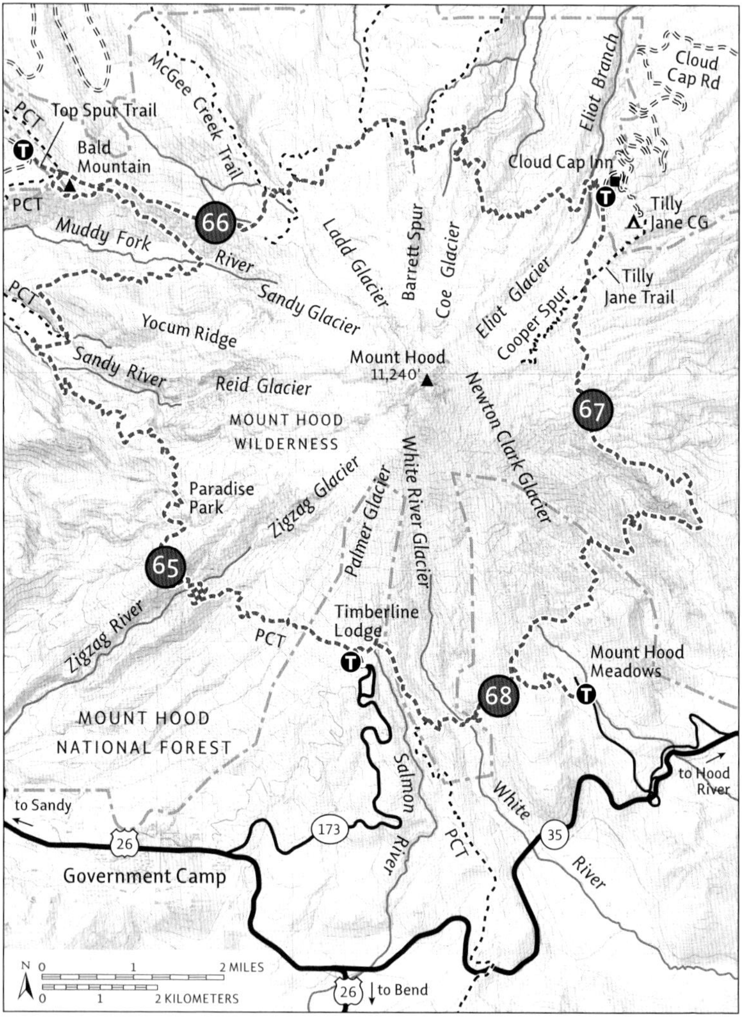

The farther one gets into
the wilderness, the greater is the
attraction of its lonely freedom.
—Theodore Roosevelt

When you're ready to graduate to a big, round-the-mountain adventure, it's time to set your sights on Mount Hood's famous Timberline Trail. This 42.8-mile loop circuits the entire mountain, tracing the tree line between the mountain's forested flanks and its upper alpine regions. An entire journey around the mountain gains 8670 feet and loses 12,040 feet of elevation (clockwise). Most hikers trek the entire loop in one outing, taking between three and five days to make an entire circuit, during which they camp on the mountain in stunning locations and enjoy a true wilderness experience. Of course, if lugging a forty-pound backpack full of gear and freeze-dried lasagna isn't your cup of tea, you can just day hike it, one segment at a time. There are four primary segments, determined mainly by the trail's easiest access points: Timberline Lodge on the south side, Top Spur Trailhead on the west side, Cloud Cap Trailhead on the northeast side, and Mount Hood Meadows ski area on the southeast side. Segments vary in distance and elevation gain/loss, with the longest segment at 15.4 miles and the shortest at 4.9 miles. (It's also possible to access the Timberline via up to ten other trails, each with varying mileage, depending on how much extra hiking you want to do.) The following segments describe a clockwise journey on the Timberline, as this direction has much less elevation gain. If you're looking for a bigger challenge, just do them in reverse.

Crossing Mount Hood's gaping Zigzag Canyon isn't as difficult as it looks.

65 Timberline Lodge to Bald Mountain

RATING/ DIFFICULTY	ONE-WAY	ELEV GAIN/ HIGH POINT	SEASON
*****/5	15.4 miles	3310 feet/ 6090 feet	July–Oct

Map: Green Trails Mount Hood #462S; **Permits:** NW Forest Pass for trailhead parking (Top Spur); self-issue wilderness permit; **Contact:** Zigzag Ranger District, MHNF; **Notes:** Requires multiple river fords; some steep, narrow stretches; **GPS:** N 45°19.842', W 121°42.630'

This is the longest segment of the Timberline Trail, because of its limited access points. It roller coasters through two of Mount Hood's biggest river canyons: the Zigzag and the Sandy. Along the way are views aplenty, gobs of wildflowers, and a couple of potentially challenging river crossings. This segment is similar to the Paradise Park route (Hike 32) and PCT leg five (Hike 73), so you may notice some of the hike info below overlaps with these other hikes. Give yourself an early start time to tackle this extra long segment so you can get the most out your day.

GETTING THERE

From Sandy, drive Mount Hood Highway (US Highway 26) east for approximately 29 miles, to the east end of the village of Government Camp. Turn left (north) on the Timberline Highway (OR 173) and head 5.5 miles up the mountain to the Timberline Lodge and ski area. Park in the main parking area. This segment ends at Top Spur Trailhead (see Getting There for Hike 66).

ON THE TRAIL

Start on the east side of Timberline Lodge and walk 0.2 mile up the service road to the Pacific Crest Trail/Timberline Trail junction; turn left (west) to get moving. Proceed through the ski area, pass the Mountaineer Trail (Hike 33) at 0.9 mile, and stop at the kiosk to collect your self-issue wilderness permit. Moving on, drop into the Little Zigzag River gully, rock-hop across, and climb out the other side. Continue downward into berry-laden forest, pass the Hidden Lake Trail (Hike 26) at 1.7 miles, then contour through a wide, open basin filled with aster and mariposa lilies. After a short ascent, you're standing at the brink of the yawning Zigzag Canyon at 2.3 miles. Pause for a moment to enjoy the view.

Now switchback down the lush south wall of the canyon, where several springs cascade down the hillside; berries and wildflowers are abundant. At 3.3 miles, drop onto the rocky floor of the canyon, and find a safe place to cross the river. In early summer, this could be a challenge; later in the season, it's usually an easy rock-hop. Once across, start climbing the canyon's drier north side to the south junction of the Paradise Park Loop at 3.8 miles. (If you're interested in this alternate route, see Hike 32.) Continue left (west) through a few more switchbacks until the trail crests the north wall of the canyon, where the grade eases and you cross the Paradise Park Trail (Hike 25) at 4.3 miles.

The Timberline now meanders north under mossy, shady conifers, crossing Lady Creek at 4.5 miles and Lost Creek at 5 miles. A little farther along, contour down into the barren canyon of Rushing Water Creek, splash across the base of a wispy waterfall, then proceed steeply up the opposite canyon

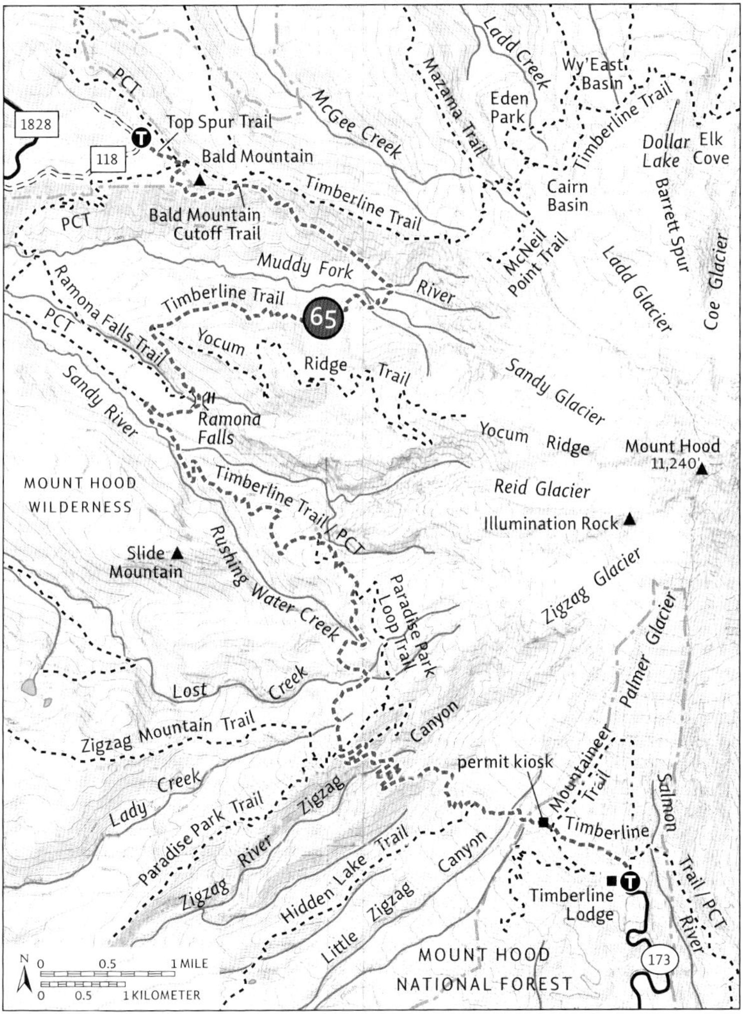

wall to dive back into more forest and wildflowers. Hop across another small stream and pass the north end of the Paradise Park Loop Trail at 6.1 miles. Now it's time to go down, down, down through a steady, switchbacking descent. Along the way, you'll get several views into a wide, flood-scoured canyon, where a streaming cascade tumbles into the rocky chasm. High above is Reid Glacier, which fills the basin between Illumination Rock to the south and Yocum Ridge to the north.

About halfway down, reenter cool, mossy forest, where rhododendron and huckleberry are abundant. The grade finally eases as you near the bottom, where the forest floor becomes thick with woody debris, and the sound of water will perk up your ears. As you get near, ferns, wild strawberry, and vanilla leaf suddenly become prolific and the trail comes right alongside Rushing Water Creek. Just beyond, pop out of the trees and onto the rocky Sandy River floodplain at 8.9 miles. The route across is marked by rock cairns. Look directly across the river, near the tree line, for where the trail continues, as you now have to find a safe place to cross.

Once you've crossed, climb out of the floodplain into dry lodgepole forest, where you'll pass a small stream and a large camp area. At 9.3 miles, the PCT veers left (northwest) and the Timberline breaks right (east). Take the right fork for Ramona Falls and continue ascending on sandy tread. Soon, you'll hear the familiar sound of falling water. Proceed through the stock control gate at 9.7 miles, then descend into a lush, shady grotto resembling the woods of Lórien, where Ramona Falls cascades down a wall of broken, columnar basalt. By now, you're probably ready for a break, so take a load off and enjoy.

When you're ready to continue, cross the bridge at the base of the falls and veer right at the fork to make a steady ascent to a junction on the lower crest of Yocum Ridge at 10.3 miles. From here, the Yocum Ridge Trail climbs steeply into Mount Hood's

Idyllic parks and wildflower meadows are an enchanting sight on the north side of Mount Hood.

alpine zone. Continue around to the north side of the ridge, and contour across the slope, where numerous seasonal springs cascade down the hillside. In some places, the path may get loose and narrow, so use caution and watch your footing. Nearing 12.4 miles, the Timberline comes to the first of three crossings of the upper Muddy Fork River. The first two are mostly inconsequential; the third crossing can be a puzzler and may require some routefinding to get across safely.

The home stretch is a long, gradual ascent of Bald Mountain's southeastern flank. Head upward under the cover of trees, and cross a few small springs where bright yellow monkeyflower is usually prolific. Pass the Bald Mountain Cutoff trail at 14.1 miles, then proceed across a slopeside meadow, often bursting with summer paintbrush, penstemon, lupine, and aster. At 14.5 miles, a rocky outcrop provides a perfect perch for taking in the wide panorama. Continue to a large junction at 14.9 miles, where the Timberline and PCT reconnect. Now, at the end of this segment, head north on the PCT for 50 yards, then veer left (southwest) on the Top Spur Trail and make a quick, 0.5-mile descent to the trailhead.

66 Bald Mountain to Cloud Cap

RATING/ DIFFICULTY	ONE-WAY	ELEV GAIN/ HIGH POINT	SEASON
*****/5	11.7 miles	4220 feet/ 6000 feet	July–Oct

Map: Green Trails Mount Hood #462S; **Permits:** NW Forest Pass for trailhead parking; self-issue wilderness permit; **Contact:** Hood River Ranger District, MHNF; **Notes:** Requires several challenging river crossings;

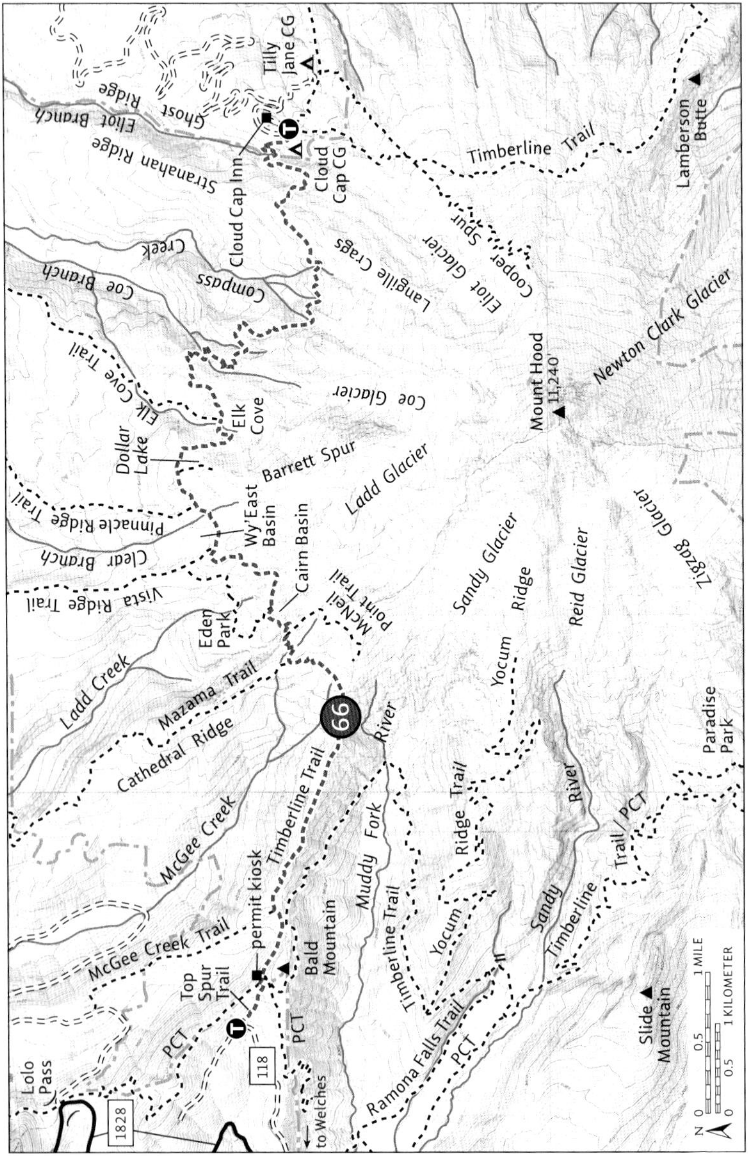

Eliot Branch
Ghost Ridge
Stranahan Ridge
Tilly Jane CG
Cloud Cap Inn
Cloud Cap CG
Timberline Trail
Lamberson Butte
Creek
Compass
Coe Branch
Langille Crags
Eliot Glacier
Cooper Spur
Newton Clark Glacier
Mount Hood 11,240'
Coe Glacier
Elk Cove Trail
Elk Cove
Dollar Lake
Barrett Spur
Ladd Glacier
Pinnacle Ridge Trail
Wy'East Basin
Cairn Basin
Clear Branch
Vista Ridge Trail
McNeil Point Trail
Eden Park
Sandy Glacier
Sandy Ridge
Reid Glacier
Zigzag Glacier
Yocum Ridge
Ladd Creek
Mazama Trail
Cathedral Ridge
66
River
Paradise Park
McGee Creek
Timberline Trail
Muddy Fork
Ridge Trail
Sandy River
Trail / PCT
permit kiosk
McGee Creek Trail
Bald Mountain
Timberline Trail
Yocum
Sandy
Timberline
Top Spur Trail
PCT
118
Ramona Falls Trail
Slide Mountain
Lolo Pass
1828
to Welches
N
0 0.5 1 MILE
0 0.5 1 KILOMETER

ELIOT CROSSING

In the winter of 2006, a massive debris flow ripped down the narrow Eliot Branch Canyon, taking out the seasonal bridge and destroying a portion of the Timberline Trail. The Forest Service officially closed that section of the trail, which rendered the full loop incomplete. That didn't stop intrepid Timberline hikers, however. They got around the closure by way of a harrowing, makeshift rope route, and even climbing above the canyon and crossing on the glacier itself. Finally, after a decade of Mount Hood's signature hiking trail being incomplete, a reroute was built across the raging Eliot. Opened in 2017, the detour added 1.5 miles to the Timberline Trail by dropping farther down the canyon to cross where the ground is more stable. Despite the opening of this new crossing, it continues to be challenging to cross the Eliot due to changes in the river's flow and constant erosion. Use extreme caution when attempting to cross.

traverses several miles of burn area; **GPS:** N 45°22.338', W 121°49.356'

This segment of Timberline Trail makes its way around Mount Hood's northern flank. There's a lot of elevation gain on this segment, but it never gets too steep, and it visits some of the mountain's more vibrant meadows and basins, all bursting with summer wildflowers. This segment also proceeds through the 2011 Dollar Lake Fire burn area. While the trail passes through pockets of burned woods, it manages to stay mostly above the charred forest, where you'll get plenty of wide views over the ghostly landscape. This segment culminates with a precarious crossing of the Eliot Branch (see sidebar), notorious for its treacherous canyon and roiling river, before making a final climb to the historic Cloud Cap Inn, perched high on the mountain's northeastern slope.

GETTING THERE

From Sandy, drive Mount Hood Highway (US Highway 26) east for 17 miles to the town of Welches. Turn left (north) on East Lolo Pass Road and proceed alongside the Sandy River for 4.2 miles. Veer right (east) onto Muddy Fork Road for 0.7 mile, then straight (north) onto Forest Road 1828 for another 5.6 miles. Where the road forks yet again, veer right (southeast) onto gravel FR 118 for 1.5 miles. Find parking on the side of the road. This segment ends at Cloud Cap Campground (see Getting There for Hike 67).

ON THE TRAIL

Begin on the Top Spur Trail and make a quick, 0.5-mile ascent under dense conifers, and among lush greenery, to a junction with the Pacific Crest Trail (PCT). Turn right (east) and proceed about 50 yards to a large trail junction where the Timberline Trail and PCT cross paths. Get your free wilderness permit at the nearby kiosk, then fork left (east) onto the Timberline Trail to get underway, where you'll proceed along the forested north slope of Bald Mountain on nice duffy tread. The surrounding forest is lush and lively and keeps the trail mostly shady. Pass the Bald Mountain Cutoff Trail at 0.9 mile, then the McGee Creek Trail at 1 mile. The latter climbs steeply from a trailhead off Lolo Pass Road.

After ascending through a viewless tree tunnel for a while, the trail pops out into the open amid a ridgetop flower garden at 2.1 miles. Here you'll find delightful summer paintbrush, penstemon, Columbia lily, mariposa lily, and pearly everlasting, as well as an impressive view of Mount Hood, Sandy Glacier, and the jagged head of the Muddy Fork Canyon. Continue back into the trees where bear grass, lupine, and corn lily become common; dip through a shallow saddle, then continue climbing more earnestly through a few switchbacks to an unmarked junction at 2.8 miles. Stay left (east) on Timberline and contour a forested slope where avalanche lilies are profuse in early summer. Proceed across McGee Creek at 3 miles, often decorated with spiraea, aster, monkeyflower, and bog gentian. This is usually an easy rock-hop.

Continue across an open heather meadow at the base of a high talus slope, then proceed up a couple of switchbacks to pass a large pond in a grassy basin. When the bear grass is blooming and the sun is shining, this meadow looks like it's illuminated with millions of flowery bulbs. Just beyond the pond, at 3.2 miles, keep right (north) at an unmarked junction, then right again (east) at the junction with the Mazama Trail. Traipse through another meadow with more flowers and views, passing the McNeil Point Trail (Hike 12) at 3.7 miles, make a quick crossing of Ladd Creek, then enter Cairn Basin at 4 miles; nearby, the Eden Park Trail drops left (northwest) into burned forest. Continue east, where the Timberline now enters burned forest, cross another wider branch of Ladd Creek, then reenter greener hillsides at 5 miles, where the Timberline meets the top of the Vista Ridge Trail.

Now you get a reprieve from climbing as the trail makes a steady descent into Wy'East Basin and proceeds to make an easy contour around the nose of Barrett Spur (Hike 8). Around 5.8 miles, a faint, unmarked trail breaks right (south) to Dollar Lake, after which, cruise down pleasant trail into Elk Cove; just beyond, at 6.4 miles, the Elk Cove Trail (Hike 7) descends left (north) to the Laurance Lake area. The Timberline then meanders around the nose of another ridge, then dips into partially burned forest to cross the Coe Branch at 7.2 miles. This one can be challenging, so look for a safe crossing. Now it's time to get your climb on again. Proceed upward through a series of wooded switchbacks, cross another stream at 8 miles, then contour along the mountainside below the remnants of Langille Glacier. The trail then reaches its high point atop Stranahan Ridge, amid more burned woodland, at 9.9 miles.

The Timberline then makes a steady descent on newer trail through alternating green and blackened forest to the Eliot Branch at 11 miles. Despite the new route across the Eliot that opened in 2017, this river canyon continues to see dynamic erosion and still presents a challenging crossing. Look for the safest possible crossing, then follow the river a short ways downstream to pick the trail back up where it reenters the trees. Finish the segment with a steady, switchbacking climb through burned woods to the Cloud Cap Campground, and wrap it up by turning left (north) onto the short trail spur to the trailhead and parking area. If you've got any juice left, wander up to the old Cloud Cap Inn for a look back at the mountainside you just traversed.

67 Cloud Cap to Mount Hood Meadows

RATING/ DIFFICULTY	ONE-WAY	ELEV GAIN/ HIGH POINT	SEASON
*****/5	10.8 miles	2680 feet/ 7340 feet	Aug–Oct

Map: Green Trails Mount Hood #462S; **Permits:** NW Forest Pass for trailhead parking (Cloud Cap); self-issue wilderness permit; **Contact:** Hood River Ranger District, MHNF; **Notes:** Requires several challenging creek crossings; traverses high-elevation cliffs and ridges; this higher-elevation segment may retain snow longer into summer; **GPS:** N 45°24.150', W 121°39.300'

This segment of the Timberline Trail traverses the high eastern slope of Mount Hood. This includes the rocky, wide-open plain at the base of Cooper Spur. Along this lofty passage, you'll be treated to some amazing panoramic views that seem to go on forever, as well as some looming in-your-face looks at Hood's rugged eastern face and its two largest glaciers. If you've got the time and energy, a

Test your water-crossing mettle with a rock hop across Newton Creek.

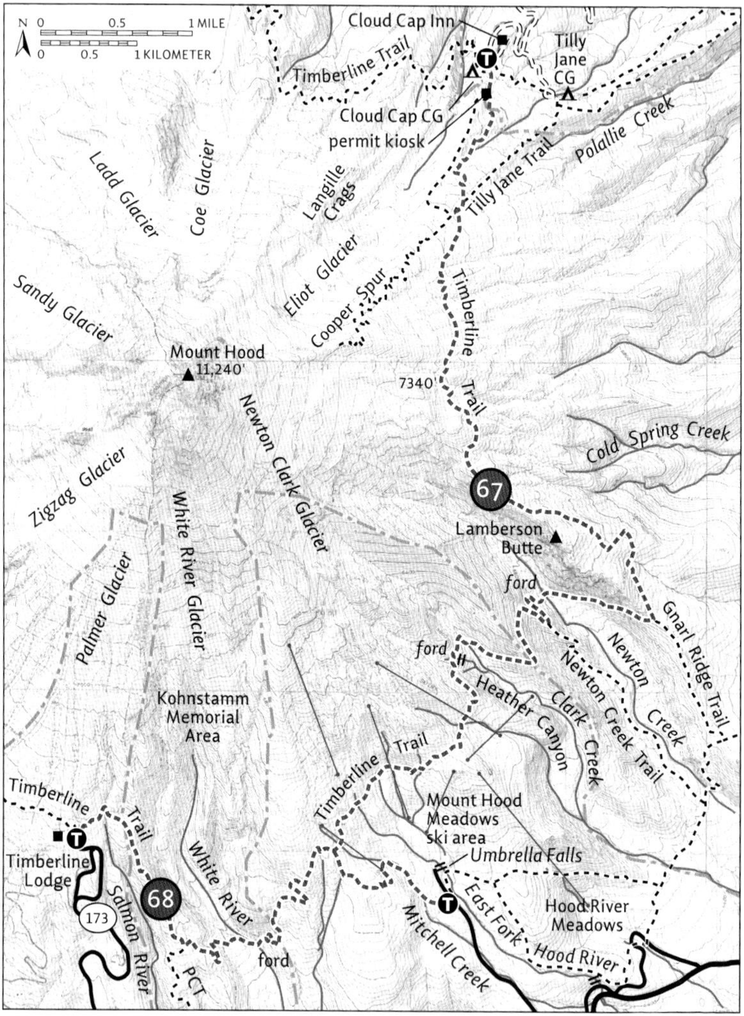

side trip to the top of the spur is a worthwhile detour. From there, the trail drops back to a median elevation and traces the tree line across a couple of big drainage canyons, then through the Mount Hood Meadows ski area. Here, the wide-open ski slopes are decorated with a bouquet of summer wildflowers, making it a fun and carefree frolic on the mountain.

GETTING THERE

From Hood River (I-84, exit 64), drive Mount Hood Highway (OR 35) south for approximately 22 miles to Cooper Spur Road. Turn right (west) and continue 2.4 miles to the Cooper Spur Resort. Turn left (south) on Cloud Cap Road and continue 8.5 miles on bumpy gravel, following signs for Tilly Jane Campground and Cloud Cap Inn. At the fork, turn right (west) and proceed 1 more mile to the Cloud Cap Trailhead and Campground. This segment ends at Mount Hood Meadows ski area (see Getting There for Hike 68).

ON THE TRAIL

Starting at the Cloud Cap Trailhead, walk through the camp area to a three-way junction with the Timberline and Tilly Jane Trails. Proceed straight ahead on the Timberline into the Mount Hood Wilderness under a canopy of old-growth hemlock and Douglas and silver firs. In just 0.1 mile, stop at the wilderness kiosk and get your self-issue permit. Continue upward on sandy tread, veering left (south) at the fork with the Eliot East Moraine Trail. The trail soon exits the trees and crosses a wide, sandy slope, then comes alongside Tilly Jane Creek's wide, shallow gully at 0.4 mile. Here's your first view of Mount Hood's northeast face; the long ridge leading right up to the mountain is Cooper Spur. Continue across a seasonal spring then follow several large, posted cairns up and out of the channel and back into the trees on the opposite ridge.

Around the 1-mile mark, just as you're getting above the tree line, you get your first big view: a sweeping panorama over eastern Oregon and southern Washington. The views only get bigger as you ascend into a vast alpine environment where rocks dominate and a few hearty plants cling to a meager existence. At 1.1 and 1.2 miles, cruise through the junctions with the Tilly Jane Trail and Cooper Spur Trail (Hike 63). The former descends to the Polallie Campground, while the latter starts a long slog up Cooper Spur—totally worth it! If you don't want to go all the way up the spur, at least take a short detour to visit the stone shelter just 0.1 mile above. Keep heading south across the desolate, windblown base of the wide spur. At 2.4 miles, you'll reach the Timberline's highest point at 7340 feet, right below the immense Newton Clark Glacier.

Now it's time to pick up some speed with a steady descent back to the tree line to make a wide circuit around the nose of Gnarl Ridge; about halfway down, the Timberline passes below 6633-foot Lamberson Butte. Nearing the bottom of your downhill sprint, pass the top of the Gnarl Ridge Trail (Hike 56), where the Timberline makes a sharp U-turn to descend the lower, forested flank of the ridge, where you'll pass several large volcanic rock outcrops and a wide scree slope. Pass a small campsite beside the trail and drop onto the wide, rocky upper channel of Newton Creek. Now follow a series of cairns (stacked rocks) across the channel and down to the water. Scout for a safe crossing location, then follow the trail back up into the trees to a chilly spring that bubbles right up out of the ground in a small clearing.

Now it's time to go up again—but not too much. Begin with a moderate ascent through a few wide switchbacks to gain the top of a long ridge. Along the way you'll pass the top of the Newton Creek Trail. From the top of this ridge, the Timberline exits the wilderness area and begins a contouring descent into the head of Heather Canyon. When you reach Clark Creek at 7.3 miles, find a safe

A big climb earns you a big view on the Timberline Trail.

crossing, then begin your ascent back out of the canyon. Across the way, you'll see a cascading waterfall. Keep this in mind, because just over 0.1 mile farther, you'll hop across the top of these falls. Safely across, proceed to the crest of a wooded ridge, then turn into the main ski area at 7.9 miles.

The next 1.6 miles traverses the ski area on a rolling path through alternating wildflower-strewn ski slopes and islands of shady trees. Along the way you'll hop across numerous creeks that feed into the East Fork Hood River, as well as Mitchell Creek. The segment nears its end at 9.6 miles, where the Timberline crosses a gravel maintenance road. Just beyond, turn off the Timberline by forking left (south) onto the Umbrella Falls Trail and meander downward though small pocket meadows, and across Mitchell Creek one more time. The trail traces the edge of the ski area and abruptly exits the woods at the resort access road near a large maintenance building. Since you've probably worked up an appetite on this journey, hop in your car and head for Government Camp, just fifteen minutes away, where pizza awaits!

68 Mount Hood Meadows to Timberline Lodge

RATING/ DIFFICULTY	ONE-WAY	ELEV GAIN/ HIGH POINT	SEASON
*****/5	4.9 miles	1860 feet/ 6020 feet	July–Oct

Map: Green Trails Mount Hood #462S; **Permit:** Self-issue wilderness permit; **Contact:** Hood River Ranger District, MHNF; **Notes:** Requires a difficult river crossing; **GPS:** N 45°19.560', W 121°39.618'

Short hikes aren't necessarily easy. This segment of the Timberline traverses only a handful of miles on the south side of the mountain but includes one of the more challenging river crossings as well as a sustained ascent on soft, sandy tread that may have you cursing every other step. The payoff is twofold: along the way, you'll get to marvel at some truly stunning views of the White River Canyon and Mount Hood, then reward yourself with a tasty snack and refreshing beverage at the historic Timberline Lodge.

GETTING THERE

From Sandy, drive Mount Hood Highway (US Highway 26) east for approximately 30 miles. Merge onto OR 35 north for Hood River and continue another 6.4 miles. Take the exit for Mount Hood Meadows ski area and proceed 2 miles to the resort area. The trail crosses the road between the Sunrise and Main parking areas. This segment ends at Timberline Lodge (see Getting There for Hike 65).

ON THE TRAIL

Access this segment of the Timberline Trail by starting with the Umbrella Falls Trail on the Mount Hood Meadows ski area access road, just north of the Sunrise parking area. Find the trailhead on the west side of the road, just north of a maintenance building driveway. Plunge into the trees and start working your way up to the Timberline, passing small pocket meadows and crossing Mitchell Creek. The path makes a lazy circuit south through a few switchbacks then tops out at the Timberline Trail at 1.3 miles. Turn left (west) to hop over the top of the ridge and proceed down, down, down toward the bottom of the White River Canyon. The upper portion of the descent meanders through an open meadow before reaching the tree line at 1.7 miles. The remainder of the descent makes a wide, circuitous curve downward and enters the Kohnstamm Memorial Area of the Mount Hood Wilderness. It then zig-zags through increasingly tighter switch-backs before dropping onto the wide, rocky, sandy river plain at 2.7 miles.

Follow the Timberline northwestward, up the river canyon. The exact route across the floodplain may vary from one year to the next as the river flow changes, so watch for cairns and other markers to help you stay on course. When you reach the river, scout for safe crossings, keeping your eye on where the trail continues on the other side. If you hike this section of the Timberline too early in the season, it might be too treacherous to attempt crossing the White River. If you don't feel safe or comfortable trying, just head back the way you came and try it again another day. Once you've made it safely across, head for the base of the western canyon wall, where the trail now starts climbing steadily upward through a few wide, sweeping switchbacks. The Timberline finally reaches the top of a wide ridge at 3.5 miles, where it merges with the Pacific Crest Trail (PCT).

Now above the tree line, looking down on the White River Canyon, the scene is all-encompassing. Your climbing isn't over yet, but take a moment to just soak it all in. Turn right (northwest) on the PCT/Timberline and start up a wide-open plain carpeted with lupine, penstemon, paintbrush, and buckwheat, intermingled with gnarled white pines. The trail tread is soft and sandy, making progress feel frustratingly slow as you trudge uphill. The plain eventually funnels into a narrow spine that separates the White River Canyon from the Salmon River Canyon, where it skirts the brink of a precipitous cliff with another "wow" view at 4.4 miles. Scan south to see how many of Oregon's Cascade peaks you can spot lined up on the horizon.

Continue your upward slog, with one eye on the trail and one taking in the views. As the trail bends westward and exits the wilderness area at 4.4 miles, dip through a wide gully channeling the upper Salmon River; crossing is usually an easy rock-hop. The home stretch to the Timberline Lodge now makes a rolling contour along the mostly open slopeside. Where the trail forks, at 4.7 miles, veer right (west) through a grove of hemlocks to a paved service road. Finish by turning left (south) and walking down the road the final 0.2 mile to the lodge where your refreshments await. Well done!

Opposite: *There's no shortage of adventure on a Pacific Crest Trail hike near Mount Hood (Hikes 69–78).*

pacific crest trail

And into the forest I go, to lose my mind and find my soul.
—John Muir

The Pacific Crest Trail (PCT) stretches for more than 2650 miles between the California-Mexico border and the Washington-Canada border. Sandwiched in the middle are 455 miles running along Oregon's Cascade Crest that circuit ancient volcanoes, traverse glaciated ridges, skirt sparkling lakes, and cross old-growth forests, alpine meadows, and rugged lava beds. The final stretch of the PCT's passage through Oregon offers a stunning tour around Mount Hood and into the Columbia River Gorge, where you can enjoy some of the best, and most dramatic, scenic eye candy in the Northwest. While usually hiked as a long-distance section- or thru-hike, the following pages will show you how to enjoy nearly 70 miles of the PCT in bite-size day hikes. Choose sections at random, or start at one end and do them sequentially until you've completed the entire journey. Once you've been bitten by the PCT bug, you may find yourself looking at going even farther!

A note about PCT section-hiking and trailheads: The descriptions for each of the following PCT segments are given in the traditional south-to-north fashion, and outline one-way hikes that start at one trailhead and end at another. This may require the arrangement of pick-ups, drop-offs, or arranging car shuttles to avoid backtracking. For each segment, you will find detailed Getting There directions to the starting trailhead. For directions to the ending trailhead, see the following segment's starting point.

Watch for songbirds flitting here and there over Timothy Meadows.

69 Timothy Lake to Little Crater Camp

RATING/ DIFFICULTY	ONE-WAY	ELEV GAIN/ HIGH POINT	SEASON
****/2	5.8 miles	330 feet/ 3410 feet	May–Nov

Map: Trails Illustrated Pacific Crest Trail, Oregon North #1004; **Permit:** NW Forest Pass for trailhead parking; **Contact:** Zigzag Ranger District, MHNF; **Notes:** Mosquitoes can be bad in early summer; **GPS:** N 45° 06.108', W 121°44.802'

This first stretch of the PCT is a mostly flat romp that begins with a pleasant walk along the verdant Oak Grove Fork Clackamas River before meandering along the eastern shores of Timothy Lake, then finishing with a stroll through stately old-growth forest. Along the way you'll enjoy plenty of lake and mountain views, abundant berries and wildflowers, and several good spots for picnics.

GETTING THERE

From Sandy, drive Mount Hood Highway (US Highway 26) east for approximately 39 miles; stay left at the OR 35 junction to continue on US 26 south toward Bend. Turn right on Oregon Skyline Road (Forest Road 42) and continue 8.2 miles to the large roadside parking area at the Pacific Crest Trail crossing. This segment ends at Little Crater Campground (see Getting There for Hike 70).

ON THE TRAIL

Begin your PCT journey at the northbound trailhead on the north side of FR 42 and plunge into shady hemlock forest, replete with lady fern, vanilla leaf, Oregon grape, and rhododendron. After an easy ramble through the trees, you'll come alongside the Oak Grove Fork Clackamas River around 0.7 mile, where the lush riverbanks are crowded with vine maple, rose spiraea, monkeyflower, and more ferns. The path proceeds alongside the river for a pleasant spell, where you'll enjoy the sound of the babbling creek before making a short ascent to the Timothy Lake Trail (Hike 51) at 1.4 miles. Just ahead, a small clearing on the left (west) side of the trail offers a picturesque view over wide, blue Timothy Lake, with Mount Hood in the distance.

Duck back under the cover of forest and continue northward, where the trail crosses a shallow drainage, which is usually dry by midsummer. Around the 2-mile mark, you'll come back alongside the lakeshore, where you'll get some partial views through the trees and find the first of several lakeside campsites. If they're empty, many of these sites make nice view spots for snack and lunch breaks. The trail then proceeds to wind along the lakeshore, at times lush and lively with rhododendron, assorted berries, pink hedge nettle, and purple penstemon, and at times lackluster with profuse and tangled woody debris. The trail completes its lakeside traverse near 4.6 miles beside a wide, grassy wetland at the head of the lake where several small springs flow into Timothy Lake's upper arm.

Continue through the dense brush, where a few more small springs cross the trail, one of which gushes right out of the rocks beside the trail. Just beyond, make haste through a swampy area filled with dark, mucky water. If it's mosquito season, you'll want to be well protected through here. At 5 miles, the Old 1916 Trail branches off right (south) for

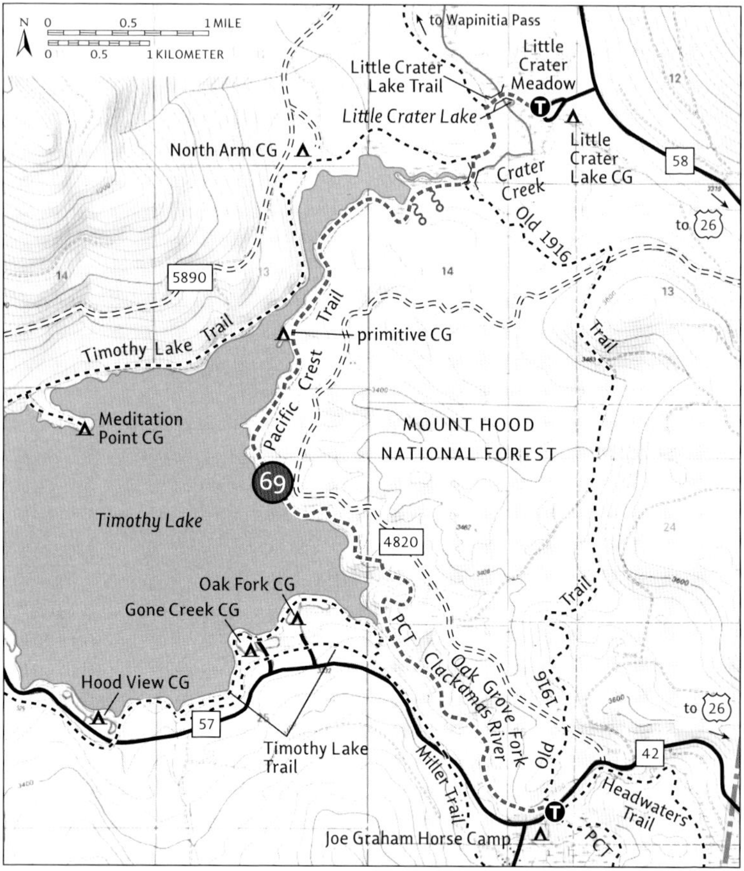

4.2 miles back to FR 42. This route is mainly used by mountain bikers for completing a full loop around Timothy Lake, as they're not permitted to ride on the PCT. Continue past this junction and over a pair of boardwalks to Crater Creek, where you can cross on a sturdy wooden bridge. In season, clusters of bright yellow monkeyflower adorn the creeksides.

Now on wide, duffy trail, stroll along under big, shady Douglas firs and Ponderosa pines to the wide northern junction of the Timothy Lake Trail at 5.1 miles. A posted sign here provides information on area permit and camping requirements—just in case you're considering a night out in the woods (Hike 49). Complete this section of the PCT by continuing north amid prolific bunchberry

HIKING THE PCT: OREGON

Once you've gotten a taste of the Pacific Crest Trail, you're likelygoing to want more. When you're ready to go farther and explore more of the PCT in Oregon, pick up a copy of *Hiking the Pacific Crest Trail: Oregon* (Seattle, WA: Mountaineers Books, 2016). This comprehensive guide provides a mile-by-mile description of the PCT through Oregon, from the expansive ridges of the Cascade-Siskiyou Mountains, to the volcanic plains of the Three Sisters Wilderness, to glacier-clad slopes of Mounts Jefferson and Hood—and everything in between. The trail is broken up into manageable pieces for hiking one section at a time, with suggested itineraries designed to help you hike at a pace that's comfortable for you. Additional features to help you plan your hikes include trail maps, elevation profiles, campsite and water locations, and tons of local resources. Start planning your next PCT adventure today! Learn more at www.pctoregon.com.

and mountain strawberry to the multisigned junction with the Little Crater Lake Trail at 5.4 miles. If you're finishing here, veer off the PCT and proceed 0.2 mile to the incredibly deep cold blue pool that is Little Crater Lake (Hike 48). The final stretch is an easy 0.1-mile walk through a grassy meadow to the Little Crater Lake Trailhead and Campground.

70 Little Crater Camp to Wapinitia Pass

RATING/ DIFFICULTY	ONE-WAY	ELEV GAIN/ HIGH POINT	SEASON
**/3	7.8 miles	1290 feet/ 4210 feet	June–Oct

Map: Trails Illustrated Pacific Crest Trail, Oregon North #1004; **Permit:** NW Forest Pass for trailhead parking; **Contact:** Zigzag Ranger District, MHNF; **Notes:** This is a dry, partially exposed section of trail; bring all the water and sunscreen you'll need for the day; **GPS:** N 45°06.108', W 121°44.802'

This section of the PCT starts the long climb from the Timothy Lake basin up to Mount Hood. The route stays mostly in dry fir and lodgepole forest with few views, making the majority of this stretch a bit lackluster. The highlight is the big panoramic view of Mount Hood and the Salmon River meadows from high on the flank of Blue Box Peak. Try to time this one for when the bear grass is blooming and the trail is lined with oodles of flowers.

GETTING THERE

From Sandy, drive Mount Hood Highway (US Highway 26) east for approximately 39 miles; stay left at the OR 35 junction to continue on US 26 south toward Bend. Turn right on Oregon Skyline Road (Forest Road 42) for 4.1 miles, then right again on Abbott Road

(FR 58) for 2.4 miles; stay right at the fork after 0.9 mile. Turn left onto FR 230 into the Little Crater Lake Campground and drive around the camp loop to the parking area and trailhead. This segment ends at Frog Lake Sno-Park (see Getting There for Hike 71).

ON THE TRAIL

Start with a pleasant walk through Little Crater Meadow on a 0.1-mile paved path to Little Crater Lake. In summer, the wide, grassy meadow blooms with blue lupine, purple camas, and pink shooting stars.

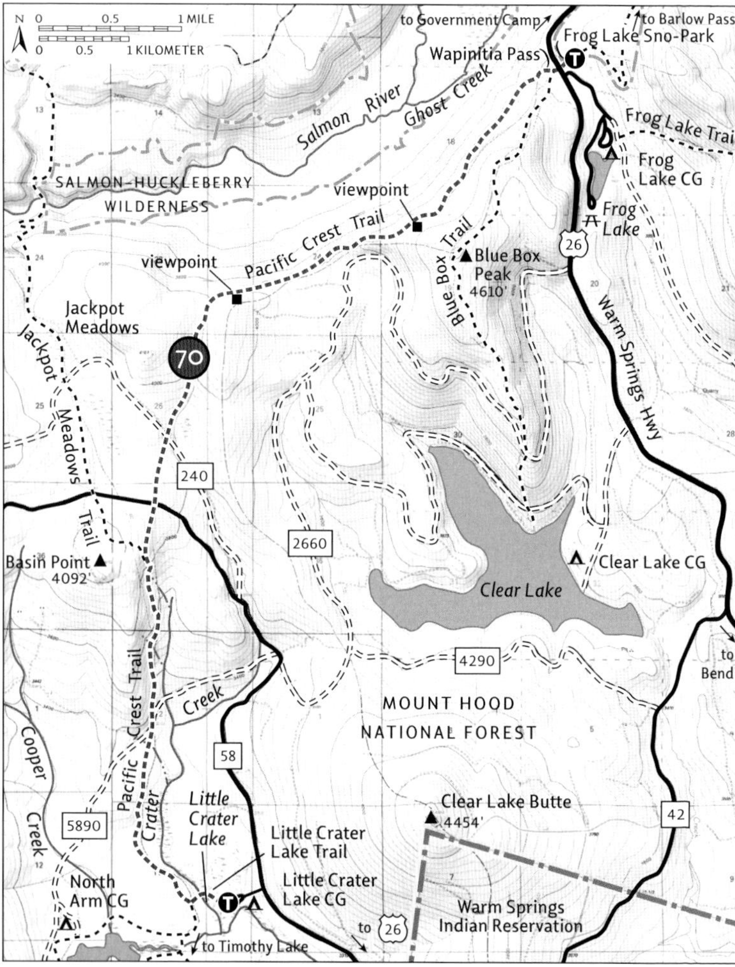

Panorama view of Mount Hood, Ghost Creek, and the Salmon River Meadows from Blue Box Peak

Pause for look at Little Crater Lake, a deep blue artesian pool in a small clearing ringed by spruce, fir, and larch trees. Continue into shadier forest of large Douglas fir and hemlock, through a boggy area choked with skunk cabbage, and around a livestock gate to a wide junction with the PCT at 0.3 mile. To the left, the trail heads south to Timothy Lake (Hike 49); to the right, it heads north to Mount Hood. Turn right and get to it.

The next mile of trail heads easily north under a shady canopy of mixed conifers, including some rather stately ponderosa pines. Along the trailside and covering the forest floor is an abundance of rhododendron, trillium, vanilla leaf, bunchberry, inside-out flower (duckfoot), Oregon grape, and wild ginger; the trail itself is pleasant and duffy for easy walking. At 1.7 miles, where the trail crosses an old logging road (FR 5890), is when it gets down to business. Now the PCT begins its steady ascent toward Oregon's highest peak, contouring upward along the eastern flank of 4092-foot Basin Point. Near the top of this first climb, at 2.7 miles, pass the Jackpot Meadows Trail (Hike 47), which branches off to the left, and continue climbing earnestly, now in more open lodgepole pine forest. A little farther on, at 3 miles, you'll reach a viewless crest on Basin Point.

The trail now levels off into denser, shadier woods, where the trailsides are lined with twinflower, bear grass, huckleberry, and rhododendron. Continue your easy walking for a spell, crossing paved FR 58 at 3.2 miles, then enter drier, open forest carpeted with bear grass. During this plant's biennial (every two years) blooming season, hundreds of stalks topped with bulb-like clusters of tiny white flowers make a spectacular sight. The trail then dips to cross a gravel road (FR 240) at 3.7 miles, where a very old trail sign indicates that US 26 is 4 miles ahead. (It's actually 4.1 miles.) After another short, easy stretch through the trees, pass a large campsite, then proceed between two low hills before turning northeast at the edge of a wide, deep, forested valley. Your viewpoint comes at 4.8 miles, where you're presented with the view you came for: the sprawling green Salmon River meadows and glacier-draped Mount Hood.

Now bearing northeast, make a gentle, contouring descent along the western flank of 4610-foot Blue Box Peak. Just upslope, tracing the crest of this ridge, is the Blue Box Trail (Hike 44). As you traverse this mostly wooded slope, you'll be treated to a few more views of the big mountain scene to the north. In actuality, these viewpoints are the edges of clear-cut patches on the forested slope below. After a half mile of easy walking, make one more moderate ascent to a crest at 6.3 miles, where you get one last look at the meadows and Mount Hood.

From this point, begin a steady, contouring descent under cover of dense hemlock and fir forest. You'll likely make quick work of this stretch until you reach the junction with the Blue Box Trail at 7.7 miles. Just beyond this junction, exit the forest onto the shoulder of Warm Springs Highway (US 26) at Wapinitia Pass. Cars and trucks race over this pass, paying little attention to hikers, so proceed across quickly and with caution. Now just follow the PCT back under forest cover for the last 0.1 mile to a spur junction to the Frog Lake Sno-Park and parking area. Hang a right (south) to exit the trail—or keep on going into the next leg.

71 Wapinitia Pass to Barlow Pass

RATING/ DIFFICULTY	ONE-WAY	ELEV GAIN/ HIGH POINT	SEASON
***/3	4.8 miles	880 feet/ 4560 feet	All year

Map: Trails Illustrated Pacific Crest Trail, Oregon North #1004; **Permit:** NW Forest Pass for trailhead parking; **Contact:** Clackamas River Ranger District, MHNF; **Notes:** This portion of the PCT is marked for winter travel, from Frog Lake Sno-Park to Barlow Pass; **GPS:** N 45°16.974', W 121°41.008'

One of the many nicknames for the Oregon portion of the PCT is the "Green Tunnel," derisively given for the abundance of forested wilderness the trail passes through. This stretch of the PCT epito-mizes that nickname. Yet while there may be a distinct shortage of panoramic mountain views on this leg, the forest is rather lovely, and at the peak of summer it is positively bursting with berries, ferns, mosses, and wildflowers.

GETTING THERE

From Sandy, drive Mount Hood Highway (US Highway 26) east for approximately 35 miles; stay left at the OR 35 junction to continue on US 26 south toward Bend. At the top of Wapinitia Pass, turn left (east) into the Frog Lake Sno-Park; the trailhead is located on the north side of the parking area, near the restroom. This segment ends at Barlow Pass (see Getting There for Hike 72).

ON THE TRAIL

Begin your trek by taking the short spur trail on the north side of the Sno-Park parking area to a signed T junction with the PCT, where you'll find a picnic table and garbage can nearby. Turn right (east) to start for the Twin Lakes (Hike 42). The trail pulls away from the intersection on duffy, level tread under a canopy of silver fir and hemlock, with a few noble firs and larger Douglas firs here and there. Underneath, you're likely to find a variety of rhododendron, trillium, vine maple, lady fern, bear grass, pipsissewa, twinflower, and vanilla leaf.

The first 0.5 mile is flat, easy walking as the trail makes a wide curve southeast. Just as the incline starts becoming noticeable, the trail switches back to make an even wider curve northeast. Contouring up the slopeside, you'll gain some elevation to reach a wide junction in a saddle between two low hills. Here, at 1.3 miles, the Twin Lakes Trail breaks off to the east (right). Many PCT hikers opt to take the Twin Lakes Trail as a detour for its access to water and good camping. At this point, you'll also find a large map board and sign that indicates entry into the Mount Hood Wilderness. There is no wilderness permit kiosk at this boundary, so forge on ahead.

Continuing north on the PCT, resume your mild ascent to contour the western slope of 4767-foot Bird Butte. You won't see any trace of the butte's upper reaches, as the surrounding forest restricts any views. Instead, look for a kaleidoscope of wildflowers decorating the trailsides: purple aster and penstemon, blue lupine, orange Indian paintbrush, pink bleeding heart and fairy slipper, and white avalanche lily and Columbia wildflower, to name just a few. You might also catch a glimpse of little Douglas squirrels darting here and there gathering nuts and seeds. Around 1.8 miles, the climbing finally subsides as the trail begins a gentle descent to pass through a wide, wooded saddle. It then bottoms out at 2.9 miles, where the PCT meets the northern junction of the Twin Lakes Trail, which dips off to the right (east).

Keep heading north on the PCT, ascending a modest grade through copious amounts of huckleberry, as the trail contours the eastern

PCT blazes, like this one on a young hemlock, mark the route from Wapinitia Pass to Barlow Pass.

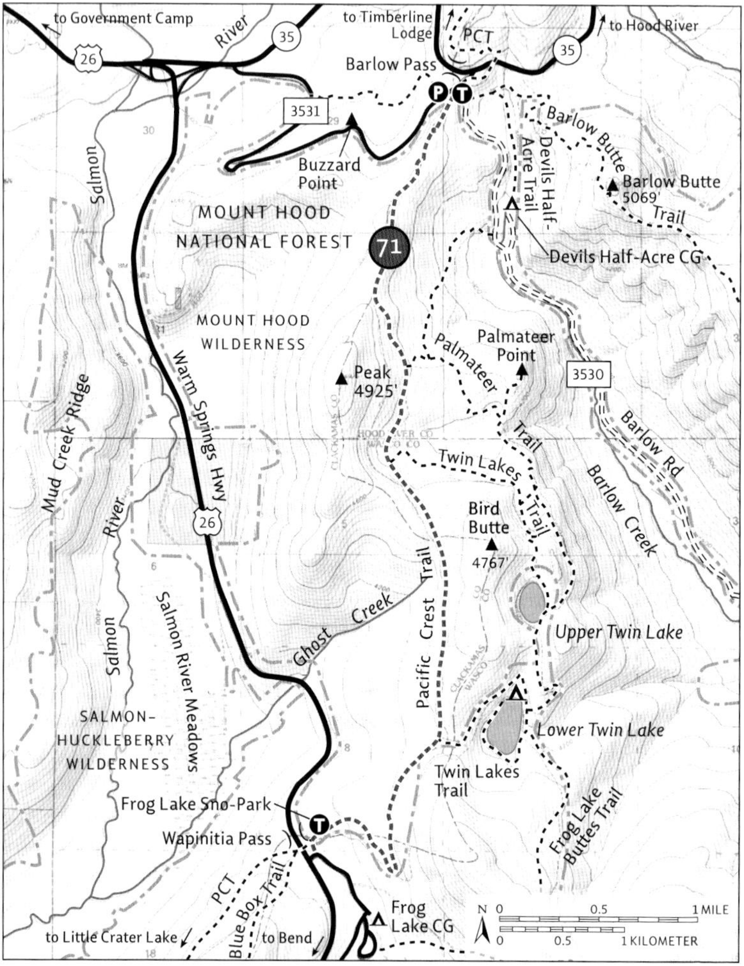

slope of aptly named Peak 4925 (its elevation). At 3.3 miles, the Palmateer Trail (Hike 41) branches off to the right (east). Continue your upward trend for another 0.3 mile to reach the viewless high point of the leg. Now it's (almost) all downhill, as you descend a wooded ridgeline. At first, the slopes to both sides fall away steeply, but as the grade eases, the slope widens out and the path meanders to the edge of the wilderness at the Barlow Pass junction at 4.8 miles. Here, between an old map board and a weathered picnic table, you can hop off the trail, keep going into the next leg, or make an about-face and return the way you came.

72 Barlow Pass to Timberline Lodge

RATING/ DIFFICULTY	ONE-WAY	ELEV GAIN/ HIGH POINT	SEASON
*****/4	5.3 miles	2200 feet/ 6020 feet	July–Oct

Map: Trails Illustrated Pacific Crest Trail, Oregon North #1004; **Permit:** NW Forest Pass for trailhead parking; **Contact:** Hood River Ranger District, MHNF; **Notes:** The upper portion of this trail traverses high, narrow ridges with sheer drops; **GPS:** N 45°16.974', W 121°41.008'

If you're up for a big climb, with even bigger mountain views, this stretch of the PCT is what you're looking for. You'll start in dense forest and climb steadily to get above the tree line, where you can take in sweeping panoramas of volcanic alpine meadows and vast river canyons, all on the doorstep of Oregon's highest peak. And if that's not enough, you can double your reward with a tasty snack or beverage when you finish at the historic Timberline Lodge.

GETTING THERE

From Sandy, drive Mount Hood Highway (US Highway 26) east for approximately 30 miles. Merge right onto OR 35 north toward Hood River and continue another 2.3 miles to the Barlow Pass Sno-Park and trailheads; turn right (south) for 0.2 mile to the large parking area. This segment ends at Timberline Lodge (see Getting There for Hike 73).

ON THE TRAIL

From the wide trail junction at Barlow Pass, find the PCT heading north behind a weathered picnic table. Proceed a few paces through the trees, then cross historic Barlow Road (Forest Road 3530). A large sign near the road gate shares some historical facts about the old Oregon Trail wagon route. Continue forward, paralleling the trailhead access road until the trail spills onto an overgrown jeep road; veer right (northeast) and follow this road to the shoulder of Mount Hood Highway (OR 35), a little more than 0.2 mile from the trailhead. Visibility is limited at this bend in the highway, so be extra alert for car and truck traffic. When safe, cross quickly and find the trail again near the guardrail on the north shoulder.

Now it's game time, as the way forward is up, up, up. Begin your ascent through prolific vine maple and thimbleberry to a sharp switchback, where the trail turns west and begins contouring the hillside on a steady upward pitch. A few gaps in the trees permit wide views over the forested hills and valleys to the south and west, including 4419-foot Buzzard Point and 4370-foot Mud Creek Ridge. The trail then turns north and becomes a narrow catwalk between an exposed rock escarpment and a precipitous drop into the head of a densely forested basin. Following this traverse, the grade eases, the forest flattens out, and the trail becomes surrounded by gobs of huckleberry and bear grass under a canopy of hemlock and silver fir draped with wispy witch's hair. As the trail zigs and zags upward, you'll find an assortment of lupine, bunchberry, mountain strawberry, and aster lining the path.

At 2.9 miles, after contouring through another drainage, pass a roomy campsite just upslope, then cross an icy creek flowing down the mountainside. Dip your hat or bandana in the water to cool off because things will start heating up going forward, beginning with a steady ascent to enter the Kohnstamm Memorial Area, part of the Mount Hood Wilderness, at 3.2 miles. As you climb on, small peeks through the trees hint at the deep, wide valley to the west. This is the Salmon River Canyon, which comes into full view at 3.6 miles. Across the chasm, you can spy the Timberline Lodge on the ridge

Mount Hood and the White River Canyon viewed from the PCT in the Kohnstamm Memorial Area.

above. From here, the trail eases to a gentler grade and the tree cover starts noticeably thinning, with small pocket meadows appearing, overflowing with aster, goldenrod, and white rhododendron. A little farther up, Mount Hood bursts into full and spectacular view, just before the PCT intersects the Timberline Trail at 3.8 miles.

Here, above the tree line, the scene is all-encompassing. Taking center stage is the vast, stark head of the White River Canyon. Above the canyon, White River Glacier spills down the mountainside. Streaming from the glacier, a large cascade tumbles down the wide, rocky basin to begin forming the White River. To the west, the groomed Palmer Glacier blankets the visible slope; to the east, year-round snowfields drape ridges and fill valley depressions. Now merged as one trail, turn left (northwest) on the PCT/Timberline. The trail surface becomes soft and sandy as it starts up a wide-open plain carpeted with lupine, penstemon, paintbrush, and buckwheat intermingled with gnarled white pines. The plain eventually funnels into a narrow spine separating the White River Canyon from the Salmon River Canyon, and skirts a precipitous cliff top at 4.4 miles. Here, high above the White River Canyon, are some pretty "wow" views. Throw a look south to see several of Oregon's Cascade peaks lined up on the horizon.

Continue grinding upward, while enjoying the views that seem to get bigger every few steps. As the trail bends westward, it exits the Kohnstamm area at 4.8 miles. Dip into a wide gully to cross the upper Salmon River, which is usually an easy rock-hop. Now nearing the end of the leg, Timberline Lodge comes into clear view. Where the trail forks, at 5.1 miles, veer right (west) through a grove of small hemlocks, then across one more small stream to a paved service road. Wrap it up by turning left (south) and walking down the road the final 0.2 mile to Timberline Lodge, where a cold, refreshing beverage awaits. Now just kick back in one of the big, cozy lounges in front of the lodge's huge picture windows and ponder your next hike on the PCT.

73 Timberline Lodge to Sandy River

RATING/ DIFFICULTY	ONE-WAY	ELEV GAIN/ HIGH POINT	SEASON
*****/5	12.2 miles	1300 feet/ 6090 feet	July–Oct

Map: Trails Illustrated Pacific Crest Trail, Oregon North #1004; **Permits:** NW Forest Pass for trailhead parking; self-issue wilderness permit; **Contact:** Zigzag Ranger District, MHNF; **Notes:** Requires multiple challenging river crossings; high water levels in spring and early summer may be hazardous; do not attempt crossing if it appears unsafe; **GPS:** N 45°19.842', W 121°42.630'

There are a lot of scenic stretches of the PCT through Oregon, but this section arguably takes the cake. After all, this one puts you right up on the western flank of 11,240-foot Mount Hood. There are a few tradeoffs for trekking through all this mountain majesty: this section is long (though it's more downhill than up), and it's busy, as this abundance of scenery definitely draws the crowds (at least partway). So if you've got the legs and don't mind the company—and can arrange a pickup on the other end—dive in and enjoy!

GETTING THERE

From Sandy, drive Mount Hood Highway (US Highway 26) east for approximately 29 miles, past the village of Government Camp. Turn left (north) on the Timberline Highway and head 5.5 miles up the mountain to the Timberline Lodge and ski area; park in the main parking area. This segment ends at the Sandy River Trailhead (see Getting There for Hike 74).

ON THE TRAIL

Start on the east side of Timberline Lodge, walk 0.2 mile up the service road to the PCT/Timberline junction, and turn left (west) to get underway. Traipse through the ski area on sandy tread, among plenty of summer wildflowers, and pass the Mountaineer Trail (Hike 33) at 0.9 mile. Just a little farther, collect your free wilderness permit at the backcountry kiosk, then hop across the Little Zigzag River and continue downward into mixed forest, where huckleberries are abundant. Next, pass the Hidden Lake Trail (Hike 26) at 1.7 miles, then contour a wide basin brimming with summer aster and mariposa lily, before ascending to the brink of the imposing Zigzag Canyon. Here, at 2.3 miles, you're treated to an impressive view of the Zigzag River, Mississippi Head, and Zigzag Glacier.

Moving on, start switchbacking down the canyon's lush south wall. Splash across several springs, which nourish an abundance of shrubs, berries, and wildflowers. At 3.3 miles, the trail spills out onto the rocky floor of the canyon, where you now have to find your way across the roiling Zigzag River. Scout up- and downstream for a safe crossing, then start up the canyon's drier north side. Climb through a few switchbacks to the south junction of the Paradise Park Loop (Hike 32) at 3.8 miles. Here, you have the option of the first of two alternates to the PCT (see Alternate Routes). Continuing upward on the PCT, climb through a few more switchbacks until the trail crests the north wall of the canyon, where the grade eases and the path crosses the Paradise Park Trail (Hike 25) at 4.3 miles.

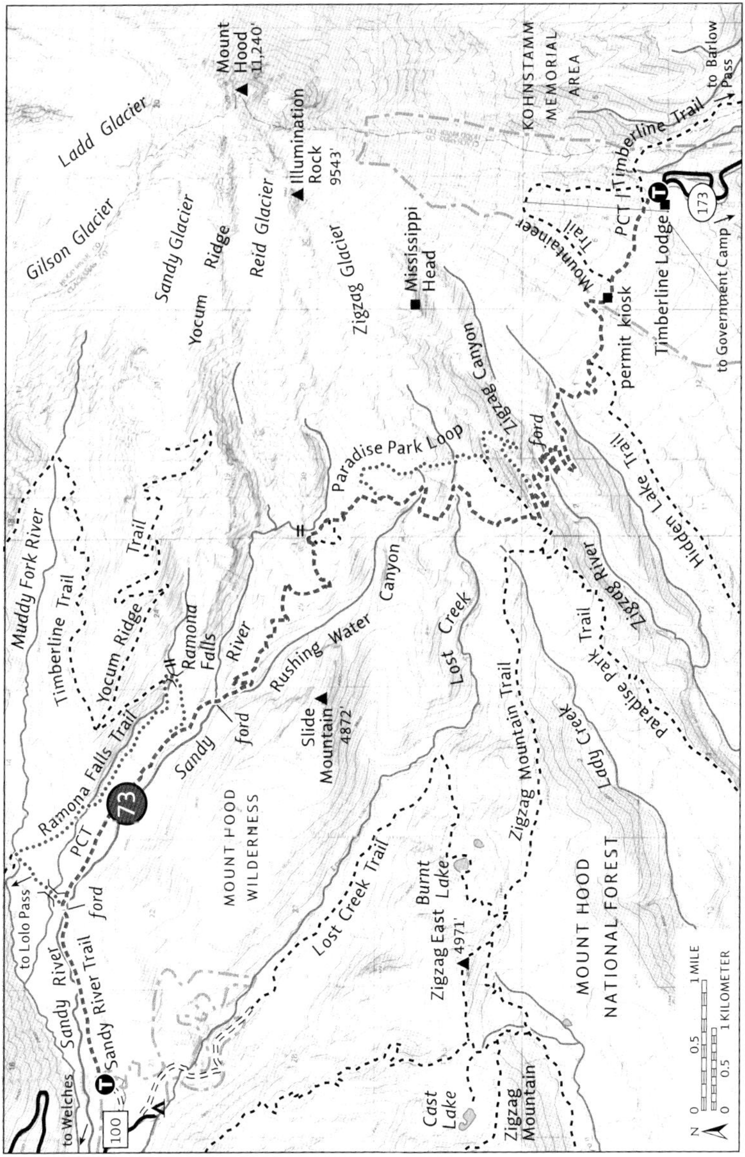
Mount Hood
11,240'
Ladd Glacier
Gilson Glacier
Sandy Glacier
Yocum Ridge
Reid Glacier
Illumination Rock
9543'
Zigzag Glacier
Mississippi Head
KOHNSTAMM MEMORIAL AREA
to Barlow Pass
Timberline Trail
PCT
Mountaineer Trail
permit kiosk
Timberline Lodge
173
to Government Camp
Zigzag Canyon
ford
Paradise Park Loop
Hidden Lake Trail
Zigzag River
Paradise Park Trail
Muddy Fork River
Timberline Trail
Yocum Ridge Trail
Ramona Falls
Sandy River
Rushing Water Canyon
Lost Creek
Slide Mountain
4872'
Zigzag Mountain Trail
Lady Creek
Ramona Falls Trail
73
Sandy
ford
MOUNT HOOD WILDERNESS
Lost Creek Trail
Burnt Lake
to Lolo Pass
Zigzag East
4971'
MOUNT HOOD NATIONAL FOREST
Sandy River
Sandy River Trail
to Welches
100
Cast Lake
Zigzag Mountain
N
0 0.5 1 MILE
0 0.5 1 KILOMETER

The PCT dips through Little Zigzag Canyon on the south side of Mount Hood.

(To ease your confusion, there are two trails that lead to Paradise Park. The Paradise Park *Loop* that connects with, and runs parallel to, the Pacific Crest Trail, and the Paradise Park *Trail* that originates at a trailhead off US 26.)

Continue cruising north under mossy, shady conifers on soft, comfortable tread. The trail crosses Lady Creek at 4.5 miles and Lost Creek at 5 miles, then curves up around the next ridge, where you'll come to the wide-open edge of Rushing Water Creek Canyon. Contour down into the barren canyon on narrow, sandy trail, where a wispy waterfall spills over a high promontory. Hop across the rocky base of the falls, then climb out of the canyon and dive back into woodland dense with paintbrush, aster, buttercup, and pearly everlasting. Hop across another small, seasonal stream, then pass the north end of the Paradise Park Loop at 6.1 miles. Now it's time to go down, down, down an earnest, switchbacking descent. Partway down, the trail crosses a wide slope of overgrown mountain ash, after which you're given a vertigo-inducing look into a wide, flood-scoured canyon, where a frothing river tumbles down a rocky chasm. High above, Reid Glacier fills the basin between Illumination Rock to the south and Yocum Ridge to the north.

Continue downward, getting a few more looks into the canyon below, or over the opposite side of the ridge into the Rushing Water Creek Canyon. The trail then plunges into cool, dense forest, where drapes of witch's hair filters the sunlight to cast an enchanting glow through the woods. Here you might imagine elves, pixies, and faeries curiously watching your passage. The grade finally eases and the forest loses a bit of its charm as it becomes thick with woody debris. Soon you'll hear the sound of water and see a profusion of ferns, wild strawberry, and vanilla leaf as the trail comes alongside

Rushing Water Creek. Finally, the trail pops out of the trees and spills onto the rocky Sandy River floodplain at 8.9 miles. The route across is marked by rock cairns. Look across for where the trail continues, as you now have to find a safe place to cross.

Once you've safely crossed, proceed into dry lodgepole forest and climb out of the river basin. The trail then makes a mild ascent to a T junction at 9.3 miles. Here, the PCT veers left (northwest) while the Timberline breaks off right (east), the latter leading to Ramona Falls (Hike 13; see Alternate Routes). Turn left on the PCT and start descending the ridge. The way down is fairly exposed and lined with dense rhododendron shrubs. At 10.7 miles, after the trail flattens out, veer left (west) off the PCT and onto the Sandy River Trail. Follow this path to cross the river again at 11 miles. Find a safe crossing, then finish your hike with an easy romp through dry forest adorned with more rhododendron, fireweed, penstemon, and pearly everlasting. The trail exits the wilderness area around 12 miles, then drops into the large trailhead parking area, where you can give yourself a high-five for a hike well done.

Alternate Routes

There are a couple of scenic alternate routes along this stretch of PCT that many hikers take for an opportunity to get out of the trees for more mountain views: Paradise Park and Ramona Falls. Both of these are day hikes by themselves, but if you're feeling ambitious you can net a two-for-one or even a three-for-one outing. The mileage and elevation gain for both is negligible, adding just a little bit to your overall journey. For the Paradise Park Loop, just veer off the PCT at 3.8 miles and follow it around to where it reconnects with the PCT a few miles later (more info in Hike 32). To visit Ramona Falls, veer off the PCT at 9.3 miles and loop back via the Ramona Falls Trail (more info in Hike 13).

74 Sandy River to Lolo Pass

RATING/ DIFFICULTY	ONE-WAY	ELEV GAIN/ HIGH POINT	SEASON
***/5	6.9 miles	2290 feet/ 4400 feet	July–Oct

Map: Trails Illustrated Pacific Crest Trail, Oregon North #1004; **Permits:** NW Forest Pass for trailhead parking; self-issue wilderness permit; **Contact:** Zigzag Ranger District, MHNF; **Notes:** Requires two very challenging river crossings; high water levels in spring and early summer may be hazardous; **GPS:** N 45°23.202', W 121°49.920'

What this short stretch of the PCT lacks in mileage, it makes up for in its long approach, elevation gain, and challenging water crossings, to turn it into a more substantial hike. The upside is some pretty fantastic views of the Muddy Fork Canyon, a lot of summer berries, and a good enough workout that you won't have to feel guilty for indulging in fries and a milkshake afterward.

GETTING THERE

From Sandy, drive Mount Hood Highway (US Highway 26) east for approximately 17 miles to the town of Welches. Turn left (north) on East Lolo Pass Road for 4.2 miles. Where the road forks, veer right (east) onto Muddy Fork Road for 0.7 mile, then turn right again to cross the Sandy River onto Forest Road 1825 for 1.7 miles, then fork left (east) on FR 100;

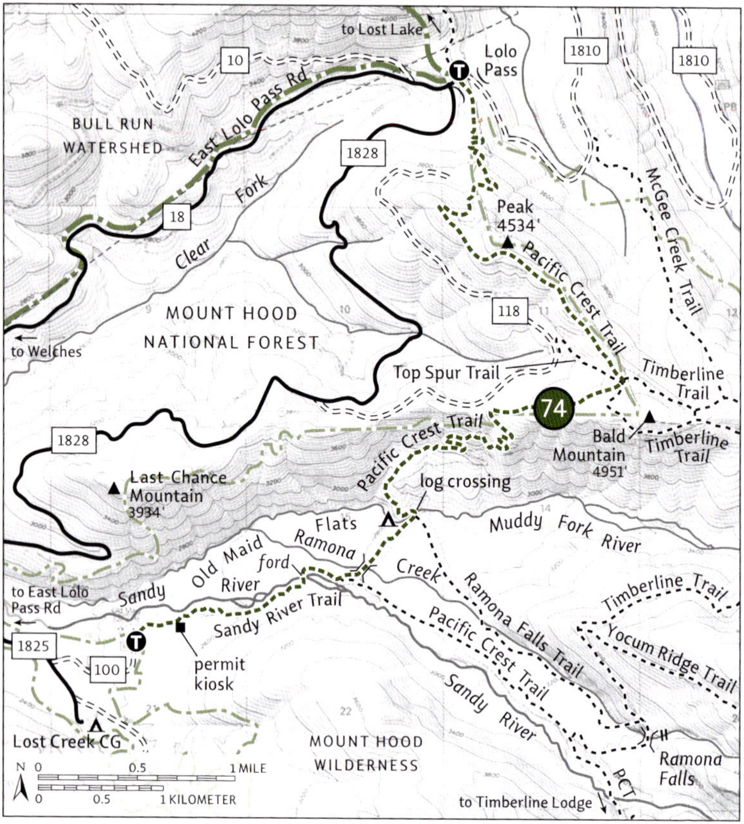

proceed a bumpy 0.3 mile to the large trailhead parking area. This segment ends at Lolo Pass (see Getting There for Hike 75).

ON THE TRAIL

This is one of the few PCT day hikes where you have to work a little extra to get to the trail. This comes in the form of a 1.5-mile approach from the Sandy River/Ramona Falls Trailhead. The nice thing is that it's easy, on mostly flat trail, with a few good views along the way. Start by heading up Old Maid Flats on the Sandy River Trail. The path dives into dry hemlock, fir, and lodgepole pine forest carpeted with manzanita and abundant mosses and lichens. Proceed through the junction at 0.2 mile to the wilderness area kiosk, collect your backcountry permit, and continue ahead (east) to the high bank of the Sandy River near 0.3 mile.

Sunlight filtered through hanging mosses illuminates Mount Hood's old-growth woods.

Here, you'll get a nice view of 11,240-foot Mount Hood. The trail, now adorned with an assortment of rhododendron, fireweed, pearly everlasting, penstemon, and thimbleberry, continues up through the forest, paralleling the river.

At 1.2 miles, drop onto the rocky floodplain of the Sandy River. There is no bridge across, so look for a safe crossing area. In spring and early summer, during peak runoff, the river may be too high and impassable. If it looks dangerous, it probably is, so don't risk it. Otherwise, take note of where the trail continues on the opposite side so you can get back on track. Once across, ascend the bank to a sandy bench and proceed through a swath of mountain ash to what looks like an unsigned junction. Turn left (north) to make a wide curve eastward, cross a rocky gully, then plunge back under the cover of trees. At 1.5 miles, meet the Pacific Crest Trail (PCT) at a signed junction. Turn left (northeast) onto the PCT and continue on duffy trail to cross Ramona Creek on a sturdy bridge at 1.6 miles. The trail then winds easily through the woods, passes the Ramona Falls Trail and a small camp area, then comes to the high bank of the Muddy Fork at 2 miles. Now you get to practice your balance beam skills by crossing the roiling brown water on a large fallen tree. A conveniently parallel second fallen tree acts as a handrail to assist your passage.

Once you've wriggled across and clambered over the rootball on the north bank, continue through a thicket of overgrown thimbleberry, where a small spring flows underneath. Then it's time to put your climbing face on where the trail turns sharply northwest and starts a steep, contouring ascent. At first, the slope is littered with deadfall and debris, but as the trail gains elevation, sword fern, rhododendron, and huckleberry begin to cover the slopeside. About halfway up, at 3.1 miles, the grade eases momentarily and the trail crosses a pretty stream that cascades down a verdant crevice choked with devil's club, wild ginger, deer fern, and sorrel. Continue your upward trajectory through a series of switchbacks until the trail finally levels out among a thick patch of rhododendron at 3.6 miles. Now atop the western ridge of 4591-foot Bald Mountain, continue east, ascending on a shallow grade through more overgrown rhododendron, bear grass, and bunchberry.

The trail tops out at a wide junction in a forested clearing where the PCT and Timberline Trail cross paths at 4.3 miles. To the immediate right (south), the Timberline heads for the rock gardens on the south slope of Bald Mountain (Hike 10); a half-mile out-and-back detour this way is worth it for the view. Straight ahead, the Timberline heads for McNeil Point, Cairn Basin, and points beyond (Hike 12). Turn left (northwest) on the PCT and commence a gentle descent that passes the Top Spur Trail, then begin a mild ascent to proceed along the spine of the ridge. The tree cover remains mostly closed in, with overgrown salmonberry and cow parsnip lining the trail, until the trees part and you're given a nice view of Mount Hood and the Muddy Fork Canyon at 5.3 miles. From here, follow the PCT down, down, down on rough, rocky, rooty tread until it bottoms out in a brushy area, where you'll pass a large campsite, then finish at East Lolo Pass Road (FR 18). When you're ready for the next section, the trail continues right across the road.

75 Lolo Pass to Lost Lake

RATING/ DIFFICULTY	ONE-WAY	ELEV GAIN/ HIGH POINT	SEASON
**/3	6.3 miles	1340 feet/ 4140 feet	June–Oct

Map: Trails Illustrated Pacific Crest Trail, Oregon North #1004; **Permit:** NW Forest Pass for trailhead parking; **Contact:** Zigzag Ranger District, MHNF; Lost Lake Resort; **Notes:** Hikers must stay on the PCT when crossing the Bull Run Watershed; off-trail exploring is not permitted; **GPS:** N 45°25.632', W 121°47.808'

If you're looking for a little solitude on the Pacific Crest Trail, you're likely to find it on this short stretch between Lolo Pass and Lost Lake, as most others starting at this point are going in the other direction. There's one good viewpoint along the way, but otherwise this section remains confined to fairly dense fern and berry-laden forest, giving you plenty of time to ponder the mysteries of the universe as you stroll along.

GETTING THERE

From Sandy, drive Mount Hood Highway (US Highway 26) east for approximately 17 miles to the town of Welches. Turn left (north) on East Lolo Pass Road and continue 10.5 miles to the trailhead at the end of the paved road. This segment ends at Lost Lake Resort (see Getting There for Hike 76).

ON THE TRAIL

Start on the north side of the road where the Pacific Crest Trail (PCT) enters the Bull Run Watershed. A large sign next to the trail

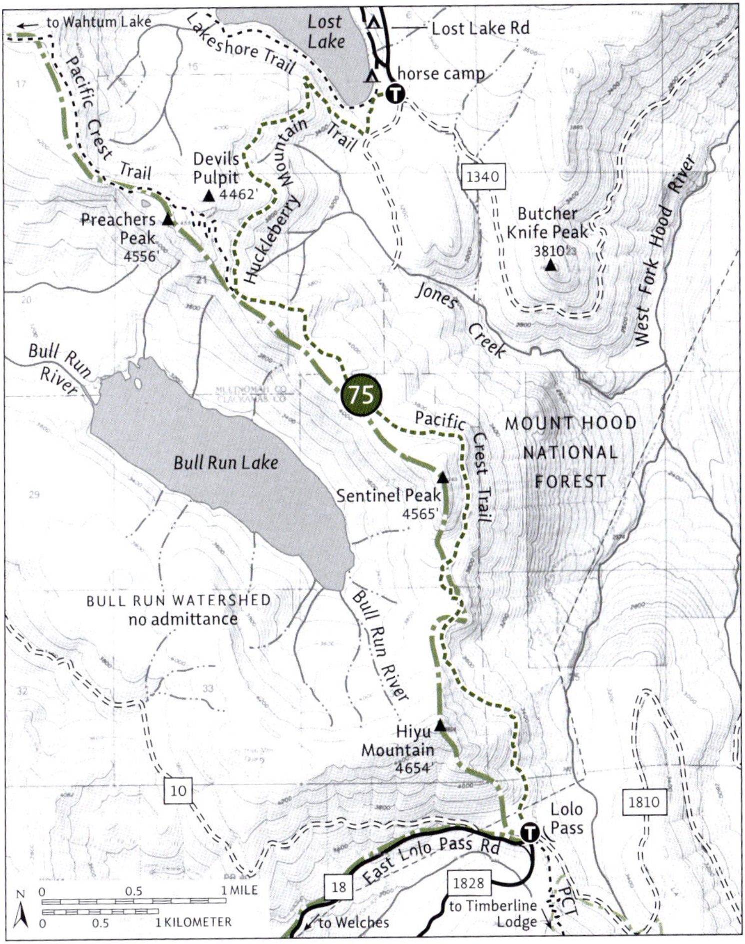

provides information and regulations about hiking through the area. The trail initially plunges into a thicket of alder and fir, before crossing a brushy powerline clearing. Here you'll find plenty of sun-loving flora, including daisies, fireweed, chinquapin, and bear grass. Just before reentering shady woods, take a look behind for a decent view of Mount Hood, only partly obscured by the numerous powerlines. Now on good trail tread, start contouring the wooded hillside, gaining elevation on a fairly moderate grade. After just 0.4 mile, make a sharp right (north) turn where a small creek splashes down a rocky chute and across the path. Just beyond, you may spy a small campsite hidden in the trees below the trail.

Continue contouring the steep eastern flank of 4654-foot Hiyu Mountain, where the trail turns into a narrow, rocky ledge. Here, you'll get a nice view of Mount Hood to the east and Mount Adams to the north. The trail then bends westward, crosses an open talus slope—with one more fleeting view of the outside world—then it's back into the trees. The forest is cool and moist, with abundant huckleberry, salmonberry, salal, vanilla leaf, and lady fern blanketing the slopeside under mossy hemlocks. Around the 2-mile mark, the ascent eases as you contour the flank of 4565-foot Sentinel Peak, where you might catch a brief look at 3810-foot Butcher Knife Peak to the north. The path then rolls along the ridge that divides the Bull Run basin from the Jones Creek valley until it crosses the Huckleberry Mountain Trail at 4 miles. With your brief journey on the PCT now at its end, turn right (north) onto this lateral trail and begin descending to Lost Lake.

The initial descent wraps around the forested flank of 4462-foot Devils Pulpit, then crosses Jones Creek at 4.8 miles. Following the next bend, traverse the base of a high scree slope, then turn west and continue descending on a more moderate grade. Views are still scarce, but berries are abundant. Nearing the bottom, at 5.6 miles, make a sharp switchback to the wooded south shore of Lost Lake. Proceeding through 6 miles, ignore the side trail right (east), which exits to an old service road, and instead turn left (north) for 0.2 mile to the Lakeshore Trail (Hike 3). Turn right (north) and follow this path about 70 yards, then proceed right up a

Get a wide view of Mount Hood from the PCT on Hiyu Mountain.

side trail, past the pavilion, to the south parking area. If you choose to finish instead at the day-use areas on the north side of the lake, continue on the Lakeshore Trail for another 1.1 miles and exit near the resort store.

76 Lost Lake to Wahtum Lake

RATING/ DIFFICULTY	ONE-WAY	ELEV GAIN/ HIGH POINT	SEASON
****/5	14.3 miles	3200 feet/ 4510 feet	June–Oct

Map: Trails Illustrated Pacific Crest Trail, Oregon North #1004; **Permit:** Lost Lake day-use or camping pass; **Contact:** Hood River Ranger District, MHNF; Lost Lake Resort; **Notes:** Hikers must stay on the PCT when crossing the Bull Run Watershed; off-trail exploring is not permitted; **GPS:** N 45°28.980', W 121°48.738'

This is the longest continuous section of the PCT between Mount Hood and the Columbia River because of limited access points. It's also the most remote segment. The 2.3-mile approach by way of Lost Lake and Huckleberry Mountain adds to the distance, lest you make it an even longer leg by starting all the way back at Lolo Pass. Either way, once you're on the PCT and rolling north, the trail traces several high ridgelines above wide, forested valleys where few but the occasional summer thru-hiker venture. If you're looking for solitude, this is where you'll find it.

GETTING THERE

From Interstate 84 in Hood River, take exit 62 for US Highway 30. Turn right on Cascade Avenue, then right on Mount Adams Avenue, then right again on Wine Country Avenue, which turns into Country Club Road. Drive 2.8 miles west then south. Turn left (east) on Barrett Drive and proceed another 1.2 miles. At the stop, turn right (south) on Tucker Road (OR 281) for 2 miles; veer right at the Odell Highway fork onto Dee Highway (OR 281) for another 6.3 miles. At the T junction, turn left on Lost Lake Road (Forest Road 13). Follow this winding road for 14 miles to the Lost Lake Resort entrance and pay your fee at the booth. Proceed 0.5 mile into the resort area and follow signs to the horse camp and pavilion area. This segment ends at Wahtum Lake (see Getting There for Hike 77).

ON THE TRAIL

Begin your trek at the trailhead at the south end of Lost Lake. Drop down past the pavilion and turn left (south) on the Lakeshore Trail (Hike 3) for a quick 70 yards to the Huckleberry Mountain Trail. Veer left (south) for 0.2 mile to another fork, then turn right (west) and begin a steady ascent through dense hemlock and huckleberry forest. The grade eases as the trail crosses Jones Creek at 1.5 miles, then meets the PCT at 2.3 miles. Turn right (north) onto the PCT and proceed on nice, duffy tread, where the slopes are blanketed with salmonberry, salal, rhododendron, and vanilla leaf. At 2.5 miles, pass the side trail to the Salvation Spring campsite, and proceed up through a series of tight switchbacks to the saddle between 4462-foot Devils Pulpit and 4556-foot Preachers Peak.

The trail soon gets narrow and brushy with overgrown berry shrubs as it makes a slippery traverse around a very steep, very deep forest basin, before making an abrupt left (west) turn at 4.5 miles. From here, the route gets a little less harrowing and dips

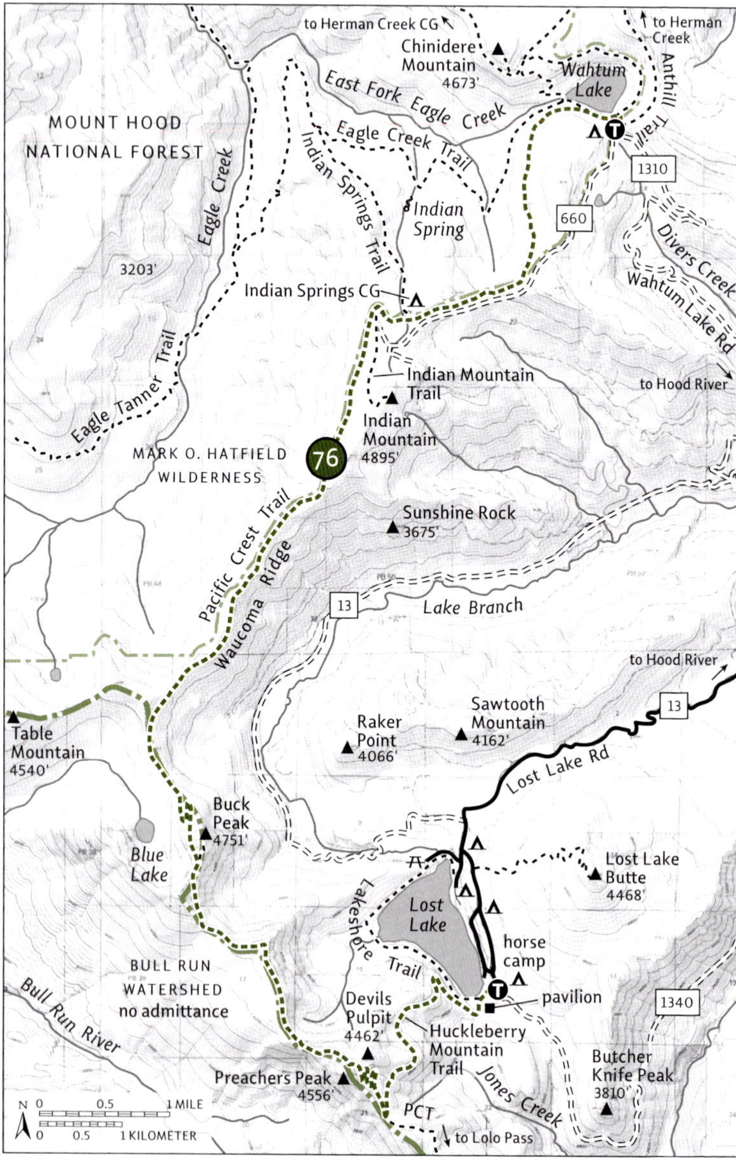
to Herman Creek CG
to Herman Creek
Chinidere Mountain 4673'
East Fork Eagle Creek
Wahtum Lake
Anthill Trail
MOUNT HOOD NATIONAL FOREST
Eagle Creek
Eagle Creek Trail
Indian Springs Trail
Indian Spring
1310
660
Divers Creek
Wahtum Lake Rd
3203'
Indian Springs CG
Eagle Tanner Trail
Indian Mountain Trail
Indian Mountain 4895'
to Hood River
76
MARK O. HATFIELD WILDERNESS
Sunshine Rock 3675'
Pacific Crest Trail
Waucoma Ridge
13
Lake Branch
to Hood River
13
Table Mountain 4540'
Raker Point 4066'
Sawtooth Mountain 4162'
Lost Lake Rd
Buck Peak 4751'
Blue Lake
Lost Lake Butte 4468'
Lakeshore Trail
Lost Lake
horse camp
pavilion
BULL RUN WATERSHED no admittance
Bull Run River
Devils Pulpit 4462'
Huckleberry Mountain Trail
1340
Butcher Knife Peak 3810'
Preachers Peak 4556'
Jones Creek
PCT
to Lolo Pass
0 0.5 1 MILE
0 0.5 1 KILOMETER

Wahtum Lake is a pleasant destination for day hikers and backpackers alike.

through another viewless saddle, after which it commences another steady ascent along the flank of an unnamed butte to a fork at 5.5 miles. The side trail right (northeast) climbs 0.4 mile to the rocky summit of 4751-foot Buck Peak (Hike 5)—a worthwhile side trip to a great view if you have the time. Otherwise, veer left (north) to continue on the PCT as it eases off the ridge, where you may catch a brief glimpse of Blue Lake in a small basin below. After descending through a few rocky switchbacks, you're back on the ridgeline and exiting the Bull Run Watershed at 7 miles. The trail then bends northeast to make a gradual ascent onto the forested spine of Waucoma Ridge.

Now back on smooth, duffy tread, the PCT skirts the Mark O. Hatfield Wilderness as it undulates along the ridgetop. A few gaps in the trees permit views east of 4066-foot Raker Point and 4162-foot Sawtooth Mountain. Where there aren't any outward views, the trailside fern, huckleberry, vanilla leaf, columbine, and devil's club offer plenty to admire. At 9.3 miles, veer left across an abandoned road and slide off the ridgetop again into dense woods. Now skirting the slopes of 4895-foot Indian Mountain, contour through the trees for a spell before popping out of the woods at 10.1 miles to cross a wide rock slope. Here, amid pockets of vine maple, thimbleberry, paintbrush, and penstemon, you're presented with a wide panorama over the upper Eagle Creek Canyon. Keep powering forward across a few more sloping rock gardens until the trail breaks out into the open at 10.6 miles, and the view becomes all-encompassing. Sadly, much of the view takes in the portion of the canyon that burned in 2017. But instead of being bummed out, try to spot cute little pikas darting around the rocks nearby.

Continue by circuiting the north slope of Indian Mountain where it meets the Indian Mountain Trail at 10.8 miles—another side trip option if you've got the legs for it (Hike 2). The PCT continues by descending an open slope, ducks through a copse of alder, then drops into the abandoned Indian Springs Campground at 11.1 miles; nearby, a seasonal spring spills cold water out of the hillside. Now continue descending on an easy grade alongside an old forest road (FR 660) and traverse a pyramid-shaped butte. As you skip down the trail, you get one more view of Mount Hood. At 12 miles, the PCT enters the Mark O. Hatfield Wilderness, where it contours the forested flank of a wooded butte adorned with fern, vine maple, vanilla leaf, false lily of the valley, and Oregon grape. The home stretch begins at 13.2 miles, as you start bending eastward above the East Fork Eagle Creek and descend to a trail junction near the wooded shores of Wahtum Lake at 13.7 miles.

Now that you're probably ready to kick off your dusty hiking boots and prop your feet up while chugging a cold, refreshing beverage, turn right (east) and follow the PCT along the lake, passing several campsites, to a fork in the trail at 13.9 miles. Veer right (southeast) off the PCT and onto a short access trail, which climbs up through a couple of switchbacks to the paved Wahtum Lake Road (Forest Road 1310) and the end of this section. Job well done. When you're ready for the next section, start right back here.

77 Wahtum Lake to Herman Camp

RATING/ DIFFICULTY	ONE-WAY	ELEV GAIN/ HIGH POINT	SEASON
****/5	13.2 miles	1630 feet/ 4300 feet	June–Oct

Map: Trails Illustrated Pacific Crest Trail, Oregon North #1004; **Permit:** NW Forest Pass for trailhead parking; **Contact:** Columbia River Gorge NSA; **Notes:** Portions of this segment of the PCT were burned in the 2017 Eagle Creek Fire, resulting in the closure of some side trails and adjacent areas; inquire with the Columbia River Gorge NSA about current conditions; **GPS:** N 45°34.632', W 121°47.568'

How you approach this long stretch of the PCT is largely dependent on how good your knees are. While there is only 1630 feet of elevation gain, there's nearly 5400 feet of elevation loss. That's more descent than going from the north (higher) rim of the Grand Canyon all the way down to the Colorado River—in about the same amount of mileage. How's that for perspective? Regardless of which direction you hike this one, you'll still get to enjoy plenty of ridgetop views and a walk across the geologic oddity that is the Benson Plateau.

GETTING THERE

From Interstate 84 in Hood River, take exit 62 for US Highway 30. Turn right on Cascade Avenue, then right on Mount Adams Avenue, then right again on Wine Country Avenue, which turns into Country Club Road. Drive 2.8 miles west then south. Turn left (east) on Barrett Drive and proceed another 1.2 miles.

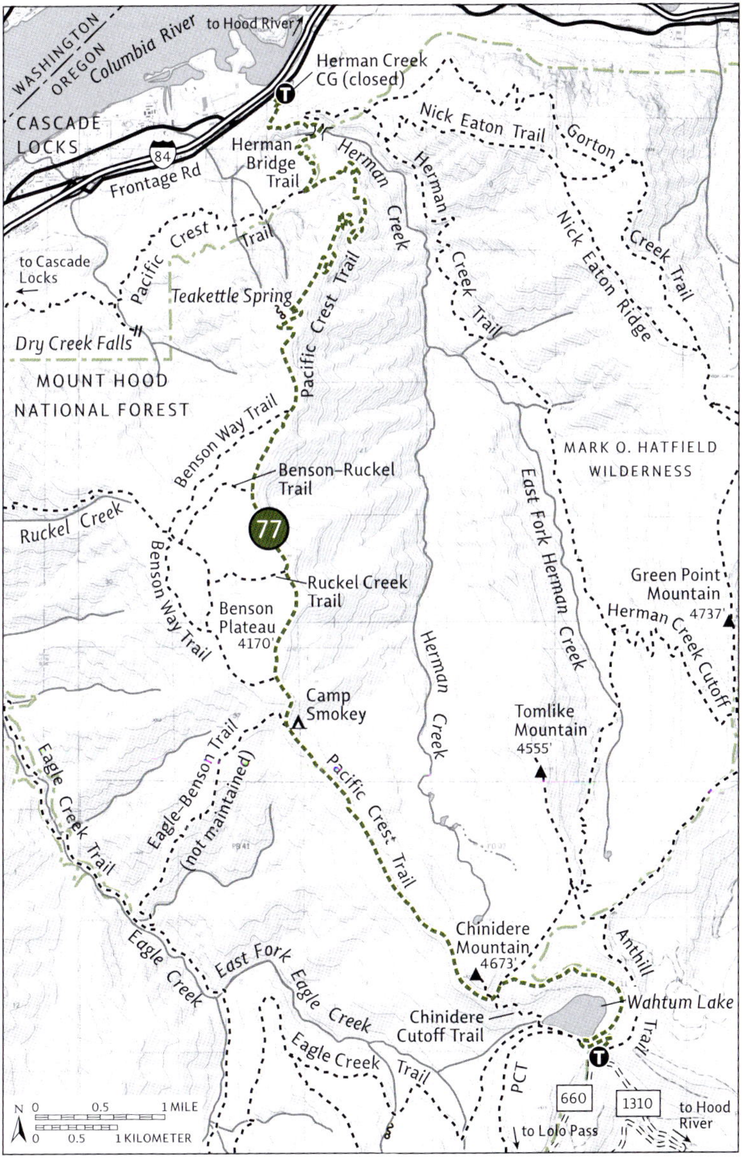

WASHINGTON
OREGON
Columbia River
to Hood River
Herman Creek CG (closed)
CASCADE LOCKS
84
Frontage Rd
Herman Bridge Trail
Herman Creek
Nick Eaton Trail
Gorton Creek Trail
Herman Creek Trail
Nick Eaton Ridge
Pacific Crest Trail
to Cascade Locks
Teakettle Spring
Dry Creek Falls
MOUNT HOOD NATIONAL FOREST
Benson Way Trail
Benson–Ruckel Trail
MARK O. HATFIELD WILDERNESS
Ruckel Creek
77
Ruckel Creek Trail
Benson Plateau 4170'
East Fork Herman Creek
Green Point Mountain 4737'
Herman Creek Cutoff
Camp Smokey
Eagle–Benson Trail (not maintained)
Eagle Creek Trail
Tomlike Mountain 4555'
Chinidere Mountain 4673'
Anthill Trail
East Fork Eagle Creek
Eagle Creek
Chinidere Cutoff Trail
Wahtum Lake
Eagle Creek Trail
PCT
660
1310
to Lolo Pass
to Hood River
0 0.5 1 MILE
0 0.5 1 KILOMETER

At the stop, turn right (south) on Tucker Road (OR 281) for 2 miles; veer right at the Odell Highway fork onto Dee Highway (OR 281) for another 6.3 miles. At the T junction, turn left on Lost Lake Road (Forest Road 13) for 4.9 miles, then veer right (west) onto FR 13 toward Wahtum Lake. Follow this narrow road 4.3 miles, then continue on FR 1310 another 6 miles to the Wahtum Lake Campground and Trailhead. This segment ends at Herman Creek Campground (see Getting There for Hike 78).

ON THE TRAIL

Starting at the trailhead opposite the Wahtum Lake Campground, take the short access trail down toward the lake. Where the spur ends at the PCT, hang a right (east) and begin traversing the lake basin. Overhead, the trail is shrouded by mossy hemlocks, while the surrounding slopes are covered with overgrown berry shrubs, ferns, columbine, bleeding heart, bog gentian, and hedge nettle. Follow the trail around the north side of the basin, where it starts steadily gaining elevation and passes several trail junctions at 2 and 2.1 miles: Herman Creek; Chinidere Cutoff; and Chinidere Mountain; this latter makes a hearty climb to a grand viewpoint (Hike 1). Bypass all of these to contour around the flank of 4673-foot Chinidere Mountain, after which the PCT begins traversing a narrow ridge. Much of this ridge was burned in the 2017 Eagle Creek Fire, so make your way across the charred, dusty crest where you'll get views east over upper Herman Creek Canyon and 4555-foot Tomlike Mountain, and north of the Benson Plateau and beyond to Mounts Adams and Rainier.

As you pass through 4 miles, notice a castle-like crag that resembles the crumbling mount of Amon Sûl—another good viewpoint. Continue past Camp Smokey and the Eagle–Benson Trail (not maintained) at 4.9 miles, right at the edge of the burn area. You'll then make a wide, curving ascent under shady woods, where you might find pretty little Scouler's bluebells on the slopeside. Finally, after another moderate ascent, reach the top of the Benson Plateau at 5.3 miles; nearby, the Benson Way Trail veers off to the left (west). Now on level ground, take an easy stroll along the plateau's eastern edge, first through a grove of scraggly white oak and silver fir, where spindly branches grope for your jacket and pack straps, then into a faerie-like forest of lush hemlock and mixed fir shading a vast carpet of bear grass. Pass the Ruckel Creek Trail at 6.2 miles, then the Benson–Ruckel Trail at 6.9 miles. From this junction, the PCT reenters burned forest at the northeastern rim of the plateau. Now it's time to go down, down, down.

Start with a steep decline to a narrow ridgetop, passing the north end of the Benson Way Trail at 7.6 miles. From here, the next 4.5 miles drops more than 3000 feet on a steady grade, turning and switchbacking down the ridge, through alternating sections of burned and unburned forest. At 8.4 miles, look for small Teakettle Spring trickling out of the hillside right below the trail. After this, the switchbacks begin, first jogging lazily back and forth down the ridge, then dropping over the east side onto the upper slope of Herman Creek Canyon. Proceed through a few more knee-grinding turns under shady conifers and vine maple as the trail zigs and zags downward, where you'll exit the Mark O. Hatfield Wilderness. Finally, passing through 11 miles, your knees will sigh in relief as the trail eases to a gentler grade, makes a sharp turn west, and comes to the Herman Bridge Trail at 11.6 miles.

Low autumn sun casts a mystical glow over the recently burned forest near Herman Creek.

It's now time to hop off the PCT, so turn right (north) and start down this spur trail to the lower reaches of Herman Creek Canyon. The trail continues descending through more sporadically burned woods that are not entirely unsightly, as ferns, shrubs, and wildflowers have begun making quick recoveries. At 12.3 miles, cross Herman Creek on a good bridge, then make a gentle, contouring ascent to the Herman Creek Trail at 12.6 miles. Now on the home stretch, veer left (northwest) and descend through a few switchbacks around a low ridge, then wind through a jumble of mossy boulders draped with licorice fern. After this, cross a wide powerline clearing, watching for trail signs to pick the route back up on the opposite side. Descend a few more switchbacks under a mossy canopy of hemlock, fir, and big-leaf maple, and finish at the Herman Creek Trailhead, where you hopefully have a tasty snack and beverage waiting for you. Now that you've done all the hard work, the final leg from this point to the Bridge of the Gods will seem like a cakewalk!

78 Herman Camp to Bridge of the Gods

RATING/ DIFFICULTY	ONE-WAY	ELEV GAIN/ HIGH POINT	SEASON
***/3	5.6 miles	1790 feet/ 960 feet	Apr–Nov

Map: Trails Illustrated Pacific Crest Trail, Oregon North #1004; **Permit:** NW Forest Pass for trailhead parking; **Contact:** Columbia River Gorge NSA; **Notes:** Portions of this hike cross recent burn areas; **GPS:** N 45°40.962', W 121°50.550'

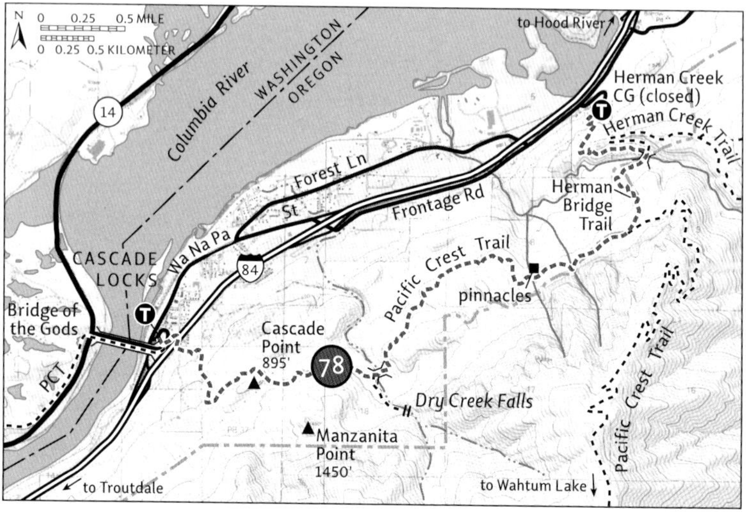

This short stretch of the PCT is one that many long-distance hikers welcome, and speed through as quickly as possible, as it ends at one of the few developed areas right on the trail's entire 2650-mile journey. That typically translates to burgers, cold beverages, showers, and a chance to recuperate for the next leg in their journey. For day hikers, it's an undemanding stretch of trail that traverses luxuriant forest, crosses gurgling creeks, and passes a few geologic oddities—and still culminates with burgers and cold beverages.

GETTING THERE

From Troutdale, drive Interstate 84 east for approximately 26 miles. Take exit 44 for Cascade Locks and merge onto Wa Na Pa Street (US Highway 30). Drive 1.5 miles through town, then fork left (east) onto Frontage Road and continue 1.7 miles to the Herman Creek Campground. The campground is indefinitely closed, but the road remains open for trailhead access. This segment ends at the Bridge of the Gods. In Cascade Locks, take the ramp for the Bridge of the Gods to Stevenson, Washington. About halfway up the ramp, turn right (south) into the trailhead parking area.

ON THE TRAIL

Your journey begins on the Herman Creek Trail, which plunges into mossy hemlock, fir, and big-leaf maple forest. Proceed upward through a few switchbacks lined with sword fern and Oregon grape to a gravel service road at the edge of a wide powerline clearing. Cross the road and follow signs for the trail, which turns right (west) on a rocky path under a pair of powerline poles. The trail then ducks back into the woods and winds through a jumble of mossy boulders draped with licorice fern and enters forest burned

Dry Creek Falls is a refreshing detour off the PCT between Herman Creek and Cascade Locks.

by the 2017 Eagle Creek Fire. The way forward now alternates through a mosaic of charred woods standing over scorched hillsides, and greener forest spared from the fire, still adorned with flowers, mosses, and shrubbery. Continue climbing around a low ridge and through a few more switchbacks to the Herman Bridge Trail at 0.6 mile. Veer right (east) onto this connector trail and descend to the bridge over Herman Creek. Cross the creek and follow the trail as it snakes its way upward through the trees to connect with the PCT at 1.6 miles; turn right (west) and get underway.

Now follow the PCT along the base of a high, rocky cliff, where it crosses a wide scree slope, then dips into a verdant notch at 2 miles. Here, a lovely stream cascades down a rocky, mossy cleft and splashes across the trail. Soon you'll notice a proliferation of mossy, volcanic boulders dotting the forest floor. This indicates that you are near the Herman Creek Pinnacles. Heading west, you may not notice them directly, but look for an obvious side trail right (north) around 2.3 miles. Here, two 50-foot-tall basalt spires—the remnants of volcanic vents—rise out of the forest floor; explore at your leisure, but use caution on the loose rocks around the base. Moving on, cross another small stream before making a winding, rising, dipping traverse around the toe of a ridge until you come alongside Dry Creek at 3.8 miles. Cross on a good bridge to the Dry Creek Falls junction. If you're in the mood for a scenic detour, turn left (south) and hike 0.3 mile up the old roadbed to Dry Creek Falls, a 74-foot waterfall that plunges out of a narrow gorge of mossy columnar basalt.

From this point, continue under the cover of pleasant, fern-choked forest, then rise to traverse the base of 1450-foot Manzanita Point, where the previously smooth, duffy tread degrades to a rough, rocky surface—watch out for ankle-rollers. At 4.6 miles, dogleg right (northwest) across a gravel service road under buzzing powerlines, then dive back under the trees to make a gently descending circuit around 895-foot Cascade Point. The rough tread eventually returns to more comfortable hardpack and the route turns and meanders down through a shady grove of big-leaf and vine maple, alder, and thimbleberry until it meets paved Harvey Road at 5.6 miles. Wrap it up by turning right (north) on the road to pass under I-84, then immediately veer left (west) back onto the PCT. Cruise through the trees beside the highway. Where the trail meets the road for the Bridge of the Gods, cross to the trailhead parking area. Well done. Your burgers and beverages are just down the road. Try the Cascade Locks Ale House—a PCT hiker favorite!

Opposite: *Once summer fades, there are still plenty of winter trails for exploring the snowy side of Mount Hood (Hikes 79–85).*

winter trails

To appreciate the beauty
of a snowflake, it is necessary
to stand out in the cold.
—Aristotle

Just because there's snow on the ground doesn't mean you can't go for a hike on Mount Hood. Pull on your puffy jacket, strap on some snowshoes, fill your thermos with hot chocolate, and get out for a winter walk in the woods. For stretching your legs and breathing in some frosty air during the snowy season, several Sno-Parks offer trails of varying lengths, mainly on the south and east sides of the mountain. Many of these trails are on old forest roads, which don't have much appeal in the snow-free seasons—but drop a ton of sparkly snow all around and suddenly those sullen old roads are paths into a winter wonderland. Many of these trails are open to cross-country skiers, and, in a few locations, motorized users, so be courteous and share the trails. The following section offers just a few winter trail suggestions. Look through the main hiking pages for more trails on Mount Hood that are open for roaming in both the sunny and snowy seasons.

Traipse through a frosty winter wonderland at the wooded Glacier View Sno-Park.

79 Glacier View

RATING/ DIFFICULTY	ROUNDTRIP	ELEV GAIN/ HIGH POINT	SEASON
***/2	1.4 miles	Up to 440 feet/ 3640 feet	Nov–April

Map: Trails Illustrated Mount Hood Wilderness #321; **Permit:** Sno-Park Permit for parking Nov. 1–Apr. 30; **Contact:** Zigzag Ranger District, MHNF; **Notes:** Portions of this route may be difficult to find following heavy snowfall; good winter navigation skills recommended; **GPS:** N 45°18.216', W 121°46.716'

For a relatively short and easy romp in the snowy woods, try one of these two forested loop trails on the outskirts of Government Camp. Both are mostly confined to forested service road corridors, but when topped with a wintry blanket, they make nice options for a enjoying a quick outdoor fix in a pretty setting—without going too far or committing your whole day.

GETTING THERE

From Sandy, drive Mount Hood Highway (US Highway 26) east for approximately 27 miles toward the village of Government Camp. Turn left into the Glacier View Sno-Park, just opposite the Mirror Lake Trailhead and entrance to Skibowl West; find parking on the side of the road.

ON THE TRAIL

The first of Glacier View Sno-Park's two loop trails uses a couple of service roads to create a 1.3-mile lollipop loop on wide track that's easy to follow. The grades on this loop are minimal, making it suitable for most snow-trompers. Start at the end of the Sno-Park road, where you'll likely need to clamber over or around a large mound of snow that's been plowed aside to clear the area. The route continues on the road itself, which proceeds on a gentle grade down a wide, tree-lined corridor, following a line of power poles. The surrounding forest is a what's-what of Northwest species, including Douglas fir, silver and noble fir, hemlock, and cedar, all sheltering an abundant understory of alder and mountain rhododendron. At 0.2 mile, the loop portion of the trail begins at a signed junction. Continue straight (west), following the power poles as the road/trail makes a quick dip to a smaller junction where Kurt's Connection branches off to the left (south). Continue your gentle descent while enjoying your snowy surroundings. There aren't any outward views to be had, but after a fresh snowfall, with the trees frosted with fresh, fluffy snow, it's quite delightful.

Approaching the half-mile mark, the path makes a short climb, then an abrupt right (north) turn to follow the powerlines down a moderate slope. Just before reaching the bottom, jog left (west), then right (north) into a partially open clearing. Turn right again and continue following the road eastward. The path now leaves the powerlines behind and the way turns into a slightly narrower corridor. Just before 0.7 mile, a blue arrow marker points the way left (north) to the Pioneer Bridle Trail (see Extend Your Trip). Keep right, following the wide track as it begins a gentle ascent on a wide, lazy S-turn through the trees. Some older maps show a smaller side loop branching off from the path here, but it's unmarked and difficult

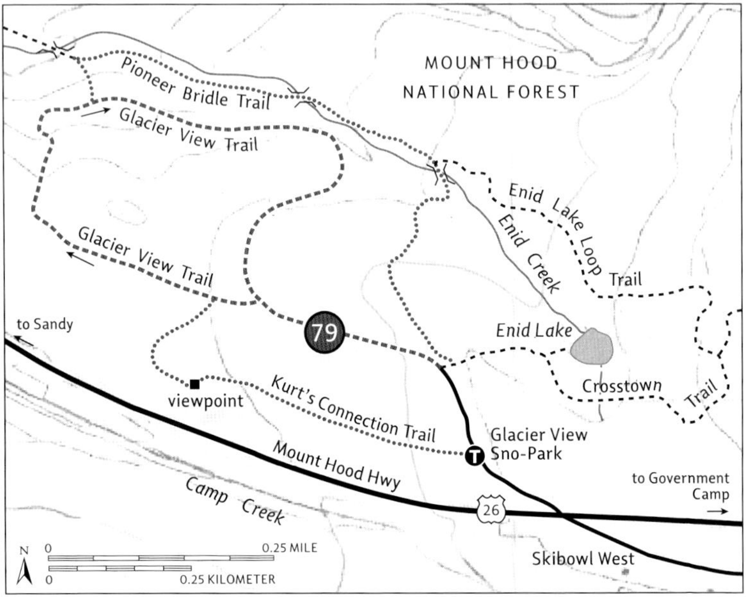

to follow, so just keep with the main route. At 1.2 miles, you'll find yourself back at a familiar junction. Now just turn left (east) and trek back up the hill to your starting point.

EXTEND YOUR TRIP

For a slightly longer romp through the winter woods, more on trail than on roadway, take this 1.6-mile loop that links Kurt's Connection Ski Trail with the Pioneer Bridle Trail. While the former is very well marked for winter travel, with abundant blue diamond markers leading the way, the latter is not, and so can be more challenging to follow after heavy snowfall. From the Sno-Park road, start on Kurt's Connection, which dips quickly into the woods and commences a nice, level walk among snowy hemlocks, cedars, and rhododendrons. At 0.3 mile, the trail makes a quick jog left (south), then right (west). At this second turn, you'll get a partial view through a clearing in the trees across the valley to Tom Dick and Harry Mountain. Just a little farther, at 0.4 mile, turn right (north), to connect with the Glacier View Trail at 0.5 mile.

Turn left (west) and follow the Glacier View Trail for the next 0.4 mile to the cutoff that leads to the Pioneer Bridle Trail (PBT). Turn left (north) off of the road and duck into the trees for a quick 100 yards to the next junction, then turn right (east) on the PBT to begin a gentle ascent, following Enid Creek upstream. Along the way, you can observe some impressively large old-growth Douglas firs right beside the trail. Cross the creek on a bridge at 1.2 miles, then come to a wide junction with the Enid Lake Loop at 1.4 miles; turn right (south) to stay on the PBT. Now well-marked again, cross the creek on another bridge, then make a sharp right (west) turn to start ascending the hillside. The path snakes this way and that as it climbs on a moderate grade and passes a sign for Barlow Road Wagon Route at 1.5 miles. Now on the home stretch on level ground, continue a final 0.1 mile to the trailhead at the end of the Sno-Park road.

80 Summit Trail

RATING/ DIFFICULTY	ROUNDTRIP	ELEV GAIN/ HIGH POINT	SEASON
**/2	4.4 miles	530 feet/ 3970 feet	Nov–Apr

Map: Government Camp Recreational Trails (see appendix II); **Permit:** Sno-Park Permit for parking Nov. 1–Apr. 30; **Contact:** Zigzag Ranger District, MHNF; **Notes:** You can also follow the summer route from the west end (Hike 29) if comfortable with winter route-finding; follow the blue diamond markers; **GPS:** N 45°18.132', W 121°46.170'

Summit Trail, located in the Skibowl East recreation area, offers three winter exploration opportunities in one: snake your way through a grove of frosty forest, traverse a ski resort base area (not ideal, but it does provide a great mountain view on clear days), and casually cruise an old road-way down a forested corridor. It's not mountaineering in the Alps, but it's easy to get to when you just want to get out for some winter wandering. The following outlines a west-to-east hike, so you're going uphill on the way out, and downhill on the way back. It can also be done vice versa.

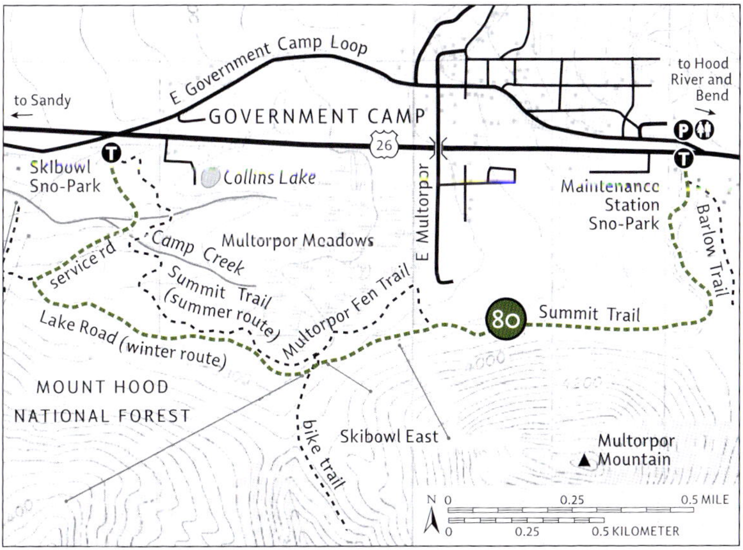

You don't have to go far to enjoy a winter trek on the Summit Trail in the Skibowl resort area.

GETTING THERE

From Sandy, drive Mount Hood Highway (US Highway 26) east for approximately 27 miles toward the village of Government Camp. For the west trailhead, turn right (south) into the Skibowl Sno-Park, opposite the left turn into Government Camp. For the east trailhead, continue another 1.4 miles to the Government Camp Maintenance Station Sno-Park; walk 0.2 mile west to the trailhead.

ON THE TRAIL

From the west trailhead, at the back of the Skibowl Sno-Park parking area, head into snowy fir and hemlock forest. The path starts out wide and flat on an old service road for easy walking. Most of the flora along the roadside will be buried under a blanket of snow, but you'll likely find some of the larger rhododendron and berry shrubs eking out their winter passage. The route narrows and starts gently ascending and bending southwest to come to the edge of the Skibowl West area at 0.4 mile. Turn left (east) onto Lake Road and head into the trees. The snowy roadway undulates upward through the trees for mostly easy tromping. Keep your eyes peeled for service vehicles using this roadway between the two base areas.

The path exits the woods at 1.1 miles and enters the Skibowl East base area beside a chairlift station. If the snow isn't too deep, you may be able to find the Multorpor Fen Trail (Hike 29) and get a look at Mount Hood and the Multorpor Meadows—an especially picturesque sight on clear winter days. Veer left (northeast) into a grove of trees and look for the side trail into the fen at 1.2 miles. If you can find it, go for a look. If not, continue east on the Summit Trail to traverse the ski area. The route passes under the Cascade chairlift, then past the Multorpor Lodge. Look for the posted Summit Trail 24 sign at the edge of the base area and continue east, passing the bottom of a couple of ski runs, and onto a snow-covered forest road.

Now out of the ski area, continue heading down the forested road corridor. After a fresh snowfall, the mix of hemlock, fir, and cedar trees flocked with fluffy white stuff creates a delightful scene. The path continues on a gentle ascent, and at 1.5 miles an open clearing appears on the right (north) side of the road. After just a little ascending, the road levels for flat, easy walking. Where the road forks, at 1.8 miles, veer left (northeast) and continue following the road as it snakes its way north toward the highway. Around 2.2 miles, the road/trail comes to an end beside a large, fenced-in building. To the right (east), the Barlow Trail continues to the Multorpor Sno-Park. At this point, make an about-face and make your way back to where you started.

81 Trillium Lake

RATING/ DIFFICULTY	ROUNDTRIP	ELEV GAIN/ HIGH POINT	SEASON
****/3	4.4 miles	500 feet/ 3600 feet	Nov–Apr

Map: Trails Illustrated Mount Hood Wilderness #321; **Permit:** Sno-Park Permit for parking Nov. 1–Apr. 30; **Contact:** Clackamas River Ranger District, MHNF; **Notes:** This is a multiuse winter trail and is open to motorized users; keep to the side of the path and stay alert for vehicles; avoid walking in ski tracks; sledding is not permitted on this trail; for the summer route, see Hike 36; **GPS:** N 45°17.160', W 121°43.772'

Trillium Lake is one of the premiere snowshoe and cross-country ski destinations on Mount Hood—and justifiably so, with its mostly flat, easy route and exceptional winter scenery. However, it's no secret, and on most winter holidays and weekends it will be mobbed with visitors. You will probably enjoy your visit more if you avoid these peak times. The winter route varies from the summer trail, as the road to the lake trailheads are not plowed during the winter season. This adds a little more mileage and a moderate hill climb

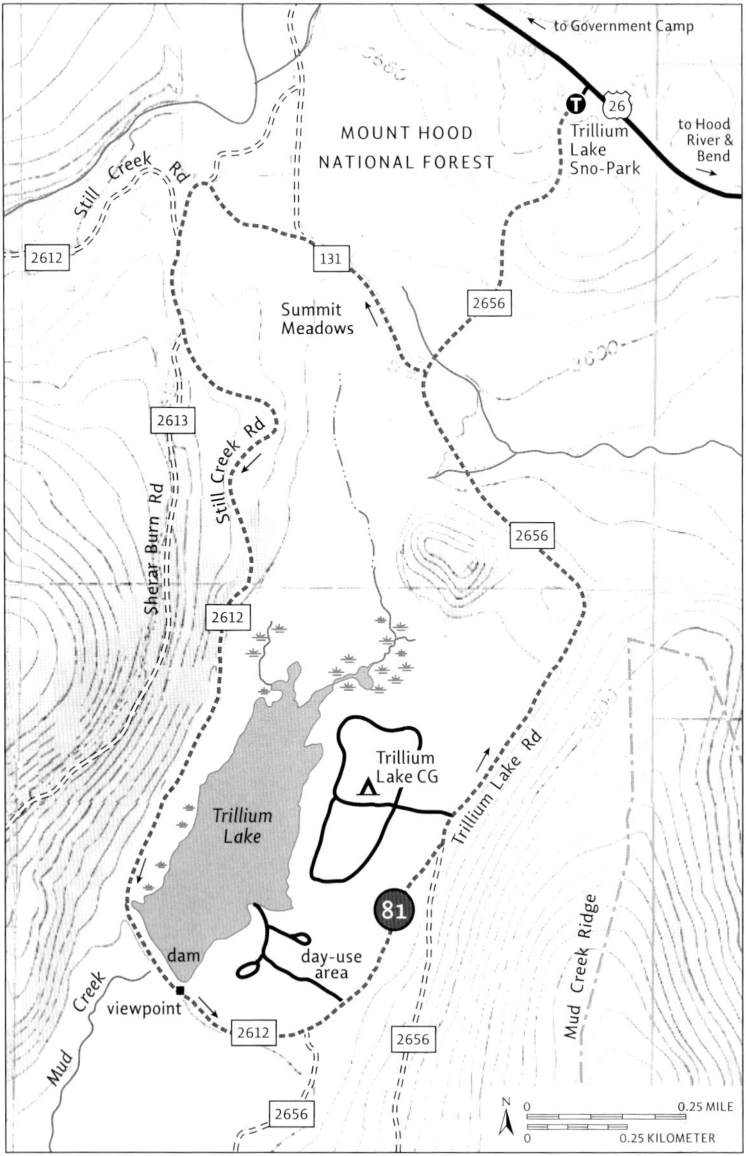
to Government Camp
26
Trillium Lake Sno-Park
to Hood River & Bend
MOUNT HOOD NATIONAL FOREST
Still Creek Rd
2612
131
2656
Summit Meadows
2613
Still Creek Rd
Sherar Burn Rd
2656
2612
Trillium Lake CG
Trillium Lake Rd
Trillium Lake
81
day-use area
dam
viewpoint
Mud Creek
2612
2656
Mud Creek Ridge
2656
0 0.25 MILE
0 0.25 KILOMETER

Mount Hood draped in winter white is a dazzling scene from frozen Trillium Lake.

at the end, but nothing worthy of deterring you from exploring this sparkling winter wonderland.

GETTING THERE

From Sandy, drive Mount Hood Highway (US Highway 26) east for approximately 30 miles to the Trillium Lake Sno-Park. Turn right into the parking area; the trail begins on the closed road.

ON THE TRAIL

Start at the gate for the snow-covered Trillium Lake Road (Forest Road 2656). Consider leaving a small donation in the box near the info board to help support the trail grooming, as you'll appreciate how nice it is to walk on this path versus some of the other ungroomed snow routes. Start heading downhill, sticking to the appropriate side of the trail, and avoid walking in ski tracks. The trail/road descends steadily for the first 0.4 mile through a corridor of evergreen conifers. Following a good snow flurry, when the trees are fabulously flocked with frosty white stuff, the setting is fantastically fetching.

The trail/road soon levels out to a nice, flat surface, crosses a small creek, and comes to an intersection at 0.5 mile. Begin the loop by turning right (west) on the signed snow route and proceeding on a barely perceptible incline through more trees until, just beyond 0.7 mile, you burst out into the wide-open Summit Meadows. (This portion follows FR 131.) Proceed across the meadow, enjoying the wintry scene. Pick up the trail again where it reenters the trees, following a narrow road northwest, then turning sharply south as the trail merges onto Sherar Burn Road (FR 2613). Just beyond this merge, at 1.2 miles, veer left (southeast) to continue on snow-covered Still Creek Road (FR 2612).

Follow this road corridor as it meanders through more snowy woods, descending gently and contouring the hillside just above but out of sight of the lake—for now. Around

1.9 miles you'll get your first look at the vast snowy plain that is Trillium Lake in winter. Finally, at 2.2 miles, drop out of the trees near the west side of the dam for a full view over the wintry scene. The panorama gets better as you plod across the dam, where on bluebird days you'll get a picture-perfect view of Mount Hood across the frozen lake. You won't get any more views once you re-enter the trees from this point, so take some time to enjoy it. A waterproof tarp can come in handy for spreading out for a winter picnic.

When the chill sets in and it's time to get moving again, start up the wide road corridor, staying on a northeastward bearing as the path proceeds through several forks. At 2.6 miles, veer left at the first junction with FR 2656; at 2.7 miles, go right at the junction with the day-use area entry; at 3 miles, continue straight past the campground entrance (left) and the second junction with FR 2656 (right). Now in the clear, continue following Trillium Lake Road through more forested winter corridor, rising and falling easily as the road crests a low saddle then drops down the other side. At 3.9 miles, you're back at the junction where you started the loop. Now just tromp your way back up the hill to the parking area and head to Government Camp for a warm beverage.

82 Frog Lake

RATING/ DIFFICULTY	ROUNDTRIP	ELEV GAIN/ HIGH POINT	SEASON
***/1	2.1 miles	160 feet/ 3950 feet	Nov–Apr

Map: Trails Illustrated Mount Hood Wilderness #321; **Permit:** Sno-Park Permit for parking Nov. 1–Apr. 30; **Contact:** Clackamas River Ranger District, MHNF; **Notes:** This is a multiuse winter trail and is open to motorized users; keep to the side of the path and stay alert for vehicles; avoid walking in ski tracks; **GPS:** N 45°13.728', W 121°41.934'

If you're hoping to avoid the crowds and packed parking area at Trillium Lake but still want an easy snowshoe around a frozen mountain lake, head for Frog Lake Sno-Park instead. This mostly flat walk around the lake is a great way to break in your snow legs on a shorter route you can do in just a couple of hours. On clear winter days, you may even get a picture- postcard view of Mount Hood.

GETTING THERE

From Sandy, drive Mount Hood Highway (US Highway 26) east for approximately 35 miles; stay left at the OR 35 junction to continue on US 26 south toward Bend. At the top of Wapinitia Pass, turn left (east) into the Frog Lake Sno-Park; the trail begins at the south end of the parking area.

ON THE TRAIL

Head down the road that starts on the south end of the parking area toward the Frog Lake Campground. The wide path starts out fairly flat for the first few hundred yards, after which it begins a mild descent. At first the way is lined with frosty hemlocks, silver firs, and winter-weary rhododendrons. As you progress, you'll begin to spot larger Douglas firs and cedars in the mix. At 0.2 mile, veer right (south) at a fork in the road to continue to the lake; the fork left (east) climbs to Frog Lake Buttes (see Extend Your Trip). Continue to the next fork, nearing 0.4 mile, and bear right (south) again. This begins the loop around the lake; the fork left (southeast) is where you will come out.

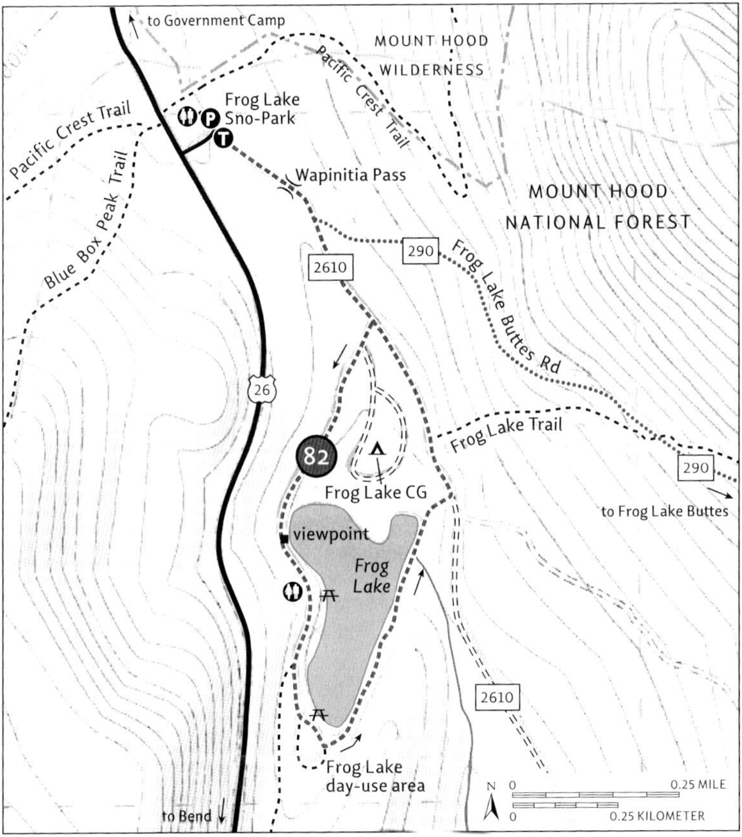

The entrance to the campground comes up quickly, veering off to the left (south). Continue straight on the road, following signs (if they're visible) to the day-use area. The way meanders easily down the wooded corridor. Look for an opening in the trees on the left (east) around 0.7 mile for your first opportunity to get a look at frozen Frog Lake. The large hills directly across are the Frog Lake Buttes. At 0.8 mile, the road passes an outhouse building on the right (west) and a picnic table on the left (east). The latter may be completely buried in heavy snow years, but if not it makes a nice place to sit and enjoy a cup of hot tea with a nice view. The road forks again at 0.9 mile. This time, veer left (south) and head into the day-use area; keep left (east) a second time when you reach the fork for the road turn-around shortly after.

A good pair of showshoes can make winter trail tromping much easier.

Now in the day-use area, lined with western red cedars, pass the boat launch area, several picnic tables (again, usable depending on the amount of snow), and another outhouse. If the skies are clear, here is where you will get a nice view of Mount Hood across the lake. Just past 1 mile, where the road bends right (south) into the trees, turn left (northeast) and begin tracing the edge of the lake along the foot of the hillside. In warmer months, the lake butts right up to the hillside (thus preventing hiking around it), but in winter, when frozen, it's possible to proceed along its frozen edge. If the lake is only partially frozen, be extra alert for holes or cracks. If it doesn't look safe, turn around and head back the way you came. If the surface looks solid enough, continue on.

Follow the rim of the lake all the way to the farthest northeast corner, where you meet the edge of the forest at 1.4 miles. There may or may not be a path leading the way from here, but in any case, make a sharp right (east) turn and climb 50 yards to a snow-covered road (Forest Road 2610). Look for an exceptionally large Douglas fir near here, amid the smaller silver firs and hemlocks; this will indicate you're on the right track. Turn left (north) on the road and begin your return journey. You'll pass the trailhead for Frog Lake Buttes (Hike 43) at 1.5 miles, then return to the fork where you started your loop near 1.8 miles. Now just follow the road you came in on back to your starting point.

EXTEND YOUR TRIP

Want more of a workout in the snow? Instead of taking the easy loop around Frog Lake, you can make the challenging climb to the top of Frog Lake Buttes. This winter trek follows an old forest road on a roundabout path to the butte's viewless summit. The round-trip is 5.4 miles with 1370 feet of elevation gain. Start the same way, heading for the lake, but veer left (east) at the first fork, at 0.2 mile, onto Forest Road 290. This road contours steadily upward, rounding the southern flank of the butte, then turns north. At 2.2 miles, fork left (north) to finish the climb beside a cellular tower. To return, just head back down the way you came.

83 Buzzard Point

RATING/ DIFFICULTY	ROUNDTRIP	ELEV GAIN/ HIGH POINT	SEASON
***/2	4 miles	530 feet/ 4150 feet	Nov–Apr

Map: Trails Illustrated Mount Hood Wilderness #321; **Permit:** Sno-Park Permit for parking Nov. 1–Apr. 30; **Contact:** Hood River Ranger District, MHNF; **Notes:** Multiuse winter trail; avoid walking in ski tracks; **GPS:** N 45°16.938', W 121°41.136'

This snow "trail" is actually a portion of the original Mount Hood Highway. Since the construction of the current highway (OR 35), this old section of road primarily serves as a short, scenic detour. From Barlow Pass, it twists and turns down around Buzzard Point, then passes the Pioneer Woman's Grave before merging with the present highway, just east of the OR 35 and US Highway 26 junction. In summer months, you likely wouldn't even consider walking this old road section, but in wintertime, when covered with snow and closed to motor vehicles, it makes a nice destination to take a leisurely romp in the winter woods.

GETTING THERE

From Sandy, drive Mount Hood Highway (US 26) east for approximately 30 miles. Merge right onto OR 35 north toward Hood River and continue another 2.3 miles to the Barlow Pass Sno-Park. Turn right (south) for 0.2 mile to the parking area; the trail begins on the closed road.

ON THE TRAIL

Unlike most trails on the mountain, this one starts high and finishes low, so you're going up on the way back. The consolation is that the grade is fairly mild the whole way, so if the snow isn't too deep, it's an easy outing for everyone. The trail begins at the unassuming Barlow Pass Sno-Park, often overlooked by the snow-play-seeking crowds. Start at the back of the parking area, where you will likely have to clamber over a large bank of snow where the plows have pushed it aside to clear the parking area. Once you're on the snow-covered road, there's only one way to go, so just start walking.

The path heads downward into snowy forest, at first dominated by hemlocks and silver firs. As you progress farther down the road, you will find an assortment of Douglas firs, cedars, and even a few lodgepole pines added to the woodland mix. After a fresh dumping, the trees can be filled with big clumps of snow. As the day warms and the breeze picks up, or gravity starts working, these heaps of snow can begin dropping out of the trees in spectacular showers of icy spray. Some of the larger masses hit the ground with resounding thumps. It's good to stay alert as you're passing under the trees that overhang the road.

About 0.5 mile down, the trail/road bends northwest and a window in the wall of trees opens up and you're presented with a glorious view of Mount Hood in all its winter splendor. If viewed in summer, the open, clear-cut areas below would be an eyesore, but in the snowy season the view is quite pleasant. Opposite the viewpoint, a seasonal spring bubbles out of the hillside, which may or may not be visible depending on the depth of the snow. Continuing down the road, near 0.7 mile, the path bends again as it rounds Buzzard Point. It's unknown how or why this point received its formidable name, but you can probably assume it had something to do with an unfortunate incident—something fairly common on early passages over the mountain.

From the point, the trail continues west, downward through the forested corridor, until, at 1.3 miles, it proceeds through a tight hairpin turn to the northeast. The road eventually flattens out where it bends north and reaches the Pioneer Woman's Grave at 2 miles (more info in Hike 38). Depending on the amount of snow, the grave monument may be visible—or it may be just another snowy hummock alongside the road. Near here, the lower junction of the Beaver Marsh Loop trail branches off to the right (east; see Extend Your Trip). This makes a suitable turnaround point. Past here, the road crosses the East Fork Salmon River then continues a final 0.3 mile to its end at OR 35 (which will likely be blocked by plowed snow). Now you just have to head back up the way you came.

EXTEND YOUR TRIP

Wanna get off the beaten path on a more challenging winter trail? Take a walk on the Beaver Marsh Loop. This 1.5-mile ski trail begins and ends near the Pioneer Woman's Grave and explores the woods and snow-covered wetlands below Buzzard Point. This path can be difficult to follow in winter conditions and requires two water crossings, so you should be proficient with

Catch a peek over the snowy Beaver Marsh area from Buzzard Point.

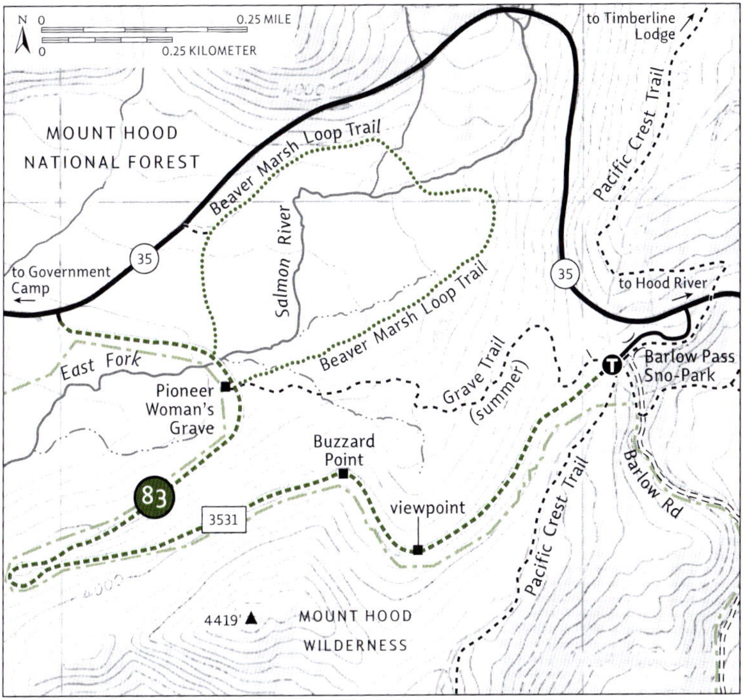

map and compass or GPS to find your way around the loop. Starting at the south end, head east into the woods and across an old clear-cut. The path ducks back into the trees for a stretch, then turns north and circuits the eastern perimeter of a wide meadow. At the top of the meadow, the trail turns west and merges into an old logging road. Follow this road northwest, then southwest, paralleling the highway. Where the road turns right (north) toward the highway, turn left (south) instead to close the loop and exit the forest to the road just north of where you started.

84 White River West

RATING/ DIFFICULTY	ROUNDTRIP	ELEV GAIN/ HIGH POINT	SEASON
****/3	3.1 miles	690 feet/ 4970 feet	All year

Map: Trails Illustrated Mount Hood Wilderness #321; **Permit:** Sno-Park Permit for parking Nov. 1–Apr. 30; **Contact:** Hood River Ranger District, MHNF; **Notes:** This route is mostly exposed, so use plenty of sun protection; also hikeable during the summer season; **GPS:** N 45°18.240', W 121°40.494'

Mount Hood takes center stage at the White River Sno-Park.

Taking a winter snowshoe on the White River is about as straightforward as you can get: walk up the river, walk down the river. Don't look for solitude here, though, as this is one of the largest and busiest Sno-Parks on Mount Hood, particularly for the huge, wide-open view of Oregon's highest peak dressed in wintry white. However, the farther you get from the parking area, the thinner the crowds get, so you can still find some serenity here by just leaving the play area behind.

GETTING THERE

From Sandy, drive Mount Hood Highway (US Highway 26) east for approximately 30 miles. Merge onto OR 35 north for Hood River and continue another 4.4 miles to the White River West Sno-Park. Turn left (north) into the parking area.

ON THE TRAIL

From wherever you park in the huge parking area, make your way over to the northeast corner and climb the berm to the high bank on the west side of the White River. In most winters, the riverbed will be a lumpy, bumpy jumble of snow-covered rocks, with the river flowing as a dark, winding ribbon down the middle. Looking up the river, Mount Hood takes center stage, rising majestically above the vast expanse. It's a good idea to stay up on the bank and out of the riverbed, as the snow can hide plenty of holes in the rocks to fall into or get stuck in.

With no formal "trail" to follow, the route essentially traces the riverbank upslope, between the riverbed on the right (east) and the high ridge to the left (west), so all you need to do is start walking toward the mountain. The grade is pretty mild the whole

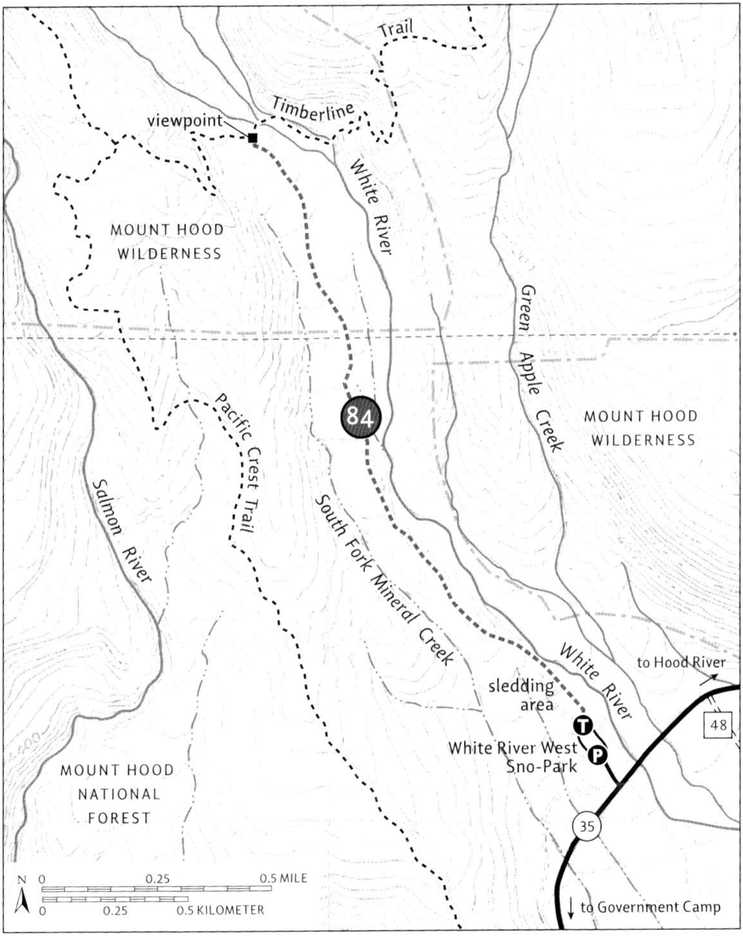

way up and back, thus mostly suitable for everyone. The first thing you'll come to, at 0.1 mile, is White River's popular sledding area. Here, families, friends, and snow-play enthusiasts of all ages enjoy careening down the snowy slope into the gully of South Fork Mineral Creek. Beyond this, the ridge on the right begins to rise and the route becomes more confined.

About 0.7 mile up, the way enters an airy forest of small trees. Keep heading upward, tracing the edge of the riverbed until you get to a clearing where a group of power-lines crosses the valley. This point, at the

1-mile mark, is a popular turnaround spot. There are more views up ahead if you feel like pressing on; however, the route starts to get a little steeper and more challenging. Just after the 1.5-mile mark, where the Timberline Trail (likely buried) crosses the White River, is another great view, and where the riverbank runs out. Going beyond this point requires expert snow travel skills, as the way forward gets into increasingly steep, rugged terrain. Call it good here and head back down the way you came.

85 Bennett Pass

RATING/ DIFFICULTY	ROUNDTRIP	ELEV GAIN/ HIGH POINT	SEASON
***/4	Up to 5.4 miles	Up to 1060 feet/ 5130 feet	All year

Map: Trails Illustrated Mount Hood Wilderness #321; **Permit:** Sno-Park Permit for parking Nov. 1–Apr. 30; **Contact:** Hood River Ranger District, MHNF; **Notes:** This is a multiuse winter trail open to motorized users; keep to the side of the path and stay alert for vehicles; avoid walking in ski tracks; **GPS:** N 45°18.582', W 121°38.454'

If the busy, crowd-magnet Sno-Parks aren't your cup of winter tea and you're looking for a quiet, leisurely stroll in the snowy woods, head for Bennett Pass. This park utilizes a network of old forest and logging roads as winter routes that spread far and wide. The longer trails require good winter backcountry experience, but the close-in routes are suitable for most casual and entry-level winter hikers.

GETTING THERE

From Sandy, drive Mount Hood Highway (US Highway 26) east for approximately 30 miles. Merge onto OR 35 north for Hood River and continue another 6.4 miles. Take the exit for Mount Hood Meadows ski area for 0.3 mile and turn right (east) into the Bennett Pass Sno-Park.

ON THE TRAIL

Start from the back of the parking area by heading east on the snowed-over forest road (Forest Road 3550). You can ignore the path that heads right (south), as this short spur just dead-ends in the trees around the bend. The road is wide and proceeds at a very mild ascent, making for easy walking (depending on snow depth) up the forested corridor, which is composed mostly of larger hemlocks and smaller silver firs. A few small gaps in the trees offer partial views over the wide valley containing the East Fork Hood River and Meadows Creek; the high hill opposite the valley is 5608-foot Elk Mountain.

The road gradually bends southward, still on a very mild grade, and contours around a wide basin, where, hidden under winter snow, a small creek plunges down into the valley. Along the trailside, small hemlocks bend toward the ground, weighed down by snow. Continue traipsing along until the road meets a wide fork at 0.9 mile. The road ahead (east) continues for miles, with increasing difficulty, to points far and wide (see Extend Your Trip). For this outing, turn right (south), making a U-turn around the ridge and continuing to another fork just past the 1-mile mark. The easy route forks to the left (south), and the less-easy route forks to the right (southwest). Both are short, out-and-back spurs that dead-end in forested clearings.

SEE A WINTER WATERFALL

Waterfalls on Mount Hood are pretty rare. Waterfalls on Mount Hood in winter are downright unique. In summer months, you can take a leisurely walk through the woods to view Umbrella Falls (Hike 54). But in winter, when soft, fluffy snow covers the trails, there's a shorter, more direct path, located right in the Mount Hood Meadows ski area. And despite being just a stone's throw from a bustling ski resort, the scene is pretty and tranquil, yet ethereal and unexpected.

For the short romp to the falls, pick up a Mount Hood Meadows snowshoe map (appendix II). The marked path starts near the lodge and descends through the trees, parallel to the parking area. Veer off the path where it makes a U-turn and proceed down an open slope. Follow the flagging—and the sound of running water—around a grove of big, mossy hemlocks and silver firs to the base of the falls, where you can admire a curtain of water cascading down a dark, rocky slope amid a wall of winter white.

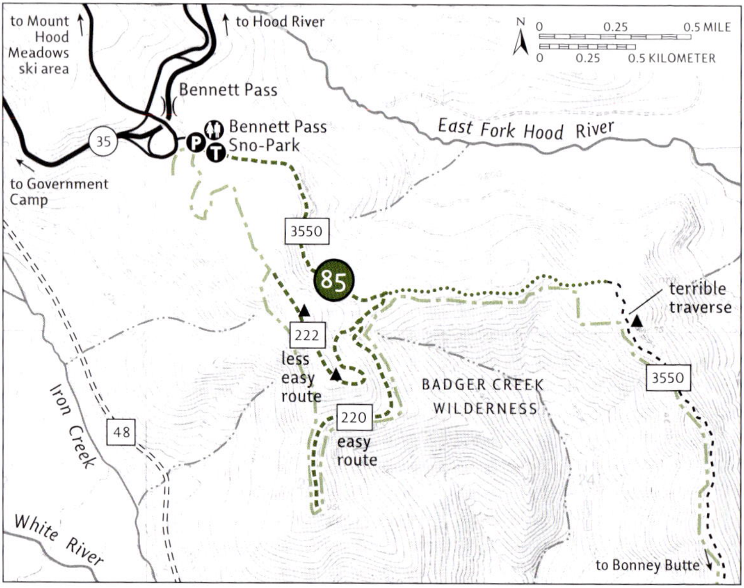

There aren't any big views to enjoy from the end of either, but the walking is pleasant through the quiet, snowy woods.

The easy route (left; south) continues another 0.9 mile on mostly flat track, skirting the boundary of the Badger Creek Wilderness. The path contours southward, winding around the top of a couple of drainage basins that feed Iron Creek. A few gaps in the trees offer partial views over the wide White River valley. The long ridge on the east side of the valley is Bonney Ridge, culminating in Bonney Butte to the southeast. As you're strolling along, look for animal tracks in the snow; bunny tracks are common and easy to identify. The last 0.2 mile of the spur climbs a moderate slope to end in a wide clearing ringed by a wall of trees.

The less easy route (right; southwest) climbs 0.8 mile to the top of the ridge above the road you came in on. The path winds upward on a steady grade for the first 0.3 mile. The partial views over the White River valley are slightly better on this route than the easier route. Once the road reaches the crest of the ridge, it makes a U-turn and proceeds northwest on a milder grade. The road reaches its high point at 0.4 mile, in a wide clearing ringed by noble firs. From here, the trail continues on narrower path, dipping along the ridgeline, then rising to another fork. The wide path right (north) heads into a clearing; the path left (northwest) narrows even more and continues another 0.2 mile to end in another tree-ringed clearing.

Enjoy quiet, snowy strolling on the winter trails at Bennett Pass.

Once you've done one or the other—or both—return to the previous wide fork and make your way back the way you came.

EXTEND YOUR TRIP

If you're interested in exploring more of the area, you can continue east on the Bennett Pass road from the fork near the 1-mile mark. The way forward gradually becomes more challenging until it reaches the "terrible traverse," a steep slope prone to avalanches. This point is about 2 miles from the trailhead, making for a 4-mile round-trip. Some older trail maps may show an 8-mile, doglegged loop that hooks south toward Bonney Butte, but this route is recommended only for experienced winter backcountry users who can assess snow and avalanche conditions and have expert winter routefinding and navigation skills.

Acknowledgments

About halfway through the development of this guidebook, at a time when I was in need of some encouragement, I made a pilgrimage to the small town of Dunbar, Scotland, birthplace of John Muir. It sounds cliché, but as I wandered the rooms of his boyhood home (which is now a nice museum that honors his legacy), and explored the castle ruins where he roamed as a child, I took inspiration from Mr. Muir's many words and deeds as he advocated the value of protecting and enjoying America's wild places. And while mine is just one small voice among thousands who walk in Mr. Muir's footsteps, I'm thankful for the opportunities I've had to explore Oregon's trails, and share these special places with all who seek recreation, relaxation, and rejuvenation in Oregon's wild places. Thank you, Mr. Muir.

Of course, I must also thank the many others who offered their support, assistance, and contributions to the development of this guidebook. First and foremost, thanks to my awesome wife, Mitzi, for enduring the development of another guidebook that required countless trips up and down Mount Hood, late nights poring over trail maps and wildflower guides, and numerous meltdowns over wildfires and trail closures—and took an entire year longer than expected. I couldn't have done it without you. You're the best, babe! The best! Thanks also to Dario Jungic, owner of Marino Adriatic Café (best cappuccino in Portland!), and his friendly staff, including Caroline, Blaine, Sonia, Anna, and Sheridan, for allowing me to occupy the corner table for nearly two years to work on this project. And a special thank-you to Margot for keeping my coffee cup filled during the whole process.

I would also like to thank fellow hiking authors Tami Asars, Brandon Fralic, Rachel Wood, Lisa Holmes, and Cassandra Mendoza for their support and encouragement, as well as Kate Rogers and Melissa Kiepke at Mountaineers Books for rolling with the evolution of this guidebook. Additional thanks go to the helpful forest and trail professionals who endured my endless questions about trail conditions, wildfire updates, and seasonal situations: Rachel Pawlitz, CRGNSA; Claire Fernandes, USFS Hood River; and Dana Hendricks, PCTA. And finally, thanks to these outdoor industry partners who kept me in comfy boots and dependable gear as I surveyed the more than 500 miles of trails in this guide: Alexa McRoberts (MSR), Julie Campagnoli (Osprey), Shelly Smith (Granite Gear), Ingrid Niehaus (Lowa), Lina Adams (Mountain Hardwear), Yusuke Igarashi (Montbell), and David Jay (NatGeo Maps).

Appendix I
Wildflowers and Shrubs

Part of the joy of hiking the forests, ridges, and meadows on Mount Hood are the many varieties of trees, shrubs, fungi, and flowering plants that grow there. While there are hundreds of species to be found, the following pages offer a visual guide for some of the most common ones you're likely to see on and around Mount Hood. Summer is the prime time for wildflowers; however, you are likely to find different varieties at different times of the summer. Flowers like trilliums, violets, and rhododendrons are common in early summer, while bog gentians and bunchberries are more common later in the summer; shooting stars and monkey flowers are often found near creeks and wet meadows, while phlox and heather occupy high, rocky terrain. Once you get acquainted with some of these regulars, consider picking up a detailed tree or wildflower guide to help you discover even more.

COMMON WILDFLOWERS

1. Arnica
2. Aster
3. Avalanche lily
4. Bear grass
5. Bog gentian
6. Buckwheat
7. Bunchberry
8. Cinquefoil
9. Columbia windflower
10. Daisy
11. Elephant's head
12. Fairy slipper

COMMON WILDFLOWERS

13. Fireweed
14. Goldenrod
15. Heather
16. Hedge nettle
17. Herb Robert
18. Indian paintbrush
19. Knapweed
20. Lousewort
21. Lupine
22. Manzanita
23. Mariposa lily
24. Monkey flower

COMMON WILDFLOWERS

25. Pasque flower
26. Pearly everlasting
27. Penstemon
28. Phlox
29. Pipsissewa
30. Rhododendron
31. Salmonberry
32. Saxifrage
33. Shooting star
34. Skyrocket
35. Spiraea
36. Trillium

COMMON SHRUBS

1. Corn lily
2. Deer fern
3. Devil's club
4. Huckleberry
5. Maidenhair fern
6. Mountain ash
7. Oregon grape
8. Skunk cabbage
9. Sorrel
10. Sword fern
11. Thimbleberry
12. Vanilla leaf

Appendix II
Permit Locations, Trailheads, and Trail Maps

WHERE TO PURCHASE TRAILHEAD PERMITS

- CJ's Foodmart, Wapinitia
- Cooper Spur Resort, Parkdale
- Hillcrest Sports, Gresham
- Joe's Donut Shop, Sandy
- Mount Hood Village Market, Rhododendron
- Mountain Shop, Portland
- Mountain Sports, Welches
- REI, Portland, Clackamas, Tigard
- Summit Chevron, Government Camp
- Timberline Lodge, Mount Hood
- US Outdoor Store, Portland
- USFS Ranger Station, Dufur
- USFS Ranger Station, Estacada
- USFS Ranger Station, Parkdale
- USFS Ranger Station, Zigzag
- www.discovernw.org
- Zigzag Mountain Store, Zigzag

TRAILHEADS REQUIRING A NORTHWEST FOREST PASS

- Badger Creek
- Barlow Pass
- Billy Bob
- Burnt Lake
- Cast Creek, Horseshoe Ridge, Sandy River
- Cloud Cap–Tilly Jane (north)
- Dog River (west)
- Eight-Mile
- Frog Lake
- Glacier View
- Herman Creek
- Hidden Lake
- High Prairie
- Hood River Meadows
- Joe Graham, PCT
- Knebal Springs
- Little Crater Lake
- Little Zigzag Falls
- Mirror Lake
- Old Salmon River
- Polallie
- Ramona Falls
- Salmon River (west)
- Surveyors Ridge
- Tamanawas Falls, East Fork
- Tilly Jane (south)
- Tollgate, Pioneer Bridle
- Top Spur
- Trillium Lake
- Umbrella/Sahale (Elk Meadows)
- Wahtum Lake

TRAILHEADS REQUIRING AN OREGON SNO-PARK PERMIT (NOV. 1–APR. 30)

- Barlow Pass
- Bennett Pass
- Cooper Spur
- Frog Lake
- Glacier View
- Government Camp
- Government Camp Maintenance Station
- Hood River Meadows

Little John
Mount Hood Meadows
Pocket Creek
Skibowl
Skyline Road
Snow Bunny
Summit Ski
Teacup Lake
Timberline
Trillium Lake
White River West/East

DOWNLOADABLE TRAIL MAPS

http://mounthoodinfo.com/recreation/trail-maps
www.skihood.com/the-mountain/trail-maps

Appendix III
Contact Information

See Mount Hood National Forest website for links to specific districts.

Columbia River Gorge National Scenic Area
Wasco Avenue, Suite 200
Hood River, OR 97031
(541) 308-1700
www.fs.usda.gov/contactus/crgnsa/about-forest/contactus

Lost Lake Resort
9000 Lost Lake Road
Hood River, OR 97031
(541) 386-6366
www.lostlakeresort.org

Mount Hood National Forest
16400 Champion Way
Sandy, OR 97055
(503) 668-1700
www.fs.usda.gov/detail/mthood/about-forest/offices
Note: Visitor services, maps, and permits not available here.

Barlow Ranger District
780 NE Court Street
Durfur, OR 97021
(541) 467-2291

Clackamas River Ranger District
595 NW Industrial Way
Estacada, OR 97023
(503) 630-6861

Hood River Ranger District
6780 Highway 35
Parkdale, OR 97041
(541) 352-6002

Zigzag Ranger District
70220 E Highway 26
Zigzag, OR 97049
(503) 622-3191

Timberline Lodge
27500 E Timberline Road,
Government Camp, OR 97028
(503) 272-3311
www.timberlinelodge.com

Appendix IV
Trail and Park Management

Oregon Department of Fish and Wildlife
(800) 720-6339
https://myodfw.com

Oregon State Parks
(800) 551-6949
http://oregonstateparks.org

US Forest Service
Columbia River Gorge
(541) 308-1700
www.fs.usda.gov/crgnsa

US Forest Service
Mount Hood
(503) 668-1700
www.fs.usda.gov/main/mthood/home

TRAIL SUPPORT, CONSERVATION, AND EDUCATION

Friends of the Columbia River Gorge
(503) 241-3762
https://gorgefriends.org

HawkWatch International
(801) 484-6808
https://hawkwatch.org

Mazamas
(503) 227-2345
https://mazamas.org

Oregon Trails Coalition
(503) 290-4569
www.oregontrailscoalition.org

Oregon Wild
(503) 283-6343
https://oregonwild.org

Pacific Crest Trail Association
(916) 285-1846
www.pcta.org

Trailkeepers of Oregon
(971) 206-4351
www.trailkeepersoforegon.org

Index

Note: Photo page references in *italics*

1% for Trails—Oregon Trails Coalition

Where would we be without trails? Not very far into the wilderness.

That's why Mountaineers Books designates 1 percent of the sales of select guidebooks in our *Day Hiking* series toward volunteer trail maintenance. Since launching this program, we've contributed more than $22,000 toward improving trails.

For this book, our 1 percent of sales is going to the **Oregon Trails Coalition**. The Oregon Trails Coalition is a cooperative body of broad-based, statewide trail interests dedicated to supporting, promoting, and advocating for the preservation, development, and stewardship of a statewide network of sustainable, world class trails. The Oregon Trails Coalition strives to ensure that Oregon's trails benefit all residents and visitors and inspire respect for Oregon's natural and cultural resources.

Mountaineers Books donates many books to nonprofit recreation and conservation organizations. Our 1% for Trails campaign is one more way we can help fellow nonprofit organizations as we work together to get more people outside, to both enjoy and protect our wild public lands.

If you'd like to support Mountaineers Books and our nonprofit partnership programs, please visit our website to learn more or email mbooks@mountaineersbooks.org.

Photo by Mitzi Sugar

About the Author

Eli Boschetto grew up hiking the high passes and alpine meadows of California's Sierra Nevada before migrating to the Pacific Northwest in 2005. Since then, he has extensively hiked, written about, and photographed trails around Oregon, Washington, and British Columbia. Over the course of his trail journeys, he has performed as a Northwest correspondent for *Backpacker* and served as the editor of *Washington Trails* magazine. In 2018, Eli was a member of the Granite Gear Grounds Keeper team and picked up trash on more than 500 miles of trails in Oregon, Washington, Idaho, and Scotland. He is also an ambassador for National Geographic Trails Illustrated Maps. In addition to *Day Hiking: Mount Hood*, Eli is the author of Mountaineers Books' *Hiking the Pacific Crest Trail: Oregon* and *Urban Trails: Portland*. He is also the founder of PCT: Oregon, an online supplement to his guidebook and a resource and information hub for Oregon's PCT hikers. Eli lives in southeast Portland with his wife, Mitzi. You can connect with him online at www.pctoregon.com, or on Facebook and Instagram at @pctoregon.